Issues and Controversies in British Electoral Behaviour

Issues and Controversies in British Electoral Behaviour

edited by
David Denver
and
Gordon Hands

HARVESTER
WHEATSHEAF

New York London Toronto Sydney Tokyo Singapore

First published 1992 by
Harvester Wheatsheaf,
66 Wood Lane End, Hemel Hempstead,
Hertfordshire, HP2 4RG
A division of
Simon & Schuster International Group

© 1992 David Denver and Gordon Hands

All rights reserved. No part of this publication may be reproduced, stored in a retrieval system, or transmitted, in any form, or by any means, electronic, mechanical, photocopying, recording or otherwise, without the prior permission, in writing, from the publisher.

Typeset in 10/12pt Times by
Keyset Composition, Colchester

Printed and bound in Great Britain by
BBCC Wheatons Ltd, Exeter

British Library Cataloguing-in-Publication Data

Issues and controversies in British electoral behaviour.
   I. Denver, David   II. Hands, Gordon
324.941

ISBN 0-7450-0975-1
ISBN 0-7450-0976-X pbk

---

1 2 3 4 5   95 94 93 92 91

Contents

Acknowledgements		*viii*
Preface		*ix*

1 *Introduction* — *1*

Part I Turnout in elections

2 *Turnout in elections: Introduction* — *15*
   2.1 Non-voting in British general elections, 1966–October 1974 — 18
       Ivor Crewe, Tony Fox and Jim Alt
   2.2 Official and reported turnout in the British general election
       of 1987 — 31
       Kevin Swaddle and Anthony Heath
   2.3 Marginality and turnout in general elections in the 1970s — 41
       David Denver and Gordon Hands

Part II Models of party choice

3 *Class and party: Introduction* — *51*
   3.1 Class and party — 54
       David Butler and Donald Stokes
   3.2 Class dealignment — 61
       Ivor Crewe
   3.3 The decline of class voting — 68
       Anthony Heath, Roger Jowell and John Curtice
   3.4 On the death and resurrection of class voting: some comments
       on *How Britain Votes* — 85
       Ivor Crewe
   3.5 Trendless fluctuation: a reply to Crewe — 97
       Anthony Heath, Roger Jowell and John Curtice

vi CONTENTS

3.6 Class dealignment in Britain revisited 107
   Patrick Dunleavy
3.7 Social class and party choice in England: a new analysis 118
   W.L. Miller

4 *Party identification: Introduction* **127**
   4.1 Parties in the voter's mind 130
      David Butler and Donald Stokes
   4.2 Partisan dealignment ten years on 141
      Ivor Crewe
   4.3 Partisan change in Britain, 1974–83 148
      Harold D. Clarke and Marianne C. Stewart
   4.4 Partisanship and party preference in government and
      opposition: the mid-term perspective 155
      W.L. Miller, S. Tagg and K. Britto
   4.5 Partisan dealignment revisited 162
      Anthony Heath, Roger Jowell and John Curtice

5 *Issue voting: Introduction* **170**
   5.1 The analysis of issues 174
      David Butler and Donald Stokes
   5.2 Policy alternatives and party choice in the 1979 election 185
      Bo Sarlvik and Ivor Crewe
   5.3 Assessing the rise of issue voting in British elections
      since 1964 198
      Mark N. Franklin
   5.4 Policy and ideology in the 1983 general election 208
      Anthony Heath, Roger Jowell and John Curtice
   5.5 Learning through a lifetime 219
      Richard Rose and Ian McAllister
   5.6 The demise of party identification theory? 230
      Anthony Heath and Sarah-K. McDonald

Part III Economic performance and government popularity

6 *Economic performance and government popularity:*
   Introduction **241**
   6.1 The parties and the economy 244
      David Butler and Donald Stokes
   6.2 The electoral cycle and the asymmetry of government
      and opposition popularity 253
      W.L. Miller and M. Mackie
   6.3 The economy and government support 264
      Jim Alt

CONTENTS   *vii*

6.4 Government popularity and the Falklands war:
    a reassessment   274
    David Sanders, Hugh Ward and David Marsh
    (with Tony Fletcher)
6.5 Recapturing the Falklands: models of Conservative
    popularity, 1979–83   289
    H.D. Clarke, W. Mishler and P. Whiteley

Part IV Recent themes in voting behaviour research

7 *Regional differences in voting behaviour: Introduction*   *301*
   7.1 Electoral developments, 1955–79   304
      John Curtice and Michael Steed
   7.2 Voting behaviour in Scotland and Wales   310
      W.L. Miller
   7.3 The changing electoral geography of Great Britain   316
      R.J. Johnston and C.J. Pattie

8 *Elections and the electorate in the 1980s: Introduction*   *322*
   8.1 Proportionality and exaggeration in the British electoral
      system   325
      John Curtice and Michael Steed
   8.2 There was no alternative: the British general election
      of 1983   334
      W.L. Miller
   8.3 The 1987 general election   343
      Ivor Crewe
   8.4 The extension of popular capitalism   355
      Anthony Heath with Geoff Garrett
   8.5 Has the electorate become Thatcherite?   364
      Ivor Crewe

Glossary of Statistical Terms   372
References   378
Index   386

Acknowledgements

The editors and publisher wish to thank the following who have kindly given permission for the use of copyright material: Basil Blackwell Ltd for Sections 3.4, 3.5, and 6.2; Butterworth-Heinemann Ltd for Sections 4.4, 5.3, 5.6, and 8.1; Cambridge University Press for Sections 2.2, 2.3, 3.7, 6.4, 6.5 and 7.1; Frank Cass and Co. Ltd for Sections 3.2, 3.6. 4.2 and 7.2; Oxford University Press for Section 8.2; Routledge for Section 2.1; Sage Publications Ltd for Section 5.5; The Macmillan Press Ltd for Sections 3.1, 4.1, 5.1 and 6.1; University of Texas Press for Section 4.3; the respective authors for Sections 3.3, 4.5, 5.2, 5.4, 6.3, 7.3, 8.3, 8.4 and 8.5.

Every effort has been made to trace all copyright holders, but if any have been inadvertently overlooked, the publishers will be pleased to make the necessary arrangements at the earliest opportunity.

Preface

Textbooks on British Government and Politics almost always include a chapter dealing with elections and voting behaviour and there are now a number of secondary texts which deal with the subject in more detail. But for students who want to go beyond this level and make use of the original material on which the secondary texts are based the relevant literature is rather fragmented and inaccessible. Much is published in the form of journal articles or chapters in edited collections, while major book-length reports are expensive. In this volume, therefore, we bring together, in an easily accessible form, some of the most important contributions to the main debates in the field of voting behaviour and elections in Britain over the past twenty years or so.

Our coverage, of course, is far from complete. There are many items that we have not been able to include because of the constraints of space (which are in turn a consequence of our desire to produce the book at an affordable price). Nonetheless, we hope that the selection made will prove useful to students and others who wish to deepen their understanding of British voting studies. They will find here many of the 'classics', as well as contributions by leading scholars to current debates, in a form which we hope will be clear and approachable. Students (and teachers too) are sometimes discouraged from using original material because of its apparent statistical complexity and to help overcome this we have provided a glossary of statistical terms used in the extracts included in the book.

All of the extracts have been heavily edited. Apart from the need to keep items short, our intention has been to bring out the central arguments as clearly as possible. In order to maintain the flow of the text we have not marked excisions in any way, although in a few cases we have drawn attention to the exclusion of the details of complex statistical calculations. For similar reasons we have made short interpolations where necessary, and these (apart from capitalisations and corrections to typographical

PREFACE

errors in the originals) are marked by square brackets. In general we have excluded footnotes, but in a few cases where they are of particular importance they have been incorporated in the text.

The format of many of the tables and figures has been altered in the interests of clarity and uniformity of presentation. It is important to note that tables and figures have been numbered sequentially within chapters and that these numbers are, therefore, different from those in the originals.

In preparing this collection we have incurred a number of debts. We would like to record our thanks to Ivor Crewe who commented encouragingly and helpfully on our original ideas; to Anthony Heath who generously made available proof copies of some chapters from the BES report on the 1987 election; to Richard Davies of the Centre for Applied Statistics, Lancaster University for help with the glossary; to Clare Grist of Simon and Schuster International for her steady encouragement and helpful advice; and to Trish Demery, Belinda Tattersfield and Maureen Worthington from our own department for their help with typing and word processing.

David Denver
Gordon Hands

Department of Politics
Lancaster University
June 1991

1 | Introduction

The study of elections and voting behaviour has now become a major component of the study of politics. During the past forty years it has expanded rapidly and has generated a large and burgeoning literature. The scholarly journal *Electoral Studies* is devoted entirely to the subject; numerous articles on elections are published in other less specialised journals; and books on the subject appear with daunting regularity. Furthermore, as well as being a major sub-field of political science, electoral analysis attracts the interest of a wide range of scholars in other academic disciplines, including sociologists, geographers, economists and psychologists, and no doubt politicians themselves pay at least passing attention to some of the controversies in the field.

This widespread interest in the electoral process is not difficult to explain. Elections are major national events and a central feature of any democratic political system. It is through open, competitive elections that the people are able to choose their rulers and hold governments accountable. Not surprisingly, then, political scientists want to examine the extent to which elections do in fact perform the functions envisaged for them in the various versions of democratic theory, and find out whether voters play the part expected of them. Sociologists and psychologists are interested in the social structural and psychological bases of voting. Politicians and journalists have rather more practical concerns: they want to know, for example, whether particular policies and campaign tactics affect the outcomes of elections, or how the mass media affect voting decisions.

But there are also rather more prosaic reasons for the popularity of electoral studies among academic social scientists. Election results are numerical in form and generate masses of easily available quantitative data. They are, therefore, singularly amenable to statistical analysis – as are surveys of voters – and investigating these data has considerable

1

2 INTRODUCTION

attractions for social scientists of a statistical bent. The rapid development of computers, and most recently of micro-computers, has enabled researchers to undertake complex analyses of voting data with remarkable speed, and this has contributed to a rapid increase in the number of books and articles in the field. Unfortunately it has also sometimes resulted in publications which are rather inaccessible to readers without highly specialised statistical training, and not a few in which the desire to display statistical virtuosity seems to have displaced any other value.

This volume focuses on a number of major issues and controversies in the study of British elections over the past twenty-five years, and brings together contributions by some of the leading scholars working in the area. Early British research on elections and voting behaviour was heavily influenced by pioneering work in the United States, but in the past twenty-five years political scientists in Britain have made significant contributions of their own, and have raised a wide range of interesting and controversial questions. In this introduction, we outline the development of British voting studies and then go on to sketch the main theoretical models which have been developed in order to organise and further our understanding of why British voters behave as they do.

Voting studies in Britain

Most studies of electoral behaviour fall into one of two categories. The first starts from election results. Elections themselves yield *aggregate data* – the results of the elections in individual constituencies (or, in local elections, wards). The basic data are the number of electors voting and the number of votes cast for each candidate in each constituency. By simple arithmetical manipulation of these figures we can produce slightly more complex statistics, such as the percentage turnout, the distribution of votes among the parties and the change in these between elections; and constituency or ward data can then be aggregated for cities, counties, regions or the whole country in order to produce corresponding statistics for these larger units.

Analysis of the basic constituency data from British general elections has a lengthy tradition. After every general election since 1945 a volume has been published (*The British General Election of . . . .*) providing a detailed descriptive account of the election campaign, and each volume has included an appendix devoted to an analysis of the results. For example, the most recent of these 'Nuffield Studies' – so called because of their connection with Nuffield College, Oxford – has an appendix by Curtice and Steed (1988) which considers such topics as changes in party support between 1983 and 1987, geographical patterns in the results, the personal vote for incumbent MPs, tactical voting, turnout change, the effects of the electoral system and so on. It is interesting to note that the methods

INTRODUCTION   3

developed by the Nuffield Studies for analysing contemporary elections have also been used with considerable effect to examine British elections in the late nineteenth and early twentieth centuries (see, for example, Blewett, 1972).

One of the best known and most important concepts developed by this kind of analysis has been that of electoral 'swing'. Swing is a measure of the net change in the relative levels of support for two parties between elections.[1] It provides a single statistic which succinctly summarises electoral change.

In the 1950s and 1960s swing was relatively uniform in general elections (that is, constituencies in different parts of the country were all likely to have roughly the same swing) and there was also a predictable relationship (known as the 'cube' rule – see p. 326 below) between the share of the votes received by a party and the share of the seats in the House of Commons that it would win as a result. In these circumstances swing was invaluable to journalists and television commentators since it enabled very accurate predictions of final election outcomes to be made on the basis of the first handful of constituency results. In the 1970s and 1980s, however, the concept has become less applicable, although it is still widely used. Swing was designed to deal with two-party competition, and the increase in third-party support after 1970 meant that it could no longer adequately summarise electoral change. And, in addition, swing has gradually become less uniform and the relationship between seats and votes is therefore less predictable.

Although the kind of analysis of basic election data that we have been describing has produced interesting and important results, it is necessarily rather limited. A fuller understanding of voting patterns can be obtained by analysing the results together with socio-economic and other data relating to constituencies. There were a number of attempts to do this for the elections of the 1950s and the early 1960s (see, for example, Allen, 1964), but before 1966 analysis of this kind was severely constrained by the fact that the relevant data were not published on a constituency basis. However, census data for parliamentary constituencies were made available for the first time following the sample census of 1966 and this was repeated for the regular censuses of 1971 and 1981. Advances in the computerisation of census data ensure that constituency-level census figures will continue to be available in the future.

The availability of these data, together with the development of computers and specialised social science statistics packages, has proved an enormous boon to electoral analysts. Despite the fact that the census data

---

1. The formula for calculating swing is $\frac{1}{2}[(A2 - A1) + (B1 - B2)]$, where $A1$ and $B1$ are the percentage shares of the vote for parties A and B at the first election, and $A2$ and $B2$ are the percentage shares at the second election.

4   INTRODUCTION

themselves have limitations – for example, they do not include figures for religious affiliation or for unemployment on a constituency basis – there has been a veritable explosion of studies of British elections using aggregate data. The possibilities for this kind of analysis were clearly demonstrated in a special appendix to the Nuffield Study of the 1970 general election (Crewe and Payne, 1971) and since then there have been numerous books and articles employing these techniques (see, for example, McAllister and Rose, 1984, and the articles by Denver and Hands in Section 2 and by Miller in Section 3 of this volume). This kind of aggregate analysis of election results together with socio-economic data can tell us a great deal about patterns of voting behaviour in different constituencies, and patterns of change over time, and now forms a routine part of academic analysis of election results.

The second type of voting study focuses upon individual voters rather than upon aggregate election results. Although there have been considerable advances in aggregate analysis techniques, this kind of analysis inevitably has its limitations. As implied above, researchers are usually limited to dealing with data that have been officially collected and published; in addition, aggregate statistics can tell us nothing about the beliefs, attitudes and opinions of voters; and, finally, aggregate data refer to collectivities – they allow the investigator to talk about wards, constituencies and regions, but not about individuals. These difficulties are overcome by studies which are based on sample surveys of the electorate – they can deal with virtually any subject the researcher is interested in, they can give us plentiful information about voters' attitudes and opinions, and of course they tell us about individuals.

Academic surveys of voting behaviour – made possible by advances in sampling theory – were pioneered in the United States in the 1940s. The first survey study of voting behaviour in Britain was carried out in the Greenwich constituency during the 1950 general election and reported in *How People Vote* (Benney *et al.*, 1956). This was followed by two similar constituency studies in Bristol in 1951 and 1955 (Milne and Mackenzie, 1954, 1958). In the late 1950s and early 1960s there were a number of other locally based survey studies, some concentrating entirely on voting behaviour (Sharpe, 1962; Budge and Urwin, 1966), while others were part of wider studies of local politics (Birch, 1959; Bealey *et al.*, 1965). There were also a number of surveys concentrating on specific groups or addressing particular questions: McKenzie and Silver (1968) explored working-class Conservatism; Goldthorpe, Lockwood *et al.*'s *Affluent Worker* studies (1968) set out to test the embourgeoisement thesis; Runciman (1966) explored the concept of relative deprivation; and Trenaman and McQuail (1961) and Blumler and McQuail (1968) examined the impact of television in election campaigns.

However, the major breakthrough in academic survey studies of voting

INTRODUCTION

behaviour in Britain occurred in 1963 when the first national survey of the British electorate was carried out by David Butler and Donald Stokes. Although 1963 was not itself an election year, this proved to be the first of a series of national surveys that have been carried out at every general election since 1964. The series is now known collectively as the British Election Study (BES). Butler and Stokes directed the studies of the 1964, 1966 and 1970 elections. The three subsequent election studies (February 1974, October 1974 and 1979) were the responsibility of a team from Essex University, headed by Ivor Crewe and Bo Sarlvik, while the 1983 and 1987 election surveys have been directed by Anthony Heath, Roger Jowell and John Curtice. Throughout the series an attempt has been made to ensure comparability over time by repeating the same questions in successive surveys, although there have also been important innovations in question wording and new questions have been introduced to cope with new political issues as they have arisen. As a further sophistication, between some sets of elections there is a substantial 'panel' element among the survey respondents – that is, the same individuals have been interviewed at successive elections. This has allowed a more precise mapping of the processes of electoral change at the individual level.

The data collected in the BES surveys are held at the ESRC Data Archive at the University of Essex. They form the basis of the three major reports on British voting behaviour which we consider below (Butler and Stokes, 1969, 1974; Sarlvik and Crewe, 1983; Heath et al., 1985), and in addition, since these data are available to other researchers in the field, they have been used in numerous other books and articles on voting in Britain.

National surveys are expensive undertakings, however, and therefore relatively rare. Not surprisingly, then, there has continued to be a steady stream of more modest local and/or specialised survey studies (see, for example, Dunleavy and Husbands, 1985; Anwar, 1986; Miller, 1988). But, in addition to academic surveys, survey data are available in another more plentiful and inexpensive form – from public opinion polls. Commercial polling firms monitor the political opinions and attitudes of the electorate on a continuous basis, although the political content in their regular monthly polls is relatively restricted. At election times, however, the pollsters undertake special polls (including 'exit' polls) and these provide a mass of survey data which has been extensively used in voting behaviour research (see Alford, 1963; Rose, 1974; Crewe, 1985; Rose and McAllister, 1986). Although they are never as comprehensive or detailed as academic surveys, commercial polls have two major advantages over the latter (besides their relative cheapness). Firstly, polling firms now understand numerous polls during a general election campaign and these can be combined to produce enormous samples, thus improving the reliability of the results and of the analysis based on them. Secondly, poll results are

6   INTRODUCTION

processed and produced very rapidly (since this is required by the people and organisations who sponsor and pay for them). Only a few days after the 1987 election, for example, commentators were able to use poll results to discuss voting patterns in the election and put forward empirically based interpretations of the results (Crewe, 1987), whereas it takes months and frequently years for the reports of major academic surveys to become available.

This brief discussion has shown the extensive use that has been made of both aggregate and individual (survey) data as the basis of electoral analysis in Britain. Each approach has advantages and limitations, and each has its own contribution to make to an understanding of elections and voting behaviour. The reader will find that this volume contains many examples of both.

Models of voting behaviour

Studying elections and voting behaviour is not just a matter of collecting facts. The bare facts may, of course, have a certain fascination on their own, but if they are to further our understanding of electoral behaviour and the electoral process they have to be organised and interpreted within some theory, framework or model. Models help us to order and relate the facts and to suggest explanations.

American influences
Early British studies of voting, up to and including the work of Butler and Stokes, were very heavily influenced, both in the methods they used and in the models of voting behaviour they adopted, by earlier work in the United States. Before describing the models that have dominated British research, therefore, it may be helpful to outline briefly the influential models developed by American scholars.

The first academic survey of voting in America was carried out during the presidential election of 1940 in Erie County, Ohio, and reported in *The People's Choice* (Lazarsfeld *et al.*, 1944). Lazarsfeld, Berelson and Gaudet had intended to analyse the effects of short-term factors, such as the election campaign, on voting choice since they believed that these were crucial. (The book is subtitled 'How the voter makes up his mind in a presidential campaign'). As their study progressed, however, Lazarsfeld and his colleagues came to realise that the social characteristics of voters, such as social class and religion, were much more important in determining party choice than were short-run political events. Their famous conclusion was that 'a person thinks politically as he is socially. Social characteristics determine political preference' (3rd edn, p. 27). In a follow-up study of the 1948 presidential election, this time in Elmira County, New York, this

INTRODUCTION

argument was reinforced and extended (Berelson *et al.*, 1954). In this second study the simple 'social determinism' account of voting was developed into what may be called an 'interests plus socialisation' model. Different social groups, it was argued, have different interests. Their members see different parties as representing these interests and, because of this, tend to vote for them disproportionately. Awareness of a group's distinctive identity and of the links between the group and a particular party is developed and sustained by regular contact among fellow group members through the family, peer groups, the local community and so on.

In the 1950s a somewhat different model – the 'Michigan' model – was developed in *The Voter Decides* (Campbell *et al.*, 1954) and *The American Voter* (Campbell *et al.*, 1960). Both of these studies were based on national sample surveys of the American electorate, the former carried out during the 1952 presidential election and the latter in 1956.

The key concept in the Michigan model is 'party identification' – indeed the model is often referred to as the 'party identification model'. Campbell and his colleagues argued that the social determinism model could not easily account for *changes* in voting patterns, since a person's social group memberships change only slowly over time, if at all. They suggested, instead, that the link between social characteristics and party choice was an indirect one – a voter's social location affects the nature of the influences that he or she will be exposed to in interacting with family, friends and so on. As a consequence of these interactions – especially those within the family – people acquire a psychological attachment to a party, a sense of being a supporter of the party rather than simply someone who happens to vote for the party from time to time. This psychological attachment is party identification. At any particular election the individual's voting choice is a product of an interaction between long-term party identification and a variety of short-term influences, such as current political issues, campaign events, the personalities of party leaders and candidates, and so on. But the long-term factor normally has predominant influence. Indeed, a person's (long-term) party identification will normally influence how he or she interprets and evaluates (short-term) issues, personalities, events and the rest.

Party identification, then, acts as a sort of psychological filter mechanism through which political messages pass to the voter; it provides a framework within which the political world is understood. It also exerts a stabilising influence upon voters. Since it is a product of long-term forces, party identification is not easily changed and its importance implies that electors will have a 'normal' vote – they will usually remain stable in their support for a particular party from election to election. From time to time, however, the events, issues and personalities of the campaign will be sufficiently powerful to lead at least a proportion of the electorate to change their normal vote.

8   INTRODUCTION

The four American studies we have referred to were major landmarks in voting behaviour research. The models which they proposed have influenced almost all subsequent voting studies, not just in the United States. In particular they had a major influence on the early development of voting studies in Britain.

Models of voting in Britain

Most of the early local studies of voting in Britain followed the model developed by Berelson and his colleagues and explained party choice largely in terms of 'social determinism'. Much of this work consisted of descriptions of who voted for which party. Voting surveys quickly established that social class was the major determinant of party support in Britain, but that some other social characteristics, such as age, sex, religion and region, also had some influence. The results of these early studies effectively debunked any idealised view of the voter as basing his or her vote on a careful weighing-up of the policy proposals of the various parties – the kind of view which might have been derived from classical democratic theory.

Butler and Stokes (the latter having been a member of the Michigan team) produced the first distinctively British model of voting behaviour in their classic study *Political Change in Britain* (1st edn 1969, 2nd edn 1974). They combined the simpler social determinism model with the more 'psychological' concerns of the Michigan model. They argued that in Britain, as in America, party identification (which they called 'partisan self-image') was central to the explanation of voting, but there were also strong links between class and party. A basic version of the model of the British voter that they developed is summarised in Figure 1.1.

As in the original Michigan model, the role of short-term factors (referred to by Butler and Stokes as 'transient variations') is played down. They do have some influence, but it is the long-term factors of class and party identification which are most important. As Butler and Stokes say, 'the voter's choice is not normally a sudden thing, but the product of months or years or even generations' (1969, p. 419).

Butler and Stokes also introduce an historical dimension into their analysis – indeed, what they have to say about long-term historical change is one of the most original and interesting aspects of the book. They show that the current alignment of the electorate is largely a product of long-established group attachments, and they emphasise the way in which these party attachments are passed from generation to generation by the processes of socialisation, especially within the family. There will be short-term fluctuations in the vote – transient variations – but they argue that the most significant form of electoral change is that which results as demographic changes slowly work their way through the electorate. On this basis (wrongly, as it has turned out) they predicted increasing support

INTRODUCTION

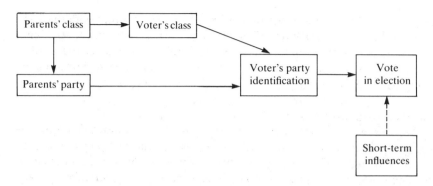

Figure 1.1 Butler and Stokes' model of party choice

for the Labour party in the 1970s and 1980s, as voters who had developed their political identities before the Labour party became a major force in British politics died and left the electorate.

The overall view of the British electorate presented by Butler and Stokes, then, was that it was divided into two great political blocs, more or less permanently aligned with one of the two major parties – Labour and the Conservatives – on the basis of class and psychological commitment. Elections were characterised by stability rather than change, and turned on the (often apparently arbitrary) behaviour of a relatively small minority of 'floating voters'. Significant electoral change was likely to be slow since it was dependent on such things as demographic change and changes in the process of socialisation.

Political Change in Britain quickly became accepted as a major contribution to the field of electoral studies, and there is little reason to doubt that Butler and Stokes provided a largely accurate picture of the British electorate in the 1950s and early 1960s. However, they themselves detected the first stirrings of change among voters. Already in the first edition they noted that 'the class basis of party allegiance is becoming weaker' (pp. 115–16) and that 'greater volatility of electoral behaviour . . . has been manifest as the postwar period has advanced' (p. 121). In the second edition they devoted an entire chapter to the weakening of class alignment (1974, ch. 9). As the 1970s progressed, electoral volatility became much more marked and support for the two major parties declined sharply. This led many commentators to argue that the general model presented by Butler and Stokes was becoming seriously inadequate. In 1974 Ivor Crewe published an article entitled 'Do Butler and Stokes really explain political change in Britain?', and he and Bo Sarlvik, as directors of the BES surveys for the elections of February 1974, October 1974 and 1979, played an important part in charting the changes that were taking place in the British electorate. Three trends were widely commented on.

INTRODUCTION

First, there was evidence of partisan dealignment. In spite of its central role in the Butler and Stokes model, the concept of party identification never achieved the importance in the British context that it had in American voting studies. There were doubts as to whether it was strictly applicable in the rather different institutional setting of British elections, and whether for the British voter party identification and the vote were really separable, as the theory demanded (Budge *et al.*, 1976). But in any case, survey evidence from the 1970s suggested that, although the proportion of the electorate acknowledging some kind of party identification remained fairly stable, there was a marked decline in the strength or intensity of party identification. The great majority of voters still acknowledged some kind of loyalty to a party in response to survey questions, but the numbers saying that this loyalty was 'very strong' fell sharply (Crewe, 1983a).

The second trend evident in the 1970s was a weakening of the link between class and party – class dealignment. This decline in class voting, which was analysed by a number of writers (see, for example, Rose, 1980a; Crewe, 1983a; Franklin, 1985a), was the result of a combination of falling working-class support for Labour *and* falling middle-class support for the Conservatives. The strong relationship between class and party, which had been the basis of British party politics for many years, now showed signs of crumbling.

These processes of partisan and class dealignment called into question the foundations of the Butler and Stokes model, and suggested – the third trend – an electorate which was becoming changeable and volatile, rather than stable in its behaviour. In *Decade of Dealignment*, the major work based on their studies of elections in the 1970s, Sarlvik and Crewe put forward a new model. They found that voters were now much more aware of political issues and party policies than they had been in the past. Voters had fairly clear opinions about the policies and performance of the parties and based their choice of party on their assessments of policies and performance. They therefore argued that the party identification model should be replaced by an issue voting model, in which voting is seen not simply as expressive of long-standing loyalty to a party, but as instrumental, being based on more or less rational assessments of party policy and performance. Different versions of an issue voting model were also advanced by other writers at around this time (Himmelweit *et al.*, 1981; Franklin, 1985a; Whiteley, 1986), and by the early 1980s the view that the electorate had become substantially dealigned and that issue voting had significantly increased had more or less become the orthodoxy of British electoral studies.

Although the results of the 1979 general election seemed to suggest that there might be a return to two-party dominance, the 1980s produced even greater change. Support for the two major parties, especially Labour,

INTRODUCTION *11*

declined further; third-party support reached heights not previously seen in the post-war period; and nationalist parties continued to be a major part of the political scene in Scotland and Wales. In 1981 a new party (the Social Democratic Party or SDP) was formed and immediately had a sensational impact in by-elections and opinion polls. The share of the vote gained by the Alliance (between the Liberals and the SDP) in the 1983 and 1987 general elections was only a few percentage points below that gained by Labour. In the European elections of 1989 the Green Party – which had previously existed on the fringe of British politics – unexpectedly obtained 15 per cent of the votes. These developments appeared to suggest that volatility, not stability, was now the striking feature of British voting behaviour, and this impression was further strengthened by violent movements in party support in monthly opinion polls and at parliamentary by-elections.

All of this seemed to many commentators to confirm the sort of interpretation suggested by Sarlvik and Crewe and others. But the new directors of the BES survey for the 1983 election, Heath, Jowell and Curtice, produced a highly controversial report, *How Britain Votes* (1985), attacking the new orthodoxy at several points. They argued, to start with, that there had been no class dealignment. They suggested that earlier commentators had misconstrued the statistical evidence and mistaken short-term political fluctuations for long-term changes in the class/party link. Their own analysis led to the conclusion that there had been no clear long-term trend in the level of class voting, and they went on to express considerable scepticism, reminiscent of the Michigan model, about the ability of voters to operate with political issues and party policies in the way that the issue voting model proposed. Like a number of other writers (Scarbrough, 1984; Rose and McAllister, 1986) they were prepared to acknowledge that voters might be swayed by broad considerations of ideology or political principle, but not that they make detailed assessments of current political issues.

In place of the issue voting model, Heath and his colleagues proposed what they called an 'interactionist' interpretation of voting. They rejected any strict social determinism, but they suggested nonetheless that class still provides a *potential* basis for party support. Class is a major source of social and political interests, and voters can be mobilised by appeals to those interests. The ideological stances of the parties will affect how much support they receive, for voters are aware of their class interests and of the link between these interests and party ideologies. But voters' perceptions of their class interests are not simply a given to which the parties must respond. The parties can play an active role – they can mould and shape voters' perceptions of their class interests. Thus Heath, Jowell and Curtice's interactionist interpretation seems to involve three main components: first, the voter's decision is based on a broad ideological affinity with a party; second, the voter's ideological position is largely a product of his or her class membership; and third, parties can play an active role in shaping the voters' perceptions of their class-based interests.

The critical aspects of Heath, Jowell and Curtice's argument are set out with considerable vigour in *How Britain Votes* and have led to a lively debate, some of the contributions to which are included in Sections 3, 4 and 5 below. Their 'interactionist' model has as yet attracted less comment, however, and it remains to be seen whether it will attain the status of the Butler and Stokes and issue voting models.

This sketch of the development of British voting studies provides the context for the readings presented in the remainder of this book. As we have seen, the central strand of debate has concerned the three major models of voting choice put forward by the successive BES studies in the 1960s, 1970s and 1980s, and the respective roles that they assign to class, party identification and issue opinions in influencing party choice. Part II of the book is devoted to this major debate. Its three sections focus in turn on the class, party identification and issue voting models. Before deciding which party to support, however, electors have to make a prior decision – whether or not to vote. In Part I, therefore, we present material which investigates non-voting at both the individual and the aggregate level.

Although the debate about the major models of party choice has dominated British electoral research, there have been a number of subsidiary areas of investigation in recent years. Part III of the book is concerned with a rather specialised area – attempts to explain levels of government popularity, especially between elections, on the basis of economic performance. Finally, in Part IV we bring together material concerned with a number of themes prominent in the 1980s – regional divergences in voting behaviour, the operation of the electoral system, Labour's heavy defeats in the 1983 and 1987 elections, and the impact of 'Thatcherism' upon the electorate.

Part I

Turnout in elections

2 | Turnout in elections

Introduction

It is obvious from general election results that the turnout of electors varies both over time and between constituencies. Figures for national turnout in British elections over the period since 1950 are shown in Table 2.1. The 'raw' figures appear to indicate a generally downward trend in turnout, but this is misleading. If the exceptionally high turnouts at the elections of 1950 and 1951 are omitted, then any downward trend is very gentle indeed. Moreover, these figures take no account of the inaccuracy of the electoral register upon which turnout calculations are based. The register is compiled each October, comes into force in the following February and remains in use until the February after that. Clearly elections which are held later in this cycle will have an artificially depressed turnout, since more people will have died or moved away from the address at which they were registered. Rose (1974) has suggested a formula for dealing with these sorts of technical problems. He proposes that the raw turnout figure should be divided by $(100 + 3.4 - 1.0 - 0.15m - 0.67m)$, where m is the number of months from the compilation of the register to the election. This takes account of electors who are registered twice $(+3.4)$, those who are accidentally not registered (-1.0), those who have died $(-0.15m)$ and those who have moved $(-0.67m)$, and produces the 'adjusted' turnout figures shown in Table 2.1. There remains some variation over time in these adjusted figures, but the impression now is not of a steady decline but of a fairly sharp break between 1964 and 1966. Turnout variation from constituency to constituency is much greater. In 1987, for example, it ranged from 84.4 per cent in Brecon and Radnor to 55.4 per cent in Hackney South and Shoreditch. Clearly variations of this sort require explanation, but to find out more about who votes and who does not we need to go beyond election results and make use of survey data.

The selections in this section address a number of important questions relating to electoral turnout, and also, incidentally, illustrate well the

15

Table 2.1 Turnout in general elections, 1950–87

	'Raw' %	'Adjusted' %		'Raw' %	'Adjusted' %
1950	84.0	84.1	1970	72.0	75.2
1951	82.5	88.3	Feb. 1974	78.1	78.8
1955	76.8	79.8	Oct. 1974	72.8	78.6
1959	78.7	85.0	1979	76.0	78.6
1964	77.1	83.3	1983	72.7	75.8
1966	75.8	77.4	1987	75.3	78.6

Source: Denver (1989, pp. 114–16).

distinction between aggregate and survey data analysis to which we drew attention in the introduction. Survey analysis of non-voting faces two initial technical problems. First, no doubt because voting is widely regarded as a civic duty, a significant proportion of survey respondents report that they have voted when they have not in fact done so. Second, since in any case the substantial majority of the electorate vote in general elections, sample surveys of the electorate yield a relatively small number of non-voters, and this restricts the possibilities for analysis.

Crewe, Fox and Alt, in an extract from a major article on non-voting, attempt to overcome the latter problem by taking as their dependent variable the number of times respondents reported voting or not voting in the four elections of 1966, 1970, February 1974 and October 1974. Starting from the argument that voting is a very 'easy' form of political participation, they derive a number of hypotheses about the factors likely to distinguish voters from non-voters and proceed to test them in a complex and rigorous piece of analysis. Among their most important conclusions are that the number of persistent and intentional abstainers is tiny; that there is no link between class or class-related variables and turnout; that the main social characteristics which differentiate non-voters are ones which are connected with relative isolation from social networks; and that the most important influence of all on turnout is strength of party identification.

Swaddle and Heath also report survey results, using the very large sample (just under 4,000) obtained by the 1987 British Election Study. However, in a novel piece of analysis they also use the official registers marked by returning officers on polling day. In the first part of their paper they are therefore able to make use of these two sets of data to show the extent to which respondents in the BES sample over-report voting, and to investigate the different causes of the over-representation of voters (as opposed to non-voters) in the BES sample. They go on to consider again the effects of social structural variables on turnout, arriving at conclusions which largely confirm those of Crewe, Fox and Alt. The one interesting difference is that Heath and Swaddle's figures do suggest that class variables are related to turnout, although the relationship is not strong.

In the last extract, Denver and Hands are concerned to examine turnout variation across constituencies and therefore present an analysis based on aggregate data, using election results together with census data. Their particular focus is on the extent to which turnout in a constituency at one election is affected by the constituency's marginality in the previous election. They find that the relationship is quite marked and has been increasing in strength, and go on to consider whether it is the product of the perceptions of voters or alternatively of the parties' campaign strategies.

Further reading

Detailed constituency turnout figures and some analysis of turnout variations are regularly presented in the appendices to the Nuffield Studies of British General Elections (see, for example, Butler and Kavanagh, 1988). But relatively little more-detailed work has been undertaken on turnout in Britain, though there are a number of articles which pursue some of the themes dealt with here.

The problem of adjusting official turnout figures to take account of the ageing of the electoral register is discussed in Rose (1974). Eagles and Erfle (1989) analyse constituency variations in turnout, introducing a measure of community cohesion as an additional explanatory variable. McAllister and Mughan (1986) use survey data in an attempt to estimate the effect that different levels of turnout would have on the parties' shares of the vote at elections. This question is also explored in some detail by Crewe, Fox and Alt in the second half of the article from which an extract is reproduced here as section 2.1. Turnout in local elections is analysed by Miller (1988) and in parliamentary by-elections by Mughan (1986). Studlar and Welch (1986) use the BES surveys to consider whether voters and non-voters have differing policy preferences.

An introduction to the complex theoretical debate arising from Downs' analysis of voting as a rational action (Downs, 1957) can be found in McLean (1982, ch. 4), and the topic is pursued further in Niemi and Weisberg (1976).

A comparative examination of national turnout trends in a variety of political systems is provided by Crewe (1981b) and by Powell (1980).

2.1 | Non-voting in British general elections, 1966–October 1974

Ivor Crewe, Tony Fox and Jim Alt

Introduction

It is clear that voting demands from the British citizen only the minimum of individual initiative or effort. It requires neither skill nor money, and rarely takes more than a few minutes' time. Registration is the responsibility of the local authorities and not the individual. Polling stations are numerous and within near distance of all electors, except in the most far-flung of rural areas [and] are also open for longer hours than [in] almost every other parliamentary democracy. In British elections, completing a ballot correctly is particularly simple. The only institutional disincentives to vote arise for those who have moved from their registered address and therefore have to apply for a postal vote or make a special journey back to their old polling station.

[However] voting provides no tangible benefit to the individual elector, either exclusively or as a member of a group. A general election result can, of course, have a direct bearing on the income, conditions of work, rights and status of particular groups and thus their individual members. But the chance of an election result in a constituency, let alone the whole country, resting on one individual's decision to vote is minute; the benefits to the individual from voting rather than abstaining are therefore equally minute.

The negligible benefits that directly accrue to the individual elector from voting have been emphasised in recent years by 'rational choice' theorists [Downs, 1957]. Their argument is that on a cost–benefit calculus voting is irrational. The benefits are infinitesimally tiny whereas the costs, whilst

From I. Crewe, T. Fox and J. Alt, 'Non-voting in British general elections, 1966–October 1974', in Crouch, C. (ed.), *British Political Sociology Yearbook*, vol. 3, pp. 38–109, London: Croom Helm.

NON-VOTING IN GENERAL ELECTIONS   *19*

small, are non-trivial and certain: time, energy and the opportunity to do other more enjoyable or profitable things. According to rational choice theorists the important question, therefore, is not 'Why do the few fail to vote?' but 'Why do the many bother?'

Rational choice theorists have had to devise a variety of ways for dealing with the awkward fact that in most democracies four electors in five 'irrationally' turn out at the polls. Usually some attempt is made to amend or augment the benefit side of the cost–benefit equation. The most satisfactory explanation of why most people defy 'reason' and vote, however, rests on a re-examination of the supposed costs of voting. If it is assumed that people only make cost–benefit calculations once costs rise above a certain minimum, and if it is assumed further that the normal costs of voting fall below this threshold, rational choice theory is saved with only a small modification. The conclusion that unavoidably emerges, then, is that voting is an overwhelmingly 'easy' form of political participation. It barely requires any individual effort, initiative, skill or sacrifice. It does not engage the participant in conflict-laden or co-operative relations with others. And a high value is attached to it in the country generally and by almost all social groups.

The ease of voting

This modification to rational choice theory sets the perspective for the analysis that follows, the theme of which is the sheer 'ease' of voting and the implications this has for the way non-voting is understood.

If voting is as costless yet culturally valued as we have suggested, a number of hypotheses about non-voting would seem to follow:

1. that a significant proportion of those not voting in any one election fail to do so because the costs of voting rise above the 'threshold';
2. that since increases of voting costs of this kind are often temporary (e.g. illness, holidays, short-term posting abroad, move of house) so too is non-voting;
3. that differences between voters and non-voters in social background and political attitudes will be negligible especially between 'once-only' non-voters and regular voters; that therefore
   (a) the normal relationship between position in the social structure and level of participation will not obtain for the act of voting; and
   (b) voters will generally be closer to non-voters in social background, political attitudes and political behaviour than they are to those who engage in more 'difficult' forms of participation;
4. that persistent abstainers will consist of either
   (a) those most isolated from cultural and social pressures to vote; or

20 TURNOUT IN ELECTIONS

(b) those who deliberately reject such pressures and spurn the opportunity to vote, i.e. reject the act of voting out of alienation from the British political system, or an important aspect of it.

There also follow implications for the way non-voting can best be studied. Non-voters constitute a small minority of the electorate but a smaller one still amongst those interviewed in a national sample survey. The result is that our dependent variable – whether or not the respondent voted – is 'highly skewed', with all the problems for analysis that that involves: insufficient numbers for more than simple breakdowns, and the absence of independent and non-tautologous variables that can adequately discriminate between voters and non-voters.

In order to alleviate these problems our measure of non-voting will consist of the number of occasions a respondent entitled to vote in the four general elections of 1966, 1970, February 1974 and October 1974 in fact did so. Our data are based on the BES February 1974–October 1974 national panel sample, i.e. respondents successively interviewed after both the 1974 elections. Reports of the 1966 and 1970 vote are based on respondents' recollections in February 1974. Respondents unable to remember whether or how they voted in 1966 and 1970 were excluded from the data base. Comparison of recall data with post-election data on the 1970 vote revealed only fractional discrepancies. It is with some confidence, therefore, that we have adopted this measure of turnout regularity.

The number of times respondents voted over the four elections is shown in Table 2.1.1. Two features are of note. First, almost three electors in four (72 per cent) claimed to have voted on all four occasions, a figure which might be taken to corroborate our view of voting as an easy and culturally valued form of participation. Secondly, amongst the minority of non-regular voters the comfortable majority (61 per cent) only missed voting once.

Table 2.1.1 Regularity of voting, 1966–October 1974, among respondents eligible to vote in all four elections

	All eligible respondents %	Respondents who failed to vote at least once %
Failed to vote:		
On no occasion (regular voters)	72	–
Once (temporary non-voters)	17	61
Twice (occasional voters)	8	27
Three times (occasional voters)	2	8
Four times (persistent non-voters)	1	5
(N)	(1,336)	(368)

NON-VOTING IN GENERAL ELECTIONS

The most striking feature of the figures on voting regularity, however, is the virtual absence of the consistent abstainer. A mere 1 per cent of those interviewed stayed away from the polls on all four occasions, and if those who at least managed to vote once are added the figure still only creeps up to 3 per cent. Non-voters in a particular election are not part of a substantial body within the electorate who persistently opt out of elections; on the contrary, the majority will have voted fairly regularly in previous elections and can be expected to resume a similar regularity in subsequent elections. Use of the term 'the non-voter' is misleading if it implies the existence of a permanent and numerically significant body of abstainers.

The social correlates of turnout regularity

Table 2.1.2 presents the relationship between social background variables and regularity of voting in the last four general elections. The percentage figures are the proportion within each social category who were entitled to vote in all four elections between 1966 and October 1974 and exercised their right on each occasion. The most striking feature of Table 2.1.2 is that the majority of social background variables fail to have any bearing on propensity to vote regularly: men and women, single and married, rich and poor, middle class and working class, minimally educated and well educated, all share similar levels of regular turnout. It is true that there are small percentage differences between these groups, but they fail to reach statistical significance, and we shall discover later that they tend to disappear once age controls are introduced. Thus voters and non-voters share the same sociological attributes.

Only three social attributes contradict these featureless findings: residential mobility, housing tenure, and age. The measure of residential mobility is simply the respondent's length of residence at his or her current address. The figures show that the level of turnout regularity only drops significantly amongst the most recent newcomers. It is lowest of all (53 per cent) amongst those who moved in the preceding twelve months. This clearly suggests that if an elector moves out of the neighbourhood the 'costs' of voting (applying for a postal vote, travelling back to one's old polling station) rise above the 'threshold' and markedly depress turnout. The fact that long-established residents display particularly high levels of regular voting suggests [however] that factors other than voting 'costs' are at play. One possible explanation is that these residents are the most likely to have established a network of friends and acquaintances and to have joined voluntary associations, which in turn reinforce the social pressures to vote.

The association between type of accommodation and regularity of turnout might be accounted for in similar terms. The important division is

22   TURNOUT IN ELECTIONS

Table 2.1.2 Regularity of voting by selected social attributes

Voted on all 4 occasions	%			Voted on all 4 occasions	%	
Sex				**Trade union membership**		
Men	74	(648)		Belongs to TU		
Women	71	(688)		household	74	(769)
				Does not belong to		
Marital status				TU household	71	(937)
Single	67	(82)				
Married	74	(1,062)		**Occupational grade (head of**		
Widowed/separated/				**household)**		
divorced	69	(177)		I Higher managerial/		
				professional	76	(112)
Age				II Lower managerial/		
Under 35	54	(180)		administrative	72	(108)
35–44	67	(290)		III Skilled/supervisory		
45–54	79	(307)		non-manual	72	(231)
55–64	78	(261)		IV Lower non-manual	70	(139)
65–74	80	(195)		V Skilled manual	73	(428)
75 and over	75	(88)		VI Unskilled manual	72	(264)
Age completed education				**Subjective social class**		
18 and over	75	(138)		Middle class	71	(446)
16–17	69	(165)		Working class	73	(834)
15 and under	73	(1,024)				
				Income		
Housing tenure				High	73	(123)
Owner-occupier	79	(712)		Medium high	73	(240)
Council tenant	77	(392)		Medium	73	(276)
Private tenant	64	(199)		Medium low	71	(229)
				Low	79	(241)
Length of residence at present						
address						
Less than 1 year	53	(90)				
2 years	59	(99)				
3 years	63	(117)				
4 years	70	(67)				
5–7 years	74	(211)				
8–10 years	70	(159)				
11–20 years	81	(318)				
Over 20 years	78	(266)				

Note: Numbers in parentheses are the percentage base.

not between owner-occupiers and tenants, but between council and private tenants. Most council houses and flats are on large, densely populated and homogeneously working-class estates where interpersonal pressures to vote (and to vote Labour) are easily exerted. Privately rented accommodation, on the other hand, tends to be geographically scattered across areas of varying social composition and less permanently available than council housing: it therefore forms a poor basis for the establishment of the kind of personal and social networks that might encourage regular turnout at the polls.

NON-VOTING IN GENERAL ELECTIONS

On the surface, the link between age and voting regularity is straightforward: the younger an elector, the less likely he or she will vote regularly. Thus barely over half the under 35s voted four times. The fraction jumps to two-thirds of those aged 35–44 and up again to four-fifths of those over 45 before dipping slightly amongst those aged 75 or older.

Residential mobility is connected with age [however]. Young electors are the most likely to have moved house recently, and older electors are the least likely to have done so. It is therefore possible that the young have relatively poor turnout records not because they are young but because they are unusually mobile; or alternatively that the mobile have poor turnout records not because they are mobile but because they are young. Table 2.1.3 categorises respondents according to both age and residential mobility and provides the proportion of four-time voters within each cross-category. It shows that both age and residential mobility independently affect regularity of turnout. Regular turnout increased with length of residence whether amongst young, middle-aged or old. And regular turnout also increased with age amongst newcomers and longer established residents alike. [But] it is amongst the very recently mobile that age makes most difference to turnout regularity; and it is amongst the youngest electors that length of residence matters most. A comparison of the four top left-hand cells in Table 2.1.3 brings out the magnitude of these cumulative trends. Of electors under 35 who had moved address within the previous three years (7 per cent of our respondents) only 44 per cent turned out at all four elections. But amongst those aged 35–44 with four to six years in the same house, the level reached 76 per cent. It appears to take only a few years of settling down for people's turnout record to approach the national average.

However, with only one exception, differences in turnout regularity between other social categories disappeared once age effects were taken into account. For example, the 3 per cent superiority of men in turnout

Table 2.1.3 Age, length of residence in present home (in February 1974), and turnout regularity

	Length of residence				
Age	Up to 3 years %	4–6 years %	7–10 years %	11–20 years %	Over 20 years %
Up to 34	44 (90)	61 (44)	59 (29)	67 (12)	75 (8)
35–44	49 (74)	76 (63)	70 (77)	75 (64)	80 (10)
45–64	74 (99)	72 (76)	76 (86)	86 (175)	77 (128)
65 and over	73 (40)	80 (30)	79 (28)	78 (64)	79 (92)

Note: Cell percentages are the proportions voting regularly in the four elections.
Numbers in parentheses are the percentage base.

24   TURNOUT IN ELECTIONS

regularity narrowed to 1 per cent once those aged 75 and over, who are disproportionately female, were excluded. Thus the well-known tendency for women to vote in smaller proportions than men is not only statistically insignificant in British elections but attributable to their greater longevity rather than to their sex.

Age effects accounted for the slender difference in regular turnout between social classes in a similar way, [and] also for the surprisingly high proportion of regular voters amongst the lowest income category. Two out of three respondents in the lowest income category were living on a retirement pension. Once [these were] excluded from the analysis, however, there appeared to be no clear relationship between voting regularity and income, and the relatively high level of consistent turnout in the lowest income category disappeared. Thus the common belief that those in the highest income and status brackets participate most in politics does not apply to [voting in] general elections in Britain.

The one exception is marital status. Within age groups differences in voting regularity between the married, the single, and the widowed, separated and divorced were always sharper than amongst respondents as a whole. The state of being unmarried or no longer married clearly lessens the likelihood of regularly turning out on election day.

There therefore appear to be four social factors associated with irregular turnout: being young, having recently moved home, housing tenure, and being unmarried or no longer married. The variables intercorrelate but each has an independent and depressive effect on regularity of turnout. Different explanations of why they should lower turnout can be provided in each case. But the most telling explanation is that which applies to all four groups: isolation from personal and national networks that by informing or exhorting exert pressure to go to the polls. Thus the young, as further analysis [below] will show, have the least developed partisan commitments and thus less incentive to vote, and are the least likely to follow politics in the press or on television. Recent movers are often newcomers to a district living in relative although often temporary isolation within the local community. And single people, whether once married or not, usually live alone and thus without the presence of somebody who might persuade them or remind them to vote, as well as discuss political affairs in general. It is social isolation, therefore, not social deprivation, to which non-voting, or at least irregular voting, should be attributed.

Turnout regularity and political commitment

If social background and economic circumstance generally fail to discriminate between voter and non-voter, what will? An obvious possibility is

NON-VOTING IN GENERAL ELECTIONS

the elector's degree of political motivation. Voters and non-voters may share similar social characteristics but diverge psychologically, that is in their intensity of political commitment.

Table 2.1.4 presents the relationship between regularity of voting in the last four general elections and six measures of political commitment and motivation. The relationships all run in the expected direction and confirm the stronger impact of motivational rather than sociological forces on turnout at the polls. None of this is surprising: indeed, it would have been remarkable had the relationships been the reverse. However, Table 2.1.4 has further features of note. Although a low level of political commitment and motivation is associated with relatively irregular turnout, this does not mean that the least motivated have poor turnout records. The vast majority of those who are quite uninvolved in political affairs vote at least occasionally. And at least half always vote.

Table 2.1.4 Turnout regularity by various measures of political commitment

	Voted four times %
Strength of party identification	
Very strong	84 (460)
Fairly strong	74 (584)
Not very strong	54 (263)
Perceived difference between the parties	
Great deal	76 (556)
Some	75 (367)
Not much	65 (394)
How much cared which party won the election	
Cared a good deal	78 (963)
Did not care very much	57 (361)
Interest in politics	
A great deal	83 (297)
Some	73 (623)
Not much	67 (324)
None at all	52 (81)
Talks about politics	
Often	78 (381)
Sometimes	75 (428)
Only rarely	66 (524)
When talk turns to politics, respondent:	
Does not care to listen	58 (85)
Usually listens but never joins in	69 (208)
Gives views sometimes but not very often	71 (404)
Usually joins in	76 (569)
Likes to start discussions	78 (55)

Note: Numbers in parentheses are the percentage base.

26   TURNOUT IN ELECTIONS

We have deliberately referred to our motivational measures in general terms. But regularity of turnout may well be related more strongly to some types of political motivation than to others. We may distinguish between apathy and alienation as the basis of low motivation. Apathy denotes an indifference to and withdrawal from political affairs, the absence of any feeling of personal obligation or responsibility in political matters, and a generally passive orientation to the political world. Alienation, on the other hand, denotes a positive rejection of the political system, the existence of interest, concern and involvement albeit in hostile and negative forms, and a generally active orientation to the political world.

We consider first the question of whether irregular voters, especially consistent non-voters, are better described as apathetic or alienated. For preliminary evidence we turn to Table 2.1.5. The six measures of political motivation it presents consist of three that refer to the political parties (strength of party identification, perceived difference between the parties, and care which party won the election) and three which measure a more general psychological involvement in politics (interest in politics, how much talk about politics, and engagement in political discussions). Low motivation on the first three measures may be considered consistent with either apathy or alienation. But poor motivation on the second group of measures would suggest that apathy rather than alienation was the basis of non-voting. For if an active rejection of the political order lay at the root of non-voting we should not expect this to affect interest in politics or readiness to talk about politics. On the contrary, we should expect the alienated, who have adopted a clear hostility to the prevailing political or party system, presumably in the face of majority opinion, to be more heavily engaged than most in political discussion and concern. Table 2.1.5 suggests that the alienated abstainer, the politically committed and purposeful non-voter, is the rare exception not only in the electorate as a whole but amongst the small minority of regular non-voters as well. The politically informed and interested abstainer who systematically avoids the polls out of hostility to the prevailing political order may be a figure of some familiarity to the academic social scientist but forms a minuscule minority of the electorate as a whole.

Acceptance of the general system of government does not preclude rejection of some of its parts, and in particular the main actors and beneficiaries in elections, the political parties. Table 2.1.4 has already shown that the level of regular voting was 30 per cent higher amongst very strong party identifiers than not very strong identifiers. The importance of partisan commitment to regular turnout is reinforced by Table 2.1.6 which categorises respondents according to their combined degree of trust in a Labour government and a Conservative government and gives the proportion of consistent four-time voters in each category. Irregular voting is markedly greater amongst those who rarely trust either party in power

NON-VOTING IN GENERAL ELECTIONS

Table 2.1.5 The political commitment of voters and non-voters

	Regular voters (four times) %	Usual voters (three times) %	Intermittent voters (twice) %	Non-voters (once or none) %
Strength of party identification				
Very strong	40	23	17	13
Fairly strong	44	47	40	20
Not very strong	15*	27	37	49
None	1	2	6	18
Perceived difference between the parties				
Great deal	45	41	38	18
Some	28	25	26	24
Not much	27	34	36	58
How much cared which party won the election				
Cared a good deal	79	61	60	33
Did not care very much	21	39	40	67
Interest in politics				
A great deal	26	17	11	7
Some	47	47	53	27
Not much	23	30	27	30
Not at all	4	6	9	36
Talks about politics				
Often	31	25	25	9
Sometimes	33	33	25	16
Only rarely	36	42	50	77
When talk turns to politics				
Likes to start discussion	4	4	2	4
Usually joins in	45	38	40	26
Gives views sometimes but not very often	30	35	28	25
Usually listens but never joins in	15	16	18	23
Doesn't care to listen	5	6	12	23

Note: The measures of political commitment refer to February 1974.

[*The figure given in the original (27%) is clearly in error and we have recalculated the correct figure from other tables.]

than in any other group. Trust in both parties, however, was not associated with particularly high levels of regular turnout. What appeared to produce persistent turnout at the polls was a double-edged partisanship: the combination of trust in one's own party and distrust in the other. It is support for one side in the party battle (and hostility to the other) that encourages people to vote; and it is indifference that keeps people away from the polls, at least sometimes. [Other evidence not shown here

Table 2.1.6 Proportion of regular (four-time) voters by combined trust in Labour and Conservative governments

Trust in Conservative government (October 1974)	Trust in Labour government (October 1974)		
	Usually	Some of the time	Rarely
Usually	72%	77%	81%
Some of the time	81%	71%	64%
Rarely	85%	71%	49%

Note: Cell percentages are the proportions voting regularly in the four elections.

confirms] the importance of partisan commitment (as opposed to support for the political system) to regular turnout. Out of the many forms taken by political commitment it is the strength of an elector's enduring psychological attachment to a party that is most likely to ensure his faithful turnout at the polls.

We have therefore discovered two particularly sturdy sources of irregular voting: relative youth and a weak or absent party identification. But these two variables are themselves related – partisanship strengthens with age. It is therefore possible that the young turn out less regularly than the old not because they are young but because their partisanship is weaker. It is equally possible that 'not very strong' identifiers turn out less regularly than 'very strong' identifiers not because their partisan commitment is less but simply because they are younger.

Table 2.1.7 groups respondents according to their age and strength of party identification and for each group gives the level of regular (four-time) turnout. It shows, first, that both age and strength of identification are independently related to turnout levels: amongst respondents sharing the same strength of partisanship the young turned out less consistently than the old. And within the same age group strong identifiers turned out more consistently than weak identifiers. The relative impact of age and partisan strength, however, was not the same. This is demonstrated by contrasting the extreme right-hand column with the bottom row. The former gives the percentage point difference in level of regular turnout between not very strong and very strong identifiers within each age group, the latter shows the percentage point difference in level of regular turnout between the young and old amongst those sharing the same strength of party identification. On the basis of this comparison strength of partisanship appears to have a greater bearing than age on turnout regularity. Indeed, after 'controlling' for the effects of partisan strength, differences in turnout regularity between the 45–64 and the 65 and over age groups completely disappear; the only important age distinction becomes that between the

NON-VOTING IN GENERAL ELECTIONS

Table 2.1.7 Level of regular turnout, by age and strength of party identification in February 1974

Age	Strength of party identification			
	Not very strong %	Fairly strong %	Very strong %	Difference between not very and very strong
Under 45	41 (109)	66 (214)	78 (130)	37
45–64	63 (111)	79 (260)	87 (189)	24
65 and over	64 (39)	78 (106)	88 (137)	24
Difference between under 45 and 65 and over	23	12	10	

Note: Cell percentages are the proportions voting regularly in the four elections.
Numbers in parentheses are the percentage base.

under and over 45s. The effects of partisan strength, however, are marked within each age group, being especially noticeable amongst the youngest respondents.

It will be recalled that a similar pattern of relationships occurred when we examined the relationship between turnout regularity and length of residence within age groups. The most crucial age distinction appeared to lie between youth and middle age after which the level of turnout regularity rose in ever smaller increments. And it was amongst the under 45s that length of residence had its strongest effect on turnout regularity just as partisan strength did. The minority of young electors who already possessed the partisan strength and residential stability of their elders displayed elderly patterns of turnout. It is as if the early settling down into both a neighbourhood and a party 'brings forward' middle age and produces a similar settling down in the habit of voting.

[What are] the long-term implications of the relationship between partisan strength and regular voting? Turnout at British general elections has steadily declined since the early 1950s. This steady fall in turnout is at first sight surprising. Coverage of the elections by the mass media, especially television, has become gradually more intensive and reached ever-growing proportions of the public. [Furthermore] none of the 15 comparable democracies in the world have undergone a postwar decline in turnout that compares with that in Britain; indeed, nine experienced steady increases in turnout.

Part of the explanation may lie in the parallel erosion of partisan commitment in the British electorate over the last decade. Although an overwhelming majority of respondents continued to volunteer a party identification, the proportion declaring themselves 'very strong' identifiers steadily fell from 41 per cent in 1964 and 1966 to 29 per cent in February 1974 and then down again to 23 per cent by October of the same year. This atrophying of party commitment has occurred in all sectors of the electorate and to a similar degree. The critical factor appears to be disillusionment by the government party's supporters with its recent performance in office. There are, of course, a variety of additional explanations, but the simple and obvious point is that persistent failure by successive governments of both parties will eventually lead to a loosening of party attachments, and this in turn weakens the resolve to vote.

2.2 | Official and reported turnout in the British general election of 1987

Kevin Swaddle and Anthony Heath

This Note looks afresh at the question of turnout in British general elections, using data gathered in the 1987 British Election Study [BES], together with information on the electoral behaviour of the sample, collected independently of the BES survey. The official rate of turnout for Great Britain in 1987 was around 75 per cent. In common with earlier surveys, the BES indicates a much higher turnout figure than the official one; 86 per cent of respondents to the survey reported that they had voted.

The aims of this Note are, firstly, to explore this discrepancy between the official and the survey-based estimates of turnout; secondly, to assess how representative the survey respondents are of voters and of non-voters; and thirdly, to reassess survey-based research on the determinants of non-voting.

Sources of data

In our analysis of turnout we have drawn on data from the 1987 BES post-election survey. Because we believed that the nature of the subject made it less than completely accessible by survey methods alone, we also sought information about the sample's turnout that would be more reliable than simply accepting the respondent's reports to our interviewers. This came from the official records showing which electors voted, compiled by the presiding officer at every polling station. These records can tell us one of three things: that someone polled in respect of a particular register

From K. Swaddle and A. Heath, 'Official and reported turnout in the British general election of 1987', *British Journal of Political Science* (1989), vol. 19, pp. 537–51.

32 TURNOUT IN ELECTIONS

entry, that no one polled in respect of that entry, or that a postal vote was issued.

The official records were successfully checked for 5,847 (all but 153) members of the BES *issued* sample, and then added to our survey data. According to the official records, 74 per cent of the issued sample voted in respect of the issued addresses and 2 per cent received postal ballots. Whatever assumption one chooses to make about the proportion of postal voters returning their ballots, the turnout of our issued sample would appear to accord closely with the 75 per cent figure for Britain as a whole.

The discrepancy between official and survey estimates

The first problem on which we are able to shed some light is the difference between the official turnout figure of 75 per cent and the figure of 86 per cent obtained in the BES. This discrepancy has been observed in sample surveys many times in the past.

There are four main reasons that can be given for this discrepancy: misreporting by survey respondents, response bias, failure to trace all movers, and redundancy in the electoral register. We consider each of these in turn.

Firstly, survey respondents may misreport their turnout; in particular, some respondents may not admit to the interviewers that they did not vote, perhaps out of embarrassment at failing in their civic obligations or perhaps genuinely misremembering whether or not they had voted.

Of the 6,000 electors named in the issued sample, 3,826 were located and interviewed. Official turnout records were available for all but 97 of these respondents, leaving 3,729 respondents for whom we have both their reports of turnout and the official records. Table 2.2.1 describes the relationship between the two measures. We see from it that misreporting generally takes the form of respondents claiming to have voted while the official records show that they did not. Twenty-eight respondents wrongly claimed not to have voted, while there were 159 respondents who wrongly claimed that they had voted. The latter amount to no less than a quarter of all the 'true' non-voters in the achieved sample.

Table 2.2.1 Official and reported turnout of survey respondents

	Reported voted	Reported did not vote
Officially voted	2,987	28
Officially did not vote	159	480
Officially voted by post	69	6

OFFICIAL AND REPORTED TURNOUT IN 1987

These misreports explain about a quarter of the eleven-point discrepancy between the survey and the official estimates of turnout. Thus 86 per cent of the respondents in Table 2.2.1 claimed to have voted, whereas (if we take the reports of the respondents issued with postal ballots to be correct) 83 per cent actually did so.

Secondly, response bias may help to explain the discrepancy between the survey and the official estimates of turnout; people who do not agree to be interviewed may be somewhat different in their turnout from those who do agree. They may, for example, be less interested in, or less knowledgeable about, politics and therefore be unwilling to spend time going to the polls or being interviewed about politics.

In 1,608 cases our interviewers were able to locate the elector named in the issued sample, but for various reasons an interview was not achieved. Table 2.2.2(a) compares the official turnout of the located non-respondents with that of the respondents. If we include postal voters along with those who voted in person, we find that 75 per cent of the located non-respondents voted compared with 83 per cent of the respondents, confirming the hypothesis of response bias. As might be expected, the bias was greatest in the case of people who were too ill or senile to be interviewed, only 42 per cent of whom actually voted, and was rather less in the case of people who personally refused to be interviewed, of whom 77 per cent voted.

We can estimate the impact of this response bias on the gap between the official and the survey estimates of turnout by adding the located non-respondents to the actual respondents to give the turnout figure for all located members of the issued sample. This is done in the third line of Table 2.2.2(a). If postal voters are again included with those who voted in person, it shows that 80 per cent of located members of the issued sample

Table 2.2.2 Turnout of located and unlocated individuals

	Officially voted* %	N
(a) Located individuals		
Located non-respondents	75	(1,608)
Located respondents	83	(3,729)
All located individuals	80	(5,337)
(b) Turnout of unlocated individuals		
Emigrated	17	(24)
Moved to unknown address	32	(301)
'Not known at this address'	44	(115)
All unlocated individuals	33	(510)

*Including those officially reported as voting by post (between 2 and 4%).

voted, which suggests that response bias could explain a further three points of the eleven-point gap between the official and the reported turnout measures.

A third source of the discrepancy is that movers are in general under-represented in surveys, but are also disproportionately likely not to exercise their right to vote. Some 234 electors who moved locally were traced while a further 75 were traced to another part of the country. But as well as the movers we managed to find, there were some 510 members of the issued sample whom we could not locate: 24 were reported to have emigrated, 301 were reported to have moved to an unknown address, 66 were reported to have died, and there were 115 people 'not known at this address' who may have been movers, but who could not be pursued any further. These non-located non-respondents have rather low levels of turnout, as can be seen from Table 2.2.2(b). Their absence from our survey has the effect of raising the figure for reported turnout artificially. The highest turnout among the unlocated non-respondents was found among those who were reported 'not known at this address', but we should be cautious here, for it seems rather improbable that all of those who voted in person in respect of the issued address were *really* movers who had returned to exercise their right to vote in the constituency. It might be wise to assume that in some cases a covert refusal to be interviewed was being made either by or on behalf of the respondent.

We cannot, however, definitively disentangle the untraced non-respondents from our fourth reason for the discrepancy between the official and the survey estimates of turnout, namely redundancy in the electoral register. Some of the movers may have left the issued addresses before the 10 October qualifying date for the new register, but may none the less have had their names carried over by the Electoral Registration Officer, and it is possible that others were legitimately registered elsewhere, and thus eligible both to vote and to be sampled in respect of their other address.

Even when it is new, then, the electoral register contains a lot of redundant or duplicate names. Comparing the 1981 census with the electoral register for that year, Todd and Butcher [1982] estimated that between 6.1 and 9.4 per cent of names on the register were redundant at the qualifying date. Our data are broadly in line with Todd and Butcher's. Our maximum estimate for redundancy in the register at the qualifying date [is] 8 per cent of the total. Since the true figure is likely to be rather lower (some people will have been resident at the qualifying date but died before the election, for example), we therefore incline towards the lower of Todd and Butcher's estimates, which is no more than 6 per cent redundancy. If we take 6 per cent as the true redundancy in the electoral register, the true turnout of individuals rises from 75 to 80 per cent, thus closing the remaining gap between the official and the survey reports of turnout.

The determinants of turnout

The evidence we have reviewed so far must clearly raise a question mark against previous survey-based research on the determinants of non-voting (or more strictly of the characteristics of non-voters). On the one hand, we have seen that the achieved sample under-represents non-voters, particularly older ones; and on the other hand, many of the non-voters who actually are in the achieved sample failed to admit that they did not vote.

We can, however, make some progress on previous research, first by exploring our data on non-respondents and secondly, in the case of respondents, by using official turnout data in place of the respondents' reports.

In their survey-based study of turnout in 1977, Crewe and his colleagues advanced four major hypotheses [see above, pp. 19–20]. We consider the first three of these in turn, but our data are not such as to shed new light on Crewe and his colleagues' fourth hypothesis.

Let us begin then with the costs of voting. Because our interviewers were asked to record a number of facts about all members of the issued sample they managed to locate, regardless of whether an interview was achieved or not, we do know something about located non-respondents and the reasons why interviews did not take place. This source of information about the determinants of turnout broadly confirms the hypothesis that turnout is related to the costs of voting. The official turnout of non-respondents, divided according to the reasons for non-response, was as follows:

Too ill or senile to be interviewed	42%	(127)
Away during interview period	61%	(77)
Appointment broken	71%	(72)
Not seen, not at home	71%	(136)
Someone refused for them	74%	(135)
Personally refused	77%	(966)

Illness and absence appear to be major causes of non-voting. Availability and/or the ease with which electors can get out to vote are clearly, and not surprisingly, important in determining the rate at which they actually do turn out.

Rather encouragingly, the same conclusions emerge from an analysis of the self-confessed non-voters in the survey. Respondents who reported that they had not voted were asked why, and their answers were distributed as follows:

Deliberately abstained	4%
Not interested	13%

Could not decide who to vote for	5%
Said voting wouldn't affect outcome	5%
Prevented by work	10%
Prevented by sickness	9%
Away on polling day	26%
Prevented by other commitments	7%
Because they had moved	8%
Other reasons	12%

The most striking thing about these figures is how few electors claim either to have deliberately abstained or to have failed to vote because they were not interested in the election. Whether their reasons for not voting are genuine or not, a substantial majority of the 480 self-confessed non-voters offered us what might be termed a 'circumstantial' explanation for their behaviour.

It would seem, then, that voting is so much a part of acceptable civic behaviour that most people are ashamed to admit not having done it without having some good cause.

Crewe and his colleagues' second hypothesis follows naturally from the first. If non-voting in a particular election is for 'circumstantial' reasons, we would expect that it is not always the same people who are unavailable to vote, and that from one election to the next the non-voters are a shifting population; we would also expect to find that the hard core of persistent non-voters is a relatively small proportion of our respondents.

Taking our official record of respondents' behaviour in 1987, together with their recalled behaviour in the 1983 and 1979 elections, we are able to produce a measure of turnout regularity. Note, however, that the following percentages are just of those respondents eligible to have voted at each of the last three general elections.

Voted three times	2,093	74%
Voted twice	468	16%
Voted once	168	6%
Did not vote	106	4%

These figures would appear to confirm our expectations about the link between availability and turnout. Although about one respondent in five failed to vote in 1987, non-voting is for most people a temporary thing, related to rises in the cost of voting, such as sickness, holidays or a change of address, which are also usually of a temporary nature. Less than one respondent in ten reported failing to vote in at least two of the last three general elections, and less than one in 25 reported that they did not vote in any of them. These findings are broadly in line with the assumptions made by Crewe, Fox and Alt in their 1977 paper on turnout.

OFFICIAL AND REPORTED TURNOUT IN 1987

We move on now to consider Crewe, Fox and Alt's third hypothesis, which was that 'differences between voters and non-voters in social background and political attitudes will be negligible, especially between "once-only" non-voters and regular voters'. We do not feel that our data allow us to add anything useful to what Crewe and his colleagues have said about persistent non-voting. It is of some interest, however, to check their other findings using the official records of turnout in place of respondents' reports.

Table 2.2.3(a) shows the turnout of our respondents according to the length of time they have lived at their present address. When Crewe and his colleagues looked at this variable they found a significant difference, with respect to turnout, between respondents who had lived at their present address for more than and for less than three years. Table 2.2.3(a), however, shows that the main difference is between those people who have lived at their present address for less than one year and those who have

Table 2.2.3 Reported and official turnout of various groups

	Reported voted %	Officially voted* %	N
(a) By length of time at present address			
Under one year	74	65	(297)
One year	87	82	(234)
Two years	89	83	(275)
Three years	86	83	(240)
Four years	89	83	(201)
Five to ten years	86	83	(830)
Over ten years	87	86	(1,611)
All	86	83	(3,729)
(b) By age			
18–24	77	66	(472)
25–44	85	82	(1,394)
45–64	91	89	(1,160)
Over 65	87	86	(672)
(c) By housing			
Owner-occupier	88	85	(2,617)
Local authority	83	79	(779)
Private tenant	82	77	(257)
(d) By marital status			
Married	89	86	(2,433)
As if married	74	66	(105)
Widowed	84	82	(340)
Divorced	83	81	(182)
Not married	79	73	(667)

*Including those who officially voted by post (between 0 and 7%).

38 TURNOUT IN ELECTIONS

lived there for one or more years. This is true regardless of whether we use respondents' reported turnout or the official records.

Table 2.2.3(b) shows the reported and official turnout of our respondents by age. Of the four variables considered, age was the one that Crewe and his colleagues found to be most important, and there does indeed seem to be a very marked relationship between youth and non-voting. Moreover, younger respondents seem much more likely to mis-report about their failure to vote than older respondents, with the result that the relationship between age and turnout is much more pronounced when we use the official records instead of the interview data.

Table 2.2.3(c) shows the reported and official turnout of our respondents according to the nature of their housing. When housing is looked at on its own, our data show the turnout of private tenants to be less than that of other groups, but the turnout of local authority tenants also seems to be significantly less than that of the owner-occupiers – especially using the official data. The low turnout of private tenants may in part be an attribute of age, but, as we note below, all effects of housing type disappear when controls for social class are introduced.

The reported and official turnout of our respondents according to their marital status is shown in Table 2.2.3(d). Crewe and his colleagues found that when they controlled for age there was a significant relationship between marital status and turnout *regularity*. It may just be a consequence of the fact that unmarried people are more likely to be young, but looking at all age groups in the one election of 1987, there does indeed appear to be a relationship between non-voting and the state of being unmarried. The relationship is especially marked when we use the official turnout data. When we control for age, we find that the voting behaviour of young respondents who are married is more similar to that of older respondents than it is to that of young unmarried respondents.

Table 2.2.4 shows the results when a multivariate analysis is carried out using the four variables age, length of residence, housing tenure and marital status. Since our dependent variables are binary, we have used logit models rather than linear regression for the multivariate analysis. The broad interpretation of logit analysis is similar to that of multiple regression: each parameter shows the strength of association between the dependent and the independent variable in question, net of the other relationships specified in the model, and a parameter needs to be twice its standard error to be significant. In both Tables 2.2.4 and 2.2.5 the figures in brackets are the standard errors.

The first column of Table 2.2.4 shows the parameters (and their standard errors) when the dependent variable is official turnout; the second column gives the parameters when reported turnout is the dependent variable. We have restricted our analysis to respondents aged under 65.

As we can see, both analyses confirm the conclusions reached by Crewe

OFFICIAL AND REPORTED TURNOUT IN 1987

Table 2.2.4 Logit model including age, length of residence, marital status and tenure

	Official	Reported
Constant	0.54 (0.04)	0.72 (0.04)
18–24	−0.25 (0.04)	−0.17 (0.05)
25–44	−0.01 (0.03)	−0.04 (0.04)
45–64	0.26 (0.03)	0.21 (0.04)
New resident	−0.17 (0.04)	−0.14 (0.04)
Married	0.11 (0.03)	0.12 (0.03)
Owner	0.08 (0.04)	0.06 (0.04)
Local authority tenant	−0.07 (0.05)	−0.07 (0.05)
Other tenure	0.01 (0.05)	0.00 (0.05)

and his colleagues. Turnout, whether measured by the official records or by respondents' reports, does have statistically significant relationships with age, marital status, length of residence and housing tenure. In general, however, relationships are rather weaker when respondents' reports of their turnout are the dependent variable. As our next step we added variables to the model which Crewe and his colleagues had found not to have significant relationships with regularity of turnout, namely, sex, class and income. Our analysis confirms theirs with respect to sex but not with respect to class and income. Both class and income have significant relationships with turnout (net of the other variables in the model) [Table 2.2.5]. Furthermore, when they are included, the net effect of tenure becomes non-significant. The common belief 'that those in the highest income and status brackets participate most in politics' is thus shown to be true after all, at least for voting in the 1987 general election.

Of course, there are several reasons why our results might be different in this respect from those of Crewe and his colleagues. Firstly, electors' behaviour may have changed between 1974 and 1987. Secondly, we have a

Table 2.2.5 Logit model including age, length of residence, marital status, social class and income

	Official	Reported
Constant	0.51 (0.05)	0.73 (0.05)
18–24	−0.25 (0.05)	−0.15 (0.06)
25–44	−0.05 (0.04)	−0.11 (0.04)
45–64	0.30 (0.05)	0.26 (0.05)
New resident	−0.18 (0.04)	−0.17 (0.04)
Married	0.12 (0.03)	0.13 (0.03)
White collar	0.18 (0.04)	0.13 (0.05)
Petty bourgeois	−0.17 (0.06)	−0.05 (0.07)
Blue collar	−0.01 (0.04)	−0.07 (0.05)
Income under £8,000	−0.07 (0.03)	−0.08 (0.03)

larger sample which makes it easier to find statistically significant results. Thirdly, our classification of the independent variables is slightly different. Fourthly, our dependent variable is different. And fifthly, we have excluded respondents aged 65 and over from the analysis because of doubts about their representativeness.

Conclusions

However, it must be emphasized how similar our results are to those of Crewe and his colleagues based on data obtained thirteen years earlier than ours. We wish to endorse their general conclusions that turnout appears to be quite high in almost all social groups and that a substantial majority of registered electors will turn out to vote if the costs of voting are not too high.

Although the use of official turnout records generally confirmed [the conclusions] of Crewe and his colleagues using respondents' reports, with the exceptions noted above, it is worth noting that the relationships between turnout and the various independent variables (age, length of residence and so on) are generally rather stronger when the official records are used. In effect, the groups with the lowest turnout are the ones who are most likely to exaggerate their turnout.

Overall, then, our results are rather comforting, both to the survey researcher and to the political theorist. We have found that misrepresenting of turnout by our survey respondents is relatively low, certainly by American standards. We have generally confirmed the conclusions of previous research on the determinants of turnout, and have shown that when better quality data are used (namely the official records of turnout) stronger relationships are found, not different relationships. For the survey researcher, who must always be concerned about the validity of data, these are comforting findings.

Our data have also tended to indicate that the level of redundancy in the electoral register is towards the lower of Todd and Butcher's estimates and yields an estimate of 80 per cent for the 'true' level of turnout. This is likely to be still some way short of the record turnout recorded in 1950. However, once one takes account of the extension of the franchise to 18-year-olds in 1969, the increased redundancy in the register, and the age of the register at the time of the election, it is unlikely that there has been much decline in turnout over the last quarter century. This suggests that alarmist fears about the collapse of the political culture, increasing alienation from the political system and so on, are rather wide of the mark.

2.3 Marginality and turnout in general elections in the 1970s

David Denver and Gordon Hands

In an article published some time ago, we analysed the relationship between constituency marginality and turnout in British general elections between 1955 and 1970 [Denver and Hands, 1974]. We were concerned with the relationship between the absolute level of turnout in constituencies in one election and their marginality at the previous election ('previous marginality' – defined as 100 minus the winning party's percentage majority over the second-placed candidate). We found that there was a consistent, significant, positive relationship between previous constituency marginality and turnout.

This conclusion was derived, in the first place, from the calculation of simple correlation coefficients showing the strength of the relationship between previous marginality and turnout. We went on, however, to examine this relationship more rigorously by constructing a series of multiple regression equations with constituency turnout as the dependent variable and a variety of social and political variables which might be supposed to affect turnout as 'predictors'. When the 'best' equation for each election was obtained, we then added the previous marginality variable in order to measure the extent to which it increased the predictive power of the equations. In each case marginality significantly increased the percentage of turnout variation explained by the regression equations. Even when other important variables were taken into account, then, marginality was found to be an important influence upon turnout. The purpose of the present note is to extend this analysis into the 1970s.

There was a major revision of constituency boundaries between the elections of 1970 and February 1974 and this led to many substantially new constituencies being created. It follows that the concept of previous

From D. Denver and G. Hands, 'Marginality and turnout in general elections in the 1970s', *British Journal of Political Science* (1985), vol. 15, pp. 381–8.

marginality cannot sensibly be applied to voting in the February 1974 election, and so our analysis concentrates on the elections of October 1974 and 1979. We have, as before, excluded constituencies in Northern Ireland and we have also omitted the Cardiff West constituency, since the Speaker was not opposed by a Conservative in that seat in 1979. This leaves a total of 622 constituencies upon which the analysis is based.

Table 2.3.1 shows the results obtained when simple correlation coefficients are computed for previous marginality and turnout in these constituencies in the 1970s together with the results previously obtained for earlier elections. In our original article we noted that the coefficients for 1966 and 1970 were rather higher than those for 1959 and 1964 and suggested that this supported the argument that electors or parties, or both, were becoming more sophisticated in their behaviour. The figures for the 1970s suggest that this trend is continuing since the correlations between marginality and turnout in October 1974 and 1979 are the strongest of the series.

As we noted above, however, the calculation of simple correlation coefficients is only a first step in the analysis. We must try to take account of other variables which might importantly affect turnout. Accordingly, we incorporated into our analysis seven social and political variables which might be expected to be related to turnout. The seven variables are, for each constituency, percentage of economically active and retired persons in professional and managerial occupations, percentage of economically active and retired persons in non-manual occupations, percentage of owner-occupier households, percentage of council tenant households, percentage share of vote obtained by minor parties, percentage change in the size of the electorate between 1974 and 1979 and the percentage of the population living in urban areas. (For precise definitions of these variables and the rationale for the inclusion of each see Denver and Hands, 1974.)

Table 2.3.2 shows the correlations between each of these variables and turnout at each of the elections considered here. Throughout the period, the occupation variables show only modest relationships with turnout. This is because the relationship between class and turnout is modified by the interdependence of class and marginality. A large proportion of either middle-class or working-class electors will tend to make a seat very safe for

Table 2.3.1 Correlations between previous marginality and turnout

1959	1964	1966	1970	Oct. 1974	1979
0.33	0.23	0.46	0.44	0.48	0.51

Note: For 1959–70 $N = 615$; for 1974–79, $N = 622$. This applies also to all subsequent tables.

MARGINALITY AND TURNOUT IN THE 1970s

Table 2.3.2 Correlations between social/political variables and turnout

	1959	1964	1966	1970	Oct. 1974	1979
% prof. & managerial	0.12	0.29	0.38	0.29	0.36	0.37
% non-manual	0.05	0.17	0.29	0.13	0.17	0.20
% owner-occupiers	0.48	0.56	0.59	0.53	0.57	0.58
% council tenants	0.03	−0.02	−0.11	−0.05	−0.13	−0.17
% minor party	0.13	0.31	0.27	0.37	0.29	0.18
% change in electorate	0.40	0.49	0.57	0.52	0.62	0.58
% urban	−0.15	−0.33	−0.32	−0.45	−0.42	−0.42

either the Conservatives or Labour. The effect is that these seats will have lower turnouts than seats in which the balance of classes leads to a more marginal political situation. The 1959–1970 data confirm the logic of this argument. Negative correlations were found between turnout and the percentage professional and managerial and the percentage non-manual in consistently Conservative seats. On the other hand, the correlations in consistently Labour seats were positive. These relationships continued to hold in the 1970s as the figures in Table 2.3.3 show.

The correlations between housing tenure and turnout are more difficult to explain. Those for percentage council tenants are weakly negative (and barely significant) while those for percentage owner-occupiers are consistently strongly positive. [This] can, however, be more easily understood if we refer to the third major category of housing tenure, privately rented housing. People living in such accommodation are likely to include a high proportion of transient, mobile and young rather than settled members of a community. Unsurprisingly, there is a strong negative correlation between turnout and percentage privately renting (−0.60 in October 1974 and −0.57 in 1979). Omitting Scotland, where the pattern of housing tenure is very different from the rest of the country, percentage privately renting is strongly negatively related to percentage owner-occupiers (−0.54, $N = 551$) but only weakly negatively related to percentage council tenants

Table 2.3.3 Correlations between turnout and occupational variables

	% prof. & man.	% non-manual	N
Con.-held seats			
Oct. 1974	−0.22	−0.33	297
1979	−0.14	−0.25	279
Lab.-held seats			
Oct. 1974	0.56	0.20	300
1979	0.61	0.28	317

$(-0.28, N = 551)$. This suggests that the overall positive relationship between percentage owner-occupiers and turnout reflects higher turnout in more stable communities and lower turnout in those characterised by larger transient populations; while the absence of a strong relationship between percentage council tenants and turnout reflects the fact that the level of council housing does not vary significantly with the stability of communities.

The share of the vote received by minor parties relates to turnout in an erratic way. It is perhaps noteworthy, however, that during the 1970s when the number of minor party candidates in elections grew substantially, the effect upon turnout appears to have steadily diminished.

Finally, two variables – percentage change in size of electorate and percentage living in urban areas – both show an increasingly strong relationship with turnout. In both cases the figures reflect low and declining turnouts in areas of rapidly declining population, most notably the centres of the large cities and conurbations.

Using these seven variables, we computed multiple regression equations for each election with turnout as the dependent variable. Using 'backward elimination' we successively removed non-significant variables until we had equations in which all variables were statistically significant. We then added the previous marginality variable in order to discover the extent to which this increased the predictive power of the equations. The results of this process are summarised in Table 2.3.4.

It can be seen that in every case previous marginality noticeably increases the predictive power of the regression equations. Moreover, the increase in variation explained is greatest in October 1974 while the figure for 1979 is larger than that for three of the four elections in the 1959–70 period. On the basis of these figures, together with the correlations shown in Table 2.3.1, we conclude that in the 1970s marginality increased in importance as a factor explaining variations in constituency turnouts.

In our original article we argued that the effect of marginality upon turnout should not be explained simply by reference to the perceptions and

Table 2.3.4 Percentage of variance in turnout accounted for by previous marginality

	1959	1964	1966	1970	Oct. 1974	1979
% variance explained by first equation	42.9	55.2	53.9	54.8	63.2	60.6
% variance explained by first equation plus marginality	50.0	60.1	63.0	60.2	72.8	67.8
Increase due to previous marginality	7.1	4.9	9.1	5.4	9.6	7.2

MARGINALITY AND TURNOUT IN THE 1970s

behaviour of electors in individual constituencies. We suggested that the perceptions and activities of the parties were probably more important. Having identified marginal seats, parties would concentrate their campaign effort on them and, in a broad way, campaign effort would be proportional to marginality. Thus electors in different constituencies would experience varying levels of local stimuli and this, more than their own perceptions of constituency marginality, would explain the relationship between marginality and turnout. To test this hypothesis we used the amount of money spent in each constituency by the parties during the campaign as a surrogate for a measure of campaign effort. It does not seem unreasonable to suggest that a party's expenditure in a constituency campaign will be roughly proportional to the effort put in by party workers.

If our hypothesis were true, one would expect a positive relationship between campaign expenditure and previous marginality. As Table 2.3.5 shows, this expectation is amply fulfilled for October 1974 and 1979 as it was between 1959 and 1970. The strong correlations found suggest that the parties do put more campaign effort into more marginal seats.

As a second step, however, we would expect campaign expenditure to be more strongly related to turnout than marginality is, and also to contribute more powerfully to accounting for turnout variation when incorporated in regression analysis. These expectations were fulfilled in our original analysis for the period 1955 to 1970 but they are not in the case of the 1974 and 1979 elections. The details are reported in Table 2.3.6.

At each election up to 1970 expenditure was more strongly correlated

Table 2.3.5 Correlations between previous marginality and campaign expenditure

1959	1964	1966	1970	Oct. 1974	1979
0.66	0.52	0.70	0.64	0.75	0.64

Table 2.3.6 Comparisons of the effect of marginality and campaign expenditure on turnout

	1959	1964	1966	1970	Oct. 1974	1979
Correlation with turnout:						
Marginality	0.33	0.23	0.46	0.44	0.48	0.51
Expenditure	0.41	0.41	0.50	0.45	0.42	0.30
Additional variation explained:						
Marginality	7.1	4.9	9.1	5.4	9.6	7.2
Expenditure	7.5	5.7	10.1	9.5	6.6	6.0

with turnout than was marginality. Similarly, up to 1970, when expenditure was incorporated into regression equations (in the manner described above in the case of marginality) the proportion of variation explained increased by more than the increment obtained when marginality was added. In 1974 and 1979, however, the position is reversed. On both tests expenditure is more weakly related to turnout than is marginality.

Although this might be explained by the weakness of campaign expenditure as an indicator of party effort, we suggest that a genuine change has probably occurred. In the days of strong party identification voters responded to the stimulus provided by the local party campaign and higher levels of party effort in marginal seats were rewarded by higher turnout. As party identification has weakened, however, the efforts of the party machines count for less; voters respond less to the stimulus of the party campaigns and more to their own independent assessments of the likelihood of seats changing hands.

This is a consequence of partisan dealignment that has hitherto been rather overlooked. The fact that the relationship between marginality and turnout is on the increase appears to be not a consequence of the increased sophistication of the parties but rather a reflection of the increased sophistication of the voters themselves. In an era of dealignment electors are not only more discriminating in deciding which party to support but also more 'choosy' about whether to vote at all. In the latter case the perceived marginality of the voters' local constituency is a factor which importantly affects the decision made.

Electors' perceptions of the marginality of constituencies may, however, be affected by perceptions of the national standing of the parties. If voters were aware – from opinion polls for instance – that one party was likely to improve its position in a forthcoming election, then seats marginally held by the likely 'losing' party would be perceived as much more 'at risk' or 'gainable' than those marginally held by the 'advancing' party. Also, seats which would seem moderately safe for the 'losing' party if the tide were running in its favour could begin to look more marginal on an adverse swing. It might be expected, then, that the relationship between turnout and marginality would be more pronounced in seats being defended by the party thought likely to lose ground in the election. This hypothesis is complex and demands a high level of sophistication on the part of the electorate, but an initial test of it is given by the data in Table 2.3.7.

Given our preceding argument, we would not expect the electorate to demonstrate sophistication of this order before the 1970s and, indeed, the most striking feature of the data up to and including 1974 is simply the increase in the strength of the correlation between marginality and turnout in Labour-held seats. This seems likely to be the result of steadily declining turnout in safe Labour seats. In 1979, however, there is a very marked drop in the strength of the correlation in Conservative seats and the highest

MARGINALITY AND TURNOUT IN THE 1970s

Table 2.3.7 Correlations between marginality and turnout in Conservative-held and Labour-held constituencies, 1959–79

	Conservative-held	Labour-held
1959	0.54 ($N = 333$)	0.18 ($N = 275$)
1964	0.36 ($N = 351$)	0.17 ($N = 257$)
1966	0.55 ($N = 290$)	0.38 ($N = 316$)
1970	0.39 ($N = 240$)	0.40 ($N = 364$)
Oct. 1974	0.38 ($N = 297$)	0.43 ($N = 300$)
1979	0.25 ($N = 279$)	0.50 ($N = 317$)

Note: The status of a constituency is determined by the party which won it at the general election preceding the ones for which coefficients are given.

correlation of the series in Labour seats. This is exactly as would be predicted by the hypothesis we have outlined, since an easy Conservative victory was generally expected in 1979.

Although this is only a preliminary test of the hypothesis, it does suggest that in assessing the marginality of a constituency electors are now influenced by their expectations regarding the overall outcome of elections. Rather than being a ritual or a response to party prodding, the decision to vote seems increasingly to be affected by a realistic appraisal of local and national political circumstances.

Part II

Models of party choice

3 | Class and party

Introduction

Our first extract in this section, from Butler and Stokes' *Political Change in Britain*, begins with a reference to a comment made by Peter Pulzer about the nature of British party politics, which must be one of the most frequently quoted remarks ever made on the subject – 'Class is the basis of British party politics; all else is embellishment and detail.' Pulzer's remark summarised admirably the findings of previous survey research on British voting behaviour, and his view – that party support in Britain was predominantly class-based – was widely shared for much of the post-war period.

Butler and Stokes used their nationwide surveys in the 1960s to demonstrate the continuing importance of this link and they build it into their model of voting behaviour. The model is essentially based on party identification and is largely derived from the Michigan model, but they see class as being such a major influence on 'partisan self-image' or 'partisanship' (the terms they use to refer to party identification) that much of their analysis actually by-passes party identification and looks directly at the class–party link. In this extract Butler and Stokes explain how they define classes (a matter which itself became controversial in later studies), set out the evidence for class voting and consider how voters perceive the links between classes and parties.

Already in the second (1974) edition of *Political Change in Britain*, however, Butler and Stokes commented on what they called the 'ageing of the class alignment', and during the 1970s class dealignment became a dominant theme in voting studies. The argument was that a steady and clear weakening of the class–party link was taking place. This argument was first fully developed in an influential article by Crewe, Sarlvik and Alt (1977). We do not reproduce a selection from this article here because many of the ideas it contains were refined, and the empirical material up-dated, by the authors in later pieces. One such piece, first published in

51

52 MODELS OF PARTY CHOICE

1983, is reproduced here as our second extract. In it Ivor Crewe provides a clear summary of what by then had become the orthodoxy about class dealignment.

This orthodoxy came under severe attack from Heath, Jowell and Curtice in *How Britain Votes* (1985). This book, which was based on the BES survey of the 1983 election, considerably stirred the psephological waters – although whether the final result has been to muddy them or make them clearer remains a matter of considerable dispute. Heath, Jowell and Curtice make two key moves: first they propose a theoretically more sophisticated operationalisation of the concept of class; secondly, they distinguish between what they call 'absolute' and 'relative' class voting. They argue that in the context of class dealignment it is the latter and not the former which should concern us, and they use odds ratios as the principal measure of relative class voting. They conclude that an analysis of post-war election results conducted in these terms shows not class dealignment but 'trendless fluctuation' in the strength of the relationship between class and party.

This argument provoked a debate among specialists in voting behaviour which has been unusually tetchy and bad-tempered. We reproduce extracts from three of the main contributions to it, by Crewe, by Heath *et al.* themselves and by Patrick Dunleavy. We hesitate to intervene in the controversy, but in our view a reasonable account of the ideas of 'class voting' and 'class dealignment' cannot be given in terms of Heath, Jowell and Curtice's notion of relative class voting. Class dealignment, as normally understood, involves changes in the levels of both relative *and* absolute class voting. If that is so, whether or not odds ratios are a good indicator of relative class voting they cannot be a good indicator of whether or not there has been class dealignment; and it also follows that log linear analysis of voting trends of the kind undertaken by Heath, Jowell and Curtice cannot decide the matter. They may have shown that there has been trendless fluctuation in the odds ratios, and possibly even in relative class voting; they have not shown that there has not been class dealignment.

Our final extract in this section sheds a different light on the debate about class dealignment. Miller's work on constituency voting trends, though it is not exactly 'user-friendly', brings to light a paradox that has attracted much attention. He shows that while (at least in conventional terms) analysis of survey data over the past twenty-five years has shown a clear weakening of the effect of class upon party choice among individual voters, analysis of *constituency* data shows that the class composition of constituencies has had a constant or even strengthening impact upon election outcomes. Miller suggests that this is to be explained as a consequence of an increasingly powerful environmental effect. People tend to adopt the dominant political norms of their neighbourhood – those

CLASS AND PARTY

living in predominantly middle-class areas are more likely to vote Conservative whatever their own class, and similarly those in predominantly working-class areas are more likely to vote Labour, whatever their own class.

Further reading

For a standard account of the relationship between class and party in Britain in the 1950s and 1960s see Pulzer (1967). Alford (1963) compares class voting in Britain, Australia, Canada and the United States, while a more recent discussion of the social bases of voting behaviour, also from a comparative perspective, may be found in Harrop and Miller (1987, ch. 7).

The first major account of class dealignment was given by Crewe, Sarlvik and Alt (1977). Sarlvik and Crewe (1983) traces the course of dealignment through the three general elections of the 1970s. Later support for the thesis is to be found in Robertson (1984) and Rose and McAllister (1986, 1990). Support for Heath *et al.*'s revisionist position may be found in Marshall *et al.* (1988) and Weakliem (1989), and there is a brief response to Dunleavy's criticisms in Heath, Jowell and Curtice (1988a).

There is a fuller – if statistically rather difficult – account of Miller's argument about the class polarisation of constituencies in Miller (1977), and the analysis is extended to include the 1979 election in Miller (1979).

In a number of publications Dunleavy has suggested that over the past twenty years sectoral cleavages have come to replace class cleavages as the main basis of party choice (Dunleavy, 1979, 1980a, 1980b; Dunleavy and Husbands, 1985), although this approach has been trenchantly criticised by Franklin and Page (1984).

3.1 Class and party

David Butler and Donald Stokes

In contemporary interpretations of British voting behaviour class is accorded the leading role. Pulzer was entirely in the academic main stream when he wrote, 'class is the basis of British party politics; all else is embellishment and detail' [Pulzer, 1967, p. 98]. There is, in fact, evidence that party allegiance has followed class lines more strongly in Britain than anywhere else in the English-speaking world.

But in view of the large amount of attention focused on the correlation between class and party in Britain, the evidence about the nature of this link remains oddly limited. Too little attention has been paid to the beliefs that link class to party in the voter's mind. The fact of partisan differences between classes is documented in a wealth of statistical evidence; the system of ideas, the attitudes, motives and beliefs which lie behind the observed differences have been largely neglected. This chapter considers some problems in the measurement of class and explores the links between class and party, including the beliefs that give meaning to politics in terms of class.

The bases of class

The identity and number of classes, the attributes characterising classes, the relationship between classes, the openness of classes to individual movements up and down between generations or within one adult lifetime – these are all matters that are seen very differently in different parts of society. We, therefore, sought to interpret the class system in the light of our respondents' own perceptions of it. We began by asking whether the

From D.E. Butler and D. Stokes, *Political Change in Britain* (1st edn, 1969), London: Macmillan, chapter 4.

54

respondent thought of himself as belonging to a class. Those, about half the sample, who said that they did were then asked in a completely unprompted way to name their class. The replies offer remarkable evidence of the primacy of the 'middle' and 'working' class designations; only one in twenty-five of such respondents failed to make use of one or other of the two.

Those who had replied to the initial question by saying that they did not think of themselves as belonging to a class were then asked whether they would place themselves in the middle or working class if pressed to do so. The overwhelming majority said that they would; indeed, we were left with only one respondent in twelve who neither volunteered nor accepted a middle or working class identification. The view that British society is divided into two primary classes is much more than a sociologist's simplification; it seems to be deeply rooted in the mind of the ordinary British citizen.

In view of the extraordinary hold of this dichotomy we sought to explore the characteristics that people attributed to members of the middle and working class. Once again we found wide agreement. Occupation provided the main basis for characterising the classes. When our respondents described the kind of people who belong to the middle class, references to occupation outnumbered references to wealth or income by three to one and references to education or manners or shared attitudes by twelve to one. When they described the kinds of people who belong to the working class the primacy of occupation was even more striking. The role of occupation in perceptions of class is matched by its primacy as a predictor of the class with which a man identifies himself. There is overwhelming evidence that occupational status is the best guide to whether an individual places himself in the middle or working class.

The measurement of occupational grade necessarily involves the investigator in some intricate problems of assessment. We have relied in our own coding of occupational level on a detailed classification of occupations into social grades proposed by a working committee of the Market Research Society, using the occupational categories of the 1961 Census Classification of Occupations. We have, however, modified these definitions to divide the lowest group of non-manual workers, those designated as C1 in conventional market-research terms, between those who have some skilled or supervisory role and those who do not. Thus the categories we have used are these:

	Market	
Our	research	
designation	designation	
I	A	Higher managerial or professional
II	B	Lower managerial or administrative
III ⎫		⎧ Skilled or supervisory non-manual
IV ⎭	C1	⎩ Lower non-manual
V	C2	Skilled manual
VI	D	Unskilled manual
VII	E	Residual, on pension or other state benefit

How do self-placements into the middle and working class differ across these occupational categories? Table 3.1.1 shows the relationship between the respondent's subjective class identification and the occupational level of the head of the respondent's household. The proportion of respondents identifying themselves with the middle class falls continuously from 78 per cent in group I to 9 per cent in group VI. The very sharp cleft between group III and group IV underlines the psychological validity of treating social stratification in terms of two main classes. But this cleft occurs not between manual and non-manual but between skilled or supervisory non-manual (III) and other lower non-manual (IV). There is a further sharp drop in middle-class identification between groups IV and V, but the self-placement of the lower non-manual group (IV) shows them to be more like the skilled manual stratum (V) than they are like the next higher non-manual grouping (III). It is plain that the combination of group IV and group III within the market research category C1 involves lumping together people who diverge markedly in their subjective class identifications.

The close alignment of occupational level and class self-image accords well with our evidence that occupation is the most important of the elements that characterise the classes in the public's mind. There are other elements, of course – education, income and occupation are, for example,

Table 3.1.1 Class self-image by occupational status of head of household, 1963

Class self-image	Higher managerial I	Lower managerial II	Supervisory non-manual III	Lower non-manual IV	Skilled manual V	Unskilled manual VI
Middle class	78%	65%	60%	32%	17%	9%
Working class	22	35	40	68	83	91
	100%	100%	100%	100%	100%	100%
(N)	(90)	(133)	(256)	(177)	(673)	(428)

CLASS AND PARTY

closely linked – but because of the pre-eminent importance of occupation we shall use it in most cases as a measure of class location.

Class cleavages in party support

Our findings on the strength of links between class and partisanship in Britain echo broadly those of every other opinion poll or voting study. The ebbs and flows of party strength over the period [of our surveys] made for some variation, but the difference between the parties' share of votes in each class remained enormous. Table 3.1.2 [which gives] the figures from our interviews in the summer of 1963 makes plain that there were strong enough cross-currents in each class for partisanship not to have been determined entirely by class. Yet its pre-eminent role can hardly be questioned.

[Table 3.1.3 shows support for the two parties across our six occupational grades, and there is a] continuous fall of Conservative strength down the occupational scale. The figure which seems most discrepant from the strong pattern of the array is that for lower non-manual (IV); the Conservatives gathered in much more than half the support of this group.

In marked contrast to the intimate ties between class and Conservative and Labour support, support for the Liberals was remarkably unrelated to class self-image and to occupational grade. The Liberals indeed constitute a standing challenge to any over-simple account of class and party [see

Table 3.1.2 Party support by class self-image, 1963

	Class self-image	
Partisan self-image	Middle	Working
Conservative	79%	28%
Labour	21	72
	100%	100%

Table 3.1.3 Party self-image by occupational status, 1963

Partisan self-image	Higher managerial I	Lower managerial II	Supervisory non-manual III	Lower non-manual IV	Skilled manual V	Unskilled manual VI
Conservative	86%	81%	77%	61%	29%	25%
Labour	14	19	23	39	71	75
	100%	100%	100%	100%	100%	100%

Table 3.1.4 Proportion Liberal by occupation level and class self-image, 1963

Class self-image	Higher managerial I	Lower managerial II	Supervisory non-manual III	Lower non-manual IV	Skilled manual V	Unskilled manual VI
Middle	12%	20%	16%	24%	12%	10%
Working	22%	14%	13%	14%	10%	5%

Table 3.1.4]. The main impression conveyed by these figures is of the breadth and evenness, in class terms, of the Liberals' appeal.

These varying patterns of class support for the main parties draw us back to the question of the basis of the ties between class and party. Here we begin to touch on questions which, to a peculiar degree, elude definitive answers: yet we feel it is worthwhile to outline three distinct models of the nature of class partisanship and to set out evidence for their validity and their relative importance.

[Three models of the link between class and party]

Politics as class conflict

The first of these models involves the conception of politics as a conflict of *opposed* class interests, with the parties attracting their support by representing those interests. Seen in terms of class conflict, the game of politics will benefit one class at the expense of the other. In the language of game theory, we might indeed say that the distinguishing feature of the class conflict model is that politics is seen as a 'zero-sum' game, in which the gains of one class are matched by the losses of the other. More is involved than a simple belief that the parties 'look after' class interests: these interests are seen as opposed and their opposition is what the party battle is thought to be about.

The simple representation of class interest

[An] alternative conception of the ties between class and party is a variant of the conflict model. Politics may be seen as an arena in which the parties do indeed represent class interests – but interests which are not necessarily seen as opposed. Politics is a *positive-sum* rather than a *zero-sum* game. [Thus] it may reflect the fragmentary nature of the perceptions of electors able to see clearly enough that their party looks after the interest of their class, but not much beyond that.

CLASS AND PARTY

Partisanship in the class culture

The individual's response to the political norms of his class milieu can also help to keep the classes politically distinct without perceptions of class interest necessarily being involved. However important the perception of interests may have been in creating the political divergence of classes in the first place or in sustaining them in the longer run, anything so pervasive as the norm of Labour voting in the working class or Conservative voting in the middle class is likely to be accepted by many members of the class simply because it is there. Within the British nation there are distinct class sub-cultures which differ as to dress, speech, child rearing and much else. The processes by which individuals accept the norms of these cultures are quite general, and it would be as absurd to see perceived class interests in all class voting as it would be to infer such interests from class differences in the time of dinner or the rituals of mourning.

This simple normative quality of party allegiance within class groupings had its origin for many electors in the childhood home. The appropriateness of a particular party to a particular class was for many children the main explanation as to why their parents voted as they did, especially in the working class. The significance of this for a sub-cultural interpretation of class voting is plain enough. An elector who absorbed in childhood a belief about a normative bond of class and party, and who finds this bond reinforced by many of the face-to-face associations in his adult life, may easily accept party allegiance as a natural element of his class culture, quite apart from any well-defined understanding of the benefits that his party may confer upon his class or himself.

A profile of beliefs about class and party

Although the difficulties are formidable, it is worth attempting some tentative estimate of the extent to which the approaches to class and party described in our three models are manifest in the electorate. We base our judgement on the evidence furnished by respondents whom we interviewed three times from 1963 to 1966 and who held throughout the period consistent class and party allegiances – either Conservative and middle class or Labour and working class. First, we inspected our respondents' verbatim comments on their likes and dislikes about the parties at each of the interviews. Second, we examined their descriptions of the reason for their party preference at each of the interviews. Third, we looked at the reasons given by respondents in the first interview to explain why their class accorded preponderant support to a given party.

Our classification of beliefs yields a very different profile for the middle and working classes, as Table 3.1.5 shows. This table makes clear how very

Table 3.1.5 Beliefs about the relation of class and party held by middle class Conservatives and working class Labour voters

Nature of beliefs	Conservative middle class	Labour working class
Politics as the representation of opposing class interests	13%	39%
Politics as the representation of simple class interests	12	47
Politics as an expression of class political norms	10	5
No interest-related or normative content	65	9
	100%	100%
(N)	(96)	(301)

much more salient to the working class are the ideas of class interest and class conflict. Seven in eight of our working class Labour supporters gave evidence of seeing politics as the representation of class interests, and almost half of these regarded such interests as opposed. Among middle class Conservatives fewer than one in three gave evidence of seeing politics in terms of the representation of class interests.

This difference of outlook between middle and working class accords well with differences of party ideology. The Conservatives can style themselves as the representatives of a more national interest, one that includes the interest of all classes within a hierarchical social order. The middle class elector can therefore identify his party with an existing social order which preserves the interest of the upper and middle classes without relying on concepts of class interest and conflict that are so evident in working class thought. In the main the working class held to a more dichotomous view of the social order, and Labour's image in the period of our work still reflected the party's explicitly working class origins and trade union connections.

3.2 Class dealignment

Ivor Crewe

In Great Britain, since World War I, 'class' has been the primary, almost exclusive, social basis of party choice. In the late 1960s [however] the first signs of a weakening in the class–party link appeared. Alternative bases of partisanship emerged (or re-emerged after decades) in some areas: language and culture in rural Wales, national identity in Scotland, race in a few cities. Butler and Stokes reported an 'ageing of the class alignment'. A new generation of electors, brought up in the relative prosperity of the 1950s and 1960s, were less likely than their parents, who had known the inter-war Depression, to think of politics in terms of class conflict or to develop a party identification that followed class lines. Nonetheless, until 1970 the overall amount of class voting remained fairly stable.

How the trend in class voting moved after 1970 is shown in Table 3.2.1 which sets out the Conservative, Labour and Liberal/other party division of the vote among manual and non-manual voters at each of the eight elections from 1959 to 1983. This is a convenient period of comparison as it begins and ends with decisive Conservative victories and is marked in the middle (1970) by another, although slightly less impressive, Conservative win: thus the trend in class voting should not be unduly affected by the trend in the election results. The second half of the period, 1970–83, was marked by minimal [economic] growth, rising unemployment and sharp cuts in public expenditure and was punctuated by outbreaks of severe industrial unrest in 1972, 1974 (coinciding with the February election) and 1978–79. During this time, therefore, a class polarisation of the vote might have been expected.

Instead, Table 3.2.1 shows that class voting declined, at first fitfully but

From I. Crewe, 'The electorate: partisan dealignment ten years on', *West European Politics* (1983), vol. 6 , pp. 183–215.

Table 3.2.1 'Class voting' 1959–83: party division of the vote in non-manual and manual occupational strata

Votes	1959 election Non-manual %	1959 election Manual %	1964 election Non-manual %	1964 election Manual %	1966 election Non-manual %	1966 election Manual %	1970 election Non-manual %	1970 election Manual %	February 1974 election Non-manual %	February 1974 election Manual %	October 1974 election Non-manual %	October 1974 election Manual %	1979 election Non-manual %	1979 election Manual %	1983 election Non-manual %	1983 election Manual %
Conservative	69	34	62	28	60	25	64	33	53	24	51	24	60	35	58	33
Liberal or minor party	8	4	16	8	14	6	11	9	25	19	24	20	17	15	26	29
Labour	22	62	22	64	26	69	25	58	22	57	25	57	23	50	17	38
Total per cent	100%	100%	100%	100%	100%	100%	100%	100%	100%	100%	100%	100%	100%	100%	100%	100%
Number of respondents	526	792	595	914	595	945	392	577	893	1,060	834	1,010	650	779	1,577	1,961
Alford Index of Labour voting	40		42		43		33		35		32		27		21	
Non-manual Conservative + manual Labour voters as % of all voters	65%		63%		66%		60%		55%		54%		55%		47%	

Source: Butler and Stokes' Election Surveys 1964, 1966 and 1970, BES February 1974, October 1974 and May 1979 Election surveys, BBC/Gallup Survey, 1983. Data on voting in 1959 were obtained from recall in the 1964 survey.

CLASS DEALIGNMENT

63

then with increasing pace. One measure of class voting, Alford's Index, is the difference between Labour's percentage of the middle-class as against the working-class vote, and ranges from 0 (no class voting) to 100 (perfect class voting). In the two elections of the 1960s it stood at 42 and 43. It dropped to 33 in 1970, stayed there in the two 1974 elections, and then fell further to 27 in 1979 and down again to 21 in 1983 – half the score of twenty years before. An alternative measure of class voting is the number of Conservative non-manual workers and Labour manual workers as a proportion of all voters. (It has the advantage of not relying exclusively on the Labour vote, and of treating Liberal and other party supporters as non-class voters.) The proportion was 65 per cent in 1959, 60 per cent in 1970, 55 per cent for the rest of the 1970s, and 47 per cent in 1983. Over the 24-year period the incidence of class voting fell from two-thirds to under half of all voters (and thus a mere third of the total electorate). The class basis of the vote has not disappeared, but it is much less visible.

In the period under scrutiny the class structure itself underwent major changes. With the gradual replacement of manual labour by machinery and of manufacturing industry by the service sector, the non-manual labour force expanded and the manual workforce contracted: in the surveys reported in Table 3.2.1 the non-manual to manual ratio shifted from 40:60 to 45:55. A change of this kind need not affect the *overall* amount of class voting, but it could be expected to alter the relative amount *within* each class. From the recruitment of manual workers' children (and wives) into the non-manual labour force, especially the rapidly expanding lower grades, and from the resulting growth in white collar trade unions, one would anticipate a gradual fall in the Conservative share of the non-manual vote. And as the manual work-force contracts, increasingly confined to those 'left behind' by economic change, one would expect it to become more solidly Labour. This is not quite what happened. Between 1959 and 1983 the Conservative share of the non-manual vote did fall, from 69 per cent to 58 per cent (which is twice the rate of the 49 to 43 per cent drop in Great Britain as a whole). But Labour's share of the manual vote, far from rising, plummeted from 62 per cent to 38 per cent.

The collapse of the working-class Labour vote is the single most significant change in the electoral sociology of Britain in recent years. In both the 1979 and 1983 elections the largest swings to the Conservatives were among the working class, not the middle classes. The Labour party's claim to be the party of the working class looks increasingly threadbare – sociologically if not ideologically. The Labour vote remains largely working class; but the working class has ceased to be largely Labour. In the 1983 election it split its vote three ways, giving Labour a mere five per cent majority over the Conservatives; among trade unionists the Labour majority was only seven per cent. Labour's share of the working-class *electorate* was down to barely a quarter (27 per cent).

By 1983 it would be more accurate to describe Labour as the party of a segment of the working class – the 'traditional' working class of Scotland and the North, the public sector and the council estates (see Table 3.2.2). Among these slowly dwindling groups Labour was still the first, if not always the majority, choice. Among the expanding 'new' working class, however, Labour support has haemorrhaged badly. In 1983 Labour ran neck and neck with the Conservatives among private sector workers. Among manual workers owning their house, or living in the South, the Conservatives had a commanding lead and Labour was *third* choice, behind the Liberal/SDP Alliance. Moreover, the 'new' working class is the increasingly preponderant group.

By 1983 twice as many manual workers were employed in the private sector as the public sector, which will contract further under the Conservative government's plans for retrenchment and privatisation. Many more manual workers are home-owners than council tenants; and over the next few years more council houses will be sold to their tenants and little new council house building will start. Almost as many manual workers live in the South as in the North and Scotland combined; as the population drift from North to South continues the balance will tip the other way. The 'traditional working class' is Britain's newest minority; it is far too small, by itself, to elect a Labour government.

In contrast, Conservative support among the working class was the same in 1983 as in 1959, having fluctuated considerably in between. The incidence of working-class Conservatism may not have changed; but its character almost certainly has. The political sociologists of a generation ago distinguished various sources of working-class Conservatism – social deference, authoritarianism, 'economic instrumentalism' – but all had in common the assumption that a manual worker who voted Conservative did

Table 3.2.2 The two working classes: % of three-party vote, 1983

	New working class			Traditional working class		
	Owner-occupiers %	Works in private sector %	Lives in South %	Council tenants %	Works in public sector %	Lives in Scotland/ North %
Con.	47	36	42	19	29	32
Lab.	25	37	26	57	46	42
Lib./SDP	28	27	32	24	25	26
Con./Lab. majority	Con. +22	Lab. +1	Con. +16	Lab. +38	Lab. +17	Lab. +10
Category as % of all manual workers	43%	66%	36%	45%	34%	38%

Source: BBC/Gallup Survey, 1983.

CLASS DEALIGNMENT

not do so out of direct, individual or group, economic self-interest. In 1979, however, it emerged that many working-class Conservatives, especially converts from 1974, were attracted by Conservative party policy to cut income tax, abandon incomes policies and encourage local authorities to sell council houses to tenants at a market discount. In all three instances Labour policy was hostile or ambivalent; in all three instances secure, high wage manual workers stood to gain. Twenty years ago the one-third of manual workers who voted Conservative arguably did so *despite* their economic interests; today most of them do so *because* of their economic interests.

The class–party relationship has gradually weakened in a second sense. Not only have the party differences between the social classes narrowed; so too have the class differences between the parties. Class voting has diminished; so have 'voting classes'. A simple measure is the difference between the percentage of the Conservative vote as against the Labour vote cast by manual workers. The score ranges from 0 (when the class composition of the two parties' vote is identical) to 100 (when each party's vote is drawn exclusively from one class). The actual score has fallen, in fits and starts, from 38 in 1959 and 41 in 1964 to 32 in both 1979 and 1983. The main reason is the gradual rise in the proportion of Labour votes drawn from non-manual workers, which was one in five from 1959 to 1966 but has been one in four since. Most of this change is due to the expansion of white collar jobs.

The class gap between the parties' supporters has narrowed in another way. At the beginning of the period the class composition of Liberal voters was almost identical to that of Conservatives: in both cases the majority were non-manual workers (57 per cent). There was therefore a clear division between Labour voters and the rest of the voting electorate. By the end of the period the social make-up of Liberal voters had diverged from that of Conservatives, having become less middle class. In their class background (43 per cent non-manual, 57 per cent manual, by 1983) they were equidistant between the two major parties. The class differences between the parties could no longer be described as a simple dichotomy between Labour voters and the rest. Not only has the class polarisation of the parties narrowed; it has also fragmented.

Analysts of British elections occasionally cast doubt on the significance of the weakening of class voting, as revealed in Table 3.2.1. Franklin (1983), Rose (1980a) and others point out that occupational status is only one, albeit the most conventional, of a number of indicators of 'social class'. Income, housing tenure, education, or membership of a trade union might capture social and economic inequalities more successfully than occupational status, and consequently prove a stronger basis of the vote. Each of these can serve to differentiate Conservative from Labour voters; and each can be used to separate an overwhelmingly Conservative or (more rarely) Labour voting group from the rest of the electorate. However, no Alford-type index of voting based on the dichotomies of self-employed and employee; owner-occupier and renter; those with and without further education; non-member and member of a trade union; and those with a 'high' as against 'low' standard of living could match the fairly modest index score of 27 (in 1979) derived from the non-manual/manual division. Moreover, an AID multivariate analysis of the contribution of different dimensions of inequality to the 1979 vote, which controls for the strong inter-correlations between these dimensions, found that the manual/non-manual distinction overrode, without entirely eliminating, the effects of the others. Thus the weakening of the class–party relationship is not an artefact of measurement or definition, but a true reflection of social and political change.

Other commentators [for example, Dunleavy (1980b)] have suggested that a new social cleavage between the private and public sectors of employment might be replacing that of social class as a basis for party choice. In both 1979 and 1983 the vote of private sector workers was indeed more Conservative and less Labour than that of public sector workers. Moreover, between 1979 and 1983, in contrast to the class convergence of the vote, there was a slight sectoral polarisation of the vote: in the private sector the pro-Conservative swing was 7.5 per cent; in the public sector five per cent. However, the Alford-type index of sectoral voting (eight percentage points) remains well below that of class voting (21 percentage points). The employment sector has grown, and might well continue to grow, in importance as a basis of party choice, but it still does not match the significance, however diminished, of the manual/non-manual divide.

Social change over the past quarter-century has placed an increasing number of electors into 'mixed class' situations. For example, in the mid 1950s only a fifth of all manual workers owned their own homes; now over half (51 per cent) do. Because income tax thresholds failed to rise as fast as money earnings in the inflationary 1970s almost all manual workers in employment pay income tax; in the 1950s only a minority did. The expansion of the public sector and rise in the number of professionally qualified employees have led to a rapid growth of white collar trade unionism: by 1980, 44 per cent of all non-manual workers held a trade union card. Intergenerational social mobility, especially upward mobility, has become much more prevalent. Already a decade ago 31 per cent of the sons of manual working men had crossed the class barrier to non-manual work; 38 per cent of men in non-manual jobs were brought up in the families of manual workers. As a result, the contraction in the number of 'pure' working-class and middle-class extended families is startling. In 1972 barely a third (34 per cent) of all households consisted of husband, father and father-in-law all in manual jobs; the figure for consistently non-manual households was 13 per cent. The remainder – over half of all extended

CLASS DEALIGNMENT

families – were mixed. Most important of all, the entry of large numbers of women into the labour force – predominantly 'white blouse' work in offices – has produced a burgeoning number of mixed-class households typically consisting of a husband in manual work with a wife in non-manual work: over a third of all two-worker households are mixed-class. If this datum is added to what we know about inter-generational mobility the proportion of pure working-class households would be smaller still.

The significance of the preceding data is that voters in mixed-class situations are subject to partisan cross-pressures. Not unexpectedly, the result is a somewhat more evenly balanced Conservative and Labour share of the vote than is found in pure-class categories. However, the balance skews in favour of the Conservatives. The vote of those in mixed-class situations reveals a consistent asymmetry: the Labour lead among manual workers exposed to some aspect of middle-class life is always smaller than the Conservative lead among non-manual workers exposed to some aspect of working-class life. Here, therefore, is one important source of the crumbling of the working-class Labour vote: the rapid erosion of the 'pure' working class.

A second result of the fragmentation of social class is electoral fickleness. People subject to any form of conflicting pressures typically meet their dilemma by compromise, procrastination, wavering and withdrawal. Politics is no exception. There is evidence from both the 1979 and 1983 elections that those in mixed-class situations were more likely to vote for the Liberal/SDP Alliance, delay their voting decision until late in the campaign, change their voting intentions and identify less strongly with any party – but the differences are slight rather than marked. Here, therefore, is a clue to increasing electoral volatility.

3.3 | The decline of class voting

Anthony Heath,
Roger Jowell
and John Curtice

Defining class

At its crudest, class can be seen as a contrast between the 'haves', who are in favour of preserving the status quo, and the 'have nots' who favour social change and the redistribution of income. The 'haves' are usually equated with white-collar, non-manual workers and their families – the middle class; the 'have nots' are taken to be blue-collar, manual workers – the working class.

This highly simplistic two-class model of the class structure is often used in political analysis. While it may have some value as a first rough approximation, we hold that it is wholly inadequate for studying the social bases of politics since it ignores important divisions which have little to do with the colour of a man's or woman's collar.

The limitations of the two-class model are widely recognised but unfortunately, when political scientists have wanted a more refined measure of class, they have turned to the highly unsatisfactory 'social grade' schema. This is commonly used in market research and in opinion polling, but we believe that it gives a misleading view of the relation between class and politics. The social grade scheme comes close to the layman's view of class as a hierarchy of social groups based on differences in income and life-style. Six social grades labelled A, B, C1, C2, D and E are usually distinguished. This focus may of course be entirely appropriate for market researchers. We would however question whether income and life-style are particularly relevant to politics, and indeed we suspect that serious errors have been made by adopting this approach to politics.

From A. Heath, R. Jowell and J. Curtice, *How Britain Votes* (1985), Oxford: Pergamon, chapters 2 and 3.

THE DECLINE OF CLASS VOTING

69

The conception of class which we shall use focuses not on income levels *per se* but on economic interests. Broadly speaking, wage labourers have different interests from those of the self-employed or from those of salaried managers and professionals. Their incomes may overlap, but the conditions under which they earn that income differ quite markedly. These employment conditions are more fundamental determinants of values and political allegiance than is life-style. It is the competitive position of different groups in the labour market which provides the basis for their differing values and political principles.

For example, manual wage-earners cannot be sure to improve their lot through *individual* action. Instead they must look to *collective* action, either through trades unions or political parties. They have a shared interest, in other words, in collective bargaining over wages and working conditions and in government intervention to reduce the risks of unemployment and redundancy. In general we would expect manual wage-earners to be more receptive to socialist or interventionist values than other groups of workers.

The salaried manager or official represents one contrast to the manual wage-earner. The salaried official has a relatively well-paid and secure job in bureaucratic employment. Even if only at the bottom of the bureaucracy, the official may reasonably hope to climb to the more lucrative and powerful positions higher up. Most importantly, he or she has a vested interest in the preservation of the social order that gives rise to this advantaged position.

A second important contrast is with the self-employed. This is a group which cuts right across the conventional manual/non-manual distinction. The self-employed include skilled artisans as well as shop keepers and farmers. They may have very different incomes, but what they share is the fact of being 'independents' who are directly exposed to market forces without the cushioning of bureaucratic employment or trade union membership. They have an interest in creating conditions favourable to private enterprise and individual success. They will be particularly receptive to individualistic and 'free enterprise' values.

The self-employed constitute the most serious challenge to the use of social grade for political analysis. They will be dispersed across the social grades from A to D, but as we shall show they are very distinctive and homogeneous in their political values and behaviour.

At the very least, then, a three-fold schema which distinguishes the manual wage-earner, the salaried official and the self-employed is required. Two further distinctions are also useful. First, we distinguish routine non-manual work from the salaried managers and professionals. Routine non-manual work as a clerk, typist, receptionist and salesworker may have some of the advantages of bureaucratic employment. In many other respects however it is poorly paid wage labour; it is subject to

MODELS OF PARTY CHOICE

managerial authority and constitutes a kind of white-collar labour force. We shall treat it as a separate class, marginal to the 'salariat' proper.

Second, we distinguish foremen and technicians from the working class proper. Again these workers are somewhat marginal in their position. The foreman, for example, is differentiated from rank and file manual employees by his (or more rarely her) limited exercise of authority which gives a modicum of managerial involvement. Nonetheless, foremen lack full membership of the managerial bureaucracy, and their interests are therefore somewhat ambiguous.

We therefore distinguish between the following five classes:

1. *The salariat.*
2. *Routine non-manual.*
3. *The petty bourgeoisie.*
4. *Foremen and technicians.*
5. *The working class.*

Class and values

Our thesis is that the five classes we have distinguished will be associated with values which to some extent express, and which have their roots in, differing [class] interests. Different positions in the division of labour will be fertile soil for distinct social or political values. Different values and principles will flourish in the different classes and will provide the basis of political allegiance. Values thus provide the crucial link between class interests and political behaviour.

In the 1983 British General Election Study we asked respondents their views on a wide range of social and political questions. These covered among other things the economy, the welfare state, trade unions, defence and civil liberties. The class differences on five [of these] questions are shown in Table 3.3.1.

The most striking feature of this table is that, in every case, it is the petty bourgeoisie which is most likely to take up what would normally be thought of as the 'free enterprise' or 'right-wing' option. Despite its members' [incomes being relatively low], and despite the fact that it contains many manual workers, the petty bourgeoisie is the class most committed to private industry and private education and the most opposed to income redistribution or job creation. This is powerful testimony to the con-gruence between market situation and political ideology.

Another feature of Table 3.3.1 is the similarity in attitudes of routine white-collar workers and of the foremen and technicians. Although they stand on different sides of the conventional manual/non-manual divide, they are almost indistinguishable in their attitudes.

Table 3.3.1 Class and values

	Percentage agreeing with 'right-wing' alternative				
	Nationalisation	Income redistribution	Job creation	TU legislation	Private education
Salariat (N = 1,021)	50	49	27	64	76
Routine non-manual (N = 923)	37	33	17	61	66
Petty bourgeoisie (N = 300)	60	60	32	71	77
Foremen and technicians (N = 277)	40	41	20	55	71
Working class (N = 1,270)	24	25	10	46	53

72 MODELS OF PARTY CHOICE

However, while Table 3.3.1 shows definite class differences in values, it would be quite wrong to think of society as polarised. Thus a majority of all classes favoured the 'left-wing' proposal of job creation and a majority of all classes opposed the 'left-wing' proposal of abolishing private schools. On both these questions there is broad consensus despite the class differences. Even on public ownership of industry polarisation was muted. Although there were big class differences in support for privatisation, the majority of the working class favoured the *status quo* rather than further nationalisation. Only on redistribution was a majority of the working class in favour but a majority of the salariat and petty bourgeoisie opposed.

Britain does not, therefore, exhibit diametrically opposite class beliefs. Rather, we should think of these questions as representing points along an ideological continuum. We are thus measuring differing degrees of support for government intervention and for free enterprise. The majority of people lie towards the centre of this continuum rather than polarised at the extremes, but it nonetheless represents the major, class-based, source of dissensus and these class values are the major source of political allegiance.

Class and party in 1983

Support for the Conservative and Labour parties follows very similar lines to those of the class values described in Table 3.3.1. Table 3.3.2 shows the pattern.

As before we see that it is the petty bourgeoisie which is the most Conservative class, and indeed by far the most united class in its politics. As we have said already, this plays havoc with the conventional manual/non-manual division and with the more detailed social grade schema. Thus our definition of the petty bourgeoisie groups together such superficially disparate groups as farmers (90 per cent of whom voted Conservative), small proprietors (70 per cent of whom voted Conservative) and self-employed manual workers (of whom 68 per cent voted Conservative).

The second striking feature of Table 3.3.2 is the contrast between the foremen and the working class. Among the foremen there is a big

Table 3.3.2 Class and vote in 1983: the political distinctiveness of the classes

	Conservative	Labour	Alliance	Others	
Salariat	54	14	31	1	100% ($N = 867$)
Routine non-manual	46	25	27	2	100% ($N = 749$)
Petty bourgeoisie	71	12	17	0	100% ($N = 245$)
Foremen and technicians	48	26	25	1	100% ($N = 220$)
Working class	30	49	20	1	100% ($N = 992$)

THE DECLINE OF CLASS VOTING

Conservative lead, bigger indeed than the Labour lead in the working class. The Labour party is certainly not the party of the blue-collar elite.

However, when we exclude the self-employed artisans and the foremen from the working class proper, we are left with a class that is somewhat more united politically than is often supposed. Even in 1983, a particularly bad election for Labour, half of working-class voters still cast their votes for the Labour party. Support for the Conservative party in the salariat was scarcely greater.

Table 3.3.2 also shows that the Alliance has more of a class base than is usually recognised. Like the Conservative party, the Alliance is quite clearly less popular in the working class and stronger in the salariat. But it is equally clear that its support does not run parallel to that of the Conservative party for its lowest popularity occurs in the Conservative stronghold of the petty bourgeoisie.

So far, we have been considering the 'political distinctiveness' of the classes, the petty bourgeoisie proving to be easily the most distinctive. However, another perspective is to consider the 'class distinctiveness' of the parties. This provides a rather different view of the class/party relation. This is done in Table 3.3.3.

Table 3.3.3 shows that the class composition of the Conservative and the Alliance vote is remarkably similar. The petty bourgeoisie makes up only a tiny proportion of the electorate, and so the Conservatives must draw the bulk of their support from elsewhere. They may be *the* party of the bourgeoisie, but they are not a 'bourgeois' party. Their vote is in fact drawn almost as evenly from across the classes as is the Alliance vote. On this criterion the Conservatives and the Alliance have almost equal claims to be called classless parties.

In comparison Labour is much more obviously a working-class party, even on our rather strict definition of class. Over half its votes come from this one class alone, and much of the remainder of its vote comes from the

Table 3.3.3 Class and vote in 1983: the class distinctiveness of the parties

	Conservative	Labour	Alliance	Others
Salariat	34	14	35	24
Routine non-manual	25	21	26	37
Petty bourgeoisie	12	3	5	2
Foremen and technicians	8	6	7	5
Working class	21	55	26	32
	100%	99%	99%	100%
$N =$	1,388	881	762	41

two 'marginal' classes of routine white-collar and supervisory blue-collar workers. It is still a party of the subordinate.

[· · ·]

The decline of class voting?

It has been widely argued that the class basis of politics has weakened in recent years, that Britain has experienced a period of 'class dealignment'. The source of the change, most commentators have argued, lies in the changing character of the classes themselves. Classes are no longer, it is claimed, the cohesive social formations that they once were. Rising standards of living, the spread of home-ownership, the decline of traditional heavy industries and their local communities, the emergence of new industries such as electronics in the affluent south, and increased social mobility out of the working class are all held to have reduced class solidarity, particularly that of the working class. Internal divisions within the classes are assumed to have become more marked, leading some commentators to coin the phrase 'the fragmentary class structure' while others have talked of a 'loosening' of the social structure.

The implication is that the parties can no longer rely on appeals to traditional class interests as they once did. The class basis of politics has changed, so it is argued, and the parties must change too or see their fortunes decline. Labour in particular must change if it is to regain power. These arguments have a remarkable resemblance to the ones put forward after Labour lost a third successive election in 1959. [But] contemporary accounts of the decline of class are no more plausible than those of the 1950s. The commentators have once again confused a decline in overall support for Labour with a decline in its relative class support. In this chapter we shall show that Labour remained a class party in 1983; it was simply a less successful class party than before.

The history of class voting

Table 3.3.4 shows the pattern of class voting over the postwar period as a whole. Owing to the shortcomings of the earlier surveys we are unfortunately restricted to the manual/non-manual dichotomy for the earlier part of the period.

Throughout the 1950s and 1960s around two-thirds of both classes voted for their 'natural' class party. Despite the alleged erosion of working-class solidarity in the 1950s, class voting remained at least as high in 1966 as it had been in 1945. Since 1966, however, there has been a much more striking decline in class voting (defining the level of class voting as the

THE DECLINE OF CLASS VOTING

Table 3.3.4 The history of class voting

	1945		1950		1951		1955		1959		1964	
	Non-manual	Manual	Non-manual	Manual	Non-manual	Manual	Non-manual	Manual	Non-manual	Manual	Non-manual	Manual
Conservative	63	29	68	32	75	34	70	32	67	30	62	28
Liberal	9	9	9	9	3	3	6	6	12	13	16	8
Labour	28	62	23	59	22	63	23	62	21	57	22	64
	100%	100%	100%	100%	100%	100%	99%	100%	100%	100%	100%	100%
Non-manual Conservatives and manual Labour as % of all voters	62		62		67		65		61		63	
Odds ratio	4.8		5.5		6.3		5.9		6.1		6.4	

	1966		1970		Feb. 1974		Oct. 1974		1979		1983	
	Non-manual	Manual	Non-manual	Manual	Non-manual	Manual	Non-manual	Manual	Non-manual	Manual	Non-manual	Manual
Conservative	60	25	64	33	53	24	51	24	60	35	55	35
Liberal	14	6	11	9	25	19	24	20	17	15	28	22
Labour	26	69	25	58	22	57	25	57	23	50	17	42
	100%	100%	100%	100%	100%	100%	100%	100%	100%	100%	100%	99%
Non-manual Conservatives and manual Labour as % of all voters	66		60		55		54		55		47	
Odds ratio	6.4		4.5		5.7		4.8		3.7		3.9	

number of non-manual Conservative plus manual Labour voters as a proportion of all voters). By 1983 less than half the voters were supporting their natural class party.

[However] the proportion of each class that votes for its natural class party is a misleading measure of class voting. As in 1959 we run the risk of confusing a decline in Labour's electoral fortunes with a change in the class basis of voting. After all, if a class party like Labour does badly at the polls, it is almost true by definition that a smaller proportion of the working class will have turned out to support their natural party. Given the large size of the working class, this in turn is likely to mean that the overall level of class voting will have fallen too. We are, therefore, simply redescribing Labour's misfortunes rather than explaining them. We are simply measuring how well the Labour party (or the Conservative party) has fared at the polls. The measure does not necessarily tell us anything very interesting about the class basis of politics.

When commentators talk about the declining class basis of politics they have a more subtle but illuminating concept in mind than just a fall in working-class support for Labour. It is an increase in *cross-class* voting that is usually taken to constitute 'class dealignment'. If Labour (or for that matter the Conservatives) begins to draw relatively more support from the opposing class than from its natural supporters, then we are indeed seeing a more interesting change in the class/party relation, one with more far-reaching implications.

Commentators were impressed by the fact that cross-class voting did seem to have increased in 1970. As Table 3.3.4 shows, Labour support dropped sharply among manual workers in 1970 but held up among the non-manual. In other words, its relative support in the two classes had changed and the character of the party seemed to have changed too. So while the overall proportion of the electorate voting for its natural class party can be thought of as a measure of *absolute* class voting, what we are really interested in is a measure of *relative* class voting. It is the latter which would tell us whether the class basis of voting has changed.

The most appropriate measure of *relative* class voting is the odds ratio. For example, the odds of a non-manual worker voting Conservative rather than Labour in 1945 were just over two to one while the corresponding odds for a manual worker were (roughly) one to two. The ratio of these odds works out at rather more than four to one [ie. $(63/28)/(29/62) = 4.8$]. An odds ratio of 1:1 would indicate that there was no class basis to voting at all, that the relative strengths of the two parties were the same in both classes. Correspondingly the larger the odds ratio, the stronger the class basis of voting. The great advantage of the odds ratio is that it clearly distinguishes relative from absolute strength. Thus the Conservatives might get twice as many votes as Labour, but providing they did so in both classes equally, the odds ratio would still be 1:1.

THE DECLINE OF CLASS VOTING

(The usual method of measuring relative class alignment has been the Alford index. To calculate this for Labour we simply subtract the percentage of the middle class supporting Labour from the percentage of the working class supporting Labour. Thus, in 1945 62 per cent of manual workers voted Labour compared with 28 per cent of non-manual, giving a score of 34 points on the Alford index. Unfortunately, the Alford index is inappropriate as a measure of relative class alignment since it confuses relative with overall support. Suppose, for example, that Labour support among manual voters fell to 33 per cent while support among non-manual fell to zero. On the Alford index this would give a score of 33 points, less than in 1945, but surely we would want to say that such a situation where Labour drew all its votes from the working class represented a much higher degree of class alignment than in 1945. The crucial point is that a decline in overall support for Labour may lead to a fall in the Alford index even if there is no change in relative class support for Labour.)

The pattern of odds ratios over time is shown in Table 3.3.4. (The ones shown relate to Conservative and Labour voting by manual and non-manual workers; odds ratio could also be calculated for Labour and Liberal, or for Conservative and Liberal, voting.) The movements are somewhat different from those in the absolute level of class voting. For example, the absolute level fell in February 1974 when the Liberals increased their share of the vote, but the relative level rose. Indeed relative class support for the Labour and Conservative parties was as high in February 1974 as it had been in 1950. True, it was markedly lower in 1979, but it is worth noting that the increased support for the Alliance resulted in a further drop in the absolute, but not in the relative, level of class voting in 1983.

In general the period from 1945 to 1974 shows no consistent trend. There are certainly ups and downs, but we would see these as having more to do with changing political events than with any underlying evolution of the classes. The mistake of recent commentators is that they have taken 1964 as their baseline. As we now see this was a rather unfortunate choice since it marked a peak in relative class voting (as measured by the odds ratio). The adoption of a longer time perspective clearly calls into question claims about any secular trend towards class dealignment.

This still leaves the question of the apparent drop in relative class voting in 1979 and 1983. That too could be no more than a temporary fluctuation as a result of specific political events, but our own view is that it is in fact almost wholly spurious, an artefact of the inadequate manual/non-manual dichotomy.

The point is a simple one. The manual/non-manual dichotomy ignores the important differences in the political interests of the three intermediate classes and runs the risk of confusing class dealignment with changing class sizes. For example, self-employed manual workers are much less likely to

MODELS OF PARTY CHOICE

vote Labour than the working class proper. But they have also been increasing in number in recent years whereas the working class has been contracting. The internal composition of the manual category as a whole has thus changed, and its declining relative propensity to vote Labour will be, at least in part, a consequence of this change in composition.

Relative class voting 1964–1983

Table 3.3.5 shows the pattern of class voting over the 1964–1983 period using the five-fold class schema. With this more complicated schema there is a large number of odds ratios that can in principle be computed. The one reported in the table is the ratio of Conservative and Labour odds in the salariat and working class.

Table 3.3.5 confirms in a more rigorous way that 1970 was an exceptional election. Cross-class voting in the salariat and working class was undoubtedly higher than in the 1960s. The 29 per cent of the salariat who voted Labour and the 32 per cent of the working class who voted Conservative in 1970 are the 'record highs' for cross-class voting in this period. But one exceptional election hardly amounts to class dealignment and is an extremely dubious basis upon which to build theories of social change.

On the other hand, Table 3.3.5 does not confirm a decline in relative class voting in 1979 and 1983. True, Labour fared worse in the working class in 1983 than it had done in previous elections, but it also fared worse in every other class as well. Labour's decline was general, not class-specific.

Over the 1964 to 1983 period as a whole the dominant impression is one of 'trendless fluctuation' rather than steady dealignment. 1964 represents the high point of relative class voting, but as we have already seen represents an unfortunate baseline. 1970 represents the low point, but can scarcely be said to have ushered in a period of continued dealignment. Faced with these short-run fluctuations the political scientist does better to search for political sources of parties' success and failure than to blame long-run changes in the character of the classes.

These conclusions are confirmed by the use of the more rigorous statistical technique of log-linear modelling. This technique analyses the full set of odds ratios and enables us to test alternative models. Taking the seven elections from 1964 to 1983 together, log-linear modelling confirms, as might be expected, that there have been statistically significant changes both in the fortunes of the parties and in the sizes of the classes. These two sorts of change are by far the most important components of the differences between the elections.

Some small variations in the relationship between class and party

THE DECLINE OF CLASS VOTING

remain, however. The model which assumes a *constant* set of class/party odds ratios over time does not fit the data wholly satisfactorily. But the deviations which remain have more of the character of 'trendless fluctuations' than steady dealignment. Perhaps most interestingly the assumption of constant odds ratios gives a rather good fit in 1983. In other words the level of class voting in 1983 (in the relative sense of class voting) was about average for the 1964–1983 period as a whole. In this one respect 1983 was not an exceptional election at all. As Table 3.3.5 indicated 1964 and 1970 were the exceptional ones. And if these two elections are excluded from the analysis, the assumption of constant odds ratios turns out to give a perfectly acceptable fit.

Changing class sizes

In focusing on class dealignment political scientists have concentrated on minor rearrangements of the furniture while failing to notice a major change in the structure of the house. Table 3.3.6 presents the class distribution of the electorate as measured by the election surveys of 1964 and 1983. It shows that Britain has been transformed from a blue-collar society into a white-collar one. Whereas in 1964 the working class was nearly three times the size of the salariat, constituting nearly half of the electorate, in 1983 the two classes were of almost the same size.

The impact of these changes upon the electoral fortunes of the parties has probably been far greater than that of any class dealignment which may or may not have occurred. There is little evidence that class differences have withered away or that the classes have changed their character, but there can be no question that the *shape* of the class structure has been gradually changing throughout the postwar period.

The implications of the two claims are very different. If class dealignment has occurred, the implication is that the political parties should stop appealing to voters' class interests. If classes have become fragmented and lack the distinctiveness they once had, class issues will be less potent sources of votes.

But if, on the other hand, as we suggest, the class structure has simply changed shape, the implication is that class interests persist. Parties must therefore continue to appeal to them, since they remain the fundamentals of electoral choice. For a party to abandon class appeals is to run the risk of losing the class votes that it still has (and in Labour's case a majority of its votes still come from the working class). According to this view Labour faces a particular dilemma. Its class base is shrinking, but it dare not abandon it for it has nowhere better to seek votes.

The impact of these changes in class structure on the fortunes of the parties can be demonstrated by means of a simple simulation. Assume that

Table 3.3.5 Class and vote, 1964–83

	Salariat	Routine non-manual	Petty bourgeoisie	Foremen and technicians	Working class	Odds ratio
1964						
Conservative	61	54	74	40	23	
Labour	20	31	12	44	70	
Liberal	18	14	13	15	7	9.3
Other	1	1	1	1	0	
	100% (N = 268)	100% (N = 256)	100% (N = 106)	100% (N = 134)	100% (N = 674)	
1966						
Conservative	58	48	66	34	23	
Labour	25	42	19	61	72	
Liberal	16	9	13	5	5	7.3
Other	1	1	2	0	0	
	100% (N = 280)	100% (N = 266)	100% (N = 102)	100% (N = 127)	100% (N = 670)	
1970						
Conservative	60	49	66	35	32	
Labour	29	42	18	58	60	
Liberal	9	8	11	5	6	3.9
Other	2	1	5	2	2	
	100% (N = 227)	100% (N = 166)	100% (N = 75)	100% (N = 82)	100% (N = 379)	
Feb. 1974						
Conservative	52	40	66	37	22	
Labour	23	35	18	38	59	
Liberal	23	24	14	24	15	6.1
Other	2	1	2	1	4	
	100% (N = 439)	100% (N = 390)	100% (N = 174)	100% (N = 134)	100% (N = 769)	

THE DECLINE OF CLASS VOTING

Oct. 1974						
Conservative	47	38	69	33	20	5.5
Labour	27	37	13	43	63	
Liberal	23	22	15	22	12	
Other	3	3	3	2	5	
	100% (N = 361)	100% (N = 344)	100% (N = 104)	100% (N = 109)	100% (N = 579)	
1979						
Conservative	59	48	76	40	30	4.9
Labour	22	36	13	44	55	
Liberal	17	15	10	13	13	
Other	2	1	1	3	2	
	100% (N = 403)	100% (N = 280)	100% (N = 123)	100% (N = 153)	100% (N = 477)	
1983						
Conservative	54	46	71	48	30	6.3
Labour	14	25	12	26	49	
Liberal & SDP	31	27	17	25	20	
Other	1	2	0	1	1	
	100% (N = 867)	100% (N = 749)	100% (N = 245)	100% (N = 220)	100% (N = 992)	

Note: The figures for October 1974 were later corrected in Heath *et al.* (1987), p. 269, note 25. As a consequence of this correction the odds ratio for October 1974 changes from 5.5 to 6.4.

Table 3.3.6 Class composition of the electorate, 1964 and 1983

	1964	1983
Salariat	18	27
Routine non-manual	18	24
Petty bourgeoisie	7	8
Foremen and technicians	10	7
Working class	47	34
	100%	100%
$N =$	1,475	3,790

the parties retained the same level of support within each class that they had in 1964. Since we can measure (as in Table 3.3.6) how the classes changed in size over the period 1964–1983, we can estimate the extent to which these changes alone would have affected the parties' fortunes. The calculation tells us how the parties would hypothetically have fared if the only source of change had been the expansion and contraction of classes described in Table 3.3.6.

On these assumptions the Conservative share of the vote would have increased by five and a half per cent. Labour's share would have fallen by seven per cent and the Liberal/Alliance share would have increased by one and a half per cent. Structural change alone, therefore, would have brought about a major decline in Labour's vote, but it does little to account for the rise of the Liberal/SDP Alliance.

These results can be put in perspective if we compare them with the actual changes in party strength over this period. Thus the Labour share of the vote actually fell from 44 per cent to 28 per cent; structural change can thus account for nearly half this decline. The Liberal share rose from 11 per cent to 25 per cent, structural change therefore telling us little about the reasons for its rise. And the Conservative share remained roughly constant, falling just one point to 42 per cent, whereas on our assumptions it might have been expected to increase to 49 per cent. Structural change [therefore] explains a large part of Labour's decline, it explains little of the Alliance rise, and it suggests that the Conservatives should have done better than they actually did in 1983.

Changing class values

Our main argument, then, is that the class basis of politics, if not the strongest it has ever been, nonetheless shows no good evidence of secular

THE DECLINE OF CLASS VOTING

decline. But it is also clear that the two main parties have both fared worse at the polls than a purely sociological theory of politics would have predicted. In our view this decline has not been due to any 'loosening' or 'fragmentation' of the classes but to political changes which have nothing at all to do with class.

The political implications of economic progress have not been well understood. *Absolute* living standards have certainly increased for many of the population, but conflicts of interest are as much, or more, about *relativities* as they are about absolutes. The cake may grow in size, but rising expectations will mean that conflicts over the size of the shares will continue unabated.

A powerful case can be made out that objective class relativities have shown little sign of change despite the undoubted economic and social progress of the 1950s and 1960s. [Furthermore], there is no evidence that subjective class awareness has declined any more than the objective inequalities have done. The evidence is unfortunately scanty, but there is a good time series on one of the key class values [nationalisation] described [above] and we can thus test whether subjective class differences, at least with respect to this one question, have declined.

Since we are concerned with relativities, Table 3.3.7 presents odds ratios. The odds in question are those of preferring privatisation to nationalisation, and we have compared these odds in the salariat and working classes respectively. The overall picture is again one of trendless fluctuation.

It would be unwise to draw conclusions about trends in class consciousness from a single time series. All Table 3.3.7 can do is place a large question mark against the claims that there has been any long-run decline in the subjective distinctiveness of the classes. Most such claims about the decline of class have been based on the intellectual equivalent of gossip and hearsay. Commentators have either assumed, without any evidence, that increases in absolute standards of living will erode class relativities, or they have inferred a withering away of class itself from the absolute decline in class voting. But this is to be guilty of a naive sociological determinism.

Our conclusion, therefore, is that class differences, whether with respect to objective inequalities, subjective values or support for the political parties, remained at much the same level throughout the postwar period. Whether for better or worse, Britain is still divided by class. On the other

Table 3.3.7 Changing attitudes towards nationalisation, 1964–83

	1964	1966	Feb. 1974	1979	1983
Salariat/working class odds ratio	2.9:1	2.5:1	2.1:1	3.6:1	4.5:1

hand the shape of the class structure has changed, with important electoral implications particularly for Labour. Its class base is clearly shrinking, and may be expected to continue to do so with the de-industrialisation of Britain. But this can account only for part of Labour's decline at the polls, and for virtually none of the Liberals' rise. Labour has changed from being a rather successful class party in 1964 to being an unsuccessful one in 1983. The Liberals, also a class party, have gained at both Labour and Conservative expense. To explain their modest success, we must look to political explanations, not social ones. The withering away of class is not the answer.

3.4 On the death and resurrection of class voting: some comments on *How Britain Votes*

Ivor Crewe

The conventional interpretation of [the relationship between class and party] is that since the mid-1960s British electors have become less willing to vote according to their class. This view has recently been challenged in *How Britain Votes*. Class dealignment, it turns out, is a mirage.

As well as being spectacularly counter-intuitive [Heath *et al.*'s conclusions] are, if correct, of obvious political and academic importance. The purpose of this article is to show that, in addition to being significant, unorthodox and undoubtedly ingenious, [they] are also highly implausible.

Heath *et al.*'s tightly compressed reasoning is not always easy to follow, but can be reconstructed as a series of steps:

1. Past studies have defined class dealignment as a decline in *absolute* class voting. This is a mistake because changes in absolute class voting are usually the mere reflection of changes in a major party's overall support.
2. Instead class dealignment should be regarded as a decline in *relative* class voting, which may be defined as the relative probability of the two classes voting *against rather than for* their respective 'natural' parties.
3. The appropriate measure of relative class voting is the ratio of two odds: (i) the probability of the middle class voting Conservative rather than *Labour* and (ii) the probability of the working class voting *Conservative* rather than Labour.

From I. Crewe, 'On the death and resurrection of class voting: some comments on *How Britain Votes*', *Political Studies* (1986), vol. XXXIV, pp. 620–38.

4. The odds ratios for non-manual versus manual voters show no clear long-term trend since 1945. It is true that they are smaller for 1979 and 1983 than previously, but this is the accidental result of changes in the size and composition of the manual and non-manual categories.
5. The odds ratios for the 'salariat' versus the 'working class' are a preferable measure. These reveal no decline in 1979 and 1983 and therefore confirm the absence of any class dealignment since the war.
6. These conclusions are reinforced by an equivalent odds ratio analysis of trends in relative class consciousness.
7. The long-term decline in the Labour vote is not, therefore, the result of an actual decline in class voting but the cause of an apparent decline. It is a political phenomenon with social consequences rather than a social phenomenon with political consequences. There is, however, a social component in the diminishing Labour vote. The contraction of the 'working class' explains a large part of Labour's electoral decline. But, to repeat, it is not the result of changing behaviour within the 'working class'.
8. These findings carry implications for Labour's strategy of electoral recovery. The lesson of a class dealignment, had it been established, is that Labour should abandon its appeal to class interests. But the absence of class dealignment within a changing class structure implies that class interests persist and that Labour must continue to concentrate its appeal on specifically working-class interests.

The aim of this note is to show that each step in this argument has serious flaws. As a result the main conclusions and inferences are dubious at best and on occasion plainly wrong.

Step 1: Past studies relied on absolute class voting which does not measure class dealignment

It is untrue that previous studies have relied on absolute class voting to establish the existence of a class dealignment. The conventional measure is, in fact, Alford's 'class index of Labour voting' – which is a measure of *relative* class voting.

Matters of record aside, Heath *et al.*'s criticisms of absolute measures of class voting are misplaced. They argue as follows:

> . . . the proportion of each class that votes for its natural class party is a misleading measure of class voting . . . we run the risk of confusing a decline in Labour's electoral fortunes with a change in the class basis of voting. After all, if a class party like Labour does badly at the polls, it is almost true by definition that a smaller proportion of the working class will have turned out to support their natural party. Given the large size of the working class, this in turn is likely

to mean that the overall level of class voting will have fallen too. We are, therefore, simply redescribing Labour's misfortunes rather than explaining them . . . (p. 31)

This passage is muddled in two ways. First, it elides the distinction between class dealignment as a description and class dealignment as an explanation. This leads to a conceptual mistake. Secondly, it confuses class voting within one class and class voting within the electorate as a whole. This leads to a statistical mistake.

Between 1945 and 1983 the proportion of manual workers voting Labour fell from 62 to 42 per cent. This decline has been accompanied by a parallel 20 percentage point decline in Labour's overall share of the vote (from 48 to 28 per cent). As a result, Heath *et al.* appear to believe that no real or genuine decline of class voting among manual workers has taken place.

This discounting of overall electoral trends is, surely, illegitimate. If words are to retain their normal meaning it is not 'misleading' but incontrovertible that class voting within the working class weakened over this period. It is irrelevant that Labour's overall vote declined in tandem. What matters is the much lower proportion of manual workers voting Labour in 1983 than 1945 – the decline of class voting within the working class. The fact that this does not necessarily *explain* Labour's electoral misfortunes does not bear on its accuracy as a *description* of working-class voting patterns.

Heath *et al.* go on to assert that Labour's electoral slide has automatically produced the decline in absolute class voting in the *electorate as a whole*. In theory this could be true but in practice it is wrong. The impact of a decline in Labour's overall vote on absolute class voting depends on the portion of the decline that occurred within the working class. This in turn is likely to reflect the size of the working class. Obviously, if the entire fall in the Labour vote took place within the working class the absolute measure of class voting must decline by the identical amount. Heath *et al.* appear to assume that something close to this has happened because of 'the large size of the working class' and the fact that Labour is a 'class party'. But this gives a very exaggerated impression of the 'size effect'.

In the passage quoted earlier it is unclear whether 'working class' refers to all manual workers or the authors' new definition which is restricted to 'rank and file manual employees' [hereafter] relabelled the 'proletariat'. Neither the proletariat nor manual workers are sufficiently numerous to have a serious size effect.

Figure 3.4.1 shows that the independent impact of working-class size on absolute measures of class voting could not have been more than marginal. Each row assumes that at election 1 the Labour to non-Labour ratio of votes was 50:50 overall and that absolute class voting was at the high level of 70. At elections 2a and 2b the Labour to non-Labour ratio has fallen to

MODELS OF PARTY CHOICE

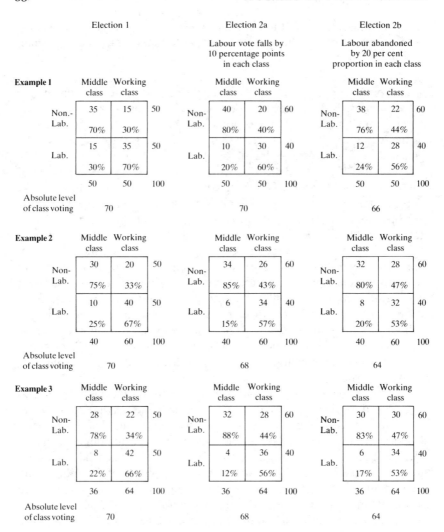

Figure 3.4.1 The independent impact of working-class size on the absolute measure of class voting

40:60 – in election 2a Labour incurs an equal percentage point decline within each class; in election 2b an equal *proportionate* decline within each class. Example 1 in the top row assumes a manual/non-manual division of 50:50 (as in 1983); example 2 in the middle row a division of 60:40 (as in the 1960s); example 3 a division of 64:36 (as in the late 1940s and early 1950s). Comparison of examples 1 and 3 demonstrates that the difference made to the absolute measure of class voting by 64:36 rather than 50:50 manual/

ON THE DEATH AND RESURRECTION OF CLASS VOTING   *89*

non-manual division amounts to a mere 2. And the difference made by a 55:45 manual/non-manual division – which existed for much of the period in which absolute class voting declined – is a tiny 0.5. Thus the decline in the absolute class vote recorded since the 1960s cannot be dismissed as the mere reflection of Labour's electoral misfortunes.

Steps 2 and 3: Class dealignment should be defined as cross-class voting and measured as an odds ratio

This note has defended the absolute measure of class voting from misplaced criticism, but its purpose is not to compare its value with relative measures of class voting. It undoubtedly has some disadvantages.

What is questioned, however, is the particular operationalization of relative class voting adopted by Heath *et al.*: 'When commentators talk about the declining class basis of politics . . . it is an increase in *cross-class* voting that is usually taken to constitute "class dealignment" . . . the most appropriate measure of *relative* class voting is the odds ratio' (p. 31).

A preliminary difficulty is the adoption of the odds ratio, rather than an Alford-style percentage point difference, as the measure of relative class voting. The odds ratio has two unsatisfactory properties. First, it is much the more sensitive to small percentage point changes. This would be a strength if we had absolute confidence in our survey estimates, but it is a weakness for data that are subject to sampling, recall and other errors of at least ±3 percentage points – and more for some sub-samples. When applied to trends in class voting the odds ratio offers a spurious degree of precision and converts tiny ripples of movement – whether real or illusory – into dramatic tides of change.

The exaggerating property of the odds ratio is compounded by a second: its asymmetrical treatment of class-consonant as opposed to cross-class voting. A change in the working-class Labour or middle-class Conservative vote has less impact on the odds ratio than the identical percentage point change in the working-class Conservative or middle-class Labour vote. The odds ratio is therefore 'driven' by changes in cross-class voting.

We now arrive at the crucial weakness in Heath *et al.*'s argument. They restrict non-class voting to Labour support in the middle class and Conservative support in the working class. Their definition of class voting silently relegates the Liberal (and in 1983 the SDP–Liberal Alliance) vote to a state of conceptual limbo where it appears to be neither a class nor a non-class vote. This procedure is unsatisfactory for a period like 1970 to 1983 in which the Liberal (and Alliance) vote fluctuated markedly, approached or exceeded 20 per cent three times and differed between the two classes. What is arguably the most important electoral change within both classes is therefore excluded from the analysis. The odds ratio is a

90 MODELS OF PARTY CHOICE

two-party measure applied to a three-party system. Not surprisingly, it leads to some very peculiar results.

Figure 3.4.2 offers three such examples. Each example assumes two classes of equal size and an increase in the Alliance vote from one election to the next. In the first example the Alliance vote rises 10 per cent between elections 1 and 2, at equal expense to the working-class Conservative and middle-class Labour vote. Thus the number voting according to their class does not change by a single elector. The absolute measure of class voting accordingly registers no change. But according to the odds ratio class voting has more than doubled, from 4.0 to 9.0. But what has actually doubled?: not the willingness to vote for the class 'enemy'.

In the second example, between elections 1 and 3, the Alliance vote rises from 10 per cent to 30 per cent. This time it gains from class-consonant and cross-class voters, though more from the latter than the former. Both the working-class Labour and middle-class Conservative vote decline from 30 to 25 per cent of the total vote. The proportion voting along class lines has *fallen* from 60 to 50 per cent and this is recorded by the absolute measure. But according to the odds ratio, class voting has *risen*, from 4.0 to 6.5.

What has actually risen, given that fewer votes have been cast along class lines? The answer is: the relative unwillingness of manual workers to vote Conservative and non-manual workers to vote Labour. But why should this decline in cross-class voting be treated as *more* significant than the decline in class-consonant voting? Is it to be regarded as *more* significant however low the manual Labour and non-manual Conservative vote falls?

These questions are prompted by the third, and most fanciful example, which illustrates the full potential for perversity in Heath *et al.*'s formulation. Between elections 1 and 4 the Alliance achieves a massive breakthrough. The Labour working class and Conservative middle class each decline to 16 per cent of the voting electorate so that *under a third* of all votes are cast along class lines. Moreover, among manual workers Labour support has fallen by more than Conservative support (while remaining higher) whereas among non-manual workers Conservative support has slipped more than Labour support (while remaining higher). Common sense says it is absurd to describe this situation as anything other than a class dealignment. But according to Heath *et al.*'s odds ratio the class alignment in the electorate has strengthened four-fold, from 4.0 to 16.0.

Perhaps Heath *et al.* would be unperturbed by this example, for they criticize the Alford index on the following grounds:

> Suppose, for example, that Labour support among manual workers fell to 33 per cent while support among non-manuals fell to zero. On the Alford index this would give a score of 33 points, less than in 1945, but surely we would want to say that such a situation where Labour drew all its votes from the working class represented a much higher degree of class alignment than in 1945. (p. 41)

ON THE DEATH AND RESURRECTION OF CLASS VOTING *91*

Election 1

Con.	Middle class	Working class	
	30	15	45
	60%	30%	
Lib./SDP	5	5	10
	10%	10%	
Lab.	15	30	45
	30%	60%	
	50	50	100

Absolute class voting   60
Alford class index   30
Odds ratio   4.0

Election 2

Con.	Middle class	Working class	
	30	10	40
	60%	20%	
Lib./SDP	10	10	20
	20%	20%	
Lab.	10	30	40
	20%	60%	
	50	50	100

Absolute class voting   60
Alford class index   40
Odds ratio   9.0

Election 3

Con.	Middle class	Working class	
	25	10	35
	50%	20%	
Lib./SDP	15	15	30
	30%	30%	
Lab.	10	25	35
	20%	50%	
	50	50	100

Absolute class voting   50
Alford class index   30
Odds ratio   6.25

Election 4

Con.	Middle class	Working class	
	16	4	20
	32%	8%	
Lib./SDP	30	30	60
	60%	60%	
Lab.	4	16	20
	8%	32%	
	50	50	100

Absolute class voting   32
Alford class index   24
Odds ratio   16.0

Notes: Absolute class voting: middle-class Conservative + working-class Labour as a percentage of the total vote; Alford class index: Labour percentage share of working-class vote *minus* Labour percentage share of middle-class vote; odds ratio: ratio of (1) odds of middle class voting Conservative rather than Labour, to (2) odds of working class voting Conservative rather than Labour.

Figure 3.4.2 Absolute, 'Alford' and odds ratio measures of class voting in four imaginary situations

But surely not. The *trompe d'oeil* in this argument is the reference to Labour '[drawing] all its votes from the working class'. The concepts of class voting and class dealignment refer to the political distinctiveness of the social classes, not to the class distinctiveness of the parties' voters. Is it seriously suggested that a halving of Labour support in the working class should be represented as a strengthening of the political solidarity, class consciousness and Labour alignment among the working class, simply because none of them is voting Conservative any more?

Steps 4 and 5: Comparison of manual and non-manual workers in recent elections is misleading and should be replaced by comparison between the salariat and the proletariat

Heath *et al.* acknowledge that their odds ratios for manual versus non-manual workers drop to record low levels in 1979 and 1983, but interpret this as 'almost wholly spurious, an artefact of the inadequate manual/non-manual dichotomy' (p. 34). In particular, they argue, Labour's apparent decline among manual workers partly reflects the growing number of Conservative-voting self-employed manual workers and the contraction of the Labour-voting proletariat. There is therefore a danger 'of confusing class dealignment with changing class sizes' (p. 34).

A recalculation of Heath *et al.*'s own data shows that the changing class composition of the manual worker category accounts for no more than a minuscule proportion of the class dealignment since 1964 and for *none* of it for the period after 1974, when the manual/non-manual odds ratios dropped to their lowest levels. This is because their 'petty bourgeoisie' of self-employed (of whom only a third are own-account manual workers) did *not* grow significantly between 1964 (7.4 per cent) and 1983 (8.0 per cent), according to their own data. Moreover, the self-employed are far too small a component of the manual worker category (about 4 per cent in 1964 and 6 per cent in 1983) to make a significant impact on its overall voting patterns. The proletariat does contract as a component of the manual worker category, but only slightly, and always constitutes the overwhelming proportion of at least 75 per cent. Changes in the composition of the manual worker category are far too slight, therefore, to have a significant impact on its propensity to vote Labour. For example, Labour's share of the manual vote fell from 64 per cent in 1964 to 57 per cent in February 1974 and to 42 per cent in 1983. If the 1983 class structure had existed throughout this period Labour's share of the manual vote would have been only 2 per cent less in 1964, and no different in February 1974. Whatever the case for comparing the salariat and proletariat after 1964 it does not rest on the alleged but unproven distortion produced by the manual/non-manual dichotomy.

There is, moreover, at least one objection to defining class voting in terms of the salariat versus the proletariat. Most previous studies have regarded the class–party alignment as a property of the voting electorate as a whole. An index based on major party voters in the salariat and proletariat excludes a large segment of the voting electorate – 40 per cent in

ON THE DEATH AND RESURRECTION OF CLASS VOTING   *93*

1964 and 1966 and the majority, 55 per cent, in 1983. Moreover, the voting categories that 'drive' the odds ratio – the Labour-voting salariat and Conservative-voting proletariat – are very small sub-categories of the electorate (in a typical election, 4 per cent and 10 per cent respectively). It cannot be assumed that the trend for these two classes represents that for the whole electorate. It might have been preferable to estimate odds ratios by combining the salariat and routine non-manual workers into one class and foremen, technicians and the proletariat into the other. This procedure would have excluded the petty bourgeoisie, and thus its confounding effects, while incorporating 90 per cent of voters.

Step 6: There is equally little evidence of a subjective class dealignment

Heath *et al.* extend their denial of a class dealignment by claiming that 'there is no evidence that subjective class awareness has declined . . .' (p. 38). In support they offer a single table of evidence consisting of odds ratios on attitudes to nationalization among the salariat and proletariat for each election since 1964. It shows that the joint probability of the salariat preferring privatization to nationalization and the proletariat preferring nationalization to privatization fluctuated without following a trend and was actually higher in 1979 and 1983 than in the 1960s. Readers are carefully cautioned against drawing too firm a conclusion from a single indicator, but, like the health warnings on cigarette packets, this caution appears to be given in the clear expectation that it will be ignored. For Heath *et al.* sweepingly assert that 'class differences, whether with respect to objective inequalities, subjective values, or support for political parties, remained at much the same level throughout the post-war period' (p. 39).

The evidence offered is surely a flimsy basis for even the most tentative conclusion. Attitudes to nationalization are, to put it mildly, an idiosyncratic indicator of class consciousness, especially when more obvious variables are as readily available over the same period. It is not self-evident, except to the narrowly partisan, that proletarians who favour privatization or members of the salariat who want more nationalization are acting contrary to either their subjective or objective class interests.

Moreover the previously mentioned problems of interpreting odds ratio measures are clearly exposed in this case. Each year's figure is typically based on a mere third of the sample (34 per cent) because, in addition to excluding their three intermediate classes, Heath *et al.* leave out the many respondents who opted for the status quo rather than privatization or nationalization. Furthermore, the two class-deviant categories that 'drive' the odds ratio together comprise a mere 12 per cent sub-group. Sampling

94   MODELS OF PARTY CHOICE

error alone could comfortably account for the apparent peaking of class values in 1979 and 1983.

The most unsatisfactory aspect of this step in the authors' thesis, however, is the false inference from these odds ratios that working-class solidarity and values have remained constant. The most that can legitimately be claimed is that the *gap* between the salariat's and the proletariat's attitude to nationalization and privatization has neither narrowed nor widened over the long term. But that is to claim very little, for it does not rule out a sea-change of attitudes among the proletariat, albeit one that finds a rough parallel elsewhere in the salariat. Heath *et al.* show later in the book (p. 132) that the balance of opinion has shifted in favour of privatization and against further nationalization in the electorate as a whole, including the proletariat. If nationalization is the 'key class value' (p. 38) that Heath *et al.* allege, then by no stretch of reasoning can its diminishing attractions and minority status among the proletariat be described as anything other than a precipitous decline in the ideological consciousness and solidarity of the working class.

Step 7: The changing class structure, not changing class behaviour, explains Labour's decline

Although Heath *et al.* deny that class dealignment can explain Labour's electoral misfortunes they accept that social change has played a role. But it is the reduced size of the working class, not its reduced willingness to vote Labour, that is the cause.

Because the working class has been radically redefined, its contraction appears all the more dramatic. Defined as manual workers, the working class shrank from 61 per cent of the electorate in 1964 to 50 per cent in 1983; defined as 'rank and file manual employees' – renamed the proletariat in this note – it declined from 49 per cent to 34 per cent. Given that Labour voting is more prevalent in the proletariat than among manual workers as a whole, Heath *et al.* understandably argue that it is the numerical and not ideological decline of the proletariat that is mainly responsible for Labour's electoral slide. However, re-analysis of Heath *et al.*'s figures suggests that this is a considerable exaggeration.

Heath *et al.* attempt to establish the precedence of a structural (over a behavioural) explanation for Labour's decline by estimating an election result which combines the 1983 class structure with the 1964 pattern of class voting. This simulation shows that structural change alone would have depressed Labour's share of the vote by 7.1 per cent (see Table 3.4.1), to the benefit of both the Conservatives (+5.7 per cent) and the Alliance (+ 1.5 per cent). They conclude that 'structural change explains a large part of Labour's decline' (p. 37). But over the same period the election surveys recorded an 18 percentage point fall in Labour's overall vote share: the

ON THE DEATH AND RESURRECTION OF CLASS VOTING 95

Table 3.4.1 The impact of changes in (a) the class structure, and (b) class behaviour on the change in the three parties' share of the vote between 1964 and 1983

	Heath *et al*.'s simulation of structural effects			Alternative simulation of behavioural effects		
	Structural effect	Actual change 1964–83	(diff.)	Behavioural change	Actual change 1964–83	(diff.)
1983 class structure 1964 pattern of class voting				1964 class structure 1983 pattern of class voting		
Con.	+5.7	+4.6	(1.1)	+1.3	+4.6	(3.3)
Lab.	−7.1	−18.3	(11.2)	−13.6	−18.3	(4.7)
Lib./SDP	+1.5	+13.7	(12.2)	+12.2	+13.7	(1.5)

Note: Figures are based on party shares of the three-party vote, to eliminate effects of minor party support. 'Actual change' is that recorded in the BES surveys, not the true electoral change.

remaining 11 per cent drop must therefore be due to changes in class behaviour. Most of Labour's decline since 1964 arises from the changing behaviour, not the changing size, of the classes.

Moreover, Heath *et al*.'s simulation tells only half the story. It needs to be compared with a second, 'reverse' simulation which estimates an election result that combines the 1964 class structure with 1983 patterns of class voting. This shows that *behavioural* change alone would have depressed the Labour vote by 13.6 per cent, to the benefit of both the Conservatives (+1.3 per cent) and the Alliance (+12.2 per cent). In other words, twice as much of Labour's electoral decline between 1964 and 1983 is attributable to behavioural rather than to structural change. This second simulation, incidentally, comes much closer to the actual 1983 result than the first simulation, on which Heath *et al*.'s argument rests. This is not to deny that the diminishing size of the working class (however defined) has contributed to the diminishing size of the Labour vote. But it is not primarily, let alone exclusively, responsible.

Step 8: Labour's advisable electoral strategy is to continue making a class appeal to the proletariat

The final chapter of *How Britain Votes* concludes that, despite the unfavourable changes in the class structure, Labour's electoral salvation does not lie in 'shifting its ground to the affluent centre'. Heath *et al*. arrive at this position by the following reasoning:

if class dealignment has occurred, the implication is that the political parties should stop appealing to voters' class interests. If classes have become

MODELS OF PARTY CHOICE

fragmented and lack the distinctiveness that they once had, class issues will be less potent sources of votes. But if, on the other hand, as we suggest, the class structure has simply changed shape, the implication is that class interests persist. Parties must therefore continue to appeal to them, since they remain the fundamentals of electoral choice (p. 36).

Even if Heath *et al.*'s substantive thesis is accepted, these are curious inferences to draw. Firstly, it is far from obvious that an electorally damaging class dealignment requires the Labour Party to abandon appealing to working-class interests. It is equally logical to infer that it should redouble such an appeal. The mere existence of a class dealignment carries no strategic implications one way or another.

Even more puzzling is the inference that the shrinking of Labour's working-class (i.e. proletarian) base should encourage it to 'remain a class party'; that is, a party largely dependent on proletarian votes. Here everything hinges on percentages.

The electoral arithmetic works out as follows. To obtain a secure parliamentary majority in the current electoral and party system Labour needs about 40 per cent of the vote. In 1983 the proletariat formed only 32 per cent of the voting electorate and in future elections the figure will be less. Labour cannot count on taking more than 70 per cent of the proletarian vote even in good election years. That would provide Labour with a vote of about 22 per cent in the 1980s, which is barely half of what it needs. The remainder must be found in other classes. The 'adjacent' class of foremen and technicians is too small a category (8 per cent of voters) to make up the difference: if Labour took as much as 60 per cent of their vote (which it has managed only once, in 1966) it is still 14 per cent short. Thus an exceptionally successful 'working class' appeal would nonetheless leave Labour far from electoral victory. Turning itself into a successful rather than unsuccessful class party is not good enough. It must in addition make a big pitch for the support of routine non-manual workers, its next best class and fully one-quarter of all voters by 1983. However, unless it can win 50 per cent of their vote – a level it has never approached since 1964 – it still needs some votes from the two remaining 'enemy' classes, the salariat and the petty bourgeoisie.

Retaining the proletarian vote is almost certainly a necessary condition for Labour's survival. But it is self-evidently not a sufficient condition for Labour's recovery. If Labour is ever again to form a secure majority government it must pitch camp on the 'affluent centre ground', not because of the class dealignment that Heath *et al.* wrongly deny, but because of the working-class contraction that they correctly assert.

3.5 | Trendless fluctuation: a reply to Crewe

Anthony Heath, Roger Jowell and John Curtice

Crewe's vigorous but extravagant critique is confined to one chapter of *How Britain Votes* – the chapter on class dealignment. Such a narrow focus might have been expected to lead to well-targeted criticism. But alas, Crewe is so far from the target that he manages to score a spectacular series of own-goals.

We shall begin by restating the central lines of our argument. We reject the version presented by Crewe (steps 1 to 8 as he calls them) which so distorts our argument as to make it unrecognizable.

Our argument restated

Between 1964 and 1983 Labour's share of the vote declined from 44.7 per cent to 28.3 per cent, the Conservative share increased marginally from 42.9 per cent to 43.5 per cent, while that of the Liberals – joined in 1983 by the Social Democratic Party (SDP) – rose from 11.4 per cent to 26.0 per cent. There are a number of rival explanations for these phenomena. Broadly speaking these explanations can be termed the sociological and the political. On the sociological side we show that there have been major long-term changes in the shape of the class structure. [The] contraction of the working class could explain nearly half of Labour's electoral decline over the period as a whole, but not the precipitate decline between 1979 and 1983. It is however a negligible factor in explaining the Liberal rise. We suggest that political factors are largely responsible for the other half.

We would not have supposed that either of these main conclusions was

From A. Heath, R. Jowell and J. Curtice, 'Trendless fluctuation: a reply to Crewe', *Political Studies* (1987), vol. XXXV, pp. 256–77.

MODELS OF PARTY CHOICE

contentious. The evidence on changes in the electorate's perceptions of the growing gap between the parties is fairly robust. And evidence on the changing shape of the class structure can be drawn from several independent sources, using various alternative schemes for measuring social class. It is surprising, therefore, that Crewe chooses to pick a quarrel over this point. It is even more puzzling as the conclusion which he eventually reaches after several pages of critique is almost identical to the one put forward in *How Britain Votes*.

The one genuinely contentious issue between Crewe and ourselves is whether there have been *additional* sociological forces at work in Labour's decline, over and above the contraction in the working class. In particular, has there been a loosening of the class structure? In *How Britain Votes* we argue that there is no good evidence of a secular decline in the social cohesion of the classes or in their ideological distinctiveness. Crewe finds this view 'spectacularly counter intuitive', but as we shall now show, the evidence supports our view, not Crewe's.

What is at issue here is the *potential* of the classes for collective political action. If the working class retains its cohesion and social character, then it remains a potential Labour stronghold, albeit one that is reduced in size. To realize that potential, Labour may need to overcome various obstacles (such as its disunity in 1983). But if our argument is sound it does not need to temper its pursuit of working-class interests or to change its overall ideology. By contrast, if Crewe is right and the working class has changed its character and lost its potential for class politics, then more radical changes in Labour's policies and ideology will be needed.

Whether or not the potential for class politics has remained unchanged is also central to the explanation of electoral trends since 1964. It has been widely argued that the rise of the Liberal/SDP Alliance, and the decline in Labour's support, have occurred *because* class has become a less important influence upon social and political life. But if we can demonstrate that the potential for class action has remained unchanged, alternative explanations of these trends must be sought. Our view is that the rise of the Alliance is due largely to political factors, with sociological factors playing a relatively minor role.

Where does class dealignment come into this? A key distinction which we make in *How Britain Votes* is between absolute and relative class voting. These concepts are importantly different. For example, if Labour loses support to the Liberals both in the middle class and in the working class, absolute class voting declines but relative class voting stays constant. By contrast, if Labour holds on to its middle-class support while losing its working-class vote, then both relative and absolute class voting will decline simultaneously.

These two cases are clearly different conceptually, and they are likely to have different explanations. For example, if the classes had indeed become looser and had lost their social cohesion and potential for class politics, then we would have expected the relationship between class and party to become more random. Instead of being relatively stronger in the working class than in the middle class, Labour might have become equally strong (or weak) in both. In other words, a loosening of the class structure is likely to lead to a decline in relative class voting. A decline in absolute class voting, if unaccompanied by a relative decline, is unlikely to have been caused by a loosening of the classes.

What we found in practice was that class voting, in the relative sense, exhibited 'trendless fluctuation' over the post-war period as a whole. There were various ups and downs, as might be expected. [But] there has been no persistent and continuing decline of the kind that would have been expected if a gradual loosening of the classes had taken place. In 1983, for example, relative class voting was about average for the period as a whole.

We also found that *absolute* class voting was particularly low in 1983, largely because one of the major 'class parties', Labour, did so badly overall. *The crucial point is that in 1983 Labour fared badly in all classes alike.* It remained relatively stronger in the working class than in the middle class; in other words, it remained a class party, but in 1983 it was an *unsuccessful class party*.

A rigorous way of testing relative class dealignment is to use log-linear modelling (as we did in *How Britain Votes*). This statistical technique enabled us to test the hypothesis that the relationship between class and party had remained constant over time once the changing shape of the class structure and the changing levels of support for the parties had been taken into account. Once we had controlled in this way, we found that relative class voting as reported in the 1964 and 1970 surveys was significantly different from that predicted by our hypothesis of a constant class alignment (1964 being significantly higher and 1970 significantly lower). But in 1983 it was very close to the predicted level. Hence we concluded that there was 'no evidence of a gradual and persistent decline in the relative strength of the class party alignment to match the steady erosion of Labour strength or the secular increase in Liberal support'. 'Spectacularly counter intuitive' as that conclusion may have been, its validity is not in serious question.

Absolute class voting – the proper meaning of class dealignment?

We certainly accept that absolute class voting has declined, and indeed show it has fallen from 63 per cent to 47 per cent over the period 1964–83. We were concerned, however, that the absolute measure was misleading as the principal way of assessing change in the class basis of politics. Crewe

100 MODELS OF PARTY CHOICE

seems to have had particular difficulty with the phrase 'the class basis of politics'. He seems to take the view that if absolute class voting has declined, then the class basis of politics must by definition have declined too. What we had in mind, however, was a distinction between description and explanation. A decline in absolute class voting may be no more than a surface change in class behaviour, largely brought about by the actions of the parties, while the underlying potential for class voting remains intact. Thus the rise in Alliance support could have been brought about by a shift of the Conservative and Labour parties away from the centre. Such a rise would necessarily lead to a decline in class voting, but this would tell us more about the class *consequences* than about the class *basis* of politics.

Crewe says that he is concerned to defend the absolute measure from misplaced criticism. Our only criticism was that it should not be misused and treated as evidence of a loosening of the class structure or a decline in the potential for class politics. That is hardly misplaced criticism. It is not clear whether Crewe now wishes to defend absolute measures as evidence of a loosening relation between class and party. We trust not, yet surprisingly he appears to reject our contention that political change alone could produce a decline in the absolute level of class voting.

That a decline in the level of absolute class voting could be brought about by political factors that have nothing to do with a loosening of the social classes is surely easy enough to demonstrate. Suppose for example that Labour moves to the left, that voters tend to be concentrated in the centre of the political spectrum, and that they respond by voting for their nearest political party, which now becomes the Liberal/SDP Alliance. Let us further suppose that these defections from Labour to the Alliance occur with the same relative frequency in all social classes, thus leaving Labour relatively stronger in the working class than in the middle class, just as it was before, but now less successful in both classes. Let us assume, in other words, that Labour has become less successful because of *political* factors, that there has been no independent loosening of the class structure, and that class voting in the relative sense has stayed unchanged. [On these assumptions] relative class voting, as measured by odds ratios [would] remain unchanged, while absolute class voting [would] decline. It seems undeniable, therefore, that Labour's loss of electoral appeal might have been responsible for the decline in absolute class voting.

The vital point is that *a decline in the absolute level of class voting does not on its own allow us to infer that the classes have lost their social cohesion or their political potential.* If the classes stay the same but the parties change, absolute class voting may decline for reasons that have nothing to do with class. In these circumstances the absolute measure would have little value for understanding the potential for class politics. Nor would it be very helpful in explaining the rise of the Liberals.

The measurement of relative class voting

We have pointed out, then, that a measure of relative class voting is preferable to an absolute measure on its own if we are concerned to test theories of a loosening of the social classes and a decline in their potential for class politics. The particular measures we use, odds ratios and log-linear analysis, enable us to say whether the relationship between class and voting has become weaker, controlling for changes in the overall levels of support for the parties. They enable us to distinguish properly between overall changes in a party's support (changes of the sort that might be brought about by political factors as described above) and a class-specific decline in a party's support.

Crewe has three major objections to our use of odds ratios. First he argues that odds ratios are unduly sensitive to small fluctuations of the kind that are bound to occur in sample surveys. Secondly, he says that the salariat/working class odds ratio which we report excludes the large section of the electorate that belongs to the intermediate classes. What is needed, Crewe suggests, is a measure of class alignment in the electorate as a whole. And thirdly he says that a defect of the odds ratio is that it is a two-party measure applied to a three-party system. *He describes this as the central weakness of our argument.* The reality is the complete reverse. On all three points odds ratios and the associated technique of log-linear analysis prove to be superior to alternatives like the Alford index.

Sampling variation

Let us begin with sampling variation. It is quite true that odds ratios, like all other estimates derived from survey data, are subject to sampling errors. It is also true that odds ratios have rather different statistical properties from more familiar measures like the Alford index, and this may be confusing for the unwary.

But it is quite misleading to say, as Crewe does, that 'the odds ratio offers a spurious degree of precision and converts tiny ripples of movement – whether real or illusory – into dramatic tides of change' (p. 626). In survey research the only sound basis for judging whether tiny ripples of movement, or dramatic tides of change, are likely to be real or illusory is to calculate tests of significance. In using sample surveys, whatever our preferred index, it is essential to use such tests, and in *How Britain Votes* we used log-linear analysis to test whether the changes over time in the full set of odds ratios were statistically significant.

The Alford index is subject to sampling error in just the same way as odds ratios are. It is quite extraordinary, therefore, that many studies which are based on the election surveys draw conclusions about changes over time without testing for significance. One looks in vain in Crewe's own

102

MODELS OF PARTY CHOICE

analyses of the election surveys for any hint that these tests have been carried out. Crewe's criticism applies forcibly to his own work but not to ours.

The salariat/working class odds ratio

[Crewe] criticizes us for measuring relative class voting solely through the salariat/working class odds ratio, ignoring the large proportion of the electorate that belongs to the intermediate classes.

Once again, Crewe has completely misunderstood our use of log-linear models to test the significance of changes in the odds ratios. He has failed to appreciate that we used log-linear analysis to examine the *full* set of class–party odds ratios. Let us try to explain more fully what this means.

In a five-by-three table [showing the five-fold class schema by party choice] there are 30 possible odds ratios that can be calculated. In order to simplify matters we decided to illustrate the trends by calculating for the reader the odds of voting Labour or Conservative in the salariat and working class. We were justified in doing so as this particular odds ratio proves to be representative of the general pattern.

To look at the trends in the 30 possible odds ratios over time might be useful but rather tedious, and it would not of course give an overall summary index. Log-linear analysis, however, provided the solution. As we explained in the book, this technique analyses the full set of odds and enables us to test the hypothesis that the strength of relative class voting does not in general vary over time. The log-linear models which we reported in the book thus take account of voting patterns in all five classes, *not* just in the salariat and working class.

Two-party measures of a three-party system?

The log-linear analysis also takes account of the Liberal Party as well as of the Conservative and Labour parties, thus disposing of Crewe's third and allegedly central criticism of our technique. It is just not the case that we apply a two-party measure to a three-party system. Once again, in fact, this criticism applies more forcibly to previous work, such as Crewe's, than to ours.

The Alford index, for example, has conventionally been applied to a two-class, two-party model of society. When Crewe (rightly) argues that Liberal (and Alliance) voting must be included in the analysis, he thus provides us with extra ammunition against the Alford index. It is no longer appropriate for analysing class alignment in Britain's multi-party political system.

Unlike the Alford index, then, our log-linear analysis fully satisfies the requirements which Crewe himself has specified. It is somewhat surprising, therefore, that there is no mention of log-linear models anywhere in his Note.

The advantages of odds ratios

Perhaps even more importantly, Crewe seems to be unaware of the advantages which odds ratios (and log-linear models) have over previous techniques such as the Alford index. Since the use of odds ratios is still relatively uncommon in British political science, it may be useful to explain in more detail why we turned to them in place of the more conventional Alford index.

The central defect of the Alford index is that the values which it can take on are constrained by the marginal totals. It therefore becomes a misleading measure in a period when the marginal totals (the distribution of support between the parties, for example) have changed markedly.

If the overall proportion [of voters who are] in the working class is 50 per cent and the overall proportion [of voters] who voted Labour is 50 per cent, then the maximum value which the Alford index can take is 100. (The maximum will occur when all working-class respondents vote Labour and all middle-class respondents vote Conservative.) But if the overall proportion who vote Labour falls to 40 per cent, then the maximum value which the Alford index can take falls to 80. (All middle-class respondents still vote Conservative; all Labour voters remain working class, but 20 per cent of working-class respondents vote Conservative.) In other words, the values which the Alford index can take are not independent of the overall distribution of the vote between the parties.

This is important because the distribution of the vote has of course changed markedly between 1964 and 1983. The Alford index indeed declined over this period too, but our suggestion is that this decline was partly due to the fall in Labour's share of the vote. It does not allow us to make any major inferences about the loosening of the class structure or the potential for class voting.

[This] limitation does not, however, apply to odds ratios. The values which they may take are not constrained by the distribution of the vote and they are therefore ideally suited to examining the relationship between class and vote, controlling for overall changes in the distribution of the vote and the sizes of the classes. If one wishes to distinguish between absolute and relative class voting in the way we did, odds ratios are clearly much more suitable than the Alford index.

The loosening of the class structure?

The evidence presented so far about the loosening of the class structure is essentially indirect. We have been making inferences about the strength of the classes and their potential for class action from the trends (or rather lack of trends) in the odds ratios. Thus the trendless fluctuation in the odds

104   MODELS OF PARTY CHOICE

ratios leads us to be sceptical about the class dealignment thesis, but as Crewe rightly suggests, direct evidence would be better.

In *How Britain Votes* we included a table on changing class attitudes to nationalization over time, and showed that class differences have not declined. Crewe criticizes this on two scores. First, he correctly points out that overall levels of support for nationalization within the working class have declined. Secondly, he criticizes us for not looking at other measures of class attitudes and values over time, in particular, attitudes towards trade-union power, big business power and self-assigned class.

Let us remedy this deficiency. Self-assigned class would appear to be the most appropriate measure of the three proposed. Table 3.5.1 shows the relationship between our five-fold class schema and the standard measure of self-assigned class in each of the election studies.

What do we find? First, we see that there has been no change at all in the proportion of the electorate who are willing to assign themselves to a class. So there appears to be no general decline in class awareness over some 20 years. Secondly, we see that there has been a decline, from 67 per cent to 60 per cent, in the proportion who assign themselves to the working class, and a corresponding increase in the proportion assigning themselves to the middle class. What we must do [however] is to control for the changing shape of the objective class structure. The results when we do so, are extremely interesting. Consider, for example, the proportion of the 'objective' working class who subjectively assign themselves to the working class. Between 1964 and 1979 this hardly changes at all, fluctuating between 81 per cent and 84 per cent.

Compared with the very large swings in working-class political *behaviour* over this period, the constancy of subjective class *awareness* in the working class seems quite remarkable. The fluctuations are far short of statistical significance and they also seem to be entirely trendless. This is, then, powerful evidence against Crewe's contention that there has been a secular decline in class awareness. Changes in subjective class awareness seem to be extremely implausible candidates for explaining political change and Crewe's contention that there has been 'a sea-change of attitudes within the proletariat' looks far from promising in the light of these data.

There is more relevant evidence, too. The notion of a 'sea-change of attitudes within the proletariat' presumably means that a range of attitudes within the proletariat all changed in similar direction and degree. This can be tested for the 1974–83 period, and the results are given in Table 3.5.2.

As can be seen, these results fail to support Crewe's hypothesis. To be sure, as Crewe himself demonstrated, there is a large (and statistically significant) shift to the right on nationalization. But this is not matched by similar shifts on other issues. There is a rather smaller shift to the right on redistribution; there is no change on poverty; and there is a rather large

TRENDLESS FLUCTUATION: A REPLY TO CREWE

Table 3.5.1 Objective and subjective class, 1964–83

Class self-image	All	Salariat	Routine non-manual	Petty bourgeoisie	Foremen and technicians	Working class
1964						
Middle	28	55	35	46	21	13
Working	67	35	63	42	74	83
None	5	10	2	12	4	4
	(N = 916)	(N = 144)	(N = 148)	(N = 58)	(N = 79)	(N = 396)
1966						
Middle	30	59	36	48	21	14
Working	67	37	60	45	76	84
None	3	5	4	7	3	2
	(N = 1,857)	(N = 332)	(N = 319)	(N = 122)	(N = 151)	(N = 801)
1970						
Middle	33	60	39	40	29	14
Working	63	34	58	50	67	84
None	4	6	3	10	4	3
	(N = 615)	(N = 120)	(N = 105)	(N = 40)	(N = 52)	(N = 236)
Feb. 1974						
Middle	34	58	39	47	29	16
Working	63	37	58	47	68	81
None	4	5	3	6	4	3
	(N = 2,443)	(N = 489)	(N = 448)	(N = 198)	(N = 157)	(N = 936)
Oct. 1974						
Middle	33	57	37	41	25	16
Working	62	37	58	52	72	81
None	4	6	4	7	3	3
	(N = 2,341)	(N = 520)	(N = 443)	(N = 176)	(N = 178)	(N = 858)
1979						
Middle	33	58	32	46	22	14
Working	62	37	64	49	73	82
None	5	5	5	6	5	4
	(N = 1,849)	(N = 458)	(N = 334)	(N = 144)	(N = 193)	(N = 580)
1983						
Middle	35	54	35	41	30	19
Working	60	39	59	51	65	78
None	5	7	6	8	5	3
	(N = 3,849)	(N = 980)	(N = 905)	(N = 289)	(N = 268)	(N = 1,250)

Notes:
1. Figures are percentages and figures in brackets give the weighted Ns.
2. In 1964 and 1970 the class self-image questions were asked of a random half sample.
3. The category 'none' includes 'don't know' and 'other'.
4. Respondents who are economically active (or retired) are assigned to a class according to their own occupation and employment status. Otherwise, they are assigned to their spouse's class (provided they are married, or living as married, and have a spouse who is economically active or retired).
5. The column 'all' includes respondents who could not be assigned to a class at all.

Table 3.5.2 Attitudes in the working class, 1974–83

Percentages agreeing that . . .	Oct. 1974	1979	1983	Change 74–83	Significance
More industries should be nationalized	37 (833)	22 (585)	23 (1,264)	−14	0.001
Income and wealth should be redistributed towards ordinary working people	67 (835)	66 (583)	61 (1,262)	−6	0.01
The government should spend more money to get rid of poverty	88 (836)	83 (585)	87 (1,262)	−1	NS
The government should give workers more say in running the places where they work	63 (838)	60 (584)	74 (1,266)	+11	0.001

shift to the *left* on industrial democracy. True, industrial democracy has not been politicized in the way that nationalization has been, but that serves to underline our point that unrealized potentials for class action may remain within the working class.

Conclusions

There is not, and never has been, any disagreement about the fact of declining *absolute* class voting. What has been at issue is the explanation of this trend and of the related trends in support for the Labour Party and the Liberal/SDP Alliance. In particular, can the decline of the Labour Party and of absolute class voting be explained by a loosening of the classes? And does this mean that the potential of the working class for radical political action has diminished?

The dispute therefore centres around the alleged decline in *relative* class voting, since the measurement of relative class voting better enables us to disentangle a long-term loosening of the classes from the transitory political fortunes of the parties. As we observed above, if the classes stay the same but the parties change, absolute class voting may decline for reasons that have nothing to do with class.

What we have shown in this paper is that Crewe scores a spectacular series of own-goals in his criticisms of our measurement of relative class voting. Unfortunately, he did not notice that we employ log-linear analysis and he failed to appreciate the relationship between odds ratios and log-linear modelling. As a result, none of his three central criticisms applies to our work. But all three forcibly apply to his.

3.6 | Class dealignment in Britain revisited

Patrick Dunleavy

Accepted interpretations of the slump in support for the Labour party, and the growth of first Liberal and now Alliance voting, have been challenged in an apparently dramatic fashion by Heath, Jowell and Curtice in *How Britain Votes*. The kernel of the book's argument is contained in its highly condensed third chapter which disputes the evidence for the decline of class voting perceived by almost all other observers.

Heath, Jowell and Curtice make four main argumentative moves. First, they reject the use of opinion poll 'social grades' for gauging class positions and opt instead for a schema derived from Goldthorpe's work on the 1972 Oxford social mobility survey, in which Heath also participated. Second, the authors use their new five-class schema to argue that occupational classes remained politically distinctive in 1983. Third, Heath *et al*. [arguing that it is trends in relative rather than absolute class voting that matter] query whether there is much evidence of 'class dealignment'. Fourth, Heath *et al*. embrace one particular measure of relative class voting, the odds ratio.

Analysing odds ratios for the non-manual/manual dichotomy, Heath *et al*. construct a time series from 1945 to 1983, from which they conclude that the 1964 election was a post-war high-point in terms of class voting. They acknowledge that the series from 1964 onward generally shows a falling odds ratio. However, they argue that the broad non-manual/manual dichotomy may be masking the effects of changes in the social composition of each side of the social divide and hence 'runs the risk of confusing class dealignment with changing class sizes'. Shifting to more detailed evidence for the 1964–83 period, they argue that the ratio of Conservative/Labour

---

From P. Dunleavy, 'Class dealignment in Britain revisited', *West European Politics* (1987), vol. 10, pp. 400–19.

108   MODELS OF PARTY CHOICE

odds across the salariat and their newly defined 'small working class' category shows no trend of any kind towards class dealignment.

Do odds ratios measure relative class voting?

Accepting for the moment Heath, Jowell and Curtice's focus upon relative class voting, their analysis assumes throughout that the odds ratio is a useful and highly reliable index of relative class voting – so much so that they seem to read significance into even minor fluctuations in this statistic. In fact, it can be demonstrated that the odds ratio is a quite inappropriate measure to use, especially in analysing the transition from a two-party to a three-party system. [This] can be demonstrated by looking at its sensitivity to quite small differences in support for the political parties, especially in a three-party situation.

Heath *et al.*'s data show how some very small changes in the parties' voting shares can produce apparently large swings in the Conservative/Labour odds ratio. Table 3.6.1 gives the 1964 and 1983 voting figures and odds ratios for the non-manual/manual and salariat/small working class comparisons. In 1964 the voting figures in the conventional non-manual group and in the salariat differed by one per cent, while the Labour vote is rated six points higher and the Conservative vote five points lower in Heath *et al.*'s small working class than in the broader conventional manual category. In 1983 the two non-manual groups show a 3 per cent difference in their estimation of Labour and Alliance voting, while in the small working class the Labour vote is seven points higher and the Conservative vote five points down compared with the conventional manual category. Yet in both cases the odds ratio looks radically different across the two sets of figures.

Two alternative measures of class voting in Table 3.6.1 show just how distorting these odds ratios are. The first is simply the Conservative share of the combined Conservative and Labour two-party vote. It indicates the relative popularity of the Conservatives and Labour across classes and time-periods. The second measure is the Alford index of class voting. On both measures the non-manual/manual and salariat/small working class contrasts yield very similar sets of figures in 1964 and again in 1983, quite unlike the odds ratios for these years. Like all such indices, these measures have drawbacks and anomalies. But precisely because they are much closer to the actual voting figures than the odds ratio they are much less likely to produce misleading results, or to create severe uncertainties in interpretation.

The obverse side of the odds ratio's peculiar property of exaggerating some small vote share differences is that the same odds ratio may conceal very different voting figures, as Table 3.6.2 demonstrates using four

CLASS DEALIGNMENT IN BRITAIN REVISITED

Table 3.6.1 The sensitivity of the odds ratio: comparing voting figures for 1964 and 1983 using alternative non-manual/manual contrasts and alternative indices of class voting

1964 election	Conventional classes		Heath *et al.* classes	
	Non-manual	Manual	Salariat	SWC
Conservative	62	28	61	23
Liberal	16	8	18	7
Labour	22	64	20	70
Con./Lab. odds	2.82	0.44	3.05	0.33
Odds ratio	6.4		9.3	
Conservative share of the two-party vote:				
	Non-manual	74	Salariat	75
	Manual	30	SWC	25
Alford index:				
	Conservative	34		38
	Labour	42		50
1983 election	Conventional classes		Heath *et al.* classes	
	Non-manual	Manual	Salariat	SWC
Conservative	55	35	54	30
Alliance	28	22	31	20
Labour	17	42	14	49
Con./Lab. odds	3.24	0.83	3.18	0.61
Odds ratio	3.9		6.3	
Conservative share of the two-party vote:				
	Non-manual	76	Salariat	79
	Manual	45	SWC	38
Alford index:				
	Conservative	20		24
	Labour	25		35

hypothetical elections. Election A resembles the configuration during the 1950s and early 1960s [and gives] an odds ratio of 6. Election B shows what happens when the Labour Party is taken over by the Militant Tendency: its support drops drastically so that over nine tenths of the electorate split their votes evenly between the Conservatives and the Alliance. It might be thought that this result represents the closest feasible approximation to identical voting patterns across the non-manual/manual divide. But

Table 3.6.2 Hypothetical situations showing a constant Conservative/Labour non-manual/manual odds ratio

	Election A		Election B	
	Non-manual	Manual	Non-manual	Manual
Conservative	72	32	48	40
Alliance	4	4	48	50
Labour	24	64	2	10
Con./Lab. odds	3.0	0.5	24.0	4.0
Non-manual/manual odds ratio	6.0		6.0	

	Election C		Election D	
	Non-manual	Manual	Non-manual	Manual
Conservative	36	72	44	13.3
Alliance	63	16	12	6.7
Labour	1	12	44	80
Con./Lab. odds	36.0	6.0	1.0	0.167
Non-manual/manual odds ratio	6.0		6.0	

because the minute Labour vote is drawn differentially from manual workers the odds ratio remains exactly the same as in election A. In election C suppose that Labour is again taken over by the Militant Tendency while at the same time the Conservatives swing radically towards a neo-Powellite line. Here non-manual support for the Alliance grows dramatically while manual workers by contrast swing vigorously towards the newly populist Tories – all without any impact on the odds ratio. Finally, suppose that in election D there is such a strong revival of Labour's electoral fortunes under Kinnock that the Alliance is squeezed into insignificance, and Labour scoops four fifths of the manual vote and achieves level-pegging with the Conservatives among non-manual voters. Again, the odds ratio remains constant at 6.0.

What (if anything) the odds ratio measures appears not at all certain. But since it is so vulnerable to distorting some small changes in absolute voting figures and disguising other major differences it should be clear that it is a useless device for comparing one election with another. Yet unfortunately in Chapter 3 of *How Britain Votes* changes in this eccentric statistic are interpreted as a critical guide to the development of 'relative class voting'.

Much the silliest example occurs where the authors seek to combat what they take to be the myths of stronger non-manual/manual voting contrasts

CLASS DEALIGNMENT IN BRITAIN REVISITED

in the 1950s and early 1960s, and to substitute instead their view of the 1964 election as a deceptive high-point in class voting. They utilise a time series for the post-war period in which there are two considerable problems. First, the 1945 election figures are of exceptionally dubious worth [and] it seems prudent to leave these data out of the time series. Second, the 1955 and 1959 figures are based upon people recalling their votes several years later, a potential source of serious error. None the less, if we retain these last two figures, the odds ratios for 1950–83 are:

							Feb.	Oct.		
1950	1951	1955	1959	1964	1966	1970	1974	1974	1979	1983
5.5	6.3	5.9	6.1	6.4	6.4	4.5	5.7	4.8	3.7	3.9

Given the sensitivity of the odds ratio statistic to small fluctuations in behaviour, the only sensible interpretation of these data is not that 1964 was some kind of zenith for class voting, but that throughout the 1950 to 1966 period the odds of a non-manual person voting Conservative rather than Labour were approximately six times greater than the odds for manual workers. From 1970 the data also suggest a considerable reduction in this odds ratio, apart from the February 1974 election, called in a crisis atmosphere by a Conservative administration on the basis of 'Who governs Britain – the elected government or the trade unions?' That there should be an isolated political reaffirmation of older occupational class allegiances among two-party loyalists in such a conjuncture, a blip which subsequently faded considerably within six months, does not seem surprising.

The second key historical argument used by Heath, Jowell and Curtice reworks the figures from earlier voting studies to fit their five-way occupational class categories. One shrewd reviewer noted that using data collected with one class schema in mind within an alternative schema devised years later must be a source of considerable coding error. In presenting their account of the evolution of occupational class sizes, Heath *et al.* strongly suggest that their data show smooth growth in the size of the salariat, the petit bourgeoisie and the routine non-manual categories, and a steady decline in the size of their narrowly defined working class. In fact there are some strange wobbles in the figures. The proportion of voters categorised in the routine non-manual, petit bourgeois and foremen/technician classes changes sharply from one survey to the next in a way which suggests that coding consistency across years is rather problematic.

Such data problems are very unlikely to be serious if attention was focused directly upon actual voting figures. But they could have an exaggerated impact on the salariat/small working class odds ratio, on which Heath *et al.* focus so much attention. For example, in the published data for October 1974 they accidentally omitted to include 314 (out of 1,811) respondents as a result of a computing error. Revised figures including the

112 MODELS OF PARTY CHOICE

missing respondents leave the small working class vote shares unchanged, but produce a two per cent increase in the Conservative vote and a three per cent decrease in the Labour vote within the salariat. That minute shift alters the odds ratio for October 1974 from 5.5 (below the median of seven ratios) to 6.7 (the third highest result after 1964 and 1966).

The combined effect of Heath *et al.*'s new class schema and reliance on the odds ratio statistic is to provide a very fragile basis for interpreting past electoral trends. By substituting a contrast between the salariat and the small working class for the conventional non-manual/manual dichotomy, they particularly restrict the numbers of voters included in calculating the odds ratio statistic used to assess class voting. No explanation is given of this step. Yet the proportion of the electorate falling within the salariat and the small working class was just three-fifths of the total by 1983. Because the Conservative/Labour odds ratio ignores third-party support, the proportions of voters whose alignments are counted in Heath *et al.*'s assessment of 'relative class voting' fell steadily from three-fifths in 1966, to less than half of men and under two-fifths of women in 1983. This restrictive basis helps explain why Table 3.6.3 shows that the salariat/small working class odds ratio behaves in a much more volatile manner than the same odds ratio across the non-manual/manual divide. As noted above, the odds ratio swings more violently than alternative measures of relative class voting across the salariat/small working class contrast, such as the class difference in the Conservative share of the two-party vote, or the Alford index of Conservative voting.

There is apparently some evidence here to support the claims by Heath *et al.* of 'trendless fluctuation' in 'relative class voting', since the class differential in the Conservative share of the two-party vote reaches its nadir in 1970 and otherwise remains fairly constant from 1966 onwards. But broadening the analysis to include all five occupational classes in

Table 3.6.3 The volatility of the salariat/small working class Conservative/Labour odds ratio compared with other indications of 'class voting'

	Conservative/Labour odds ratios		Conservative share of the two-party vote		Alford index for Con. vote across salariat/SWC
	Salariat/ SWC	Non-manual/ manual	Salariat	SWC	
1964	9.3	6.4	75	25	38
1966	7.3	6.4	70	24	35
1970	3.9	4.5	67	35	28
1974 Feb.	6.1	5.7	69	27	30
1974 Oct.	6.7	4.8	67	24	27
1979	4.9	3.7	73	35	29
1983	6.3	3.9	79	38	24

CLASS DEALIGNMENT IN BRITAIN REVISITED

Figure 3.6.1 shows that there was a continuing trend for occupational class differences in the Conservative share of the two-party vote to lessen in the late 1970s, despite the rewidening of differences in the February 1974 election. It is the fairly consistent gap between the salariat and the small working class which is the odd thing out in this picture. Even in their own terms of focusing on 'relative class voting', Heath *et al.* have been misled by their focus on a very partial comparison of trends in their five occupational classes.

The log linear analysis of class voting

The case for the stability of class voting is not based solely upon odds ratio analysis. Heath, Jowell and Curtice were clearly aware that it would be better to measure electoral change using an index or type of analysis which could tackle multi-party voting as well as a two-party configuration; which would include all voters in the assessment of change; and which could cope

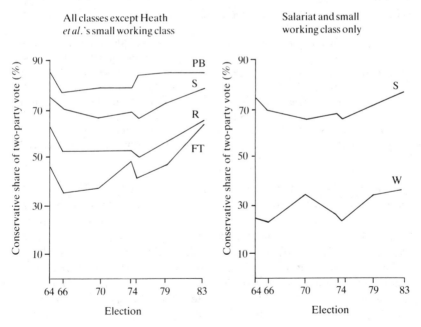

Note: PB petit bourgeoisie; S salariat; R routine non-manual; FT foremen and technicians; W small working class.

Figure 3.6.1 The evolution of the Conservative share of the two-party vote across five occupational classes, 1964–83

114 MODELS OF PARTY CHOICE

with multiple classes instead of just two. Consequently the final element in their empirical case is a log linear analysis of voting, class, and elections. However, the analysis is unfortunately relegated to the footnotes and described in an extremely abbreviated way.

Log linear analysis is a technique for understanding what is going on inside large contingency tables. It resembles chi-square procedures in using the column and row marginals of a table to estimate the scores which should be found in each cell of the table, but unlike the normal chi-square it can tackle multiple variables. Fitted scores and observed values are then compared to assess whether deviation from expected scores are likely to have arisen by chance. The technique allows one to determine how good a fit to the observed data is achieved by various models including only some of the possible explanatory variables. Comparing different partial models also gives an estimate of the significance which attaches to each term in the final model chosen. Comparing the differences between observed and fitted scores also allows the technique to estimate the direction and effect of particular explanatory variables. Finally, of course, a cell-by-cell analysis of deviations can shed light on those effects which the chosen model does not explain.

Heath *et al*. argue that their conclusions from the analysis of odds ratios:

> . . . are confirmed by the use of the more rigorous statistical technique of log linear modelling. Some small variations in the relationship between class and party remain, however. The model which assumes a constant set of class/party odds ratios over time does not fit the data wholly satisfactorily. But the deviations which remain have more of the character of 'trendless fluctuations' than steady dealignment . . . As [the odds ratio analysis] indicated, 1964 and 1970 were the exceptional ones. And if these two elections are excluded from the analysis, the assumption of constant odds ratios turns out to give a perfectly acceptable fit.

A rather different picture emerges in the footnotes. The constant class/party model which 'does not fit the data wholly satisfactorily' in the text, in fact 'does not give a good fit to the data', with a significance (or p) value of under one per cent; while the 'perfectly acceptable fit' for the constant class/party model for the five elections leaving out 1964 and 1970 itself gives a p value of only 13.7 per cent. (By contrast the p values for the authors' own more complex models given in a later chapter exceed 30 per cent, which is a reasonable fit for log linear analysis.) And while proclaiming their ability to dispense with a class/vote/election interaction term in their three variables analysis, Heath *et al*. do not explain that such a term would create a 'saturated model' – which automatically produces a full fit with the data, and hence indicates the inconclusive termination of the log linear analysis.

Readers must make their own judgements about the wisdom of fitting

CLASS DEALIGNMENT IN BRITAIN REVISITED *115*

models to only some of seven elections and simply leaving out those elections which present difficulties for the analysts' preferred models. Certainly no evidence is presented of the results which class dealignment enthusiasts might be able to achieve if they could similarly pick and choose the data to be modelled.

In a later log linear analysis of only the 1964 and 1983 elections but expanded to take account of housing tenure as well as occupational class, the change in the relative sizes of tenure groups within classes 1964–83 emerges as a significant variable in explaining changing vote trends. A fair summing up of these findings might run as follows: 'In a three-variable analysis (looking at class, vote and election) the model which assumed a constant class-vote linkage, failed to fit the data, and no other models short of the saturated model could be analysed. In a four-variable analysis including housing locations, tenure change was a significant factor explaining vote change across elections. The effect of the housing tenure change was to cross-cut the class–party linkages.' Such a summary hardly constitutes a refutation of previous findings about class dealignment.

The meaning of class voting and class dealignment

Heath, Jowell and Curtice suggest that if their five occupational classes had gone on voting as they did in 1964 over the next two decades, but class sizes had simply changed in line with observed trends, then both Conservative and Labour support has been below expectations, while third-party voting has grown far more than would have been expected.

The obvious question is one of explanation. Is the growth of third-party voting a factor which we must discount before trying to assess changing class alignments, or is it the most fascinating symptom of class dealignment? Heath *et al.* answer that since only 'relative class voting' counts as class voting, then the growth of third-party voting and the under-performance of Labour and the Conservatives has to be explained by other factors. 'In our view [these shifts] have not been due to any "loosening" or "fragmentation" of the classes but to political changes which have nothing at all to do with class' (p. 38). The point to recognise here is that this stance is an assertion, a definitional fiat about the meaning of 'class voting' and 'class dealignment'. It is not established by empirical analysis, but simply by a particular use of vocabulary.

There are three possible meanings of 'class voting' and 'class dealignment'. 'Absolute class voting' is the proportion of all voters who are non-manual and vote Conservative combined with those who are manual workers and vote Labour. Class dealignment in these terms is simply a decline in this percentage. 'Relative class voting' as used by Heath *et al.* is measured by the Conservative/Labour odds in the non-manual group

116 MODELS OF PARTY CHOICE

divided by the same odds among manual workers, and class dealignment occurs if cross-class voting increases. Both these meanings (together with other constructs such as the Alford index) are specialised psephological constructs which bear little relation to what might be termed the 'intuitive' view of class voting – which is simply that there are clearly divergent patterns of voting across the non-manual/manual divide. The 'intuitive' meaning of class dealignment is simply that non-manual and manual classes have become more similar or less clearly contrasted in their voting patterns over time. In this 'intuitive' sense it is obviously undeniable that the relatively uniform growth of Liberal and Social Democratic Party voting across occupational classes constitutes class dealignment, with an additional effect if cross-class voting increases.

What considerations should influence our choice of meaning to give 'class voting' and 'class dealignment'? An important objection to both the absolute and relative class voting concepts is that they focus solely on the Conservative and Labour contrast, which seems inappropriate in a period when explaining the transition to a three-party system is the central analytic problem. Public perceptions of class dealignment are especially serious for Labour's viability as a party of government, given its much greater dependence on single-class support. The incentive for non-manual people to vote Labour depends very heavily upon the party's ability to retain manual workers' allegiances. If Labour's grip upon working-class loyalties obviously weakens we should expect its marginal non-manual supporters to respond to its reduced electoral viability by defecting to Liberal/Alliance voting in a three-party system.

This suggests a crucial reason why the Heath *et al.* approach of focusing on relative class voting could be misleading. Dynamic processes of class dealignment operating between one election and another may produce an even decline in support for 'class parties' across the non-manual/manual dichotomy. Class dealignment might cause a drop in Labour support across-the-board within a three-party system.

In Chapter 2 Heath *et al.* argue that all three major parties have a skewed social base which justifies the 'class party' label. They also promise to demonstrate 'that Labour remained a class party in 1983; it was simply a less successful class party than before' (p. 29). But unfortunately no data are presented about the evolution of the class distinctiveness of the political parties' support bases over time.

This record can be analysed, however, by recomputing Heath *et al.*'s data, and using an index of dissimilarity. To calculate this index for the Conservative and Labour parties, it is necessary to work out the differences between the share of each party's support which is drawn from each occupational class, sum these differences across all five classes (ignoring the positive and negative signs involved), and divide the resulting figure by two. This process creates an index which runs from 0 (minimum

CLASS DEALIGNMENT IN BRITAIN REVISITED 117

dissimilarity) to 100 per cent (maximum dissimilarity). Comparing the class distinctiveness of the Conservative and Labour vote bases [the index] shows a marked reduction from 43 to 29 up to 1970, but thereafter a rise again to the mid-30s, although with a downward dip in 1979. Creating a single non-Labour series for comparison with Labour's support base shows a much clearer picture of weakening class distinctiveness, with the index falling from 43 in 1964 to fluctuate around the 30s thereafter.

Thus there are four general grounds for rejecting Heath, Jowell and Curtice on relative class voting. Their discounting of the growth of third-party support is an unargued definitional manoeuvre. By focusing on an index which matters to no one except a few psephologists, they ignore the impact of the 'intuitive' trend towards class dealignment upon voters. Once we recognise this possibility, there is good reason to believe that class dealignment need not show up as a class-specific decline in a 'class' party's vote, but instead becomes manifest as an across-the-board reduction in support. Furthermore, the meaning of 'class party' is anyway obscure in their account, and does not recognise the evidence that once we incorporate reference to growing Liberal/SDP support, the class distinctiveness of major parties' support bases has appreciably declined since the mid-1960s.

Conclusion

By sceptically reopening the debate about class voting in Britain, and by striking a note of caution about the continuing occupational class differences in voting which underlie the transition from a two- to a three-party system, Heath, Jowell and Curtice have performed a valuable service. The trouble is that their own contribution in *How Britain Votes* is itself a compressed and misleading piece of analysis, which should carry a government health warning about the definitional manoeuvres and statistical indices included. Clearly, it is important to knock on the head exaggerated interpretations of how changing political allegiances bespeak the end of 'class' as a political influence. But it is no less important that we do not substitute in its place a new myth about 'trendless fluctuations' in an arcane concept called 'relative class voting' and measured by a virtually meaningless odds ratio statistic.

3.7 | Social class and party choice in England: a new analysis

W.L. Miller

It is common knowledge that party support in England is strongly polarized along class lines. But how strongly? And is the degree of class polarization increasing, decreasing, or approximately constant? It is to these questions that this article is devoted. [It] will compare survey-derived individual-level results with degrees and trends of class polarization at the constituency level, as indicated by Census data and constituency election returns and, most crucially, it will attempt to clarify and refine both the concept and the measurement of class polarization.

Class polarization in recent survey studies

Class polarization has traditionally been defined in two stages. First some definition of class is used to assign all or most individuals to classes. Then these classes are dichotomized into a set of 'middle' classes and a set of 'working' classes and some measure of the difference between middle- and working-class partisanship is taken as a definition of class polarization.

In Britain class is usually defined by occupation and occupation alone. On the basis of head of household's occupation respondents are assigned to a number of classes. Butler and Stokes' six 'social grades' are typical. There are [then] a number of pressures towards simplifying this classification by dichotomizing it at some point.

Class polarization has usually been defined in terms of dichotomous, all-inclusive classes. Even with this simplification, however, there are

From W.L. Miller, 'Social class and party choice in England: a new analysis', *British Journal of Political Science* (1978), vol. 8, pp. 257–84.

SOCIAL CLASS AND PARTY CHOICE IN ENGLAND 119

several ways in which polarization could reasonably be [measured]. In a pure two-party system [if we imagine a regression line fitted to a plot of class against party] we could measure the degree of class polarization as a degree of 'fit' [to the line], or of 'slope' [of the line]. According to the 'fit' definition a strong class alignment would mean that both cross-cutting alignments and random deviations from the class alignment were slight. According to the 'slope' definition a strong class alignment would mean that there were large class differences in partisanship irrespective of whether these were overlaid by other structured or random partisan variations. It is theoretically possible for one of these definitions to show a high degree of polarization when the other indicates little. More important, one definition may indicate a rising trend while the other indicates a declining trend.

Butler and Stokes, and later Crewe, Sarlvik and Alt, defined class polarization as the difference between the Conservative share of the two-party (i.e. Labour plus Conservative) vote in the middle and working classes. That is a 'slope' definition, exactly equal to the unstandardized regression slope in a dummy variable regression where the dependent variable is vote, coded 1 for Conservative and 0 for Labour, and the predictor variable is class, coded 1 for middle and 0 for working. A corresponding 'fit' definition would be the R^2 value for that regression, the proportion of partisan variation explained by class.

Although it is seldom stated explicitly, one reason why the manual/non-manual dichotomy is favoured for survey analyses of class polarization is that it is the least skewed of the class dichotomies and so gives the best fit even when it does not produce the largest partisan difference (i.e. slope). Table 3.7.1 illustrates this.

[In a three-party system] there are two obvious ways of measuring bipolar alignments. Liberals and others may be excluded and class

Table 3.7.1 Slope and fit in dummy variable regressions on survey data, 1966

Class dichotomy	Slope	Fit (R^2)
12/3456	41.2	8.7
123/456	44.9	16.5
1234/56	42.7	17.3

Note: Based on the 1966 BES survey. In this and all subsequent tables figures are for English respondents only. The class dichotomies are based on different divisions of Butler and Stokes' social grades, here numbered 1 to 6. Slopes are expressed in terms of percentages of the vote; fit is expressed in terms of percentage of the variance explained.

120   MODELS OF PARTY CHOICE

polarization defined as the class difference in Conservative shares of the Conservative plus Labour vote. Alternatively we may calculate separately the class differences in Labour, and then in Conservative, shares of the total vote, finally averaging the two differences. This is the same as using half the Conservative lead over Labour as a partisan measure. We regard the measure based on the total vote as the more valid for trend analysis. However, all our conclusions are strengthened if the other measure is used. We think it overstates our case.

When Butler and Stokes originally pointed to a weakening of the class alignment they based their conclusion on trends in the bipolar measure based on two-party support but applied to party identification rather than voting. In Table 3.7.2 we show our own calculations of the trends in class polarization since 1963 using the [BES] series of surveys and applying both bipolar measures to both party identification and voting. Although the trends are not completely in agreement they suggest that both voting and party identification were most polarized in the early or mid-'sixties and have declined thereafter.

Using our preferred measure of polarization – that based on half the Conservative lead (the fourth line in the table) – there was a substantial decline in the class polarization of survey respondents. We shall now consider in what sense that finding indicates a 'decline in class polarization' without the qualifying phrase 'amongst survey respondents'.

Social interaction and class polarization

The classic statement of the likely effect of social interaction on partisan differences is that 'contact is a condition for consensus', [but] it is easy to imagine circumstances where contact intensifies differences rather than eliminates them.

Table 3.7.2 Four survey-based measures of class polarization, 1963–74

Bipolar polarization		1963	1964	1966	1969	1970	1974 (Feb.)	1974 (Oct.)
Using two-party total	I[†]	47.3	38.0	41.9	32.3	35.7	35.6	33.3
	V	–	41.1	42.7	–	35.8	39.8	35.7
Using half Con. lead	I	40.9	32.9	37.2	28.1	32.2	30.0	27.4
	V	–	36.1	39.1	–	33.2	31.3	28.7

Note: Based on reanalysis of SSRC Election Study Surveys directed by Butler and Stokes (1963–70) and Crewe and Sarlvik (1974).

[†]I, party identification; V, vote. Note that votes were always a little more polarized than identifications. Only votes are comparable with the election returns. All polarizations are expressed in terms of percentages of votes or identifications.

SOCIAL CLASS AND PARTY CHOICE IN ENGLAND

Some contacts are certainly more likely to produce consensus rather than reaction. People with similar characteristics and interests are more likely to come into contact with one another and these contacts, if not all contacts, are likely to produce discussions leading to consensual tendencies in political attitudes and partisanship. Thus, working-class people are likely to have a pattern of contacts biased towards the working class which will reinforce the working-class influence on their partisanship. And the same is true, in the opposite direction, for middle-class people. A class polarization that might be small if each individual evaluated the parties in isolation from his fellows is likely to be magnified as a result of individuals making class-structured contacts.

Two major factors influence the composition of the individual's set of contacts. His selection of contacts from within his environment is biased towards those similar to himself but that bias is not sufficient to prevent the spatial environment having a considerable effect. If Mr A and Mr B have similar social characteristics but Mr A lives in an area where the middle class form twice as large a fraction of the local population as in the area where Mr B lives, then Mr A is likely to have more middle-class contacts than Mr B.

The consequences of this bias depend upon how people respond to contact with those who do not have the same characteristics as themselves. [One] possibility is that people will be influenced towards agreement with their contacts, whether or not these contacts have similar characteristics to themselves. Both middle- and working-class individuals [would be] more Conservative in middle-class areas because both sets of individuals have fewer working-class contacts and more middle-class contacts than if they lived elsewhere. We shall present evidence to show that this model does describe class polarization in England, and we shall attempt to quantify this model's parameters.

Quantitative implications

If there were no environmental effects on class polarization the slope measure used by the survey analyses would equal the slope relating constituency partisanship to constituency class. Suppose that fractions a of the middle class and b of the working class voted Conservative. The survey-based measure of class polarization is therefore $(a - b)$. If these fractions held for each constituency electorate the proportion Conservative of the two-party vote in each constituency would be CON where

$$CON = aM + b(1 - M)$$
$$= b + (a - b)M$$

and M is the proportion middle-class in the constituency. In a scatterplot of constituency partisanship against constituency class all the data points would lie exactly on a line whose slope would be $(a - b)$. Random variations between constituencies in the partisanship of the two classes

122   MODELS OF PARTY CHOICE

would make the fit to a line rather less than perfect but a regression through the scatter would still have a slope equal to $(a - b)$.

The degree of fit to the constituency data regression would be a second measure of class polarization which gauged the importance of spatially distributed deviations from the class alignment. It need not be related to the fit measure of polarization based on survey data. Constituency regressions should show the same slopes as shown in Table 3.7.1 but not the same fits, not even the same rank ordering of fit. Table 3.7.3 compares the survey-based and constituency-based measures of slope and fit.

The model of class polarization that excludes environmental influence is clearly wrong. The constituency-based slopes are all higher than the survey-based slopes by a multiple of between two and six times. In 1966 the manual/non-manual class dichotomy gave a 42.7 per cent slope with survey data but an 87.5 per cent slope with constituency data. Every 1 per cent increment of non-manual middle class made a constituency 0.88 per cent more Conservative in 1966.

Suppose now that we let the partisanship of individuals depend upon their own class characteristics and also upon the class mix in their local constituency. The simplest form which such a dependence could take is represented by two linear functions which may be regarded as simple approximations to a more complex reality. Within the middle class we now suppose that the probability of an individual voting Conservative is $a_0 + a_1 M$, where a_0 and a_1 are constants while M is, as before, the proportion of the local constituency which is middle-class. Similarly we take $b_0 + b_1 M$ with b_0 and b_1 constants, as the probability that a working-class individual, living in an environment defined by M, will vote Conservative. For individuals living in the same constituency the class polarization is

$$(a_0 + a_1 M) - (b_0 + b_1 M) = (a_0 - b_0) + (a_1 - b_1) M$$

If individuals in both classes are equally responsive to the environment

Table 3.7.3 Slope and fit in constituency regressions and survey regressions, 1966

Class dichotomy	Slope		Fit (R^2)	
	Survey	Constituency	Survey	Constituency
12/3456	41.2	246.2	9	70
123/456	44.9	156.8	17	64
1234/56	42.7	87.5	17	51

Note: Slopes are percentages to make them comparable with earlier tables. In purely constituency data analyses it is more natural to quote them as fractions, e.g. 2.462 instead of 246.2. In later tables we use fractions except when comparing survey and constituency results. R^2 fits are percentages of variation explained.

SOCIAL CLASS AND PARTY CHOICE IN ENGLAND

then $a_1 = b_1$ and the class difference within any one constituency reduces to $(a_0 - b_0)$ which we may call the individual effect of class on partisanship.

In a constituency where the proportion middle-class is M, the statistically expected proportion Conservative under this environmental effects model is

$$CON = (a_0 + a_1 M)M + (b_0 + b_1 M)(1 - M)$$
$$= b_0 + (a_0 - b_0 + b_1)M + (a_1 - b_1)M^2$$

If both classes are equally responsive to the class mix in the environment then $a_1 = b_1$ and the last term in this equation is eliminated. Then the linear regression we have already calculated has a slope equal to

$$a_0 - b_0 + b_1 = (a_0 - b_0) + b_1$$
$$= \text{individual effect} + \text{environmental effect}$$

(recall that $b_1 = a_1$ by assumption, so that there is only one environmental effect that operates equally in both classes).

It is tempting, but fallacious, to regard $(a_0 - b_0)$ as equal to $(a - b)$, the survey-based slope measure of class polarization. After all, survey data are often described as individual-level data. So we might assume that they reveal individual-level effects. Alas, when environmental influences operate they corrupt or bias survey-based estimates of individual-level effects. However, we can calculate the degree of that bias and hence eliminate it. [Statistical operations not shown here.]

Table 3.7.4 shows our estimates of individual and environmental components of class polarization at each of the last five elections. These estimates suggest:

(1) Survey-based estimates were inflated by about 3 per cent compared to individual class polarization. Survey estimates averaged 36.3 per cent, while individual class polarization averaged 33.7 per cent.
(2) Individual class polarization was not the major component of constituency class polarization. The environmental component averaged 52.3 per cent against the individual component's 33.7 per cent.
(3) As the individual component trended downwards the environmental component trended upwards so as to offset the individual-level depolarization. Consequently constituency polarization did not decline and, indeed, increased.

Qualitative implications

So far we have kept our model of class polarization as close as possible to the traditional survey-based approach, which simply contrasted the partisanship of manual and non-manual respondents. Yet without introducing much more complexity its theoretical structure can be rendered more plausible and its predictive power greatly improved.

MODELS OF PARTY CHOICE

Table 3.7.4 Trends in components of class polarization, 1964–74

	1964	1966	1970	1974 (Feb.)	1974 (Oct.)
Using two-party total:					
Raw survey-based measure	41.1	42.7	35.8	39.8	35.7
Individual component	38.6	40.3	33.1	36.6	32.2
Area/environmental component	48.0	47.2	52.7	63.4	71.5
Constituency polarization	86.6	87.5	85.8	100.0	103.7
Fit (R^2) to constituency regression	51	51	48	51	52
Using half Con. lead:					
Raw survey-based measure	36.1	39.1	33.2	31.3	28.7
Individual component	34.0	36.9	30.8	28.8	25.8
Area/environmental component	41.9	42.9	47.0	50.3	57.9
Constituency polarization	75.9	79.8	77.8	79.1	83.7
Fit (R^2) to constituency regression	52	52	49	54	54

Note: Slopes are percentages of votes. R^2s are percentages of variation explained.

[One] modification is suggested by some of the results quoted in Table 3.7.3. That table showed that the best class prediction of constituency voting was given by per cent employers and managers rather than per cent non-manual. Numerous other constituency analyses point to the same conclusion. Moreover, this did not occur just because high concentrations of employers and managers correlated with high levels of other non-manual classes. Stepwise regressions were [calculated for each election using various occupational classifications of occupied males, in addition to per cent employers and managers].

A typical set of results [for 1966] shows:

(1) The best single predictor [of constituency vote] is the per cent employers and managers.
(2) Its predictive power is high, explaining 70 per cent of partisan variation in 1966.
(3) No other class predictor could explain more than one per cent of the deviation from this alignment.
(4) Even when all the other class predictors were allowed into a multiple regression the fit was only improved by half a per cent.
(5) In multiple regressions the slope coefficient of 'employers and managers' was not much different from its slope in a simple bivariate regression.
(6) The slope coefficients on the other class variables in the multiple regression were small in size and did not always have the expected sign.

In summary, class polarization at the constituency level differed qualitatively as well as quantitatively from the survey-based findings. Not only was class polarization well over twice as great at the constituency

SOCIAL CLASS AND PARTY CHOICE IN ENGLAND

level, not only did it follow different trends from those suggested by survey findings, but it was also clearly and almost exclusively related to an employers and managers/others dichotomy rather than a manual/non-manual dichotomy.

Table 3.7.5 shows the trends in constituency class polarization over the last five elections using the per cent employers and managers as the measure of class. Apart from this change in class measure it replicates the constituency parts of Table 3.7.4. Although the fit is much better and the slope much steeper the trends in Table 3.7.5 are broadly similar to those in Table 3.7.4. The constituency patterns in Table 3.7.4 should be viewed as imperfect surrogates for those in Table 3.7.5, not as a truly separate finding.

The employers and managers category is [what may be called] a core class or, in Rose's terminology, an ideal-type class. They are controllers. Their antithesis, the opposite core class, is not the totality of the controlled, but the anti-controllers, those who actively oppose that control. The occupational categories in the Census capture one of these core classes very well, but not the other. Consequently we believe that one reason why the Census category 'employers and managers' is unrivalled as a class predictor of Conservative/Labour partisanship is that while there are two core classes, only one is measured by a Census occupational category.

We are now ready to state a model of class polarization which is both theoretically plausible and gives an optimal or near-optimal fit to the data. It has six elements:

(1) There are some positions or activities which merit the title 'core' classes and these are responsible for the class polarization of Labour/Conservative partisanship.
(2) A few people are so closely linked to these roles that they can be described as 'belonging' to these core classes.

Table 3.7.5 Constituency regressions, 1964–74, using core class predictor

	1964	1966	1970	1974 (Feb.)	1974 (Oct.)
Using Con. share of two-party vote as dependent variable:					
Constituency polarization	2.41	2.46	2.46	2.58	2.66
Fit (R^2)	69	70	69	77	77
Using half Con. lead as dependent variable:					
Constituency polarization	2.08	2.21	2.21	1.99	2.11
Fit (R^2)	68	70	69	77	78

Note: See note to Tables 3.7.3 for definitions of units.

126 MODELS OF PARTY CHOICE

(3) The class position of the bulk of the electorate is defined by the relative strength and quantity of their links to these core classes.

(4) These links depend on personal occupations, including the individual's past and present occupation and his expectations about his future occupations.

(5) These links also depend upon contacts with other people. Contacts are structured by purely personal characteristics – family, voluntary association and workplace – but also by the local spatial environment.

(6) One of the two core classes is so much easier to define and measure that in empirical analyses its variation must do duty for variation in the balance between core classes.

If this model did apply we should expect that the partisanship of all individuals would be more or less responsive, in a consensual way, to the ratio of core classes in their local environments but members of the core classes would be the least responsive. Analysis of the election survey data by the local concentration of employers and managers suggests that this is so. Employers and managers, particularly in small establishments, were politically insensitive to their environments as were manual trade unionists, particularly unskilled trade unionists.

Conclusions

[First] we have had to reject the idea of class polarization as simply the difference between the partisanship of different classes. Analysis shows that this group difference is only a minor component of constituency class polarization. The major component comes from the power of the environment to structure social contacts plus the empirical fact that contact across class boundaries makes a consensual impact on partisan choice. Social interaction contributes the major component of constituency class polarization.

Second, analysis suggests that as the difference between group partisanship has declined, the environmental component of class polarization has increased sufficiently to offset all of this decline.

Third, our analyses have led us to give much greater emphasis to the notion of core classes, which include few individuals but which are relatively unambiguously linked to partisanship. We suggest that ultimately it is the degree of contact with core class occupations that is critical for partisan choice. In particular, the occupational mix in the local environment influences the occupational mix amongst the individual's contacts, but our analysis shows that the local mix of core classes has much more effect on party choice than the local mix of middle and working classes, as conventionally defined.

4 | Party identification

Introduction

The concept of party identification, developed in the United States in the 1950s, was also of central importance in British voting studies in the post-war period. It is used to refer to the lasting psychological attachment to a party which many voters acquire and it forms the basis of the model of voting behaviour put forward by Butler and Stokes (although, as noted earlier, they generally use the terms 'partisan self-image' or 'partisanship' instead of 'party identification').

In the first extract in this section, which is taken from the second edition of *Political Change in Britain*, Butler and Stokes explain the value of the concept and consider whether it can in fact be transferred from its original context in American politics to the rather different circumstances of British elections. They argue that, although British voters in the 1960s were more likely than Americans to change their party identification when they changed their vote, nonetheless most British voters did have an enduring attachment to a party and that this was an important determinant of how they voted in elections. Butler and Stokes go on to show how individuals acquire a party identification in their early years in the family, and how this identification strengthens the longer a voter remains committed to a particular party.

But as with the class/party link, Butler and Stokes' discussion of party identification was almost overtaken by events. By the elections of 1974 there were clear signs of a marked weakening in the strength of party identification in Britain. In the major article to which we have already referred Crewe, Sarlvik and Alt (1977) argued that 'whereas the two-party vote had been subject to almost continuous decay since the 1950s, major-party identification held steady throughout the 1960s before crumbling abruptly in February 1974' (p. 182). They explored the possible causes of this development and concluded, first, that it was not a 'generation' effect arising because new voters joining the electorate in the 1970s had

128 MODELS OF PARTY CHOICE

markedly weaker party identifications than earlier generations – the decline was common to all generations; second, that there was some evidence to suggest that 'partisan decline reflected a continuing erosion of the class–party tie' (p. 183) – the weakening of the class link facilitated the weakening of party identification; and third, that declining partisanship was to a considerable extent a response to the extraordinary political events preceding the February 1974 election. They found 'overwhelming support' for the claim that the weakening of Conservative partisanship was a response to these events. In the case of Labour, although declining partisanship 'had its origins in a growing rejection of the Labour party's basic tenets on the part of its own rank and file during the late 1960s', nonetheless 'for a substantial number of Labour identifiers, February 1974 appears to have been a "last straw" election, confirming doubts and fears that had originated in the previous decade' (p. 182).

In the second of our extracts here, from an article published in 1983 and entitled 'Partisan dealignment ten years on', Crewe plots the continuing weakening of party identification and also argues that it has led in a variety of ways to increased electoral volatility. With the electorate's party loyalties no longer so securely anchored, swings in general elections and by-elections have become much greater, while opinion polls have also indicated much greater intra-election volatility.

Clarke and Stewart, in the third extract, use some of the same techniques as the original Crewe, Sarlvik and Alt article to show that the continuing decline in party identification in the 1974–83 period can still not be interpreted as a generation effect. They go on to argue that what they call the 'proximate cause' of declining strength of partisanship was such short-term political factors as party leader images and voters' issue perceptions.

Miller, Tagg and Britto suggest an important modification to Crewe, Sarlvik and Alt's original analysis of the decline in the strength of party identification. Using data from surveys conducted between elections, in the mid-term, they argue that the collapse of Labour partisanship occurred not in 1974, but in the later 1960s in response to the performance of the Wilson government.

Finally, Heath, Jowell and Curtice sound a cautionary note. The 1987 BES survey results show no reversal in the trend in party identification, but they argue that the consequences of declining partisanship are not as had been predicted. They argue that there is no clear evidence that voters have become more hesitant about which party to vote for, that there has been no increase in volatility or 'turbulence', and that there has been no tendency for party identification to become a less powerful influence upon voting choice.

PARTY IDENTIFICATION

129

Further reading

The classic account of party identification is given in *The American Voter* (Campbell *et al.*, 1960) while various applications of the concept are explored in a follow-up volume by the same authors (Campbell *et al.*, 1966). Asher (1984) surveys later developments in the study of party identification in America.

Useful summaries of the party identification model are given in Harrop and Miller (1987, ch. 6), who also provide a useful set of references, and in Dunleavy and Husbands (1985). A fuller account of the partisan dealignment thesis is to be found in Sarlvik and Crewe (1983).

A critical collection of essays edited by Budge *et al.* (1976) examines the cross-national validity of the concept of party identification. It includes an essay by Crewe which expresses doubts about the ability of the model based on party identification to account for developments in British electoral behaviour. Mughan (1981) questions whether it is valid to use the concept in the same way across different political systems. Cain and Ferejohn (1981) argue, however, that party identification *can* be measured and interpreted in Britain in broadly the same way as it is in the United States. In a recent article, part of which is reproduced in our section on issue voting (see below, pp. 230–8), Heath and McDonald (1988) demonstrate the continuing powerful effects of party identification among British voters.

4.1 | Parties in the voter's mind

David Butler and Donald Stokes

The role played by parties in giving shape and direction to the behaviour of voters is so taken for granted that its importance is easily missed. Without it, however, the mass of the people could scarcely participate in regular transfers of power. Graham Wallas [1910] suggested half a century ago that the parties loomed large in popular perceptions of politics because the electorate required 'something simpler and more permanent, something that can be loved and trusted, and which can be recognized at successive elections as being the same thing that was loved and trusted before; and party is such a thing' (p. 83).

The intrinsic values of party

As long-established actors on the political stage it is natural that parties should have become objects of mass loyalty or identification. As a result, the success of a given party and the confounding of its enemies has a value in its own right for many electors, quite apart from the uses which the party might make of power. Commentaries on politics are rich with sporting metaphors, and the values of partisan loyalty may be as intrinsic to the contest as the values of loyalty to a team. Our view of the 'intrinsic' values of party should be broad enough to include a number of psychic or social utilities that party may have for the voter that are distinct from the values government may supply. The intrinsic values of partisanship may, for example, be those of preserving harmony in the friendship group or the home or the nuptial bed. Or they may be those of reducing the costs to the individual of obtaining the information he needs to discharge his civic duty

From D.E. Butler and D. Stokes, *Political Change in Britain* (2nd edn, 1974), London: Macmillan, chapters 2, 3.

PARTIES IN THE VOTER'S MIND

as elector. We speak of a variety of such personal and social uses of party allegiance as 'intrinsic' values to set them off from the utilities which may flow from the actions of government.

This aspect of party support is more easily understood when it is seen how early in life partisan inclinations may appear. The child who knows nothing of the uses of power may still absorb a party preference from his home. This early role of the family has its counterpart in the influence of a succession of associations in adolescence or adulthood. Many of the groups found at work or church or public house may foster a common political inclination among their members, perhaps through reinforcing the intrinsic values of party.

Electoral history suggests that strong new primary forces can sweep away political attachments that depend mainly on the intrinsic values of party. Yet it would be unwise to discount the importance of accustomed loyalties. Among other things, they enter in at least two ways into the motives that induce citizens to go to the polling station. The elector has the *instrumental* motive of voting: the casting of his ballot may contribute to the election of a government whose outputs he values. He may also have the *expressive* motive of voting: the casting of his ballot shows support for the party he identifies himself with, and has an intrinsic value of its own.

Yet we must also allow for the *normative* motive of voting; the casting of the voter's ballot may reflect primarily a sense of civic obligation. But those who are drawn to the polling station in this way must support some party when they are there. The elector who possesses a firm attachment has a basis for preferring one party programme, one set of political leaders, and indeed one interpretation of current political reality to its rivals. The psychological convenience of such a habitual tie adds to the values that are intrinsic to being a party supporter.

Partisan self-images and electoral choices

The values which the individual sees in supporting a party usually extend to more than one general election. There may be strong continuity in the outputs of government, such as the welfare of a class, which provide the individual with the same basis for his choice over successive contests. Moreover, the values involved in party support of the intrinsic sort tend by their very nature to be enduring ones. As a result, most electors think of themselves as supporters of a given party in a lasting sense, developing what may be called a 'partisan self-image'.

This phenomenon is a familiar one in many party systems. The United States has produced the most intensive studies of such dispositions towards party; these have demonstrated that there is a remarkable degree of independence between electors' generalized identification with party and

132   MODELS OF PARTY CHOICE

their behaviour in particular elections, especially in the choice of a President. From the time when comparable measurements of these identifications began to be taken on a nationwide scale in the early 1950s, the distributions of party loyalty have fluctuated only modestly from sample to sample despite massive swings in the presidential vote.

There is no doubt that the partisan dispositions of British voters tend to be generalized ones. Looking back over their own past voting in general elections, in 1963 well over four-fifths of our respondents said that they had always supported the same party. Moreover, our repeated measurements of the preferences of our panel showed the majority holding fast to the same party from 1963 to 1970.

To study more closely the nature of our respondents' partisan self-images, we asked them at each interview, quite separately from questions about their voting, to describe their partisan inclinations in a more general way and we were able to divide the sample into those who described themselves as Conservative, Labour or Liberal in this more general sense. (Two questions were asked: i) Generally speaking do you usually think of yourself as Conservative, Labour or Liberal (or what)? ii) How strongly [chosen party] do you generally feel – very strongly, fairly strongly, or not very strongly?) At least 90 per cent of the sample accepted such a generalized partisan designation at each interview, except in 1969, when at a time of extreme government unpopularity the figure fell to 85 per cent.

One of the clearest evidences for the generalized nature of partisan dispositions in Britain comes from local government elections. In 1963, for example, those who went to the polls in local elections that were fought on a party basis voted to an overwhelming degree in line with their expressed party self image, as Table 4.1.1 shows. Well over 90 per cent of our respondents stayed with their generalized tie to the national parties, though local elections might be thought to be fought on entirely special local issues.

In view of the generality and continuity of partisan dispositions it is natural to wonder whether a partisan self-image may not survive in the elector's mind during a temporary defection to non-voting or even to support of another party. This sort of tenacity of generalized partisan identifications is one of the most central findings in American studies. Large numbers of voters have defected to the presidential candidate of the opposite party in every recent election. But their proclaimed party allegiance has remained remarkably undisturbed during such defections; in fact, it continues to be a better predictor of what the voter will do in future elections than is his current presidential vote.

Has this pattern any parallel in Britain? The answer is that, in the main, partisan self-images and electoral preferences travel together in Britain far more than in America. This is sharply evident when we examine a series of elections. Table 4.1.2 compares the stability of self-image and vote in the

PARTIES IN THE VOTER'S MIND

Table 4.1.1 Local election vote in May 1963 by partisan self-image

	Partisan self-image		
	Conservative	Labour	Liberal
Local election vote			
Conservative	85%	1%	2%
Labour	3	95	4
Liberal	6	2	88
Independent	4	1	6
Other	2	1	0
	100%	100%	100%

Note: This analysis is limited to people identifying themselves with one of the three main parties who were also qualified electors in wards where candidates of their 'own' parties contested the local council elections in May of 1963.

American congressional elections of 1956, 1958 and 1960 and British parliamentary preferences in the summer of 1963 and the elections of 1964 and 1966. The contrast is clear. Although roughly three-quarters of each of these national electorates held to their established (and consistent) party loyalties and vote preferences over the three points in time, the dominant mode of change in America was for party self-image to remain fixed while voter preference changed. In Britain, by contrast, the dominant mode of change was for party self-image and vote preference to change in tandem. Indeed, half as many British electors changed their partisan self-image while keeping to the same vote preference as the other way round, whereas in America only one-eighth as many did so.

Table 4.1.2 Stability of partisan self-image and voting preference between three points in time in America and Britain

		Party preference in voting for Congress			Party preference in voting for Parliament		
		Stable	Variable		Stable	Variable	
Partisan self-image	Stable	76	16	92	75	8	83
	Variable	2	6	8	4	13	17
		78	22	100%	79	21	100%

Note: The American data are drawn from the University of Michigan panel study of the 1956, 1958 and 1960 elections. The British data are drawn from our 1963–64–66 panel.

134 MODELS OF PARTY CHOICE

The more durable nature of the individual's party self-image when voting for the opposite party in America must largely be due to the different challenges faced by the elector in the two countries. On polling day the British elector votes only for a single office at a single level of government. The American has to cope simultaneously with a vast collection of partisan candidates seeking a variety of offices at federal, state and local levels: it is small wonder that voters are conscious of generalized beliefs about their ties to party, although some of their individual choices are not guided by these.

Without this prompting from the electoral system, British voters are less likely than the American to make distinctions between their current electoral choices and more general partisan dispositions. The majority of voters do in fact have general dispositions towards party which give continuity to their behaviour in a succession of specific choices. But in transferring their vote from one party to another they are less likely to retain a conscious identification with a party other than the one they currently support.

The contrast we have drawn between Britain and America held throughout our studies. Yet the slippage between self-images and votes was enough for the British pattern to look increasingly like the American as the shifts of strength between the Labour and Conservative Parties became more and more massive in the later 1960s.

The changing pattern of relationship between self-image and vote is perhaps clearest when we contrast the slippage between the two at different points in the decade. Table 4.1.3 sets out the joint distribution of self-images and vote preferences in the summer of 1963 [and the summer of 1969]. It is clear from the table that [in 1963] the two were linked exceedingly closely and that neither party held an advantage in votes beyond what might have been expected from the then-current distribution of party loyalties.

Table 4.1.3 Vote preference by partisan self-image, 1963 and 1969

	Partisan self-image 1963				Partisan self-image 1969			
	Con. %	Lab. %	Lib. %	None %	Con. %	Lab. %	Lib. %	None %
Vote preference								
Conservative	86	2	4	11	95	8	11	26
Labour	4	91	2	14	1	71	9	10
Liberal	4	2	88	11	1	5	67	7
None, don't know, other	6	5	6	64	3	16	13	57
	100	100	100	100	100	100	100	100

PARTIES IN THE VOTER'S MIND

135

During the period of Labour's greatest disarray later in the decade a very different pattern emerged. When we examine the joint distribution of self-images and preferences in the summer of 1969 we find a much greater disparity between the two. We also see at once that the Conservative Party did far better in 1969 in terms of vote preferences than would be expected simply from the division of the electorate's partisan self-images. In particular, the party won support from 8 per cent of Labour's partisans, while giving away to Labour only 1 per cent of its own. Moreover, only 3 per cent of Conservative identifiers were unsure how they would vote, while fully 16 per cent of Labour identifiers were unsure. As a result, the Conservatives outmatched Labour by almost two to one in vote preferences in 1969 but by less than nine to seven in terms of party self-images.

Hence, the evidence from the 1960s emphasizes both the similarity and dissimilarity of the role played by partisan self-images in Britain and the United States. In the decade's later years an increasing portion of the British electorate seemed capable of retaining partisan self-images to which their electoral choices returned after a period of disenchantment. But this pattern was much less marked in Britain than in America.

Whatever the role of party loyalties in guiding the behaviour of those who shift their preferences, it is clear that millions of British electors remain anchored to one of the parties for very long periods of time. Indeed, many electors have had the same party loyalties from the dawn of their political consciousness and have reinforced these loyalties by participating in successive elections. The manner in which partisan self-images take root and strengthen is an essential aspect of the individual's experience over the political life cycle, which we shall now examine.

The political life cycle

The impressionable years
W.S. Gilbert's quatrain about everyone's being born 'either a little Liberal or else a little Conservative' is often cited in acknowledgement of the deep childhood roots of partisanship in Britain, amounting to the inheritance of party allegiance. A child is very likely indeed to share the parents' party preference. Partisanship over the individual's lifetime has some of the quality of a photographic reproduction that deteriorates with time: it is a fairly sharp copy of the parents' original at the beginning of political awareness, but over the years it becomes somewhat blurred, although remaining easily recognizable. The sharpness of the first reproduction is shown by Table 4.1.4(a), which examines the early preferences of those who remembered each of their parents as either Conservative or Labour partisans. Children of parents who were united in their party preference

136   MODELS OF PARTY CHOICE

were overwhelmingly likely to have absorbed the preference at the beginning of their political experience.

The progressive blurring of this first reproduction can be seen by examining the current preferences of the same respondents. The preferences of these respondents as adults in the mid-1960s are shown in Table 4.1.4(b). The imprint of the family's partisanship is still clear but it is more blurred than it was in Table 4.1.4(a).

But the family is not the sole influence in the impressionable years, especially those of adolescence and early adulthood. The plasticity which renders the young open to so deep an impress from their parents also renders them more open to influences from other quarters than they will be later, when set in their adult ways. Many of these influences are lodged in a wider social milieu of school or work. In particular, the widening contacts of the young must often bring them the values and norms which connect party to class.

Such a process is reflected in the entries of Table 4.1.5(a), which have been built up by comparing the first remembered party preferences of children from Conservative and Labour homes with those of their parents and comparing their parents' party preferences with the dominant political tendencies of their class – Conservative in the case of middle class families, Labour in the case of working class families. The table shows a greater erosion of family political traditions where they are inconsistent with those of class. But the table shows equally the strong continuity of these

Table 4.1.4 Earliest and present party preference by parents' Conservative or Labour preference, 1963

	Parents' partisanship		
	Both parents Conservative %	Parents divided %	Both parents Labour %
(a) Respondent's own first preference			
Conservative	89	48	6
Labour	9	52	92
Liberal	2	–	2
	100	100	100
(b) Respondent's own present preference			
Conservative	75	37	10
Labour	14	49	81
Liberal	8	10	6
Other	–	–	–
None	3	4	3
	100	100	100

PARTIES IN THE VOTER'S MIND

Table 4.1.5 Agreement of earliest and present preferences with parents' partisanship among children from Conservative or Labour families by whether parents' partisanship was aligned with class, 1963

	Parents supported party:	
	Dominant in class %	Opposite party %
(a) Respondent's earliest party preference		
Agrees with parents' preference	91	70
Differs from parents' preference	9	30
	100	100
(b) Respondent's present party preference		
Agrees with parents' preference	85	58
Differs from parents' preference	15	42
	100	100

traditions even when dissonant with a class milieu. The first preferences of fully 70 per cent of respondents whose families were not aligned with the majority of their class agreed with their parents' preference.

Indeed, the survival value of these minority political views was still very evident at the point of our respondents' adult lives when we first interviewed them. The evidence of this is set out in Table 4.1.5(b), which substitutes our respondents' current preferences for those they remember holding when they first became aware of politics. It is seen that the present allegiance of fully 58 per cent of respondents whose families were not aligned with the majority of their class continued to coincide with the preference to which they were exposed in the home as children.

The relative impressionability of the young also means that they will be unusually open to the influence of issues and events which dominate national politics at the time of their entry into the electorate. If strong forces move the country towards one of the parties we can expect these forces to be most clearly evident in the behaviour of the youngest electors, on whom the weight of prior loyalties sits most lightly. The profile of the main parties' support among new voters over a generation suggests in a remarkable way the ebbs and flows of party fortune. These proportions are reconstructed from the reported first votes of our sample in Figure 4.1.1, which plots the Labour Party's share of new votes for the two main parties in each election from 1935 to 1970. This profile of the behaviour of the youngest electors indicates clearly the surge in Labour's strength during the Second World War and its aftermath, the decay of its strength during the Conservative years of the 1950s, and the fresh Labour surge in the early and middle 1960s.

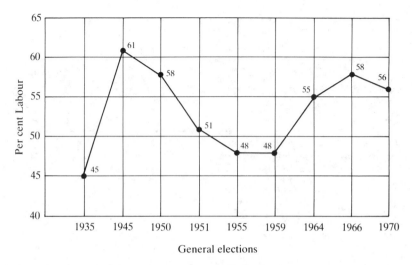

Note: The 1970 figure refers to new electors who would have been qualified under the law as it stood in previous contests. Electors aged between 18 and 20 who were enfranchised by the 1969 Act are excluded. If all new voters were included the figure for 1970 would be 59 per cent.

Figure 4.1.1 Labour's share of support for the two main parties from new electors, 1935–70

These formative influences have carried over into later voting. The greater Labour feeling of the Second World War and its aftermath could still be seen in the support for the two leading parties in the mid-sixties. Among those who first voted in the Labour years of 1945 and 1950 the proportion voting Labour in the General Election of 1964 stood at 60 per cent; among those who first voted in the Conservative years of 1951, 1955 and 1959, at only 53 per cent. With the ageing of the voter the relatively plastic attitudes of youth tend to harden and the acquired habits of the early voting years begin to become more deeply fixed.

The later years
The hardening of partisanship in the mature elector is a tendency which has been very generally observed in various countries and party systems. The strengthening of the British elector's partisan self-image with age is suggested by the entries of Table 4.1.6, which shows proportions within successive age groups describing themselves as very or fairly strongly attached to a party.

There is evidence [however] that what determines the strength and unchangeability of partisan ties is not so much the voter's age in years as the duration of his attachment to one party. Younger voters tend to be more

PARTIES IN THE VOTER'S MIND

Table 4.1.6 Strength of partisan self-image by age, 1970

	Age							
	17	18–24	25–30	31–40	41–50	51–60	61–70	71–
Percent describing selves as 'very strongly' attached to party	17	23	35	43	47	52	63	64

plastic because their party preferences tend to be more recent. But older voters who have supported a party for as brief a time prove to be just as weak and changeable in their partisanship. When the strength and duration of partisanship are examined within age-levels, it is quite clear that what counts is the duration of the party tie and not the age reached by the elector. This finding is reflected in Table 4.1.7. Among those with long established partisanship, age made no difference to its strength. Among those with a more fickle voting record, the old were, if anything, more weakly attached to their current party than the young.

That psychological attachments become stronger the longer they are held is a fairly general finding in the social sciences. Furthermore it is easy to sense how the recurrence of election campaigns can progressively deepen the partisanship of the committed voter. Each general election confronts the voters once again with the necessity of acting on distant and complex matters about which they are very imperfectly informed. In this situation an established partisanship provides voters with a simple means of sorting political leaders into the worthy and less worthy, and making judgements on the merits of conflicting party claims. Moreover, a partisan commitment simplifies their choice between rival candidates for Parliament whose party label may be their most salient or their sole characteris-

Table 4.1.7 Proportion strongly partisan by age and by duration of party tie, 1964

			Age	
		25–39	40–59	60+
Duration of present party tie	13 years or more	81%	80%	82%
	Less than 13 years	64%	70%	54%

Note: Each entry of the table shows the proportion describing themselves as very or fairly strongly attached to party within a group jointly defined by age and duration of present partisanship.

tic. Every time a partisan tie functions in this way it is likely to become stronger. The voter's experience over a series of campaigns can indeed be regarded as a kind of 'learning' in which the rewards of increased clarity and simplicity reinforce the party ties that supply them.

The psychological processes that underlie the strengthening of partisanship with time must be fairly complex [but] the longer a given tie with party is held and the more experience the elector has in coding new messages consistently with it, the less likely is it that information about new issues and events will lead him to revalue the parties.

4.2 | Partisan dealignment ten years on

Ivor Crewe

In the mid 1970s observers of British elections began to revise their assumptions about the nature of the electorate. The 1970 election, it was argued, marked the close of a quarter-century of 'stable two party voting'; the two elections of 1974 the beginning of a new era of 'partisan dealignment'. The initial diagnosis of partisan dealignment was inevitably tentative because there were only two elections, held a mere eight months apart, on which to rely for evidence. But the passing of two more general elections, in 1979 and 1983, provides an opportunity to re-examine the central tenets of partisan dealignment.

[The best] measure of partisan commitment is the direction and strength of an elector's self-declared party identification. This has consistently proved to be the strongest single correlate of long-term party loyalty and of party political involvement, including turnout.

Figure 4.2.1 and Table 4.2.1 display the level and strength of Conservative and Labour party identification from 1964 to 1983, and reveal a marked drop in the electorate's long-term commitment to the two parties. In 1964, 81 per cent of the electorate identified with one of the two governing parties, the large majority at least 'fairly strongly' and half 'very strongly'. The two-party system appeared to rest on a bedrock of unswerving commitment. Twenty years later the portion of the electorate with a 'very strong' Conservative or Labour partisanship had dwindled from being a substantial minority (40 per cent) to being a clearly insubstantial one (23 per cent). The staunch, automatic Conservative or Labour supporter has become a member of a small and rapidly dwindling group.

From I. Crewe, 'The electorate: partisan dealignment ten years on', in *West European Politics* (1983), vol. 6, pp. 183–215.

MODELS OF PARTY CHOICE

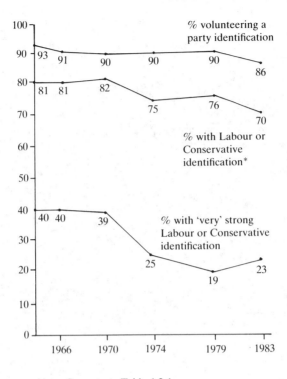

Note: See note to Table 4.2.1.

Figure 4.2.1 Incidence and strength of Conservative and Labour partisanship, 1964–83

The general picture of declining loyalty to the two parties needs to be qualified in various ways. First, the willingness of respondents to give themselves some kind of party identification, weak or strong, major or minor, has lessened only slightly and remains remarkably widespread. Positive repudiation of the party alternatives, or indifference between them, has not grown to significant levels (much smaller proportions of the electorate volunteer, or after pressing yield, a class or religious identification). Indeed, identification with the minor parties, despite their eruptions of support at elections, has barely changed over the twenty years. In 1964 it stood at 12 per cent; in 1983 at 16 per cent. The proportion identifying with the two main parties has fallen, but not by much, from 81 to 82 per cent in the 1960s to a still high 70 per cent in 1983. In the era of partisan dealignment many more electors continue to think of themselves as Conservative or Labour than actually vote for them; many more neglect or defy their party loyalties than abandon them.

PARTISAN DEALIGNMENT TEN YEARS ON
143

This phenomenon invites two interpretations. It suggests, firstly, that as an influence on the vote old-established party loyalties have increasingly been overridden by other, short-term, factors in recent elections. One possibility is that the emergence of television as the main mass medium of politics has made the short campaign period – and the issues, people and events it brings into prominence – a more powerful determinant of the vote. But, secondly, it draws attention to the considerable reserves of partisan loyalty and habit in the electorate, accumulated over many decades, from which the Conservative and Labour parties can still draw to re-establish their electoral ascendancy. In the major party ranks electoral obedience has become less automatic; major rebellions more frequent, but permanent desertion on a large scale has not yet happened. Residual attachments to the two major parties remain widespread.

The point to stress, however, is that they are increasingly residual. For what has markedly declined over the past two decades is *strength* of

Table 4.2.1 The incidence and strength of party identification, 1964–83

	1964	1966	1970	Feb./Oct. 1974 (combined)	1979	1983
% with a party identification	93	91	90	90	90	86
% identifying with Con.	38	35	40	35	38	38
% identifying with Lab.	43	46	42	40	38	32
	81	81	82	75	76	70
% All electors						
Very strong identifiers	44	44	42	26	22	26
Fairly strong identifiers	38	38	37	40	46	38
Not very strong identifiers	11	9	11	14	23	22
No identification	7	9	10	10	10	14
% Conservative identifiers only						
Very strong identifiers	48	49	50	29	23	34
Fairly strong identifiers	41	39	40	50	53	43
Not very strong identifiers	11	12	10	21	24	23
% Labour identifiers only						
Very strong identifiers	45	50	47	37	27	32
Fairly strong identifiers	43	41	40	44	50	39
Not very strong identifiers	12	9	13	19	23	29
	(100)	(100)	(100)	(100)	(100)	(100)

Note: The figures for 1983 are derived from a survey conducted on the eve and the day of the general election; the figures for all other years are taken from surveys conducted in the 6–8 weeks after the election. Self-declared strength of party identification tends to be higher in surveys conducted close to general elections.

Sources: Butler and Stokes' elections surveys, 1964, 1966, and 1970; British Election Studies, February 1974, October 1974 and 1979; BBC/Gallup survey, 1983.

partisanship. The proportion of 'very strong' Conservative and Labour identifiers in the electorate has almost halved, from 40 per cent in the 1960s to 23 per cent in 1983; the proportion of 'not very strong' Conservative and Labour identifiers has almost doubled, from nine to 17 per cent. Only one elector in five can now be described as a truly committed, unswerving, Conservative or Labour loyalist.

The decline of partisanship has shadowed the electoral fortunes of the Conservative and Labour parties and has not, therefore, been even-handed between the two. The proportion of Conservative identifiers has fluctuated over the two decades but was the same at the end as at the start (38 per cent). In Labour's case, however, the proportion has fallen from 43 per cent in 1964 (and 46 per cent in 1966) to 32 per cent in 1983 – a loss of one-third. In 1983, for the first time on record, Conservative identifiers outnumbered Labour identifiers. Until then Labour had been the 'natural majority' party in the sense that, although it often lost elections, it enjoyed a small headstart over the Conservatives in the instinctive allegiances of the electorate.

Trends in the strength of Labour as opposed to Conservative identifica-tion tell a similar story. The electorate's commitment to both parties has weakened, but more so in Labour's case. Moreover between 1979 and 1983 there was a marked recovery in the strength of Conservative identification but none overall in that for Labour. This contradicts what one might have expected, for it would be natural to assume that a contraction of Labour identifiers would involve the dropping away of the least committed, leaving a smaller but at least more steadfast group. In fact the opposite has occurred. In this sense the public's loosening of attachment to Labour has taken a toll in morale as well as numbers.

This dilution of partisanship has occurred with remarkable uniformity across the social and demographic spectrum: men and women, rich and poor, working class and middle class, young and old have gradually distanced themselves from the two main parties at about the same rate. There is one significant exception. Partisan weakening has proceeded further and faster among the younger generation of university graduates and professional people than in any other category. These groups are likely to be the opinion leaders and agenda setters of the next three decades and as such the avant garde of the political culture of the 1990s.

Moreover, the incidence and strength of partisanship is directly related to age (as indeed it always appears to have been). The younger the age category the higher its proportion of weak partisans. In 1983, 46 per cent of party identifiers aged 65 and over described themselves as 'very strongly' partisan; among 18–22 year olds (i.e. new voters) the figure was 13 per cent. In line with the electorate's overall weakening of partisanship, each 'entry cohort' of new electors has become progressively less partisan since 1964. Scoring 'very strong' identifiers three, the 'fairly strong' two, 'not

PARTISAN DEALIGNMENT TEN YEARS ON 145

very strong' one and those with no party identification zero, the mean partisan strength score for each batch of new electors since 1964 has declined as follows:

1964	1966	1970	Feb./Oct. 1974	1979	1983
1.97	1.95	1.82	1.72	1.77	1.58

In the absence of a sharp reversal of this trend among future entry cohorts, the overall proportion of strong partisans in the British electorate is likely (although not guaranteed) to continue falling as older generations die out.

Electoral volatility

In the quarter-century after 1945 general elections displayed a rock-like stability in the major parties' division of the vote. As partisan and class ardour cooled, however, considerations other than habitual party and class loyalties began to influence the voting decisions of more and more electors. In particular, campaign-specific factors – the outgoing government's record, the major issues of the day, the party leaders' personal qualities, specific and perhaps quite trivial incidents – took on a greater significance. Judging from the opinion polls, the three- to four-week campaign has had a stronger impact in recent years. In both 1970 and February 1974, the campaigns undoubtedly decided which party took office. Moreover, even the votes of those adhering to their usual party in the campaign are prone to waver more. Between 1964 and 1979 the proportion of voters who left their final voting decision until the campaign jumped from 17 per cent to 28 per cent, and the proportion claiming to have thought seriously of voting differently in the course of the campaign rose from 24 per cent to 31 per cent. The committed electorate has begun to make way for the hesitant electorate.

The weakening of partisan ties has produced more switching between parties from one election to the next, and in by-elections and the opinion polls in the intervening period (see Table 4.1.2). The mean fall in the governing party's vote share at by-elections, compared with the same constituencies at the preceding general election, rose from two per cent in the 1950–51 and 1951–55 governments, to nine per cent in 1955–59, 14 per cent in 1960–64 and 17 per cent in 1966–70 – a harbinger of the growing electoral volatility of the 1970s. In fact the fall in the governing party's share of the vote at by-elections in the 1970s and 1980s appears to be slightly less serious than in the 1960s. However, when adjustment is made for the lower general election base against which the by-election support is compared, the fall turns out to be *proportionately* more serious, not less.

146   MODELS OF PARTY CHOICE

Oscillations in the opinion polls have also become sharper, again usually at the expense of the governing party. The trend is cyclical rather than linear, but clear enough. In the three governments of the 1950s the average annual fluctuation was 11 per cent, 9 per cent and 14 per cent respectively; in the three governments of the 1960s, 11 per cent, 18 per cent and 19 per cent respectively. In the 1970s they reached new heights – an annual average of 26 per cent under the 1974–79 Labour government. And under Mrs Thatcher's first government the record was broken again. The opinion polls recorded 20 per cent leads for each of the Conservative party, Labour party and Liberal/SDP Alliance at some point between May 1979 and May 1983. The average annual fluctuation over the four years was 27 per cent.

Inter-election volatility is more important than intra-election volatility. The British Election Study's 1974–79 panel survey showed that over the four elections of the 1970s – a mere nine years – half the electors entitled to vote on all four occasions changed vote or abstained at least once, and often more. Volatility between pairs of consecutive elections was lower, but rising. In the three elections of 1964, 1966 and 1970 it averaged 32 per cent; in the three of February 1974, October 1974 and 1979 it averaged 37 per cent. Panel data are not available for the 1983 election but a comparison of recall data in 1979 and 1983 leaves little doubt that volatility in 1983 went up, equalling or exceeding the exceptional level of February 1974.

Much of this switching cancels out, but not all. The two-party swing at general elections has steadily risen, from 2.0 per cent in the four elections of the 1950s, to 3.2 per cent in the two elections of the 1960s, 4.0 per cent in the 1970s (5.3 per cent if the two 1974 elections are counted as one) and 6.3 per cent in 1983 (see Table 4.2.2). The 12.9 per cent two-party swing to the Conservatives between October 1974 and 1983 is the sharpest turnround in a major party's fortunes since Labour's revival between 1935 and 1945. The 'increasing volatility of the electorate' might be a cliché, but like many clichés it is true.

PARTISAN DEALIGNMENT TEN YEARS ON

Table 4.2.2 Indicators of volatility of support between the Conservative and Labour parties in general elections, by-elections and opinion polls, 1945–83

Year	National swing[1] %	Mean fall in support for government party in by-elections %	Range in monthly opinion polls[2] %	
1945–50	+3.3	4.5	n.a.	
1950	+1.1	2.0	8.0	10.5
1951			13.0	
1952	+2.1	1.9	11.0	8.5
1953			6.0	
1954			9.0	
1955			8.0	
1956	+1.3	8.8	8.0	13.6
1957			18.0	
1958			16.0	
1959			12.5	
1960	−3.4	13.5	9.5	11.0
1961			12.0	
1962			11.5	
1963			9.5	
1964			12.5	
1965	−3.0	1.8	18.0	18.0
1966			18.0	
1967	+5.2	16.8	27.0	18.9
1968			19.0	
1969			17.5	
1970			12.0	
1971	−1.3[4]	13.1	20.5	15.3
1972			10.5	
1973			15.0	
1974 (Feb.)	−2.8	0.5[3]	23.0	23.0
1974 (Oct.)				
1975	+6.6	9.5	21.5	25.7
1976			31.0	
1977			21.5	
1978			16.5	
1979			28.0	
1980	+6.3	11.4[5]	13.0	26.8
1981			36.0	
1982			31.5	

Notes:
1. The national swing shown relates to the relevant pair of consecutive elections, e.g. 1951–55, 1966–70. Two-party swing is adopted, i.e. the change in the Conservative share of the two-party vote.
2. Range is measured by the difference between the highest and the lowest support for the Conservatives in any one month *plus* the difference between the highest and lowest support for Labour in any one month.
3. There was only one by-election between February and October 1974.
4. This is a misleading figure since there was a substantial fall in the vote shares obtained by both the Conservative (−7.4%) and Labour parties (−5.9%).
5. If the three by-elections held during the Falklands War are excluded, the fall is 13.7 per cent.

4.3 | Partisan change in Britain, 1974–83

Harold D. Clarke
and Marianne C. Stewart

This paper uses data from the 1974, 1979, and 1983 national election studies to investigate patterns of stability and change in the direction and strength of Labour and Conservative partisanship. It makes extensive use of the panel design of these studies to assess the role of conversion processes in effecting partisan change. The paper focuses on the impact of short-term forces, and finds that public reactions to parties' perceived or anticipated performance on salient issues and changing levels of affect for party leaders have affected the strength of party ties.

The time series provided by the 1964–83 survey data [shows] that there have been two relatively clear trends in party identification in Britain over the past two decades. The first is the declining percentage of Labour identifiers in the electorate. Between 1964 and 1983 the net decrease in Labour strength was 11 percent. This decrease, however, has not been accompanied by substantial growth in the percentage of Conservative or other identifiers.

The second, and more striking, trend is the progressive weakening of attachments to the two major parties. Among Labour identifiers, the percentage of very strong partisans decreased from 50 percent in 1964 to 32 percent in 1983, and the percentage of weak identifiers almost tripled (from 13 percent to 35 percent). Comparable figures for the Tories are 47 to 33 percent (very strong) and 13 to 35 percent (weak).

From H.D. Clark and M.C. Stewart, 'Dealignment of degree: partisan change in Britain, 1974–83', *Journal of Politics* (1984), vol. 46, pp. 689–718.

148

Explanations of dealignment

How has this 'dealignment of degree' occurred? One possibility is replacement, i.e. processes of demographic change in the voting public. Over time the entrance of successive cohorts of young persons into an electorate, accompanied by the exit of older generations, can radically transform the balance of partisan forces. [In addition] the reduction of the age of majority from twenty-one to eighteen in 1970 increased the proportion of young persons in the electorate, [and this] may have weakened aggregate levels of partisanship over the past decade.

The presence of a relatively large number of younger voters in recent elections, however, has not been the only source of weakening partisanship. In an age cohort analysis using 1964–October 1974 data Crewe and his colleagues concluded: 'The picture that emerges clearly is one of uniform partisan decline across the entire electorate . . . with no suggestion that it was particularly rapid amongst the young . . .' (Crewe, Sarlvik and Alt, 1977, p. 164). The 1974–79 and 1979–83 survey data suggest a similar conclusion. As Table 4.3.1 (column 5) shows, for virtually every age group the mean strength of partisanship in 1979 was less than it had been five years earlier. Cohort differences (column 4) also tend to be negative, with overtime decreases being registered by nine of the fourteen equivalent age groups. Moreover, [where there are] increases in partisan intensity [they] are very small, and three of them occur among the youngest groups. Similarly, the 1979–83 comparison (not shown in tabular form) indicates that partisanship decreased in strength across several age

Table 4.3.1 Mean strength of party identification by age cohort, October 1974–79

Age group	Oct. 1974	1979	Age cohort difference (79–74)	Age group difference (79–74)
18–25	1.59	1.52	–	−0.07
23–30	1.63	1.66	0.07	0.03
26–33	1.69	1.65	0.02	−0.04
31–38	1.87	1.70	0.01	−0.17
34–41	1.92	1.81	−0.06	−0.11
39–46	1.87	1.83	−0.09	−0.04
42–49	1.84	1.85	−0.02	0.01
47–54	1.91	1.89	0.05	−0.02
50–57	1.96	1.85	−0.06	−0.11
55–62	2.02	1.88	−0.08	−0.14
58–65	2.02	1.99	−0.03	−0.03
63–70	2.13	2.04	0.02	−0.09
66–73	2.16	1.98	−0.15	−0.18
71–78	2.10	1.95	−0.21	−0.15
74–81	2.11	2.04	−0.06	−0.07

cohorts. The observed weakening of partisanship across a number of widely separated age cohorts is sufficient to suggest that tendencies toward dealignment in the post-1974 period cannot be attributed solely to changes in the electorate's age distribution or the presence of a new generation of weak partisans.

The second possibility involves changing partisan orientations among 'established' voters, i.e. persons eligible to vote in a series of successive elections. To determine if such changes produced a net decrease in the intensity of partisanship panel data are essential. Recall data on partisanship, although suggestive, are subject to bias, and cannot be relied upon to gauge accurately the magnitude of change. The 1983 survey, however, does not incorporate a panel design, and we must confine our attention to the 1974–79 panels. They are sufficient to establish two important points about partisan attachments in contemporary Britain. First, the diminished intensity of partisanship has been accompanied by substantial individual level instability. Second, individual level partisan change reflects the impact of short-term forces, namely voters' judgements about party performance on important issues and their reactions to party leaders.

Regarding the first point, sizeable numbers of voters failed to maintain directionally stable partisan ties across each pair of elections. Between October 1974 and May 1979, for example, 15 percent switched identifications and another 7 percent moved to or from nonidentification. Percentages for the two earlier election pairs are similar. Many more in every panel varied the intensity of their partisan ties. Between October 1974 and May 1979, for example, 43 percent did so. The net effect of these variations was to promote the aggregate decrease in strength of party ties documented previously.

Regarding the second point, explanations of partisan change may be subsumed under the rubrics of long- and short-term forces. Consideration of the former suggests two possibilities. One of them, demographic replacement, already has been investigated and found wanting. The second focuses on relationships between class and party. Several studies have documented that relationships between class location and voting declined steadily from the mid-1960s to the mid-1970s. Analyses of data on party identification paint a similar picture.

If there has been a significant and generalized erosion of the ties between class and party, one might expect that voters in all class categories would be equally susceptible to partisan change during a particular time interval. Consistent with this argument, the 1974–79 panel data indicate that various objective and subjective measures of class location and salience had very weak correlations with partisan change across this period.

The finding that class-related variables are unrelated to the weakening of partisan ties is consistent with the proposition that a general 'class decomposition' may have facilitated partisan dealignment. It is important

PARTISAN CHANGE IN BRITAIN, 1974–83

to recall, however, that preceding analyses have shown that although there was an erosion of the class/party alignment in the 1970s, this was accompanied by different patterns of partisan change across the three interelection periods of the decade. This, in turn, suggests that a progressive diminution of traditional bonds between class and party was not the proximate cause of the specific patterns of change (and dealignment) observed in particular time intervals. Shorter-term forces have overlaid longer-term trends.

Thus, to comprehend the patterns of partisan change which have occurred during the past decade, it is necessary to examine [short-term] forces operating in the electoral arena during various interelection periods. Here, we will confine our investigation of these forces to a consideration of the impact of party leader images and issue perceptions between October 1974 and May 1979.

In Britain it is conventional wisdom that, although many voters have clearly defined party leader preferences, these have negligible effects on electoral choice once other factors are controlled. It might seem unlikely, therefore, that public feelings about party leaders would have a significant impact on partisan change. Yet, there are reasons to believe that reactions to party leaders may have been of some importance in the late 1970s. First, observers of recent British elections have commented on the growing tendency of the mass media to focus their campaign reportage on party leaders. In so doing, the media emphasize not only leaders' policy pronouncements but also their personalities and styles. Second, polls conducted prior to and during the 1979 campaign revealed marked differences in public perceptions of which leader would make the better prime minister. These differences may have been sufficiently pronounced to affect the direction and intensity of partisanship.

Empirically, relative levels of affect for leaders of the major parties were strongly associated with the strength of partisanship in the 1979 cross-sectional survey. Conservative identifiers liking Thatcher more than Callaghan recorded a mean party identification intensity score of 2.1; among Tory identifiers preferring the Labour leader the equivalent score was 1.6. Among Conservatives liking both leaders equally the mean was 1.7. [These scores are calculated by scoring very strong identifiers as 3, fairly strong as 2, not very strong or close to a party as 1, and nonidentifiers as 0.] Comparable patterns for Labour identifiers are virtually identical. Moreover, the 1974–79 panel data clearly show that changes in relative affect for party leaders were associated with dealignment at the level of the individual voter. Among 1974 Labour identifiers preferring the leader of their party in both 1974 and 1979, 25 percent had weakened or abandoned their Labour identification by 1979 (see Table 4.3.2). In contrast, among Labour partisans favouring the Labour leader over his Tory rival in 1974, but preferring the latter to the former in 1979, 44 percent were tied less

152

MODELS OF PARTY CHOICE

Table 4.3.2 Partisan dealignment and relative party leader affect, October 1974–May 1979 (%)

	Respondent favours Labour leader in:			
	1974 and 1979	1974, not 1979	1979, not 1974	Neither year
% Labour identifiers who weakened or abandoned Labour identification between October 1974 and May 1979	25	44	21	50
	Respondent favours Conservative leader in:			
	1974 and 1979	1974, not 1979	1979, not 1974	Neither year
% Conservative identifiers who weakened or abandoned Conservative identification between October 1974 and May 1979	16	31	16	40

Note: Respondents changing to a new party identification between October 1974 and May 1979 have been eliminated from the analysis.

closely to the party or had left it completely by then. Among 1974 Labour identifiers consistently favouring the Conservative leader, fully 50 percent had weakened or abandoned their allegiance to Labour by 1979. Patterns of party leader affect and partisan dealignment among 1974 Conservative identifiers are very similar. In sum, these data suggest that changing feelings about party leaders were associated with variations in the strength and durability of voters' party ties.

Unlike party leader images, issue perceptions and concerns normally are accorded a prominent role in explanations of electoral choice in Britain, and recent research suggests that evaluations of parties' issue positions and performance also may affect voters' partisan attachments (see Cain, 1978; Alt, 1984). Generally, it seems plausible that issues associated with the economic and political circumstances of the 1970s could affect long-standing patterns of partisan allegiance.

The hypothesis that voter dissatisfaction with one or both major parties' issue positions or performance prompted partisan change at the individual level in the late 1970s can be investigated by measuring changes in panel respondents' assessments of parties on different issues, and by determining if such changes are related to alterations in the direction and strength of party identification. Although the October 1974 and 1979 surveys included several issue questions, only five of them were asked identically in both studies. They concerned prices (inflation), strikes, social services, nationalization, and the common market. For the first two, respondents were asked to rate each party's ability to cope with them; for the latter three, they were requested to indicate their party preference.

PARTISAN CHANGE IN BRITAIN, 1974–83

153

Table 4.3.3 uses data from [the 1974–1979] panel to demonstrate that changing party preferences on issues were strongly related to weakening party ties. Persons moving away from their 1974 party on a given issue were more likely to weaken or abandon their partisan attachment than were those who consistently preferred their party on the issue or moved to a position of approval between 1974 and 1979. For example, among 1974 Labour identifiers who judged in that year that their party handled strikes effectively but had changed their minds by 1979, 34 percent weakened or abandoned their partisanship. Among Labour identifiers who were consistent in their belief that their party had performed 'very' or 'fairly' well in the area of strikes or had adopted this belief by 1979, the equivalent

Table 4.3.3 Partisan dealignment and evaluations of parties on issues, October 1974–May 1979

Oct. 1974 party identification	Issue	Party identified with in 1974 would handle issue 'very' or 'fairly' well			
		1974 and 1979	1974, not 1979	1979, not 1974	Neither year
Labour	Prices	26	33	32	35
	Strikes	25	34	21	35
Conservative	Prices	17	41	16	22
	Strikes	18	23	18	22

Oct. 1974 party identification	Issue	Pattern of preference for Labour party on issues			
		1974 and 1979	1974, not 1979	1979, not 1974	Neither year
Labour	EEC	18	42	20	–[a]
	Nationalization	18	52	33	43
	Social services	23	47	33	33

Oct. 1974 party identification	Issue	Pattern of preference for Conservative party on issues			
		1974 and 1979	1974, not 1979	1979, not 1974	Neither year
Conservative	EEC	16	25	14	25
	Nationalization	16	–[a]	–[a]	–[a]
	Social services	13	44	14	50

Note: Entries are percentages of respondents who weakened or abandoned their party identification between October 1974 and May 1979. Respondents changing to a new identification between October 1974 and May 1979 have been eliminated from the analysis.

[a]Insufficient cases for analysis.

154   MODELS OF PARTY CHOICE

percentages are 25 percent and 21 percent. The behaviour of 1974 Conservative identifiers on prices provides a second example. Of those who moved away from their party on this issue, 41 percent weakened their partisan attachment. In contrast, only 17 percent judging their party positively on prices in both years weakened their partisanship, and only 16 percent of those making such an assessment in 1979 but not 1974 did so. The prevalence of these patterns strongly indicates that negative evaluations of parties' issue performance were associated with the erosion of partisan ties in the late 1970s.

To investigate the effects of changing feelings about party leaders and changing party/issue judgements in greater detail, multivariate analyses are required. The results [not shown here] reveal that changing party/issue evaluations have statistically significant effects on the strength of partisanship [in 1979] among 1974 Labour and Conservative identifiers. Among both groups changing feelings about party leaders also have significant effects, as does strength of partisanship in October 1974. Taken together, the three predictor variables are able to explain an estimated 25 percent of the variance in the strength of 1979 partisanship among 1974 Labour identifiers, and 21 percent for 1974 Conservatives.

[These findings] strengthen the argument that changing public feelings about leaders and issues played a role in the dealigning trends over the 1974–79 period.

4.4 Partisanship and party preference in government and opposition: the mid-term perspective

W.L. Miller, S. Tagg and K. Britto

Except when an indecisive result forces an early re-run, British general elections occur only once in every four or five years. But political life goes on in the intervals between these elections. Trends evolve and crises break, without much regard to electoral timing. A balanced description of political and partisan change over the last two decades [therefore] has to give as much weight to non-election times as to elections themselves.

Survey research has largely focused upon elections; [but] any brief description of change as inter-election change can be as much misleading as enlightening. The typical progress of the electoral cycle means that British governments tend to lose support in the earlier part of the parliament and regain it later on. So the overall change between one election and the next usually has at least two major components which offset each other. Net inter-election change depends upon how badly things went early in the parliament and how well the government recovered later on. So even a *two*-stage account of political change over the parliamentary cycle can be a considerable advance over a single-stage inter-election description.

Our essential argument is that a mid-term perspective will alter and

From W.L. Miller, S. Tagg and K. Britto, 'Partisanship and party preference in government and opposition: the mid-term perspective', *Electoral Studies* (1986), vol. 5, pp. 31–46.

156 MODELS OF PARTY CHOICE

deepen our understanding of political change in Britain. We shall illustrate this argument by presenting some new data on the changes in party identification over the period 1965–74. Our data come from a panel survey commissioned by the Conservative party. It used similar questions to the ESRC's panel survey directed by Butler and Stokes [but] it focused on the mid-term rather than election times. Election-time surveys did form part of our panel but they were to some extent conceptualized as follow-ups to more extensive surveys taken in the mid-term. In addition to surveys at every general election [between 1966 and October 1974], there were mid-term surveys in 1965, 1967–9 and 1972. Since 1965 is not an entirely typical mid-term period, our interest focuses on 1967–9, the true mid-term of a Labour government and on 1972, the mid-term of a Conservative government.

Party identification at election times

In their immensely influential paper on 'Partisan dealignment in Britain', Crewe, Sarlvik and Alt (1977) concentrated their attention on election times and this led them to some very strange conclusions which we shall investigate further. They were concerned with aggregate levels of party identification. In particular they drew attention to the declining proportion of party identifiers who identified *strongly* with the parties and they stressed the *timing* of that decline:

> Up to 1970 both the level and the strength of partisanship *held serenely steady*, despite the decline of the two-party vote over the same period. And *within each party it held steady* despite the parties' strongly fluctuating electoral fortunes. But in February 1974 it *crumbled* . . . thus *Labour partisanship, which had weathered six disappointing years of Labour Government, declined after four years of Labour Opposition* . . . The election of February 1974 does appear, therefore, to mark a significant loosening of public adherence to the two main parties . . . the very *abruptness* with which partisanship crumbled might be thought strong evidence for holding responsible the unusual circumstances of the February 1974 election. (Crewe, Sarlvik and Alt, 1977, pp. 146–8, our emphases)

They found 'overwhelming support' for the proposition that the decline in the strength of Conservative partisanship was a 'response to the extraordinary events preceding the February 1974 election', but 'the decay in Labour partisanship, while owing much to events surrounding the February 1974 election, had its origins in a growing rejection of the Labour party's basic tenets on the part of its own rank and file during the late 1960s'.

The mid-term perspective

These findings have been conditioned by a focus on election times and on change as inter-election change. They are partial and, at times, misleading truths. A focus on the mid-term and on the continuous nature of political change can lead to rather different conclusions.

Tandem change and the party identification model

Butler and Stokes' claim that when votes or identifications changed the 'dominant mode of change was for partisanship and vote to change *in tandem*' was based upon their data for 1963–4–6. In that time period over half the changers changed *both* their vote and their identification, about a third held on to their partisanship while changing their vote and a sixth changed their partisanship without changing their [vote]. By the 1970s this dominance was no longer clear. Our own analyses of the Conservative party surveys show that change in accord with the party identification model came to equal or exceed tandem change. Between February and October 1974, for example, our data indicate that over half the changers changed only their vote, while only a quarter changed both their vote and their partisanship.

Over the full parliament of 1966–70 our data show that tandem change continued to predominate, but that was not true for the sub-periods of 1966–70. During the first part of that parliament, and again during the latter part, changing votes combined with stable partisanship were as frequent as tandem changes. Quite simply, many Britons kept their partisanship all the way through that parliament but first defected and then returned home in terms of voting preferences. During the period of the 1966–70 parliament, if not between the two time-points of 1966 and 1970, British electors behaved more like American voters of the 1950s, changing their voting preferences while retaining their party identification (see Table 4.4.1).

The homing tendency through the mid-term

Despite their finding that tandem change was the norm in the early 1960s, Butler and Stokes also detected a strong 'homing tendency'. They found that those electors who changed their voting preferences once were particularly likely to change again and revert to their original party preference. Sarlvik and Crewe (1983) have updated this analysis of homing tendencies through all the general elections up to 1979 and qualified Butler and Stokes' finding in one important respect. Overall, roughly 40 per cent of Conservative and Labour vote switchers at one election reverted to their original party at the subsequent election, but about the same percentage stayed with their new vote preference.

158 MODELS OF PARTY CHOICE

Table 4.4.1 Tandem change and the party identification model in the mid-term

	Stable id. + changed vote	Stable vote + changed id.	Changed both	Stable both	
1965–1967/9	10	3	11	76	100%
1967/9–1970	9	4	9	79	100%

Note: Since the party identification question was only put to one quarter of the sample in 1966, we have taken change from 1965 rather than from 1966.

In addition, Sarlvik and Crewe found that the balance between the numbers who stayed with their new vote preference and the numbers who reverted varied sharply from year to year. Reversion predominated amongst former Conservative defectors in 1970, February 1974 and 1979; and amongst former Labour defectors in 1966 and February 1974. [Otherwise] defectors tended more to stay with their new party.

So according to Sarlvik and Crewe's analysis, February 1974 was the *only* election when reversion predominated amongst both Labour and Conservative defectors. Now that may seem an odd conclusion, since the election of February 1974 is remembered for the sudden surge in the Liberal vote and a sharp decline in both Labour and Conservative votes. It is not remembered as a high point of Labour and Conservative loyalty. But we have to recall the inter-election perspective that informs the Sarlvik and Crewe analysis. High reversion rates in February 1974 occurred amongst those Labour and Conservative voters of 1966 who had defected at the 1970 general election and were reverting in 1974 to their original 1966 vote.

A mid-term perspective tells a different story. Our concern is not with those voters who changed their votes between two elections, but with those electors who changed their voting preference between a general election and the mid-term: how did they actually vote in the following general election? We look at three parliamentary cycles: 1964–6, 1966–70 and 1970–February 1974 (see Table 4.4.2).

First of all, a plurality of those Liberal voters in 1964 and 1966 who switched to a Conservative vote preference in the mid-term went on to vote Conservative in the next election. Although a homing tendency was clearly evident, it did not predominate. The major parties fared better – though they had more voters to start with and more mid-term defectors at risk. In all three parliaments, Labour recovered a plurality of its mid-term defectors, though its rate of recovery varied. Relatively few former Labour voters who expressed a mid-term preference for the Liberals actually went on to vote Liberal. Rather more of them voted Conservative, but a very high proportion – up to 69 per cent – went back to Labour. Labour defectors to the Conservatives were markedly less likely to return to Labour. During

PARTISANSHIP: THE MID-TERM PERSPECTIVE

Table 4.4.2 The collapse of the homing tendency

			Con.		Lab.		Lib.	
	1964 vote	=	Con.		Lab.		Lib.	
	1965 preference	=	Lab.	Lib.	Con.	Lib.	Con.	Lab.
Subsequent vote in 1966	Con.		*	52	24	10	47	*
	Lab.		*	5	60	69	9	*
	Lib.		*	19	2	12	40	*
	Non-vot.		*	23	14	9	5	*
				100%	100%	100%	100%	
	1966 vote	=	Con.		Lab.		Lib.	
	1967–9 preference	=	Lab.	Lib.	Con.	Lib.	Con.	Lab.
Subsequent vote in 1970	Con.		*	58	37	13	57	*
	Lab.		*	15	47	62	11	*
	Lib.		*	11	3	5	20	*
	Non-vot.		*	17	13	20	12	*
				100%	100%	100%	100%	
	1970 vote	=	Con.		Lab.		Lib.	
	1972 preference	=	Lab.	Lib.	Con.	Lib.	Con.	Lab.
Subsequent vote in Feb. 1974	Con.		18	26	*	25	*	*
	Lab.		42	15	*	55	*	*
	Lib.		20	54	*	20	*	*
	Non-vot.		20	5	*	0	*	*
			100%	100%		100%		

*Too few cases for analysis.

the 1966–70 parliament when Labour was in government 37 per cent of Labour's mid-term defectors to the Conservatives went on to vote Conservative in 1970 while Labour only recovered 47 per cent. Things went even worse for the Conservatives when they were in government between 1970 and 1974. Although a substantial majority of the Conservatives' mid-term defectors during Labour governments had returned to vote Conservative in 1966 and 1970, only a small minority of the Conservatives' mid-term defectors in the 1970–4 parliament voted Conservative at the end. A plurality of former Conservatives who stated a Labour preference in 1972 voted Labour in 1974 while a plurality of those who stated a Liberal preference in 1972 voted Liberal in 1974.

In short, far from being an occasion when reversion rates were unusually high, February 1974 was an election when – in terms of the mid-term swings and roundabouts – the well-established homing tendency broke down.

160   MODELS OF PARTY CHOICE

Sarlvik and Crewe's inter-election analysis suggests a strong homing tendency in February 1974, yet a collapse in October 1974. Our emphasis on the mid-term shows that the collapse happened at the crisis election in February and merely continued in October.

Dealignment in the mid-term
Overall, Sarlvik and Crewe noted that roughly 47 per cent of British party identifiers expressed a *very strong* sense of identification at each of the elections in 1964, 1966 and 1970. But in February 1974 the figure fell to 33 per cent and dipped further to 25 per cent in 1979. Hence the justification for their conclusion that dealignment in Britain was so '*abrupt*'. And they stressed that this sharp decline in 1974 affected all the parties at the same time.

Our own data point to a less dramatic trend. In the Conservative party surveys partisanship also declined in strength but the decline was more gradual. In 1966, 42 per cent of identifiers had a *very strong* identification but this figure had already fallen to 37 per cent in 1970 before dropping to 33 per cent in February 1974 and 32 per cent in October 1974.

A mid-term perspective sharpened our findings. In mid-term waves of interviews the percentages of identifiers with a very strong identification were only 32 per cent in 1965, 31 per cent in 1967–9 and 30 per cent in 1972. But our mid-term data also show that this was not merely a cyclical pattern, not just the natural consequence of a more relaxed, less campaigning atmosphere in the mid-term. When we break identifiers down by party, and look both at election times and the mid-term, our data show that Conservative or Labour partisanship peaked in strength when the party won a major electoral victory and plunged to an all-time low in the mid-term that followed that victory. In 1966 the percentage of Labour partisans with a very strong identification peaked at 49 per cent before collapsing to 32 per cent in 1967–9. Similarly the percentage of Conservative partisans with a very strong identification peaked at 40 per cent in 1970 before collapsing to only 28 per cent in 1972. By contrast Liberal partisanship did not vary in strength with the electoral cycle and the alternation of governments (see Table 4.4.3).

It is totally misleading to claim that 'up to 1970 both the level and the strength of partisanship held *serenely steady*' or that 'Labour partisanship, which had *weathered six disappointing years* of Labour Government declined after four years of Labour Opposition'. Partisanship and especially Labour partisanship was anything but 'serenely steady' during those 'six disappointing years of Labour Government'. Whatever the net inter-election change in the parliament of 1970–4, the most dramatic collapse of enthusiasm for Labour occurred in response to the Labour government's performance in 1967–9, *not* in response to the party's performance in opposition during 1970–4 nor its performance at the 1974 election itself.

Table 4.4.3 Trends in the strength of party identification (percentage of identifiers with 'very strong' identification)

	1965	GE 1966	1967–9	GE 1970	1972	GE 1974F	GE 1974O
All identifiers	32	42	31	37	30	33	32
Amongst Con. id.	33	36	33	40	28	33	34
Amongst Lab. id.	34	49	32	39	33	37	35
Amongst Lib. id.	23	26	21	22	24	17	15

Labour partisanship was *stronger* in 1974 than it had been seven years earlier and we should not dismiss this contrast simply because it compares an election time with a mid-term. Labour suffered in 1967–9 not just from the lowered tempo of politics in the mid-term but from positive reaction against its performance in government. Labour suffered a decline of one third in the numbers with 'very strong' identifications in that mid-term while the strength of Conservative identification scarcely dropped.

Conclusion

Our investigation of the mid-term has challenged standard interpretations of recent political change in Britain and highlighted the significance of the years 1967–9. Contrary to previous findings which have been focused mainly on election times, partisan dealignment did *not* occur 'abruptly' in February 1974, [and] the homing tendency amongst voting defectors did not work particularly well in February 1974. The key to an understanding of the sea-change that has occurred in British politics is *not* the miners' strike election of 1974 but the disillusionment with Wilson's Labour government seven years earlier. Our analysis does not reveal the nature of the disillusionment, but we have shown that dealignment was linked to government performance of some kind.

4.5 | Partisan dealignment revisited

Anthony Heath, Roger Jowell and John Curtice

A theme running through much recent electoral research is that of partisan dealignment – the suggestion that we are in an era where the electorate has weaker allegiances to the parties.

We do not, of course, challenge the findings [of, for example, Crewe (1983a) and Rose and McAllister (1986)] on the crumbling of partisanship in 1974, although we shall bring the trends in level and strength of partisanship up to date with material from the 1983 and 1987 Election Studies. Instead, we shall focus on the possible consequences of this crumbling. We therefore propose to examine two major claims, first that the electorate has become more volatile and, second, that habitual party loyalties have become less important influences on the vote. We believe that these two suggestions are central to the hypothesis that there has been a secularisation of the vote or a shift to 'open' elections in Britain.

Sources of data

Our sources of data are the British Election Studies. For updating the trends in partisanship we rely on the cross-section surveys. For measuring trends in volatility and in the influence of party identification on vote we rely on the panel studies, in particular the four panel studies for March 1966–June 1970, June 1970–February 1974, October 1974–May 1979, and June 1983–June 1987 conducted as part of the British Election Studies. These four panels were chosen because they cover roughly similar durations and we are thus comparing like with like.

From A. Heath, R. Jowell and J. Curtice, 'Partisan dealignment revisited', unpublished paper presented to the PSA annual conference, 1988. Tables 4.5.2 and 4.5.3 below are taken from a revised version of this paper which appears in Heath *et al.* (1991).

PARTISAN DEALIGNMENT REVISITED

Trends in partisanship

The major pieces of survey evidence for the partisan dealignment thesis have been the trends in the proportion of the electorate who identify with a party and in the strength of their party identification. Tables 4.5.1 and 4.5.2 bring these trends up to date with results from the 1987 election survey.

As can be seen, the 1987 results seem to continue the modest decline in party identification that has been apparent throughout the election study series. As previous commentators have noted, there was no particular discontinuity or crumbling in 1974 but rather a steady and continuing erosion throughout the period. The overall picture seems clear enough. And while the trend is modest in magnitude, it is considerably greater than would have been expected on the basis of chance.

More dramatic changes have of course been reported in the strength of party identification, particularly the spectacular fall in 1974. Table 4.5.2 shows that this decline has continued too, albeit on a more modest scale.

Two further pieces of evidence have been mentioned in support of the notion that the electorate has become more hesitant and less attached to

Table 4.5.1 Trends in party identification

% with a party identification

	1964 %	1966 %	1970 %	Feb. 1974 %	Oct. 1974 %	1979 %	1983 %	1987 %
	93	91	92	90	90	87	86	86
(N)	(1,757)	(1,860)	(1,796)	(2,460)	(2,356)	(1,868)	(3,923)	(3,788)

Source: British Election Study cross-section surveys.

Table 4.5.2 Trends in strength of party identification

	% of identifiers who felt:				
	Very strongly	Fairly strongly	Not very strongly		N
1964	48	40	12	100%	(1,623)
1966	48	42	11	101%	(1,688)
1970	47	41	13	101%	(1,651)
February 1974	33	48	19	100%	(2,162)
October 1974	29	52	19	100%	(2,063)
1979	25	53	23	101%	(1,621)
1983	25	47	28	100%	(3,231)
1987	23	48	29	100%	(3,134)

Source: British Election Study cross-section surveys.

MODELS OF PARTY CHOICE

the established parties, namely the trends in the proportions who left their final voting decision to the campaign and who seriously thought of voting for an alternative party. [The first column of] Table 4.5.3 [relates to] the timing of the vote decision.

Unfortunately, there was a major discontinuity in the question wording in 1974. In the 1964 survey respondents were asked 'How long ago did you decide to vote that way?' It appears that this was an open-ended question. A similar format was used in the 1966 and 1970 studies.

In the February 1974 study, however, a new format was introduced. Respondents were asked the following closed question: 'How long ago did you decide that you would *definitely* vote the way you did – a long time ago, sometime this year, or during the campaign?' This format has been followed, with some very minor changes, ever since.

The change in the format from open to closed and the introduction of the word 'definitely' mean that we cannot easily interpret the discontinuity in 1974. All we can be sure of is that there was no trend between 1964 and 1970 and no trend between 1974 and 1987. With the exception of the 1979 figure, all the differences within the two periods could be explained (at the 5% level) by sampling error.

Our final piece of evidence from the cross-section surveys refers to those who wavered in their vote decision, that is who thought of voting for an alternative party. Again, unfortunately, there was a change of practice in 1974. In the preceding surveys the question asked was: 'Did you think of voting for any other party?' But in 1974 this was changed to: 'Was there any time during the election campaign when you *seriously* thought you might vote for another party?' While the addition of the word 'seriously' might be expected to reduce the number who reported wavering, the specification of 'during the election campaign' might act in the opposite direction.

Table 4.5.3 Trends in hesitancy

	% of voters who decided during the campaign	% of voters who thought of voting for another party	N
1964	12	25	(1,504)
1966	11	23	(1,517)
1970	12	21	(1,431)
February 1974	23	25	(2,071)
October 1974	22	(21)	(2,008)
1979	28	31	(1,597)
1983	22	25	(3,188)
1987	21	28	(3,280)

Notes: The Ns are the numbers answering the question on when the vote was decided. The percentage in brackets is of doubtful validity for technical reasons.

Source: British Election Study cross-section surveys.

PARTISAN DEALIGNMENT REVISITED

If we are prepared to assume that these two factors cancel out, we might conclude from [the second column of] Table 4.5.3 that there has been a very modest increase in wavering. The differences are greater than would be expected from sampling variation, but no clear pattern emerges.

The cross-sectional evidence, then, has not told a particularly clear story. On partisanship we have seen a very modest continuation in the 1980s of the trends towards lower levels and weaker strength. But the other data give no great support to the notion that the electorate has become more hesitant or wavering. The changes in question wording mean that there is no clear evidence of a major discontinuity in 1974, and even in the post-1974 period when question wording was retained unchanged there is no evidence of a trend towards a more hesitant electorate.

Trends in volatility

Our major interest in this paper is what, if any, have been the consequences of the erosion of partisanship. In general, strength of partisanship is associated with the stability of the respondent's vote over time. (In the 1983–7 panel for example, 79% of very strong identifiers were stable, 75% of fairly strong identifiers, and 59% of not very strong identifiers.) It is therefore not unreasonable to expect that a decline in the average strength of partisanship would be associated with an increase in volatility, and this appears to be the assumption lying behind the theory of dealignment.

It has been customary to distinguish between *net* volatility and *overall* volatility. Net volatility refers to the change in the distribution of the vote between two elections. Overall volatility refers to the total amount of vote switching, and can most simply be calculated by summing the percentages lying off the main diagonal in a vote (t_0) by vote (t_1) table drawn from a panel study. As we know from the election result, net volatility was relatively small in 1987, but this leaves open the question whether the underlying 'turbulence' in the electorate has remained high. Overall volatility is therefore the concept of greater interest to us in the present context.

Before turning to the summary statistic of overall volatility, however, it is of some interest to look at the details of the vote (t_0) by vote (t_1) tables for the four panel studies. Table 4.5.4 presents the percentages on the main diagonal of these tables, that is the 'retention rates' of the parties in the four panel studies. (The retention rate for a party is calculated simply as the proportion of respondents voting for a given party in the first wave of the panel who reported casting a vote for the same party in the final wave. The analysis is restricted to those who participated in both waves of the panel, less those who refused to disclose their vote in either wave.)

MODELS OF PARTY CHOICE

Table 4.5.4 Trends in retention rates

	1966–70	1970–Feb 74	Oct 1974–79	1983–87
Conservative	85 (366)	75 (380)	90 (228)	83 (366)
Labour	69 (476)	76 (425)	80 (284)	79 (158)
Liberal (Alliance)	50 (86)	64 (75)	46 (118)	65 (194)
Abstention	42 (147)	21 (166)	41 (82)	25 (120)

Note: Figures in brackets give *N*s.

The results of Table 4.5.4 are much as one might expect. Not surprisingly, parties tend to show higher retention rates over election periods when they gained votes than when they lost votes. The Conservative party generally has a higher retention rate than the Labour party, again not surprisingly as it has maintained its share of the vote rather better over the 21 year period as a whole. And the Liberal/Alliance, despite gaining votes, shows the lower retention rate expected given the often-reported 'softness' of its vote.

Table 4.5.4 does not however suggest that retention rates have declined over time. While the very high Conservative and Labour retention rates in the 1974–79 panel may be questioned, given the high attrition rate in this panel, comparison of the other three panels suggests that there has been no secular trend in retention rates. One is tempted to say that the figures display trendless fluctuation.

To be sure, the distribution of votes between the three parties has changed over the period, hence the need to weight these figures if we are to obtain a picture of overall volatility. If we weight the retention rates according to the actual distribution of the vote in the first wave of the panel, we obtain an estimate of overall stability and volatility. [Including] consistent abstainers among the stable, the overall percentage stable becomes 66% for 1966–70, 59% for 1970–February 74, 65% for October 74–79 and 61% for 1983–87. Again no clear trend is apparent.

If we wish to look at the underlying turbulence in the electorate, it is [also] necessary to control for the changes in the distribution of the vote. This can be done using the technique of proportional marginal adjustment described by Mosteller (1968). Using this technique we can adjust the marginal totals of the vote (t_0) by vote (t_1) tables from the four panels so that they are identical (and symmetrical), but without changing the internal structure of the table. That is to say, the pattern of odds ratios within the original tables is preserved.

Table 4.5.5 shows the retention rates in the 'Mostellerized' tables. They can be thought of as showing the underlying 'stickiness' or 'turbulence' of the parties' vote. The picture is a fairly clear one. Turbulence, defined and measured in this way, was slightly higher in the 1970–74 period. For all four

PARTISAN DEALIGNMENT REVISITED

Table 4.5.5 Retention rates after proportional marginal adjustment

	1966–70	1970–Feb 74	Oct 1974–79	1983–87
Conservative	70	65	71	69
Labour	67	63	75	70
Liberal/Alliance	72	65	66	65
Abstention	53	45	69	50

categories of vote, retention rates fell in this period. But this increase in turbulence seems to have been a once-and-for-all phenomenon, restricted to the rather unusual election period of 1970–February 1974. There is no sign whatsoever of turbulence continuing to increase in the later 1970s and 1980s, nor indeed of turbulence remaining at the new higher level of 1970–74.

In this respect, then, Table 4.5.5 tells much the same story as Table 4.5.4, and indeed as Table 4.5.3. Over the period covered by the election studies, we see no clear evidence of an increase in volatility or turbulence to match the decline in strength of partisanship.

Trends in the determinants of voting behaviour

But perhaps the most interesting way to test the effects of weakening partisanship is to look at the changing predictive power of party identification. If partisanship has weakened, then we would surely expect party identification to play a more minor role in influencing how people vote. This is what we take it Rose and McAllister mean when they say that the electorate has become more open or what Crewe and his colleagues mean when they say that the electorate has become more secular.

One of the central claims of party identification theory is that there will be a 'homing tendency'. That is to say, 'Electors who are influenced by the short-term forces of a particular campaign to vote against the party with which they identify normally retain their partisanship and return to it in subsequent elections' (Harrop and Miller, 1987, p. 134). If habitual party loyalty has indeed become a weaker force in influencing the voters' choice, we would expect this homing tendency to have become weaker too.

Consider Table 4.5.6. This covers respondents who *did not* vote Conservative in 1983 and includes non-voters as well as voters for Labour, the Alliance and other parties. As can be seen, respondents who reported a Conservative identity in 1983 were markedly more likely to cast a Conservative vote in 1987 than were respondents who reported Labour, Liberal/SDP, other or no party identity in 1983. To get a simple and interpretable measure of the size of this effect, let us collapse the categories

MODELS OF PARTY CHOICE

Table 4.5.6 The homing tendency: respondents who did not vote Conservative in 1983

Identity in 1983	Vote in 1987					
	Con.	Lab.	All.	Other	None	N
Conservative	53	0	20	0	27	(51)
Labour	8	71	11	1	9	(202)
Liberal/SDP	11	9	71	0	9	(140)
Other	19	43	10	24	5	(21)
None	23	18	36	4	17	(69)

of Table 4.5.6 into two dichotomous variables, namely Conservative identity versus non-Conservative identity in 1983 and Conservative vote versus non-Conservative vote in 1987. We can then carry out a logit analysis of the effect of identity on vote.

The same procedure can be carried out for the other parties too. For example, we can look at all respondents who did not vote Labour in 1983 and, for these respondents, look at the effect of a Labour identity in 1983 on Labour voting in 1987. In this way we can compare the homing tendency for different parties. We can further repeat the analysis for the other three panel studies, and the results are shown in Table 4.5.7.

Table 4.5.7 shows rather conclusively that the homing tendency has not declined. In general, the logit coefficients for the four panel studies are remarkably similar, and in most cases the differences are within sampling error. The one notable exception is the Labour homing tendency in 1987, which shows a marked increase. This is not altogether surprising given the rather exceptional circumstances of the Labour result in 1983. The results of this analysis, then, are exactly in line with those of volatility.

Table 4.5.7 Logit coefficients for the effect of ID on vote in the four panel studies

	1966–70	1970–F74	O1974–79	1983–87
Conservative	0.43 (0.07)	0.56 (0.06)	0.38 (0.06)	0.53 (0.08)
Labour	0.55 (0.08)	0.47 (0.05)	0.43 (0.09)	0.79 (0.08)
Liberal/SDP	0.47 (0.09)	0.43 (0.07)	0.53 (0.09)	0.42 (0.10)

Note: Figures in brackets give the standard errors.

Conclusions

The results reported here leave us with something of a paradox. Over the period with which we are concerned, the levels and strength of partisanship have declined and have tended to continue their decline even into the 1980s. This has led many commentators to expect that voters would become more hesitant and volatile, and less inclined to vote on the basis of party loyalty. These expectations appeared all the more reasonable as strength of partisanship is correlated, at the individual level, with stability. None of these expectations, however, has been borne out. There has been no clear increase in hesitancy, volatility or turbulence, and no tendency for party identification to become a less powerful influence on vote.

The paradox can, we think, be resolved if we distinguish between the electorate's evaluations of the parties on the one hand and the way the electorate decides how to vote on the other. [We need to] consider the meaning of [changes in the] strength of party identification. Miller, Tagg and Britto (1986) showed that the proportion of Labour partisans with a very strong identification peaked at 49% in 1966 before collapsing to 32% in 1967–9. They suggested that this dramatic collapse of enthusiasm for Labour was in response to the Labour government's performance in 1967–9.

Miller's assumption, with which we would agree, is that measures of the strength of identification are in part measures of support for the party, measures which change in line with the party's performance. In other words, changes in [strength of] partisanship are in part functions of the parties' performances in office or in opposition. Such changes should not, therefore, be taken as evidence of changes in the way in which the electorate makes up its mind. *How* voters decide may stay constant, but *what* they decide may change.

5 | Issue voting

Introduction

Early American voting studies attached little importance to electors' opinions about policies or issues in explaining party choice in elections. The authors of the Michigan studies did include 'issue orientation' in their model of the American voter, but they concluded that 'many people fail to appreciate that an issue exists, others are insufficiently involved to pay attention to recognized issues, and still others fail to make connections between issue positions and party policy' (Campbell *et al.*, 1960, p. 183). Even among the few voters who were able to make such connections, the predominant pattern was not one in which the voter chose a party on the basis of the match between his or her opinions and the policies of the parties. Rather, such voters tended to assume that the party they supported on other grounds had policies congruent with their opinions. In addition, the authors of *The American Voter* found that where voters did have opinions and attitudes these were weakly developed and unstructured.

This line of argument was pursued in greater detail in a well-known later article by Phillip Converse, a member of the original Michigan team (Converse, 1964). In this article, which is referred to a number of times in the extracts in this section, Converse pointed out that although voters were generally willing to indicate their positions on political issues when asked to do so in survey questionnaires, their opinions were very unstable from one interview to the next. He argued that this probably indicated that many voters did not have 'real' attitudes towards current political issues. If this were the case, then voters could not base their party choice on their policy opinions.

In their analysis of the effects of issue opinions on party choice in *Political Change in Britain*, Butler and Stokes were heavily influenced by the ideas put forward in *The American Voter* and they came to similar conclusions about British voters. In the first extract in this section, Butler

ISSUE VOTING

and Stokes show that, on the whole, voters in the 1960s failed to meet the conditions for issue voting. Their data suggest that voters' opinions, even on the most central of issues, were remarkably unstructured and inconsistent over time, and that the proportion of voters having even a rudimentary understanding of the concept of a left/right political continuum, along which the issue positions of parties and voters could be arrayed, was very small. This view, that the great majority of voters were simply too ignorant of the issues of the day and too ill-equipped conceptually to deal with complex political issues, came to be widely accepted as an accurate picture of the British, as of the American, voter in the 1960s. The 'ideal' voter of liberal democratic theory – concerned, informed, basing party choice upon a careful weighing-up of the parties' positions on important issues of the day – was consigned to the political theory textbook.

In the 1970s, however, the view that voting was largely 'issueless' began to be called into question in the United States (Pomper, 1972; Nie *et al.*, 1976). Similarly in Britain, as class voting declined, party identification weakened and voter volatility appeared to increase, researchers began to look again at the possibility that party choice was based on voters' assessments of the parties' policies and performance. A milestone in the development of this renewed interest was Sarlvik and Crewe's study of the 1979 general election, *Decade of Dealignment*, from which our second extract is taken. Sarlvik and Crewe argue that in 1979 there was a good fit between voters' attitudes on individual issues and their party choice and that it was possible to predict party choice successfully on the basis of voters' overall policy preferences.

In our third extract, Mark Franklin uses causal modelling techniques to assess changes in the level of issue voting between 1964 and 1983. Although the statistical methods involved are complex, Franklin's general argument is not difficult to follow. His analysis leads to the conclusion that there was a marked increase in issue voting between the elections of 1966 and 1970, but that after 1970 there was no very clear trend in levels of issue voting.

In *How Britain Votes*, Heath, Jowell and Curtice criticised the view, which had become generally accepted by the early 1980s, that there had been a sharp increase in issue voting. In the extract reproduced here they use the 1983 BES survey to argue that if voters had made their party choice on the basis of their opinions then the election would have been a relatively close-run thing between Labour, the Conservatives and the Alliance, rather than a resounding Conservative victory. They take this as evidence of the weakness of the issue voting model. Heath *et al.* argue, in addition, that there are serious theoretical problems with the commonly accepted version of the issue voting model – what they call 'consumer' voting. In particular, they reject the procedure (used for example by Franklin and by Himmelweit *et al.* (1981) in constructing their statistical models) which assumes that all voters employ the same 'counting rule' to trade off a preference for one party on one issue against a preference for another party on another issue. This leads Heath and his colleagues to reject the conventional model of issue voting and to propose a model of what they call 'ideological' voting. It is through broad ideological preferences, which are based at least partly on class position, that voters' opinions influence their choice of party.

Rose and McAllister also reject the conventional issue voting model, although their reasons for doing so are not explained at any length. They use factor analysis, a statistical technique which can be used to discover patterns in responses to survey questions, to show that people's opinions on issues, as reported in BES surveys, tend to go together in distinctive ways. This suggests that electors share common underlying political 'principles', and Rose and McAllister then develop a model of 'lifetime learning' in which these principles are a significant element in determining party choice.

Finally we reproduce an extract from a more recent article by Heath and McDonald which, although focusing mainly on party identification theory, also offers some further evidence about the extent of issue voting. Here Heath seems to have abandoned some of his earlier objections to conventional issue voting models, for the analysis employs an index of voters' issue positions very similar to those used by Sarlvik and Crewe and Franklin. Heath and McDonald call their model 'principled voting', however, arguing that their index is tapping broad ideological orientations, and they explicitly draw a parallel with the model put forward by Rose and McAllister. They argue that there is little evidence to support the view that issue voting in Britain has increased, even in the guise of principled voting.

These last three extracts reflect a recent decline in support for a straightforward issue voting model among commentators, in favour of models which put greater weight on broader, underlying principles or ideologies. There has been something of a return to the Michigan school's scepticism about the level of voters' knowledge about, and ability to think in terms of, current political issues. These critics of issue voting claim, however, that voters do have political principles or ideologies and that they are able, in some more rudimentary way than the issue voting model suggests, to make connections between the parties and these principles or ideologies.

We have ourselves examined this line of argument in some detail in a recent article (Denver and Hands, 1990). We firstly argue that neither Heath *et al.* nor Rose and McAllister give adequately detailed accounts of the models that they have in mind. Since ideologies can only be understood as made up of sets of principles, Heath, Jowell and Curtice's ideological voting model has to be understood, in practice, as a form of principle voting, as in Rose and McAllister's model. That model in turn, although

ISSUE VOTING

inadequately described, seems to have the same basic structure as the standard issue voting model, with principles substituted for issues – voters choose the party which is, on balance, closest to their own position across a range of principles. Secondly, we test a principle voting model defined in this way (admittedly using a somewhat narrow sample) and find no statistical reason to suppose that it is superior to a conventional issue voting model. We conclude that there are as yet insufficient grounds for dismissing the issue voting model and replacing it with models based on ideology or principles.

Further reading

A useful summary of the extensive literature dealing with the attitudes and opinions of voters in a comparative context is given in Harrop and Miller (1987), while the literature on issue voting in Britain is reviewed in Denver (1989).

Research on issue voting frequently acknowledges an intellectual debt to Anthony Downs (1957) whose influential work developed a model of the 'rational' voter. The debt is clear in Himmelweit *et al.* (1981), although this study has been widely criticised, partly on account of the small number of voters on which it is based. The most extensive investigation of issue voting in Britain is to be found in Sarlvik and Crewe (1983). This is a major contribution to the debate and readers may find Part II in particular worth further study. Strong support for the view that opinions and judgements have come to be more important than social location in determining party choice is given by Whiteley (1986).

Scarbrough (1984) puts forward a complex and thoroughly worked-out model of ideological voting, though unfortunately the sample which she uses to test her theory is very small. Rose and McAllister (1990) use basically the same techniques as their earlier book to update their analysis to include the 1987 election. Denver and Hands (1990) offer a general critique of models of voting based on principles and ideology.

The American literature on issue voting is immense. Abramson (1983) provides a good general account, but of particular interest is Nie, Verba and Petrocik's *The Changing American Voter* (1976) and the debate to which it gave rise (see Bishop *et al.*, 1978, and Sullivan *et al.*, 1978).

5.1 | The analysis of issues

David Butler and Donald Stokes

Analyses of political issues often tend to cast the public in the role of an informed spectator at the game of government, one who sees policy issues much as they are seen by the political leaders who play the game. But the simplest evidence about the extent of popular attention to the affairs of government must challenge any image of the elector as an informed spectator.

[This is] persuasively attested to by the fluidity of opinion on questions which have been at the heart of the party battle for many years. An impressive example of this is provided by the nationalization of industry, a matter that for a generation has never been far from the centre of political controversy. At each round of interviews [in 1963, 1964 and 1966] we asked our respondents to choose one from an ordered set of positions on nationalization – or to say that they had no opinion. The overall responses remained quite constant over our three rounds of interviews. The distribution of views among those with a declared view seemed quite stable.

When individual responses are examined, however, the truth is found to be very different. Table 5.1.1 shows the full turnover of views between our first and second interviews. A glance at the squares in the main diagonal shows that only 39 per cent stuck to an identical and definite position on the broad lines of nationalization policy. There was a good deal of wavering between having and not having an opinion and even more between different opinions. By any standard statistical measure, the stability of the entries is decidedly modest. The turnover of opinion carried many respondents across the line between those who believed in more

From D.E. Butler and D. Stokes, *Political Change in Britain* (1st edn, 1969), London: Macmillan, chapters 8 and 9.

THE ANALYSIS OF ISSUES

175

nationalization and those who did not, the critical divide in the struggle over nationalization at the elite level.

This line is blurred still more when we lengthen our time interval and examine the movements of opinion over our three interviews. Even when we collapse our four alternatives into two and consider only whether a respondent was for more nationalization or not, an intricate pattern of change emerges. Fully 26 per cent said in one or more interviews that they had no opinion on nationalization. Only 50 per cent were consistent in either supporting or opposing further nationalization over the three interviews. It seems plausible to interpret the fluidity of the public's views as an indication of the limited degree to which attitudes are formed towards even the best-known of policy issues.

The extent to which the changeability of attitude is a reflection of the sheer uncertainty that surrounds many people's beliefs emerges from another property of opinion revealed by repeated canvassing of individual views. Substantial short run reshuffling of views fails to yield the longer run movement of individual position which we would expect from real and cumulative attitude change.

This aspect of popular response to policy issues emerges clearly from the turnover of opinion on nuclear weapons policy. Individual attitudes towards the Bomb were as fluid as those towards nationalization. The correlation between opinions on nuclear weapons expressed in 1963 and 1964 was only +0.33 and between 1964 and 1966 only +0.38. But what is

Table 5.1.1 Turnover of opinion towards nationalization of industry, 1963 to 1964

		Autumn 1964					
		Lot more	Few more	No more	Less	No opinion	
	Lot more	3	3	3	1	1	11
	Few more	1	6	6	1	1	15
Summer 1963	No more	1	5	21	6	3	36
	Less	1	1	10	9	1	22
	No opinion	7	2	5	2	6	16
		7	17	45	19	12	100% ($N = 1,473$)

176   MODELS OF PARTY CHOICE

significant for our present purpose is a comparison of the rate of change between the two pairs of closer interviews (1963–4 and 1964–6) with the rate between the more distant pair of interviews in 1963 and 1966. If changes of response reflected only genuine attitude change and occurred at a rate fast enough to have produced the very modest correlations between the first and second, and second and third, interviews, then the correlation between the first and third interviews ought to be almost non-existent. Indeed, on these assumptions we would expect the correlation between 1963 and 1966 to be only +0.13 [i.e. 0.33 × 0.38]. In fact, however, the observed correlation was +0.31, not much lower than the correlation between opinions at the two closer pairs of interviews. The slower rate of decay may therefore be seen as further evidence that the circulation of opinion is substantially due to mere uncertainty of response and not to genuine attitude change.

Analysing the effect of issues

It is possible to lay down two conditions that will have to be met if an issue is to exert genuine force on the individual elector.

The first involves the individual's orientation to the issue itself. This must entail something more than simple awareness. If an issue is to sway the elector it must not only have crossed the threshold of his awareness; he must also have formed some genuine attitude towards it. The more an issue is salient to him and the subject of strong attitudes, the more powerful will be its influence on his party choice. Indeed, given the multiplicity of influences upon the individual elector, only issues that excite strong feeling are likely to have much impact.

[But] the influence of an issue on the elector's choice depends also on the links in his mind between the issue and the parties. However well-formed the individual's attitudes towards an issue, they will not affect his party choice unless he sees the connection between the issue and the parties.

In some cases, this link need involve only one of the parties, especially when it mainly involves judgements upon the government of the day. But the link may involve a differing perception of the parties, with the elector judging the relative chance of achieving certain values if one or if the other comes to power.

The bonds suggested by our [analysis so far] indicate the conditions that must be fulfilled if an issue is to sway the individual elector. But we cannot say what impact an issue may have over the whole country without extending our framework of analysis to the electorate as a whole. Let us see what conditions must be met before an issue can be said to have made a net alteration to the strength of the parties.

A first condition is a straightforward extension of the need for the

THE ANALYSIS OF ISSUES

177

individual to perceive an issue and to form some attitude towards it. For an issue to have much impact in the whole electorate the bond of issue to self must be formed in the minds of a substantial body of electors. The greater the proportion of people to whom an issue is salient and the subject of strong attitudes, the more powerful the impact it can have on the fortunes of the parties.

A second condition has to do with the balance or skewness of attitudes towards [issues]. What this condition entails is most easily seen in the case of an issue that poses only two clear alternatives. If, for example, the issue of Britain's entry into Europe comes down to a choice between 'In' or 'Out', the issue is likely to affect the relative standing of the parties only if there is a surplus of opinion for one or other of these alternatives.

The importance of the skewness of opinion calls attention to issues involving values that are widely shared in the electorate. Many issues present alternative policies or conditions whose value is a matter of disagreement in the country. Nationalization is one of these, but other issues involve a virtual consensus in the electorate, and indeed among the parties as well, on the values entailed by different alternatives. The issues connected with the state of the economy offer outstanding examples. There is no body of opinion in the country that favours economic distress, and thereby cancels some of the votes of those who want better times; the whole weight of opinion lies on the side of prosperity and growth. Issues of this sort do not find the parties positioning themselves to appeal to those who favour alternative policies or goals. Rather the parties attempt to associate themselves in the public's mind with conditions, such as good times, which are universally favoured, and to dissociate themselves from conditions, such as economic distress, which are universally deplored. Such a distinction between *position* issues, on which the parties may appeal to rival bodies of opinion, and *valence* issues, on which there is essentially one body of opinion on values or goals, is too often neglected in political commentary. The potential [of valence issues] derives from the fact that they satisfy so well the second of our conditions for an issue to have impact on the strength of the parties: that the distribution of opinion be strongly skewed.

The third condition for an issue to alter the net strength of the parties is that it be associated differently with the parties in the public's mind. Unless there is a difference of this sort, an issue will not sway the electorate towards one party or the other, however strongly formed and skewed opinion may be.

Issues do in fact vary widely in the degree to which they differentiate the parties in the public's mind. The extent of these contrasts is illustrated by the issues of nationalization and of Britain's entry into the Common Market. These issues were alike in the low degree of attitude formation towards them in much of the electorate. But they differed profoundly in

178   MODELS OF PARTY CHOICE

terms of the separation of parties they achieved in the public's mind. This contrast is set out in the entries of Table 5.1.2. As the gap between the first two percentages in each column shows, the consensus on the party difference was almost four times greater over nationalization than over entry into Europe.

The conditions of an issue's influence imply the conditions under which that influence will change. The net 'force' which an issue exerts on the party balance can be altered by a change in the strength of the public's feeling, the distribution of that feeling across alternative policies or goals, or the way the parties are linked to these alternatives in the public's mind. Because each of these conditions is necessary for an issue to have effect, all three must be considered before we can say whether a change in one will alter the issue's influence.

Patterns in political attitudes

Political change – whether in the individual elector or in the mass electorate – will seldom be provoked by a single issue, standing on its own. Most voters have attitudes towards many issues, and these may fall into discernible patterns. Indeed, one of the most familiar frameworks for interpreting change – the schema of left and right – assumes that the public sees a number of political issues in terms of an ideological spectrum and responds to leftward and rightward movements of the parties along this spectrum.

Table 5.1.2 Perceived party differences on nationalization and the Common Market, 1964

	Party more likely to extend nationalization	Party more likely to enter Common Market
Labour	90%	22%
	84% difference	22% difference
Conservative	6	44
Not much difference	3	21
Don't know	1	13
	100% ($N = 1{,}563$)	100% ($N = 1{,}161$)

The structure of stable opinions

The fact that weakly formed attitudes will tend to change over time suggests an analytic step for us to take in searching for pattern in the attitudes of those who do hold genuine issue beliefs. If we exclude from consideration those whose views wavered between interviews and examine the interrelationships of the attitudes only of those whose views remained fixed, we will be able to clear away most responses that had a random element and [this will] allow us to detect any pattern in the beliefs of the minority whose views were more genuine and stable.

What in fact emerges from the correlations obtained in this way is that there is no strong pattern linking the attitudes even of those who do have stable attitudes. Compared with the expectation that any reader of the *Economist* or *New Statesman*, say, would have about political positions that naturally go together, the actual correlations are strikingly low.

The main impression left by Table 5.1.3 is of the weakness of the links between attitudes. These figures are based on the drastically reduced groups of electors who held stable opinions on each of two issues over two or three interviews. On average something like 70 per cent of our full sample has been cut away. Yet even when we go to such lengths to confine our attention to the minority of people who have well-formed and enduring views, the association of attitudes is relatively feeble. An occasional correlation, such as that between nationalization and trade union power, rises to an impressive level. But most of these figures are notable mainly for their modest size. There is a mild tendency here for opinion to organize along the left–right lines which would be recognized by political insiders. But by the standards of elite opinion the tendency is very mild indeed.

This aspect of popular thought inevitably raises the question of how important the left–right framework is to the public's appraisal of politics.

The left–right framework of issues

The notion that policies and leaders can be ranked on an ideological scale running from left to right is perhaps the commonest of all political abstractions. It is not just a piece of academic conceptualization; the words 'left' and 'right' are constantly used in everyday political comment and reporting.

In this left–right model the parties take their place along the spectrum according to the stands which they adopt on issues. Voters too take their place according to their position on issues. The central assumption of the model when it is taken as a theory of electoral behaviour is that a voter's preference for a party depends on how far its position is from his own along

Table 5.1.3 Correlations of stable attitudes towards issues

	Nuclear weapons	Common Market	Too many immigrants	Death penalty	Big business power	Queen and Royal Family	Trade union power
Nationalization of industry	0.14	0.10	0.06	0.18	0.37	0.26	0.65
Retention of nuclear weapons		−0.26	0.07	0.20	0.09	0.23	0.12
Entry into Common Market			−0.07	0.20	0.00	−0.01	−0.02
Whether too many immigrants let in				0.33	−0.06	0.10	0.18
Abolition of death penalty					0.09	0.14	0.18
Whether big business too powerful						0.10	0.17
Importance of Queen and Royal Family							0.18

Note: The entries are Kendall's tau-b rank order correlation coefficients. For further details of how the figures were arrived at see the original.

THE ANALYSIS OF ISSUES

the left–right dimension. Thus, he will most prefer the party that is closest to him and least prefer the party that is farthest from him; any other parties will enjoy an intermediate degree of preference. Because of the central role that this idea of a left–right spectrum plays in most ideological discussion, we should explore in detail how far the left–right spectrum provides a realistic model of the relationship between parties and voters.

A natural approach to the problem is to see how far the assumption that the elector judges the parties by the distance from his own position does in fact fit the preferences felt by voters towards the Conservative, Labour and Liberal Parties. Our respondents who said that they thought of the parties as being to the left, centre or right politically were virtually unanimous in placing Labour to the left, the Conservatives to the right and the Liberals somewhere in between. Fewer than one in twenty ranked the parties in an order that differed from the conventional one.

[However] if ideological closeness were in fact the basis of preference, all voters [to] the left would like Labour best, the Liberals next best and the Conservatives least. Similarly all voters [to] the right would like the Conservatives best, the Liberals next best and Labour least. Voters in the centre would like the Liberals best but their second and third choices would depend on whether they were to the left or right of a point halfway between Labour and the Conservatives.

There are, however, two other sequences in which a voter might order his preferences:

1	Labour	1	Conservative
2	Conservative	2	Labour
3	Liberal	3	Liberal

But to have either of these orders of preference would be to contradict the assumption that ideological closeness is the basis of party choice.

Yet in fact many voters do order the parties in this way. Among Labour supporters in the summer of 1963 fully a third preferred the Conservatives to the Liberals as a second choice and among Conservatives more than a quarter preferred Labour to the Liberals. How are these inadmissible orderings to be explained?

One possibility is to imagine that preference is related to ideological distance in some much more complicated way. But a much simpler explanation is that many electors do not in fact see politics in terms of a single ideological dimension. There is no point in devising complex reasons why the left–right model fails to account for popular preferences if in fact a substantial proportion of the public is quite innocent of the left–right distinctions that are so constantly employed by insiders. Let us therefore try to measure more directly the extent to which the notions of left and right are comprehended by British electors.

Recognition of the concept of left and right

A first indication of the limited extent of ideological thinking at the mass level comes from the electors' answers to the question 'Do you ever think of the parties as being to the left, the centre or the right in politics or don't you think of them in that way?' Not many of them do – only 21 per cent of our respondents answered 'Yes'. Given the opportunity to confess the remoteness of such terms most people took it.

In a widely separated place in our interview we asked our respondents if they ever thought of themselves personally as being to the left, centre or the right in politics. Only 25 per cent said that they did so. This contrasts sharply with the fact that 96 per cent of our respondents concede readily enough to some degree of party commitment. Allegiance to party is one of the central facts of the British elector's political awareness. Identification with the ideological symbols of left and right is clearly one of the more peripheral facts of such awareness.

These sobering proportions do not of course show the full extent to which these ideological symbols are recognized. In order to see how many among that vast majority of electors who do not think in these terms nonetheless have some awareness of them, we included in our interviews an alternative approach to the question. Our respondents were asked to rate the parties along a series of scales involving such polar extremes as United/Split, Expert/Clumsy, Middle Class/Working Class and, among a number of other qualities, Left-wing/Right-wing. Our respondents found [eleven of] these questions quite comprehensible. But on the Left-wing/ Right-wing scale more than one elector in five was too baffled to give any reply at all, a proportion which suggests the difficulty the public has in using these terms.

Let us look more closely at the places given to the Labour Party along this Left-wing/Right-wing scale for evidence of the limits of ideological awareness.

Of the respondents who were asked [in] both the summer of 1963 and the autumn of 1964 to place Labour along the left–right scale, we find 29 per cent who confessed at one interview or the other that they were unable to do so. We find another 28 per cent who at one interview or the other placed Labour at the middle or to the right. Moreover, since 3 per cent put Labour on the right both times, we can assume that a further 3 per cent were guessing when they put Labour on the left both times. Thus we end up with approximately two-fifths of the electorate who can be presumed to connect the left and right symbols with the Labour Party in a meaningful way. The arithmetic by which we would identify the proportion correctly placing the Conservatives gives very similar results.

THE ANALYSIS OF ISSUES

Total sample asked to place Labour at both interviews		100%
Said 'don't know' at one interview or other	29	
Placed Labour in middle or on the right in at least one interview	28	
Placed Labour on the left both times by guessing	3	60%
Genuinely perceived Labour as on the left		40%

In other words, in addition to the 20–25 per cent who said that they thought in terms of left and right, there was an additional stratum of 15–20 per cent who showed some ability to link these ideological symbols with the parties. But we are still left with a substantial majority of the British people unfamiliar with these concepts.

Levels of ideological interpretation

To probe [further] what meaning the words left and right imparted we asked those of our respondents who said they thought of the parties in such terms what they had in mind when they said a party was to the left, centre or right politically. Their replies could be sorted into three levels of ideological sophistication. The highest involved a well-elaborated interpretation, one in which the concepts of left and right seemed to organize the respondent's attitudes to several issues at once. Such interpretations seemed also relatively 'dynamic', in the sense of providing the grounds on which the elector might decide the parties, or he himself, had moved to the left or the right. By a fairly generous classification not more than one in ten of those who associated the words with the parties (which means only two in a hundred of the entire electorate) gave answers at this level.

A second level involved a less developed interpretation in which the concepts were given meaning in terms of only one kind of content, usually identifications with a social class. Interpretations at this level seemed not only less capable of organizing attitudes towards various issues at once but also more static in the sense that the parties' behaviour in relation to contemporary issues, or changes of the voter's own issue beliefs, would be unlikely to change his placement of the parties or himself on the left–right spectrum. Just under three out of four of those who associated the terms with the parties gave answers at this level (or about 14 out of 100 of the entire electorate).

A third level of interpretation was provided by respondents who seemed unable to give any meaning to the concepts other than a purely nominal

Table 5.1.4 Levels of interpretation of left–right concepts

Fully elaborated dynamic interpretation	2%
Partially elaborated static interpretation	14
Nominal interpretation	4
Minimal recognition	20
No recognition	60
	100%

one. They had learned to know which term was linked with which party – but nothing more. In all, nearly one in four of our respondents who said they thought of the parties as being to the left or to the right could offer only an empty, nominal interpretation of this sort.

By adding to these three levels of ideological sophistication the two remaining categories into which the electorate can be placed – those who can at least connect the terms left and right correctly with the parties when obliged to do so and those who cannot – we summarize in Table 5.1.4 the ideological awareness of the mass public. Even with full allowance for the approximate nature of the methods leading to this distribution, we must regard it as a remarkable profile of popular acceptance – or rather non-acceptance – of the left–right framework.

From all that has been said, it is clear that the theory that a voter chooses among parties on the basis of their distance from his own position along a left–right spectrum is very far from describing how the great bulk of British electors make their choice. The assumption that people order their preferences for the parties according to the parties' distance from their own position is contradicted by the preferences expressed by many of our respondents. The assumption that voters see themselves or the parties on a left–right dimension at all is contradicted by our evidence on the slightness of the role that the words left and right play in the political thought of the British mass public. A thin layer of the most ideologically aware does seem to use left and right to organize their views about where they and the parties stand on current issues. But such people are vastly outnumbered by those who have more impoverished and static interpretations of the concepts. And a large majority of the electorate apparently give left and right no political meaning at all.

It follows from this that the classical model of ideological distance offers little towards the explanation of British electoral trends. For a tiny minority, the model may render a useful account of partisan change. But electors who obeyed the assumptions of the basic left–right model, applied as a theory of electoral change, seemed virtually non-existent.

5.2 Policy alternatives and party choice in the 1979 election

Bo Sarlvik and Ivor Crewe

Our survey measures of voters' opinions on the policy alternatives in the 1979 election consist of a series of interview questions devised to record both the voters' own policy preferences and their perceptions of what the two major parties actually stood for. Each of the [six] questions contained two statements which comprised different policy alternatives and in some instances also suggested different ways of looking at a given issue. [The issues were: tax reductions vs. government services; the best way to tackle unemployment; how wages and salaries should be settled; trade union legislation; the EEC; and immigration and race relations.]

For most issues it was possible to formulate statements that could easily be identified with either a Conservative or a Labour point of view. A third statement expressing lack of concern – 'it doesn't matter much either way', or a phrase of similar meaning – was also included. The respondents were asked which one of the three statements came closest to their views. Respondents who agreed with one of the policy alternatives were asked: 'How strongly are you in favour of this statement: 1. very strongly, 2. fairly strongly, 3. mildly in favour?'. This question format makes it possible to array respondents on a seven-point scale [ranging from very strongly in favour of statement 1 to very strongly in favour of statement 2].

With the same question format, the respondent was then asked what the views of the Conservative and Labour parties were on the matter concerned. Using these responses we are thus able to locate each respondent's perceptions of the stands of the two major parties on the seven-point scale for each issue.

From Bo Sarlvik and Ivor Crewe, *Decade of Dealignment* (1983), Cambridge: Cambridge University Press, chapters 9 and 11.

186   MODELS OF PARTY CHOICE

The steps in the enquiry

(1) For a matter to become an issue in an election, it is a first requirement that the parties' policies are seen [by the electorate] to differ. We [therefore] begin with an exposition of the voters' views of what the parties stood for in 1979.

(2) In the next step of the enquiry, we will review the division of opinion on the main issues in the electorate and explore the relationships between the voters' policy preferences and their party choice.

(3) In the third step of the analysis we make use of our data both on the individual policy preferences and on the perceptions of the positions of the parties on the issues. Voters' opinions on the issues are defined in terms of the 'distances' between their own opinion positions and their perceptions of the parties' positions. We will thus be looking at the relationships between opinions and party choice from the individual voter's own point of view and in terms of his own appraisal of the choice situation.

(4) Finally, we shall explore how the salience and the importance of the issues to the individuals operate as weighting factors in the making of voting decisions.

The electoral choice – as seen by the voters

What did the parties stand for in the 1979 election? The data are set out in Table 5.2.1. For the sake of clarity, the table shows only the percentages of the voters who identified the parties with either side of the argument. With regard to three of the four economic policy choices, there was a near consensus in the electorate about the nature of the differences between the parties.

There was much less agreement about where the parties stood on incomes policy [and] we find a similar lack of agreement about the Conservatives' and Labour's attitudes towards the economic policies of the EEC.

[The table shows] that the differences between the parties did not stand out with equal clarity on all issues; there is always more or less room for different perceptions of party positions, and some voters simply do not know what one or both of the major parties stand for. This is not surprising, given that party positions are more ambiguous on some issues than on others, and that some issues attract more public attention than others. All the same, the parties did have easily recognised profiles on many of the most important policy issues and on other issues there emerges at least a distinctive tendency for the two parties to be associated with opposing policies.

Table 5.2.1 Voters' perceptions of the Conservative party's and Labour party's views on policy alternatives in the May 1979 election (%)

Policy alternatives	Conservative voters		Liberal voters		Labour voters		All respondents	
	Con. party view	Lab. party view	Con. party view	Lab. party view	Con. party view	Lab. party view	Con. party view	Lab. party view
Tax cuts vs. government services								
Cut taxes	66	11	76	8	72	12	68	12
Keep up government services	25	71	16	80	15	76	20	72
Tackling unemployment								
Allow companies to keep profits to create more jobs	86	4	83	6	73	13	78	8
For government to use tax money to create jobs	7	81	9	82	11	72	9	75
How wages and salaries should be settled								
Firm government guidelines	39	59	30	69	35	60	34	58
Leave it to employers and unions to settle	52	22	54	22	47	22	48	22
Stricter laws to regulate trade unions								
For stricter laws	92	9	86	12	83	22	86	15
Against stricter laws	1	79	4	71	4	60	4	69
EEC economic policies								
Britain should be more willing to go along with EEC economic policies	44	21	52	22	53	21	48	21
Britain should be readier to oppose EEC economic policies	33	49	29	49	23	55	28	49
Best way to improve race relations								
Stop further immigration	64	7	66	7	64	13	63	10
Tackle the problems of jobs and housing	19	45	13	46	13	53	16	46
Number of respondents	(728)	(728)	(212)	(212)	(583)	(583)	(1,871)	(1,871)

Note: Entries are the percentages of voters who thought that the views of the Conservative party and the Labour party, respectively, were closest to each of the two statements for each issue. The remainder up to 100% consists of respondents who didn't think the party favoured any of the alternatives or 'didn't know' what view the party had.

Source: In this and all subsequent tables data are from the BES May 1979 Election Survey.

The voters' views

Which side of the argument on each of these issues had most support in the electorate? The basic data are given in Table 5.2.2 which sets out the distribution of opinions on each of the six policy issues within the electoral bases of the three main parties as well as in the electorate as a whole. The overall pattern in this table suggests that Conservative and Labour voters alike sided with their own party's stand more often than did the supporters of other parties – but not overwhelmingly so and with noteworthy exceptions. There were strong electoral majorities in support of the Conservative view on the best ways of tackling unemployment and creating more jobs, and also on the need for stricter trade union legislation. On these issues Conservative voters endorsed their party's view with near unanimity. Labour voters were fairly evenly divided on both issues, but a

Table 5.2.2 Voters' views on policy alternatives at the May 1979 election (in %)

Policy alternatives	Conservative voters	Liberal voters	Labour voters	All respondents
Tax cuts vs. government services				
Cut taxes	36	20	13	25
Keep up government services	51	69	77	62
Tackling unemployment				
Allow companies to keep profits and to create more jobs	81	66	41	63
Government to use tax money to create jobs	11	13	37	22
How wages and salaries should be settled				
Firm government guidelines	36	45	37	37
Leave it to employer and unions to settle	53	41	51	50
Stricter laws to regulate trade unions				
For stricter laws	90	71	47	70
Against stricter laws	5	15	32	17
EEC economic policies				
Britain should be more willing to go along with the economic policies of other countries in EEC	26	17	15	20
Britain should be readier to oppose EEC economic policies	58	65	66	60
Best way to improve race relations				
Stop further immigration	55	50	49	51
Tackle problems of jobs and housing	33	38	39	36

Note: The table shows, for each interview question, the percentage in favour of each of the alternatives offered; the balance to 100% consists of respondents who have no preference for or do not support either alternative, or have given a 'don't know' answer.

POLICY ALTERNATIVES AND PARTY CHOICE, 1979   *189*

slight plurality actually came out in favour of the Conservatives' policies. When it came to choosing between tax reduction or government services, on the other hand, the majority of the electorate gave priority to public services. On that issue it was the Labour voters who showed very strong support for their party's viewpoint, and even among Conservative voters the balance of opinion was in favour of public services rather than tax reductions. On incomes policy, the EEC, and race relations, the electorate was clearly divided, but not along the expected party lines.

We give [in the first column of Table 5.2.5 below] correlation coefficients that indicate the strength of the relationship between voting for the three main parties and the voters' positions on the six seven-point scales of opinion on policy issues. For comparison we have included also two [other] policy issues, nationalisation and social services (marked with asterisks). As can be seen from these coefficients, opinions on trade union legislation are nearly as strongly correlated with voting as are the voters' opinions on nationalisation. The questions concerning social services and benefits, the best way to create more jobs, and tax reductions form a second group: the correlations with voting are, by comparison, only moderately strong. For the three remaining issues (EEC, race relations and incomes policy), only weak relationships, or none at all, can be discerned.

Voters' opinions, perceptions of party positions and party choice

If the emphasis of our enquiry [is on] accounting for the way people vote in an election, we need to look at the voters' opinions in relation to their own perceptions of what the parties actually stood for.

The voter who can see no difference between the major parties on a particular issue is obviously not facing the same choice as a voter who thinks that their policies differ. Likewise, two voters who both wish to support the same policy may have different perceptions of which party is in favour of that policy and therefore come to support different parties.

As will be recalled, our measures of opinions and perceptions of the parties' positions are such that the individual has indicated both his own view and the position he thinks the two major parties occupy on seven-point scales. We have made use of [these scales] for two purposes. Firstly, we have constructed a classification which represents the individuals' perceptions of the parties' positions relative to each other. The classification was constructed so as to distinguish between voters who placed Labour 'to the left' of the Conservatives and those who placed Labour 'to the right' of the Conservatives on the scale.

Our second classification pertains to the degree of proximity between an individual's own view and the position on the scale which he has given to

190 MODELS OF PARTY CHOICE

each of the parties. For each of the issues, we obtain one category of voters who have placed themselves closest to Labour on the scale and another who placed themselves closest to the Conservatives. We assume that, given the choice, the individual will prefer the party policy that he perceives to be closest to his own view on the relevant scale. The classification is based entirely on the individual's own understanding of the choice he faces [even if he is objectively wrong].

Table 5.2.3 shows how Conservative, Liberal and Labour voters perceived the distances between their own opinion positions and the stands of the two major parties. It is instructive to compare this table with the

Table 5.2.3 Party vote and perceived distance to party positions on policy alternatives (in %)

	Party voted for in 1979		
Policy issue	Conservatives	Liberals	Labour
Tax cuts vs. government services			
Closest to Labour	29	54	65
Closest to Conservatives	44	27	11
Tackling unemployment			
Closest to Labour	8	18	40
Closest to Conservatives	77	55	29
How wages and salaries should be settled			
Closest to Labour	14	30	42
Closest to Conservatives	60	41	26
Stricter laws to regulate trade unions			
Closest to Labour	5	21	41
Closest to Conservatives	82	59	28
EEC economic policies			
Closest to Labour	22	37	45
Closest to Conservatives	38	29	15
Best way to improve race relations			
Closest to Labour	18	30	35
Closest to Conservatives	49	38	31
Social services and benefits			
Closest to Labour	11	28	46
Closest to Conservatives	65	45	22
Nationalisation			
Closest to Labour	3	13	34
Closest to Conservatives	83	54	30

Note: This table comprises only voters who voted for one of the three main parties. The table shows, for each party, the percentage of voters who placed themselves closest to the perceived positions of the Labour party and the Conservative party, respectively, on each of the 'policy scales'. The remainder to 100% for the issue concerned consists of voters who could not place both of the parties, or were at the same distance to both parties, or had no opinion on the issue.

opinion distributions in Table 5.2.2. We found in Table 5.2.2 that, on most issues, there were substantial proportions of Conservative and Labour voters whose views differed from their parties' official policies. Table 5.2.3 not only confirms this but also demonstrates that many voters clearly recognised that they did not wholly agree with the policies of their parties.

In some instances the picture changes significantly when the voter's perceptions of party positions are taken into account. These changes have mainly to do with divisions of opinions among Labour voters. Thus we now find that Labour voters were definitely more likely to be closer to the Labour party than to the Conservative party with regard to the best way of tackling unemployment, incomes policy and trade union legislation. In Table 5.2.2 the opposite appeared to be the case. To some extent, and notably in the case of incomes policy, the explanation is that some voters had actually reversed the parties' positions in their own perceptions. A less drastic but also important factor is that some Labour voters have placed themselves and their party at or near the midpoint of the seven-point scale, whilst projecting the Conservatives' position towards the extreme right on the scale. They did not exactly endorse their party's view, but were nevertheless nearer to Labour than to the Conservatives, or equidistant from the two.

On most of the policy issues Conservative voters sided more often with their party's view than Labour voters did with theirs. We have summarised the data by calculating the average proportion of respondents who were closest to the Conservative and Labour parties, respectively, on all of the eight issues taken together. On average, as is shown [in Table 5.2.4], nearly two out of three (62 per cent) of Conservative voters sided with their own party, whereas this was true for only 44 per cent of Labour voters. In the electorate as a whole, an average of 43 per cent were closest to the Conservatives' positions, whereas 27 per cent were closest to Labour's. The difference is as good an indicator as any of the strength of the Conservatives' appeal in the 1979 election.

The relationship to voting

Measures of perceived 'distances to parties' yield stronger relationships to voting behaviour than respondents' actual opinion positions. The effect is summarised in Table 5.2.5. The table gives three sets of correlation coefficients for the relationship between issue opinions and voting for either of the three main parties. The first two columns comprise the entire sample and contain the coefficients for opinions measured by scale positions and opinions measured by distances to parties, respectively. The third column includes only those respondents who placed the Labour party 'to the left' of the Conservatives on the issue concerned.

192 MODELS OF PARTY CHOICE

Table 5.2.4 Average percentages of voters who were closest to the Conservative and Labour parties on eight policy issues (in %)

Voters' policy opinions	Conservative voters	Liberal voters	Labour voters	All respondents
Closest to Conservatives	62	44	24	43
Closest to Labour	14	29	44	27

Table 5.2.5 The relation of opinions on policy issues to voting for the three main parties

	Correlation coefficients[1]		
Policy issue	Opinion positions	Distances to parties	Left/right perceptions of parties: Distances to parties:[2]
*1. Nationalisation	0.45	0.48	0.52
2. Stricter laws to regulate trade unions	0.41	0.47	0.52
3. Tackling unemployment/ creating jobs	0.35	0.42	0.46
*4. Social services and benefits	0.28	0.39	0.44
5. Tax cuts vs. government services	0.25	0.33	0.40
6. How wages and salaries should be settled	0.00	0.32	0.34
7. EEC economic policies	0.11	0.24	0.33
8. Best way to improve race relations	0.07	0.19	0.23

Notes:
1. Correlations in this and subsequent tables are measured by Kendall's tau-b coefficients and are based on the three party vote.
2. As explained in the text, this column includes only respondents who placed Labour 'to the left' of the Conservatives on the appropriate policy scale.

As the table shows, all relationships are strengthened when opinions are measured by distances to parties rather than by the original scales of opinion positions. The effect is striking in the case of opinions on incomes policy. Fairly substantial correlations with voting also come to light for opinions on the EEC and race relations.

Among voters who perceived Labour as occupying a position 'to the left' of the Conservatives on a policy issue, the strength of the relationship between opinions and voting is consistently stronger, as is shown by the third column in the table. In most instances, the apparent explanation is that these are the voters with the best grasp of the policy issue concerned. We have, in effect, excluded a category of persons many of whom had little

POLICY ALTERNATIVES AND PARTY CHOICE, 1979 *193*

knowledge about the political context of the issue and possibly little interest in the matter.

With the exception of incomes policy, the rank ordering of the issues with regard to the correlation coefficients comes out as almost exactly the same, irrespective of how the relationship between opinions and voting is measured. If we take this connection between individuals' opinions and their voting as our criterion on which to judge the relative importance of the issues in the election, these data yield therefore a distinctive rank ordering of the issues. Nationalisation and stricter laws to regulate the trade unions emerge again as the issues most strongly connected with party choice in 1979. A second group is formed by the questions about the best strategy to tackle unemployment and create new jobs, social services, and the choice between tax reductions and maintaining the standard of government services. Opinions on incomes policy and the EEC show comparatively weaker correlations to voting even when opinions are measured by 'distances to parties'. Finally, race relations and immigration come at the bottom of the list in this rank-ordering.

The voters' views on the importance of the issues

All issues are not equally important to all voters. Individuals do their own weighting of the matters that bear upon their voting decisions. No analysis model could replicate all the variations in these individual voting decisions. [But] if voters' ratings of the importance of the various questions on the political agenda affect their voting decisions, one would expect a stronger relationship between issue opinions and voting among those who consider a given issue important than among those who are less concerned.

Those interviewed were asked how important they rated [each issue] at the time when they 'were deciding about voting'. Table 5.2.6 shows the percentages of voters who rated each of the policy issues as 'extremely important' and also the percentages who considered it either 'extremely' or 'fairly important'. In general there is only a feeble relationship between the proportion rating an issue as 'extremely important' and the strength of the correlation between opinions and voting. The issues are ordered in the table according to the strength of that correlation, and it is readily apparent that a rank ordering with regard to ratings of importance would look quite different. For example, the nationalisation issue, which showed a strong correlation with party choice, is rated as 'extremely important' by only 19 per cent of voters.

It is all the more noteworthy that individuals' ratings of the importance of an issue emerge as a powerful mediating (or intervening) factor when we look at the relationships between opinions and voting for each policy issue separately. As can be seen from the columns on the left side of Table 5.2.6,

Table 5.2.6 Opinions on policy issues, rating of the importance of issues, and party vote

| Issues | Correlation of issue opinion to vote | | | | Per cent considering the issue 'extremely' important | Per cent considering the issue either 'extremely' or 'fairly' important |
| | Issue rated as: | | | | | |
	Extremely important	Fairly important	Not very important	All respondents		
Policy alternatives						
1. Nationalisation	0.60	0.55	0.38	0.48	19	51
2. Stricter laws to regulate trade unions	0.62	0.47	0.38	0.47	23	63
3. Tackling unemployment	0.46	0.41	0.46	0.42	33	71
4. Social services	0.51	0.41	0.36	0.39	23	63
5. Tax cuts vs. government services	0.44	0.33	0.25	0.33	33	78
6. How wages and salaries should be settled	0.42	0.37	0.28	0.32	25	69
7. EEC economic policies	0.47	0.31	0.11	0.24	17	52
8. Best way to improve race relations	0.36	0.24	0.14	0.19	14	46

POLICY ALTERNATIVES AND PARTY CHOICE, 1979 *195*

the strength of the correlations between opinions and voting increases regularly with increases in the importance rating for all of the issues but one. In most instances the increase is quite sharp. Opinions on nationalisation, for example, show a rise from 0.38 to 0.60 from the lowest to the highest level of importance ratings, and for opinions on tax reduction there is an increase from 0.25 to 0.44. Among the voters who rate an issue extremely important, we find substantial correlations in all instances.

We have thus found that the correlation between voting and opinions on a political issue, almost without exception, increases with increasing rating of the importance of that issue. Yet, when comparing correlations and importance ratings in the entire sample for several issues, we found only a slight tendency for issues with high importance ratings to show comparatively high correlations between voting and opinions. Why is that? It is likely that individuals, when they answered the importance rating questions, were often thinking of how much attention a particular issue attracted during the campaign or how heated the debate between the parties had been. We have thus measured 'importance' in the sense of *saliency*. But a party's position on an issue can also be more or less important in the sense that it is seen as a more or less *decisive reason* for voting for it or not voting for it, independently of whether the issue was seen to play a prominent role in the campaign. To take nationalisation as an example, no major nationalisation proposal was put forward in the election campaign, and this may be the reason why not many voters thought it was a very important issue at the time when they made their voting decisions. But someone who was strongly opposed to nationalisation would, nevertheless, be comparatively unlikely to consider voting for Labour, and we will therefore find a strong correlation between issue opinions and voting at all levels of salience rating. The degree of 'decisiveness' will be different for different issues. The salience of an issue to individuals will then have the function of a weight factor: it will amplify the correlation between opinions and voting among the voters for whom the issue is salient. When the level of salience for a particular issue is high in the electorate as a whole, the correlation between opinions and voting with regard to that particular issue will thus become higher *than it otherwise would have been* for that issue – but not necessarily higher than the correlation for a less salient issue; this would depend on the relative 'decisiveness' of the issues concerned.

Opinions on the issues and party choice – the overall account

The question naturally arises whether one could not account for individuals' voting decisions by somehow summing each individual's views across the entire array of opinion measures. Rather than looking at the relation between opinions and voting on each issue taken separately, we would then be in a position to determine the strength of the relationship between voting and the individual's opinions on all of the issues taken together.

If we do this, we would in a sense replicate the overall judgement made by the voter when he made his voting decision. Of course, we cannot observe directly how the individual was summing up his reasons for liking and disliking each of the parties. What we can do is sum up the opinions he has expressed on the many political issues which are known to bear upon many voters' party choices and then establish (using some 'counting rule') whether he is most likely to vote Conservative, Liberal or Labour. Needless to say, it cannot be assumed that all individuals actually carry out such calculations for themselves as a deliberate thought exercise. [But] whilst it would be unrealistic to imagine that individuals in general decide their party choices in the style of calculating machines, it would be a great deal more unrealistic to assume that they thoughtlessly repeat their party choices from election to election without any regard to their experiences of governmental actions or the arguments in the political arena.

The analysis model

The statistical technique we will employ is multiple regression. The essence of our multiple regression model is that it 'predicts' individuals' party choices by summing up their responses to a number of interview questions which are treated as 'predicting' measures of opinions.

The underlying summation model is bound to be based on the 'average effect' of each of the issue opinions in determining individuals' decisions. It does not portray the entire variety of 'counting rules' that individuals would apply if they were to sum up their positions across a number of issues through analogous, individual calculations; individual variations could emerge only as 'errors' in our prediction. As a further caveat, the model presumes what we know is only partially true: namely that issue opinions are the causes and the individuals' party choices are the result.

Our analysis model also requires that voting, like the opinion measures, be treated as a scale of numerical values for Conservative, Liberal and Labour voting, in that order. We are, in effect, presuming that individuals perceived the three parties as being positioned on a scale, with the main adversaries – the Conservatives and Labour – at a long distance from each other and with the Liberals halfway between them. In the logic of the analysis model, individuals will be predicted to vote Liberal if they have neither strongly Conservative nor strongly Labour opinions on many issues, or if they combine pro-Conservative views on some issues with pro-Labour views on about as many other issues.

POLICY ALTERNATIVES AND PARTY CHOICE, 1979

The model applied
Our enquiry comprises three broad groups of opinion measurements: one is concerned with the voters' views on the Conservatives' and Labour's performances in office when it comes to handling the economic problems the country is facing; the second was intended to record electoral responses to societal change; and the third was concerned with the main policy alternatives that the parties offered in the 1979 election. The interview questions in these groups are different with regard to format but to some extent the groups are overlapping in the sense that questions in different groups elicit opinions on the same issues from different viewpoints. How strong is the joint relationship between the political opinions recorded in each of these groups and party choice? And how far can all of these measurements, when taken together, account for voting in that election? The answers are given in the form of multiple correlation coefficients in Table 5.2.7.

The bottom row of the table shows that the entire array of opinion measures has a multiple correlation of 0.77 with party choice. This constitutes a far greater 'explanatory power' than could have been achieved using any single opinion measure. It is also greater than the multiple correlations for each of the three groups of questions taken separately, as is shown by the table.

A multiple correlation of 0.77 for the relationship between a set of opinion measures and voting behaviour is undoubtedly very reassuring [and] this lends credence to the two basic assumptions in this analysis: that voting decisions can be realistically described by a model that summarises individuals' opinions across several aspects of politics, and that the matters which bear upon most individuals' overall judgements of the parties can be adequately represented by a parsimonious set of interview questions about the current issues in party politics. In short, the model has done very well.

Table 5.2.7 Multiple correlations between groups of opinion measures and voting in the 1979 election

Group of opinion measures	Multiple correlation (R) between voting and each group of opinion	Explained proportion of the variance (R^2)
Assessment of the Conservatives' and Labour's ability to handle economic problems: strikes, unemployment, prices	0.69	0.48
Responses to change: 'left/right' and 'social welfare' attitude dimensions	0.57	0.32
Policy alternatives in the 1979 election	0.68	0.46
All opinion measures	0.77	0.59

5.3 Assessing the rise of issue voting in British elections since 1964

Mark N. Franklin

One of the best substantiated findings of recent voting studies is the decline in the power of social class to explain voting choice. [But] the decline of class voting leaves important questions unanswered. In particular, if class has declined as a determinant of partisanship, what, if anything, has taken its place?

It seems reasonable to hypothesize that the decline of class voting will have opened the way, at least to a limited extent, for a rise in issue voting to take place, and the purpose of the present paper is to investigate this hypothesis.

Certainly, on the basis of casual observation, issues do seem to have increased in importance in recent years; and respondents to post-election surveys now appear better informed about political issues than they did 20 years ago. Asked to name the important issues that helped them decide how to vote, fewer than 6 per cent of respondents to a series of surveys conducted following recent elections were unable to name a second issue. Twenty years ago, 40 per cent of respondents were unable to name as many as two important questions facing the country.

The data

The data for this study come from [the BES] surveys of the British electorate, conducted following the General Elections of 1964, 1966, 1970, 1974, and 1979. From each of these surveys, in addition to measures of party identification and voting choice, five variables were chosen as being

From Mark N. Franklin, 'Assessing the rise of issue voting in British elections since 1964', *Electoral Studies* (1985), vol. 4, pp. 36–55.

representative of different social influences connected with the concept of class voting, and a number of variables representing the importance of issues. Each of the five [class variables] serves as an indicator for the general direction of political influences that individuals can be expected to experience. During childhood they will have been influenced by the political atmosphere in the home and neighbourhood (indicated by parents' party and parents' class). During adulthood they will have been affected by their neighbours at home and their colleagues at work (indicated by type of housing, occupation and union membership).

At the time of writing [the BES] survey of the 1983 General Election is unavailable for secondary analysis. However to verify as far as possible the continuity of trends established in previous years a seventh dataset was also analysed, deriving from pre-election and election day surveys conducted by the Gallup Organization in 1983. These data are in many ways not comparable to the data available for other elections, and so will be used sparingly in the investigation that follows.

In contrast to previous practice, two dependent variables have been employed. One of these, voting choice, is derived by dichotomizing supporters of the Labour party against the rest. The other is a measure of party identification. Again this was dichotomized to distinguish supporters of the Labour party from others. All subsequent analyses reported in this paper exclude non-voters but include minor party voters, along with those who voted Conservative or Labour.

The problem of issue voting

The study of issue voting is complicated by a number of factors. In particular, it is not at all clear to what extent issue preferences are independent of party identification. On the contrary, [there is] considerable evidence that issue preferences are mediated by party preference. The classic solution to this problem is to look at the issue preferences of those members of the electorate who switched [in consecutive elections] from support of one party to support of another [since] 'switchers' are those least likely to have their issue preferences contaminated by longstanding party identification. This procedure does not permit the sort of multivariate analysis which is necessary in order to disambiguate the effects of issue preferences from those of class and social milieu. For the latter purpose it is necessary to be able to build a causal model in which the effects of issue preferences are measured for the whole electorate and not just those who switched parties.

The measurement of issue preferences is itself a vexed question. [But] an index can be constructed measuring the extent of issue-based support for any political party by establishing, for each of a number of issues, the

200 MODELS OF PARTY CHOICE

extent to which each respondent considers it a salient issue, the position he takes on that issue, and the identity of the party (if any) which he views as taking the same position. Issue-based preference for a party could then be calculated by taking a simple sum of the number of times that a party is preferred in regard to important issues.

Unfortunately, changes in questionnaire design over the years mean that these three things cannot be established in precisely the same manner for each of the elections considered here. Whether my indices of issue-based party support are in fact comparable from year to year is a question that cannot easily be resolved; but the fact that the measures are almost completely identical for the two elections of 1966 and 1970, and for the three elections of 1974 and 1979, gives some firm ground upon which to build in considering whether any trends discerned are at least plausible.

The rise of issue voting in British elections

At the individual level, viewed in a simple-minded fashion in terms of voting in accord with issue-based party preferences, it is clear that issue voting increased between 1964 and 1983. If the index of issue-based preference for the Labour party is correlated with Labour voting in 1964 and 1983, the Pearsonian correlation increases from 0.418 in 1964 to 0.771 in 1983. The correlation of the corresponding Conservative index with Conservative voting increased even more, from 0.328 to 0.797, so that by 1983 issue-based preference was explaining some 63 per cent of the variance in Conservative voting. However, these studies at the extreme ends of the time period being considered are not comparable in a number of respects. Not only were the data collected for different purposes and at different times in relation to the elections concerned but they are also subject to bias because different parties gained most votes. A better match for 1964 is February 1974, in which the corresponding correlation was 0.713.

But these perspectives on issue voting are much too simple to be of much use. In the first place, they skirt the question of whether issue-based preferences reflect rather than cause a prior decision on how to vote, and in the second place (rather more subtly) they ignore the fact that issue-based preferences may themselves be partial consequences of prior influences (for example, from early socialization or social status).

Towards a model of issue-based voting in British elections

Goldberg (1966) [analysing American data] proposed a model of class and issue voting that can be used here as a particularly suitable starting point. It

ASSESSING THE RISE OF ISSUE VOTING SINCE 1964

made issue preferences dependent in part on party identification which was in turn dependent on class and socializing influences. The model attempts to overcome the first problem by separating out the vote decision from party identification and positing that the former is partially determined by political attitudes, which in turn are partially determined by party identification.

Applied to British voting data from the elections of 1964 to 1979 this model [Model A] does quite well. Small but sometimes statistically significant influences from respondent's social class both to respondent's attitudes, and also to his voting choice are found. These influences are at their greatest in the election of 1966, whose coefficients are those illustrated in Figure 5.3.1. The coefficients are beta weights derived from multiple regression analysis which treats each variable (except Parents' Social Class) as dependent in turn on all those variables prior in causal sequence.

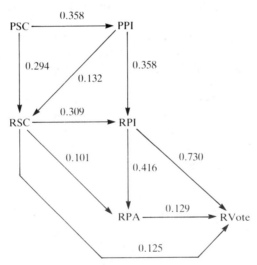

Table of symbols:
PSC   Parents' Social Class
PPI   Parents' Party Identification
RSC   Respondent's Social Class
RPI   Respondent's Party Identification
RPA   Respondent's Political Attitudes
RVote Respondent's Voting Choice

Figure 5.3.1 A tentative model of British voting behaviour, with additional paths discovered empirically (RSC to RPA and RSC to RVote) and coefficients for all voters, 1966

202 MODELS OF PARTY CHOICE

The illustration shows that the direct effects of Respondent's Political Attitudes on voting choice was 0.129, only some 13 per cent of the total effect on 1966 voting choice, most of which came from party identification (see Table 5.3.1). Moreover, the coefficients on the paths leading to Respondent's Political Attitudes indicate that this variable was itself largely determined by prior influences $(0.101 + 0.416 = 0.517)$. In 1966, it seems, voters' perceptions of party stances were largely coloured by their own class and especially by their party identification. Thus any balanced view of the independent contribution of issue preferences to voting choice has to subtract transmitted influences of some 7 per cent (the product of 0.101×0.129 plus the product of 0.416×0.129). Table 5.3.1 summarizes the gross and net effects of issue-based party preferences on voting choice estimated on the basis of Model A, for all years 1964 to 1983, and shows that on the basis of this model, far from an increase in issue voting between 1964 and 1979, what is found is negligible issue voting at any time.

But is Model A a plausible model of British voting behaviour? In the American context, the relatively small influence of Respondent's Party Identification on voting choice together with the relatively large direct effect of attitudes means that any reciprocal causation between attitudes and identification would only make a modest difference to the overall effect of attitudes on voting choice. But in the British context the reverse is the case, and even a modest effect of attitudes on party identification would make a very large relative difference to the apparent overall effect of attitudes.

[How can these reciprocal effects be measured?] If advantage is taken of the fact that any influence of Parents' Party Identification on Respondent's Attitudes must (according to my model) arise indirectly through Respondent's Social Class or Respondent's Party Identification, then it is possible to arrive at an algebraic result for the effect of Respondent's Party Identification on his attitudes and in the other direction.

Table 5.3.1 Gross and net effects of political attitudes on voting choice estimated from Model A for 1964–83

	1964	1966	1970	1974*	1979	1983
Direct effects of RPA (a)	0.086	0.129	0.128	0.149	0.244	–
Effects of RSC on RPA (b)	0.067	0.101	0.025	0.108	0.111	–
Effects of RPI on RPA (c)	0.412	0.416	0.405	0.677	0.654	–
Transmitted (ab + ac) (d)	0.041	0.067	0.055	0.117	0.187	–
Net effects (a − d) (e)	0.045	0.062	0.073	0.032	0.057	(0.061)

Note: Symbols as in Model A.

*Figures for 1974 are averages of those obtained for each of the two election studies conducted in that year.

(–) Calculations for 1983 not comparable because of different question formats and different available variables.

Model B [which takes account of these reciprocal effects] is presented in Figure 5.3.2 with coefficients derived from the election of 1970. The first thing to notice about this model is that, as suggested above, the indirect effects of even quite modest influences on party identification from political attitudes can be considerable. Table 5.3.2 estimates these effects, and then calculates the net effects of attitudes in the same manner as was done in Table 5.3.1. As can be seen, Model B produces net attitude effects that are quite respectable, and even shows a modest rate of increase over the period. But even this model may be defective in at least one important respect. A single measure of political attitudes does not allow for the fact that disenchantment with the potential of one political party may not be matched by enchantment with the potential of the other. Respondents may have issue-based preferences for both political parties at the same time, or for neither. In particular the latter possibility would appear to be one for which allowance should be made when respondents have the option of voting for a party other than Conservative or Labour; and my analyses do include minor party voters even though I have not estimated their issue preferences.

With these considerations in mind, Figure 5.3.3 presents Model C which differs from Model B in providing two measures of issue-based party

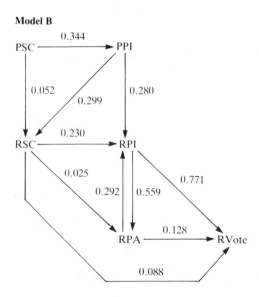

Note: Symbols as for Fig. 5.3.1.

Figure 5.3.2 A second tentative model of British voting behaviour with reciprocal causation between Party Identification and Political Attitudes, and coefficients for all voters, 1970

Table 5.3.2 Gross and net effects of political attitudes on voting choice, both direct and indirect, estimated from Model B for 1964–83

	1964	1966	1970	1974*	1979	1983
Direct effects of RPA (a)	0.086	0.129	0.128	0.149	0.244	–
Indirect via RPI (b)	0.219	0.215	0.225	0.277	0.282	–
Total effects (a + b) (c)	0.305	0.344	0.353	0.426	0.525	–
Includes effects ** (d)	0.055	0.087	0.081	0.151	0.241	–
Net effects (c – d) (e)	0.250	0.257	0.272	0.276	0.284	(0.303)

Note: Symbols as in Model A.

(–) Coefficients for 1983 non-comparable.

* Average of effects in two 1974 elections.
** Sum of paths RSC, RPA, RVote + RPI, RPA, RVote + RSC, RPA, RPI, RVote.

preference. So in this model, Respondent's Political Attitudes have been recast as Respondent Pro-Labour and Respondent Pro-Conservative, and the layout has been somewhat re-arranged in order to accommodate the extra linkages. The model does not perform much better than Model B in terms of explaining variance in voting choice. Largely because of the powerful impact of party identification, both models explain some 76 per cent of the variance in 1970, with the more complex model explaining an additional half of one percentage point. However, the additional paths

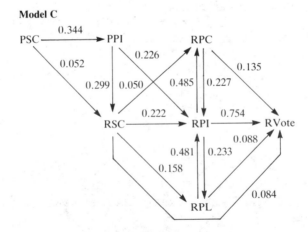

Note: Symbols as for Fig. 5.3.1 except
RPC = Respondent Pro-Conservative on issues
RPL = Respondent Pro-Labour on issues

Figure 5.3.3 Proposed model of British voting behaviour with reciprocal causation and dual attitude measurement, and with coefficients for all voters, 1970

ASSESSING THE RISE OF ISSUE VOTING SINCE 1964 *205*

provided for the indirect effects of issue-based preferences can make a lot of difference to the apparent impact of the attitude variables, and do so especially from 1970 onwards, as can be seen in Table 5.3.3 which provides the same information as did Table 5.3.2, but for the more elaborate Model C.

In this table for the first time a progressive increase can be seen in the total effect of issues, by 5 per cent or more per general election, from a low of 0.389 in 1964 to a high of 0.632 in 1979. However, the proportion of this total effect which is properly attributable back to class and party identification because of the dominant influence of these characteristics on issue perceptions also varies from year to year, in such a way as to give greater net effects of issues in 1970 than in any later year. But the major implication of Table 5.3.3 is that issue voting rose suddenly between 1966 and 1970, with smaller fluctuations thereafter.

Class constraints on issue voting

Whatever one may feel about the propriety of algebraic manipulation of regression coefficients in order to untangle the problem of reciprocal causation between political attitudes and party identification, it is virtually certain that some reciprocal causation does take place. In Model C it is found to be very consistent from election to election, with party identification having about twice the impact on issue-based party preference that the latter has on party identification. Even if for some reason the effect of

Table 5.3.3 Gross and net effects of political attitudes on voting choice, both direct and indirect, estimated from Model C for 1964 to 1983

	1964	1966	1970	1974*	1979	1983
Direct effects of RPC + RPL (a)	0.111	0.170	0.223	0.249	0.280	–
Indirect effects via RPI (b)	0.278	0.271	0.350	0.326	0.352	–
Total effects of RPC + RPL (c)	0.389	0.441	0.573	0.575	0.632	–
Prior effects included ** (d)	0.134	0.167	0.156	0.230	0.247	–
Net effects of issues (e)	0.256	0.274	0.417	0.345	0.385	(0.410)
Percent of all effects***	25.8	26.7	39.1	36.3	40.1	(39.6)

Note: Symbols as in Model C.

(–) Calculations for 1983 non-comparable.

   * Average effects of two 1974 elections.
  ** Using the same logic as described in note **to Table 5.3.2.
*** Total effects of all variables taken together varied slightly, from 0.959 in 1979 to 1.067 in 1970. These differences corresponded to differences in variance explained running from 69.3 per cent to 76.2 per cent in the same two studies. The final row attempts to take account of these overall variations by looking at the extent to which issues contribute to the total of all effects on voting choice.

issues on party identification is being overestimated, it is implausible that this effect should be less than half what has been estimated, in which case, feeding through the indirect paths in Model C and adding the direct effects of issues will still give a low of 0.250 and a high of 0.391 in total effect of issues before deduction of (much reduced) transmitted effects. At any level of indirect effects, the general pattern observed in Table 5.3.3 seems likely to hold good because it is dominated by the direct effects of issue-based preferences. Indirect effects remained remarkably constant throughout the period, with a single step up in 1970 (row b).

The fact that this pattern of rise and fall in the effects of issue voting roughly reciprocates the pattern of fall and rise in the corrected effects of class voting (Franklin, 1982) is suggestive of a possible relationship between issue-based voting choice and class-structured voting, where the level of one is constrained by the level of the other, so that when class voting is high issue voting is necessarily low, and the reverse is also true (see Figure 5.3.4).

But while the correspondence shown in Figure 5.3.4 is striking, it must be emphasized that both of the trends depicted there are highly corrected for contaminating influences. [Nonetheless] it can certainly be said that the degree of correspondence adds verisimilitude to the procedures, and also suggests that class voting and issue voting are indeed inversely related.

Conclusions

It would be comforting to be able to conclude that British voting behaviour became more rather than less rational over the decade from 1964 to 1974, as issue voting rose to fill the vacuum left by a decline in the class-structuring of voting choice; but while the evidence that has been presented in this paper is consistent with such a conclusion, it does not lead inevitably to it. Conditions have been established that are necessary for an increase in rational voting behaviour, but not sufficient for such an increase.

My less than definitive findings arise from two deficiencies in the analysis. In the first place, algebraic manipulation of causal paths is not an altogether satisfactory means of resolving problems in reciprocal causation. In the second place, I have not even addressed the question of whether there might be reciprocal causation involved in the relationships between party identification and voting choice, and between political attitudes and voting choice. Any such reciprocity would attenuate the effects of political attitudes which have been measured, though they would be unlikely to change the direction of the trends established unless they were so strong as to completely remove the effects of issues.

Finally, concern was expressed as to the comparability of the measures

ASSESSING THE RISE OF ISSUE VOTING SINCE 1964   207

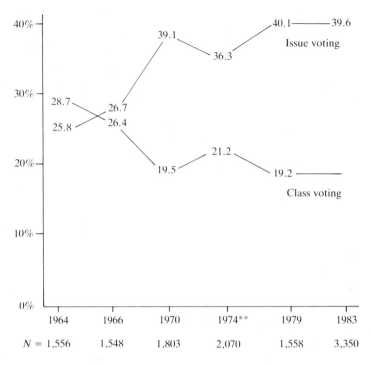

Notes:
*Decline of class voting taken from Franklin (1982) Fig. 10 which contains no coefficients for 1983. Increase in issue voting taken from this paper, Table 5.3.3, bottom row.
**Average of two elections for 1974.

Figure 5.3.4 Correspondence between change in percentage effects of issues from Model C with changes in class structuring of voting choice from other research

of issue-based party preference between 1964 and 1983. However, the major change detected occurred between two elections (1966 and 1970) for which problems of comparability do not arise, and the fit between this finding and previous research (Franklin, 1982) adds plausibility to a supposition that comparability problems have not affected any of the findings reported here.

What has certainly been established in this article is that different models of issue voting give rise to different implications for the extent and direction of change in issue voting. The model that has been considered to be most plausible shows issue voting to have increased in step with the decline in class voting.

5.4 Policy and ideology in the 1983 general election

Anthony Heath,
Roger Jowell and
John Curtice

Policies

Party policy, particularly Labour party policy, has been singled out by many commentators as an explanation of political success or failure. It has been argued that Labour had unpopular policies in 1979, failed to learn the lessons of defeat, and so went down to even worse defeat in 1983. Similarly, whereas the Conservatives may have had unpopular policies on unemployment, they more than made up for this by their popularity on other important issues of the day. This line of argument has been suggested as an explanation not only for the Labour defeat in 1983 but also for the long-run decline of Labour and the rise of the Liberals and the Alliance.

[However] the evidence we present here suggests that, had people voted according to the detailed stances of each party on the most important issues of the day, Labour would not in fact have gone down to defeat at all. Its policies on the important issues were not nearly so unpopular as commentators have imagined. As we shall show, if voters had decided between the parties according to their policy preferences, there would actually have been a dead heat between Conservative and Labour.

The consumer theory of voting
The view that election results are determined by the detailed stands which the competing parties take on the issues of the day has become the vogue in recent years. This vogue has been largely a result of the failure of the previous orthodoxy (the 'expressive' theory of voting) to account for the electoral changes of the 1970s. The old orthodoxy had emphasised the importance of childhood socialisation in the development of political

From A. Heath, R. Jowell and J. Curtice, *How Britain Votes* (1985), Oxford: Pergamon, chapters 7 and 8.

POLICY AND IDEOLOGY IN THE 1983 GENERAL ELECTION *209*

allegiance. Long term political change occurred as one political generation was replaced by another – as older voters died, young voters with different identities and allegiances entered the electorate. In an elegant piece of analysis Ivor Crewe and his colleagues (Crewe, Sarlvik and Alt, 1977) showed that this theory failed to account for the results of the 1970 and 1974 elections. The consumer theory of voting then filled the resulting vacuum.

The consumer theory in essence is based on the axiom that individuals vote for the party they prefer; no limit is set in principle on the range of party characteristics that may be taken into account. On this account, the act of voting is analogous to the purchase of a consumer good. Parties are treated as competing products; voters are assumed to be discriminating consumers who weigh up their likes and dislikes about the alternative parties and choose accordingly. Emotional ties such as party identification or class loyalty do not come into it.

Were Conservative policies really preferred?

[In formulating questions] to determine whether it was party policy that determined the [1983] election outcome, we used a set of scales to measure the respondents' own views and their perceptions of the parties' positions on each of the major issues of the election. For example, in the case of unemployment and inflation we gave respondents a 21-point scale (running from -10 on the left through zero to $+10$ on the right) and introduced the question by saying that 'people who are convinced that *getting people back to work should be the government's top priority* will put a tick in the last box on the left [the -10 box] and those who are convinced that *keeping prices down should be the government's top priority* will put a tick in the last box on the right [the $+10$ box]'. People who held intermediate positions were asked to tick a box somewhere in between. We then asked respondents where they would place themselves and where they would place the Conservative party, the Labour party and the Alliance respectively.

As can be seen from Figure 5.4.1, there was broad consensus among our respondents that [on this issue] the Labour position lay on the extreme left of the scale. In that respect the perceived thrust of Labour's policies apparently got across to the electorate rather better than did that of Conservative or Alliance policies. Among those who claim[ed] to know where the [Conservatives and the Alliance] were there was more disagreement about the Conservative position. The median respondent placed it about halfway between the centre and the extreme right, but there was a substantial minority who placed it well over to the left.

In itself this is an important result. It shows that perceptions of party positions are themselves variable. Party policy is not an objective phenomenon universally recognised by the electorate. It cannot therefore

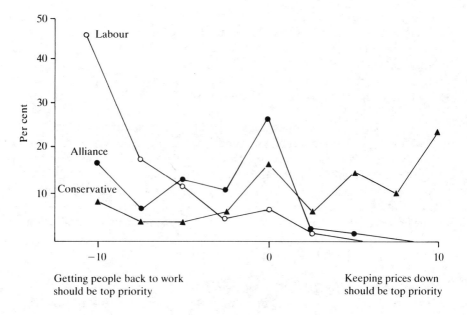

Figure 5.4.1 Where the parties were believed to stand

be 'the' cause of election results, as implied by the consumer theory, for there must be further causes of the variation in perception.

One of the major correlates, and a possible cause, of variations in perception is where the voter places him- or herself on the scale. The distribution of our respondents on unemployment and inflation is shown in Figure 5.4.2 together with the parties' positions (as seen by the median respondent).

On all the issues that we covered in the scales, there were peaks in support at the centre and at the two poles, but on the unemployment–inflation scale there was a particularly pronounced peak on the left, close to the perceived Labour position, with only a very minor peak on the right. At first sight, therefore, Figure 5.4.2 suggests that the Labour party was, by a wide margin, the electorate's first choice on unemployment and inflation, the two issues which our respondents claimed were the most important to them in deciding their vote. Indeed 49 per cent of the sample placed themselves closer to the median Labour position than to either of the other two parties; next came the Alliance – 32 per cent placed themselves closest to the median Alliance position; and the Conservatives trailed in third with only 16 per cent.

However, these calculations ignore the fact that where one places

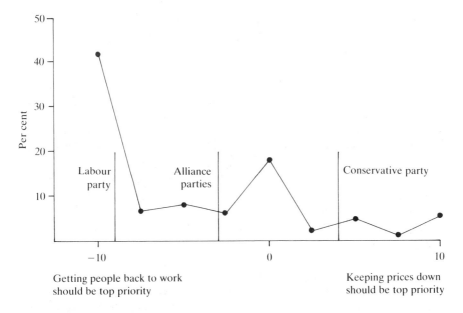

Figure 5.4.2 Where the electorate stood on unemployment and inflation

oneself and where one places the parties are not independent phenomena. In particular, Conservative voters who placed themselves on the left of the scale were quite likely to place the Conservative party there as well. Labour voters who placed themselves on the left were quite likely to place the Conservative party well over to the right. Party preference seems to influence how party policy is perceived. We cannot, therefore, conclude that Labour's policy on unemployment was so overwhelmingly preferred by the electorate as our initial calculation implied.

A second set of calculations is therefore required, based on where the *individual* respondent rather than the *median* respondent placed each party. These calculations reduce the Labour party's lead on unemployment and inflation, but still leave it well ahead. 40 per cent now placed themselves closest to Labour, compared with 32 per cent to the Alliance, while the Conservatives were still in third place with 28 per cent. Whatever the causal processes that lay behind these perceptions and evaluations, there has remained a clear preference for Labour policy on the two (apparently) most important issues of the 1983 election. If people had voted on the basis of these two issues alone, there would have been a Labour landslide.

After unemployment and inflation, the next most important issue in the

212 MODELS OF PARTY CHOICE

election was judged by our respondents to be government spending on health and social services. We pitted this against its natural opponent – tax cuts – to create another set of scales.

As with unemployment and inflation [the distribution of the sample shows] three peaks, at the centre and at the two poles. And as before the electorate tends towards the left rather than the right of the scale, although the peak at the centre is now much the largest. Superficially, this suggests that the Alliance position was the most popular, but many people (19 per cent) did not know where to place the Alliance, while many supporters of the other two parties also placed them at the centre.

Once again, then, we must compare the individual respondent's position with where he or she placed the parties. On these calculations the Alliance position is still preferred by 38 per cent with Labour and the Conservatives sharing second place on 31 per cent. We have yet to find a Conservative victory on an issue, leave alone a wide margin of victory.

The Conservatives did, however, fare rather better on the next most important issue, defence. Unilateral nuclear disarmament did not prove to be a popular policy. Labour's views were generally perceived to be perilously close to the extreme of the scale while the electorate found the centre to be a much more attractive resting point.

As with the first two scales, the respondents on average placed Labour nearer to the extreme left than they did the Conservatives to the extreme right. But while on the first two scales a position near the extreme left did not seem to be a particular electoral handicap, in the case of nuclear disarmament it did seem to be one. Only 26 per cent placed themselves closest to the Labour position on disarmament whereas 37 per cent preferred the Conservative position and a further 37 per cent preferred the Alliance position. All the same, this could hardly have been the grave electoral handicap that commentators at the time supposed. Even on Labour's apparent Achilles' heel, the Conservatives had still failed to win an outright victory. Since they tie with the Alliance on nuclear defence, even this issue can hardly explain the margin of their electoral success. We have reached the fourth most important election issue, according to our respondents, before the Conservatives even so much as share the lead.

These results seem to challenge the consumer theory's contention that the policies of the parties on the important issues of the day determine election results. True, on the other scales we included, a nationalisation–privatisation scale, and a law and order scale, the Conservative party did well. But these were comparatively minor issues in relation to the other four [and] on none of [the four] was the Conservative party clearly in the lead.

What the result might have been
It is interesting to speculate what the result of the election might have been if the consumer theory had been literally correct. Let us suppose that

POLICY AND IDEOLOGY IN THE 1983 GENERAL ELECTION *213*

people vote solely on the basis of their preferences for party policies. Let us assume too that the six issues covered by our scales had been the only ones that really mattered.

The calculations necessary to pursue this hypothetical question involve rather heroic simplifying assumptions [which] we ought to make explicit in advance. First, and most heroically, we have assumed that people vote for the party that comes closest to their own position on the issue they regard as most important. Thus in accordance with the spirit of consumer theory we asked our respondents 'Which one of the six issues on the card would you say was most important to you in deciding about voting?'. For each issue we have included in our analysis only those people who regarded it as most important.

Next, we have calculated the distances (assuming an equal interval scale) between people's own position and the position that they themselves assigned to each party. The closest party is then taken to be the party of their choice. If two or more parties were equidistant from their position, we have split the vote equally between the equidistant parties. Finally, if people were unable to nominate a most important issue, we have simply excluded them. This applied to fewer than 5 per cent of the respondents.

The result [of these calculations] is more or less a dead heat between the Conservative and Labour parties with the Alliance only barely behind [Conservative 35%, Labour 35%, Alliance 31%].

We explored the effects of changing the most heroic of our assumptions. We realise that it is a gross over-simplification to pretend that people vote on the basis of their one most important issue. Two or three 'quite important' issues might outweigh one 'extremely important' issue.

The consumer theory allows that people do make this kind of rational calculus of competing policies. But how are we to ascertain what trade-offs people make? The consumer theory is not very helpful on this. The usual method in studying how people choose real consumer goods is to observe a series of actual choices under different conditions and infer their trade-offs. But in the analysis of an election we have only one choice to study – the vote itself. It would be unjustified to tinker with hypothetical trade-offs until we were able to make them generate the 'right' election result. This would render the analysis circular as we would have to assume the truth of the theory in order to test it! What we need is *independent* evidence about trade-offs in order to test the consumer theory.

We do in fact have some independent evidence ourselves since we asked our respondents not only which issue was most important to them when deciding about voting but also which came next. If we give equal weight to the two issues judged most important by the respondents, we are probably erring on the side of generosity. In so doing we allow trade-offs a good opportunity to display themselves.

The main consequence of such calculations is to pull the Alliance up at Labour's expense. The expected outcome now becomes 35 per cent of the vote for the Conservatives, 32 per cent for the Alliance and 33 per cent for Labour. This is still a long way from the actual election result.

One could go on tinkering with the assumptions *ad infinitum* in order to get a closer approximation to the actual result, but, as it turns out, the most effective way of getting the 'right' answer is to ignore respondents' own judgements of importance altogether. As we shall show [below], issues like nationalisation, which respondents almost universally described as unimportant in deciding their vote, actually prove to be the best predictors of voting behaviour.

It seems to us that this is bad news indeed for the consumer theory of voting. The theory surely cannot rely on respondents' reports of their policy preferences but then reject their reports of their relative importance. Why should one set of reports be so unduly privileged?

In our view, the consumer theory is based on the misconception that voting is based on a discrete, deliberate decision. The fact that people will answer a survey question that asks them what was 'the most important issue in deciding about voting' does not mean that they actually reach their decision in that way. It is well known that respondents have an infuriating (and gratifying) habit of answering questions that have little or no relevance to their behaviour simply in order to be cooperative.

Our data suggest to us that voting choices are not made on the basis of a conscious weighing in the balance of alternative policies. Electoral choice is based on a much broader, more 'synoptic' evaluation of parties than the consumer theory allows for. We accept the conclusions of the 'expressive' theory that these electoral choices and evaluations will in many cases be long-standing ones, perhaps even inherited from childhood socialisation. But they are not solely inherited. We do not want to replace a one-sided instrumental theory with a return to a one-sided expressive theory. Events and personalities may also shape perceptions: there is a 'political construction of reality' as well as a 'social construction of reality'.

But these constructions are not detailed appraisals of party manifestos and policies. Rather they are more global or 'synoptic' perceptions of the overall character of a party. Factors such as policies, record in office, putative ability to implement a programme, leadership, unity of purpose may all come into it, but none is paramount. It is the fit between the general character of the party and the voter's own general ideology which, we believe, best accounts for electoral choice. But we do not believe that there is any one simple causal process that underlies this fit. The expressive theory held that parties shape electors' values; the instrumental theory held that electors' attitudes determine party choices. Both are right but both are too simple.

Ideology

We have suggested that it is unsound to view the voter as a consumer in the marketplace, choosing between parties on the basis of their detailed policy proposals. The notion that the elector makes up his or her mind in the course of the election campaign on the basis of the important issues of the day simply will not do. But we do not want to revert to the old orthodoxy. People do not, and probably never have, voted simply out of loyalty to a party. Our theory is that it is also the 'fit' between the voters' general values and their overall perceptions of what the parties stand for – their general ideologies rather than their specific policies – which affects how they vote and how strongly they are attached to a party. It is not the small print of the manifesto but the overall perception of the party's character that counts.

In general, we believe the character of the parties to be rather stable. Benney, for example, writing in the 1950s, saw the Labour party as standing for public ownership of the means of production and for the development of the National Health Service, while the Conservative party stood for tax cuts and privatisation (Benney *et al.*, 1956). A very similar account would be given today, some thirty years on. The emphases which the two parties place on these different aspects of their underlying ideologies may change from time to time. [But] these general philosophies are both enduring and fundamental aspects of the Labour and Conservative parties' characters. The electors' attitudes towards these political philosophies provide a key to their voting behaviour not only in 1983 but also in all the earlier general elections on which we have the relevant data. They are of course attitudes and appeals which derive to a large extent from the class basis both of the electorate and of the two major parties. We must however emphasise that the relationship is a two-way one: the parties' appeals may help to shape class values too.

Conservative and Labour voters

Let us begin by comparing the attitudes of Conservative and Labour voters towards these general features of party philosophy and ideology. We asked our respondents not only about the campaign issues but also about a range of less prominent policies on which the parties take fundamentally different stands. The questions on which Conservative and Labour voters expressed the most divergent attitudes are shown in Table 5.4.1.

In Table 5.4.1 we report the percentage of Labour and Conservative voters who expressed agreement with the 'right-wing' alternative on each question. In the third column we give the index of dissimilarity [computed by summing the differences (of the same sign) between the percentages of Conservative and Labour voters in each category – 'right-wing', 'left-wing' *and* 'not sure'. (For further details, see Heath, Jowell and Curtice (1985), p. 125, note 5.)]. This is an overall measure of the difference between

MODELS OF PARTY CHOICE

Table 5.4.1 The attitudes of Conservative and Labour voters

	Percentage agreeing with 'right-wing' alternative		
	Conservative voters	Labour voters	Index of dissimilarity
Nationalisation	66	12	54
Trade union legislation	84	29	55
Income redistribution	59	12	49
Defence spending	82	37	45
Private education	87	43	44
Job creation	35	2	42
N (minimum)	1,383	837	

Conservative and Labour voters on each question. The index takes into account the proportions who were 'not sure', or who could not choose between the options given, in addition to those who gave 'left-wing' responses. This is important in the answers to the job creation question and in this case the index gives a better guide to the difference of opinion than the first two columns in Table 5.4.1 provide on their own.

As we can see, the two sets of voters differ most in their attitudes towards nationalisation and trade union legislation, followed by income redistribution, defence and private education. The major issue of the campaign – unemployment – comes relatively low in the list. Few respondents described nationalisation as an important issue in the election, and hardly any had said that trade union legislation was important (although it figured quite prominently in the Conservative manifesto). But the close relation between the unions and the Labour party is not only part and parcel of its constitution, it is also widely recognised as part of its character. People's perceptions of the party reflect this (just as they reflect each party's general stance on public ownership) almost regardless of manifesto commitments.

Income redistribution and the abolition of private education were also largely absent from the explicit campaign debate. But again these issues sharply divide Conservative from Labour voters, more so indeed than does job creation, which was a campaign issue. Both are also long-standing concerns for the two parties.

These themes of public ownership and free enterprise, the reform of trade unions and private schools, social equality and individual incentives have been persistent sources of disagreement between the parties since the Labour party's formation. Along with defence they are also the themes on which their supporters diverge most strongly. They constitute the main ideological divisions between the parties. They should be distinguished from issues such as full employment or the National Health Service where the parties agree on the overall goals but disagree on the means.

POLICY AND IDEOLOGY IN THE 1983 GENERAL ELECTION *217*

The ideological content of different policies varies, therefore. And it is those where ideology is most visible that differentiate most strongly between the rival sets of voters. This was true not only in 1983 but also in 1979. Trade union reform, nationalisation and income redistribution headed the list in both years. Their importance (as predictors of vote) does not seem to vary according to their prominence in the electoral campaigns.

We do not however interpret any of these findings as evidence that people consciously weighed up nationalisation or trade union reform instead of (or as well as) the campaign issues they claimed were on their minds. Instead, we interpret these questions as tapping people's under-lying values, values which they most often take for granted but which nonetheless shape their perceptions and evaluations of specific events, personalities and policies. Our questions on nationalisation, income redistribution and private education are not so much tapping discrete issues as a general ideological dimension the respective poles of which are support for government intervention on the one hand and free enterprise on the other.

Positions along this ideological dimension are probably quite stable, but by no means immutable. They derive from, among other things, people's class positions. The list of questions in Table 5.4.1 that differentiates Conservative from Labour voters has a striking resemblance to the list in [Table 3.3.1 on p. 71 above] which differentiates members of the five classes.

The presence of these 'taken-for-granted' class values in the background of voters' thinking helps to explain (although only in part) why Labour has done so badly of late, despite the electorate's favourable attitude towards its stand on unemployment and the welfare state. Our interpretation is that in 1983 there were relatively few people towards the left-wing end of the interventionist–free enterprise continuum. Changing the details of policy would not have affected matters greatly.

Nor do we wish to imply that changing Labour's left-wing character is the only remedy available for the party. The consumer theory of political choice may treat attitudes as 'independent' variables which 'determine' voting behaviour; its proponents conclude from this that the Labour party must change its policies if it is to regain office. But our conception of political choice treats values as 'dependent' variables which can be shaped, both by political and by social processes.

Voting histories
Just as the consumer theory failed to predict the election result, greatly underestimating the Conservative total, so our ideological theory is not sufficient on its own. People remain attached to their previous parties even when they have moved out of line with them on major political principles. Even after we have taken account of where people stand on the major

principles, how they voted before (and even how their parents voted before them) is still a good predictor of how they will vote in the future.

To this extent we support the expressive theory rather than the instrumental theory of voting. Loyalty to one's party is not a vacuous concept. However, theorists of the 'expressive' school of thought have tended to exaggerate the importance of childhood and early adulthood socialisation into a 'party identity' and have been wrong to look to the replacement of one generation by another as the major source of electoral change. In that respect we agree with the critics of the expressive theory. Party loyalty may act as a brake on electoral change, but it slows it down rather than stopping it altogether. Loyalty is unlikely to be wholly unconditional and none of the parties should count on the loyalty of those who lie far away from its [ideological] heartland.

5.5 | Learning through a lifetime

Richard Rose and Ian McAllister

The first object of this chapter is to examine the extent to which the British electorate does have political principles, and to identify their salient characteristics and relevance to parties, including potential conflict between popular principles and party positions. Secondly, the chapter sets out a lifetime-learning model of voting, which systematically incorporates the influence of pre-adult socialization, socio-economic interests, political principles and current party performance.

The principles of voters

The term political *principle* is here used to describe underlying judgements and preferences about the activities of government. Principles are general enough to be durable (for example, favouring the poor, or a strong national defence) and thus applicable in many different contexts (to public spending and taxation, or to the Falkland Islands or Russia). Just as the elements of a party image (good for the working class, stands up for the national interest) reflect durable features of parties, so political principles are lasting because they concern persisting problems of public policy. It is reasonable to think of voters using their principles to guide decisions about voting at a particular election, for principles come first in time.

Political principles are plural not singular; a voter holding one principle need not endorse another. Because of this, an analysis of the electorate in terms of principles differs from an analysis of ideology. An *ideology*

From R. Rose and I. McAllister, *Voters Begin to Choose* (1986), London: Sage, chapter 7. The ideas put forward in this extract have been more fully developed by the authors in *The Loyalties of Voters* (1990) London: Sage.

consists of a number of logically consistent principles that can be related to nearly every issue facing a government. An ideology represents the ultimate in closed political thinking, for conclusions are deduced rather than tested against experience and evidence. In a pure model of closed electoral competition, voters would not only have their votes determined by their class, but also their political principles determined by the ideology of their class.

Political principles must be distinguished from topical *issues* of the moment, which are transitory by definition. The problems posed by a particular strike, a particular sterling crisis or a furore about a crime or scandal are important at the moment, but lack the durability of political principles.

Political *attitudes* differ from principles and issues since attitudes are relatively non-specific in their relevance to government actions. For example, a list of voters' likes and dislikes about a party will catalogue many attitudes that are not on the agenda of public policy. The response of voters to questions asking for a series of adjectives to be applied to parties (for example, extreme/moderate; united/divided) or to party leaders (for example, determined, likeable or caring) may reflect something about the feelings of voters towards political objects. But the expression of such attitudes and feelings is not the same as the choice of party. Only if the electorate is moved by appeals to emotions rather than actions will such attitudes influence voting.

Because political principles are durable, they can properly be considered prior influences upon the choice of the vote at a particular election. By contrast, many questions about topical issues reflect judgements made after a person decides which party to support. Demonstrating a correlation between what people think about topical issues and party choice leaves open the direction of causation. Post-election analyses of issues may show a correlation between how people voted and answers to issue questions, but *post hoc* explanation is not a satisfactory basis for understanding future voting.

The raw materials for identifying major political principles in the minds of the electorate are readily available – a battery of British Election Studies' questions about political phenomena. Once it is clear what one is looking for – underlying, durable political judgements held by the mass electorate – the task of excluding as well as including questions is greatly simplified. Principles are meant to have a persisting quality; so too should the questions used to measure them. Analysis here is concentrated upon those questions that could be asked at each election over a decade or more. [Our analysis makes use of the BES] surveys [of] October 1974, 1979 and 1983.

Factor analysis provides an appropriate statistical method for deriving political principles from the responses of voters to a host of questions about

LEARNING THROUGH A LIFETIME

public policies. Factor analysis can identify what is common in a number of questions: this commonality is the underlying principle causing people to give similar responses to questions about different topics. For example, if a voter favours nationalization, trade unions, and a more equal distribution of wealth, we would consider these answers as reflecting a single underlying socialist principle, not a random association.

Insofar as voters make principled judgements about public policy, then a factor analysis should explain most of the variance in answers given to a variety of survey questions. Insofar as thinking is ideological, only one factor will be prominent, reducing views about many different questions to a single dimension. Insofar as thinking is principled but non-ideological, then several unrelated factors would be identified. Insofar as voters' minds are blank, then no underlying principle should appear and the proportion of variance explained would be low.

The first step in a factor analysis is to identify a variety of public policy questions suitable for testing whether and in what ways responses reflect underlying political principles. Initially, a pool of 14 different questions asked across a decade was factor analysed. Questions that did not correlate with others to form a common factor were excluded from analysis.

The factor analysis consistently identifies eleven views reflecting four political principles, which together account for 58 per cent of the variance in 1974, 59 per cent in 1979, and 54 per cent in 1983. The four factors are readily related to political principles: socialism, welfare, traditional morality, and racialism. Since there is a very high degree of stability in the principles elucidated, only the results of the 1983 study are discussed here (see Table 5.5.1).

The principles in [the voters'] minds refer to two socio-economic concerns, socialism and welfare, and two cultural concerns, traditional morality and race relations.

Socialism (Factor I: 23 per cent of variance)
There is empirical evidence of an underlying principle linking views about the nationalization of industry, comprehensive schools, trade union power, the reduction of military strength, and the redistribution of wealth. Positive answers to these questions can properly be called socialist.

Welfare (Factor II: 12 per cent)
British voters view the public provision of welfare as a principle too. Views about spending on the health service, from which everyone benefits, are strongly correlated with views about the reduction of poverty, from which only a minority benefit. Equally, people who are against public action to reduce poverty, from which they do not benefit, also oppose spending more money on a health service that benefits everyone.

222 MODELS OF PARTY CHOICE

Table 5.5.1 Factor loadings for political principles, 1983

	Factor loadings			
	I	II	III	IV
I Socialism				
1. Should be more nationalization	**0.71**	−0.14	−0.01	−0.01
2. Trade unions do not have too much power	**0.63**	0.02	0.15	−0.10
3. Government should redistribute wealth	**0.62**	−0.28	0.05	−0.06
4. Government should establish comprehensive schools	**0.61**	−0.12	0.12	0.01
5. Reduction of military strength not gone far enough	**0.55**	−0.04	−0.08	−0.26
II Welfare				
1. Important to reduce poverty	0.18	**0.77**	−0.02	0.06
2. Government should spend more money on the health service	0.19	**0.75**	0.02	0.02
III Traditional morality				
1. Availability of abortion on NHS gone far enough	0.04	−0.06	**0.78**	0.04
2. Nudity and sex in media gone far enough	0.07	0.05	**0.75**	−0.06
IV Racialism				
1. Racial equality gone too far	0.02	0.25	0.21	**0.75**
2. Important to repatriate immigrants	−0.17	−0.13	0.14	**0.74**
Variance explained	22.6	11.6	10.3	9.4
(Eigenvalues)	(2.5)	(1.3)	(1.1)	(1.0)
Total variance explained, 53.9 per cent				

Note: Varimax rotated factor loadings from a principal components factor analysis with unities in the main diagonal. No other factor had an eigenvalue greater than one.

Source: British Election Study, 1983.

Traditional morality (Factor III: 10 per cent)
Traditional moral principles are independent of such party principles as socialism and welfare. This is hardly surprising, given that parties consciously try to avoid becoming entangled in debates about moral issues. The efforts of parties to keep a subject off the political agenda do not mean, [however], that it is outside the popular mind. Morality accounts for as much variance in popular attitudes as do questions of welfare.

Racialism (Factor IV: 9 per cent)
Replies to questions about coloured immigrants and the promotion of racial equality identify a factor important in the minds of voters and independent of the principle of socialism. People who evaluate govern-

LEARNING THROUGH A LIFETIME

ment actions according to socialist principles are as likely to hold racialist as anti-racialist principles, and racialists are as likely as anti-racialists to endorse socialist views.

The extent to which underlying principles account for voters' views rejects the proposition that the mind of the electorate is blank. If that were the case, then there would be no coherence in views, and no meaningful factors could be identified. As it is, more than half the variation in views can be accounted for by four principles. Each is clear enough to be widely understood by voters, and general enough to provide the basis for the electorate to judge a host of problems facing government.

The variety of principles rejects the assumption that voters' minds are committed to a closed partisan ideology. If that were the case, views about socialism would be integrally related to views about welfare, morality and racialism, forming a single factor statistically. But there is very little correlation between a voter's views on one principle and another.

It is sometimes argued that political principles are not so much the reflection of the minds of voters as they are of socio-economic interests. If principles are simply derivative of socio-economic interests then middle-class voters should differ substantially from working-class voters. In order to test this hypothesis, it is necessary to create a standardized score summarizing the views of voters about the multiplicity of questions that constitute each principle. [The scores for each year were calculated by summing the items in each factor, respecting signs. They were then standardized and transformed into a 1 to 100 scale.] If a group of voters completely endorses a principle, its score will be 100, and if a group completely rejects it, the score will be 0. For political principles to be distinctive between social groups, one group's views should approach 100, and the other 0.

Middle-class and working-class voters structure their political thinking in much the same way. There is only a three-point difference in the mean scores of the two classes about traditional morality (69 and 72 respectively) and about racialism (52 and 55 respectively). Very positive endorsements of welfare are given by both the middle class and working class (85 and 91). The mean scores for socialism are relatively close, 33 for the middle class, and 45 for the working class; the distance between the two classes is small by comparison with divisions about socialism within the working class. For the four principles the average class difference is only six points, thus rejecting the theory that political principles are derived from location in the class structure.

For principles to produce closed competition between parties, Conservative, Alliance and Labour voters should have very different positions on each principle. Insofar as those voting for different parties have much the same principles, then the electorate is open. Voters find movement

224 MODELS OF PARTY CHOICE

between parties easier when there is not the inhibition of differences of political principles. *Inter*-party similarity is greater the closer mean scores are to each other, whether high, low or in the middle. *Intra*-party consensus is greater the closer the score approaches either 100 or 0.

For three of the four principles, there is inter-party consensus among voters (Table 5.5.2). There is intra-party consensus on the welfare principle; the mean score is 97 for Labour, 92 for the Alliance and 80 for the Conservatives; and about traditional morality too for the factor scores are Alliance, 69; Labour, 70; and Conservatives, 72. The principle of racialism divides the electorate and creates intra-party disagreement; the mean racialism score is 50 for Labour, 48 for the Alliance, and 43 for the Conservatives. The closeness of the scores shows inter-party similarity in divisions about race.

Only one of the four [principles] – socialism – shows much difference between supporters of the different parties; the distance between Labour and Conservative voters is 37 points, with Alliance voters halfway between. Socialism divides Labour voters. There is less unity in the Labour Party in support of socialism (mean, 61) than there is among Labour voters in supporting traditional morality (mean, 70). Moreover, Conservatives

Table 5.5.2 Similarities between partisans in political principles, 1974–83

	Con.	Lib./All'ce	Lab.	Difference Con.–Lab.
	(Mean score for party's voters)			
Socialism				
1974 Oct.	27	38	56	29
1979	23	34	50	27
1983	24	43	61	37
Welfare				
1974 Oct.	77	80	86	9
1979	57	61	61	4
1983	80	92	97	17
Traditional morality				
1974 Oct.	71	66	67	4
1979	71	66	72	1
1983	72	69	70	2
Racialism				
1974 Oct.	53	47	48	5
1979	50	43	44	6
1983	57	52	50	7

Note: All answers standardized on a scale from completely negative (0) to completely positive (100).

Source: Calculated from factor analyses reported in Table 5.5.1 and similar analyses for October 1974 and 1979.

LEARNING THROUGH A LIFETIME

are closer to rejecting socialism completely than Labour voters are to endorsing socialism completely.

Inter-party consensus has been consistent among voters for the past decade. At all three elections since October, 1974, the views of Conservative and Labour voters on traditional morality and racialism have been within a few per cent of each other, and attitudes toward welfare have also been close (Table 5.5.2). In 1983 they appeared to move apart only because of the extremely high degree of endorsement of welfare principles in all three parties. Only socialism has shown a tendency toward increasing disagreement. As Labour's vote declined drastically in 1983, Labour voters became a little more socialist. From the evidence of the 1970s, an increase in the Labour vote would attract more voters who do not subscribe to socialist principles, increasing inter-party agreement and dissensus within Labour's ranks.

The best way to describe the relationship between the principles of the electorate and the parties is to say that no party represents the constellation of principles widespread in the electorate. Voters have minds of their own, and blocs of voters can readily be identified who have distinctive political principles. But the bundles of principles common in the electorate are not consistently linked with the choices that the parties offer voters.

Lifetime learning

The division of academic labour normally concentrates attention upon a single set of influences upon voting behaviour, whether pre-adult socialization, social structure, political principles, or the relatively transitory events of a Parliament or election campaign. However, the distinctive feature of an election is that voters are subject to all these influences *simultaneously*. In order to understand voting, we need to think in terms of the accumulation of influences through a lifetime of learning (Figure 5.5.1).

In testing the lifetime learning model, it is important to order the analysis of influences in the sequence in which they occur in the life of the voter, starting with pre-adult socialization. Hierarchical stepwise multiple regression is here used to discriminate between those experiences in a life history that affect electoral behaviour, and those that do not [see Table 5.5.3].

I Pre-adult socialization (15 per cent of variance explained on average)

Influences that come first in time remain of some importance throughout a lifetime. Consistently, father's party is the single most important early influence upon adult party choice. But its effect is limited, and in decline. It explained 10 per cent of the variance in Conservative versus Labour voting in 1974, and 7 per cent in 1983. Father's class, religion and education each

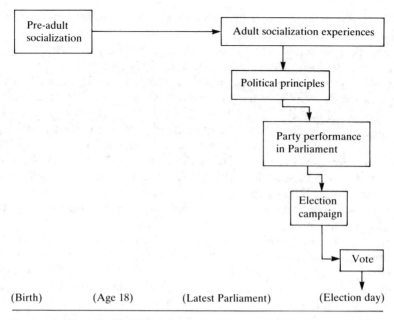

Figure 5.5.1 A cumulative lifetime learning model of voting

have a little effect; none can be regarded as by itself of substantial importance.

II Socio-economic interests (12 per cent)
Current occupation, housing, nation and union membership can exercise an independent influence upon a voter's current party choice. Housing is the most important. Altogether, these four interests accounted for 13 per cent of the variance in Conservative versus Labour voting in 1983, after allowing for the full impact of pre-adult influences.

III Political principles (24 per cent)
Political principles explain nearly as much of the vote as do pre-adult socialization and current socio-economic interests combined, and the influence of principles has been increasing. In 1974 principles accounted for 22 per cent of the vote, as against 30 per cent for social structure influences, and in 1983 for 29 per cent, against 27 per cent for social structure influences.

The importance of political principles is particularly striking, since their effect is calculated only *after* allowing for the full impact of social structure.

LEARNING THROUGH A LIFETIME

Table 5.5.3 The cumulative effect of determinants of Conservative vs. Labour voting, 1974–83

	Conservative vs. Labour			
	1974 Oct.	1979	1983	Change 1974–83
Influences	(% variance explained)			
I Pre-adult socialization	(20)	(12)	(14)	(−6)
Father's party	10	7	7	−3
Father's class	6	3	3	−3
Education	2	2	2	0
Religion	2	0	2	0
II Socio-economic interests	(10)	(12)	(13)	(+3)
Housing	4	4	5	+1
Union membership	4	4	3	−1
Nation	0	3	3	+3
Current class	2	1	2	0
III Political principles	(22)	(22)	(29)	(+7)
Socialism	22	19	27	+5
Welfare	0	0	2	+2
Racialism	0	2	0	0
Traditional morality	0	1	0	0
IV Current performance of parties	(18)	(17)	(21)	(+3)
Leaders	14	16	6	−8
Evaluation of governing party	4	1	7	+3
Event evaluation[a]	0	n.a.	1	+1
Campaign	0	0	0	0
Future expectations	0	0	7	+7
V Current party identification	(9)	(20)	(3)	(−6)
Total variance explained	79	83	80	+1

[a]Common Market in 1974; Falklands in 1983.

Source: British Election Studies, 1974, 1979 and 1983.

One principle, socialism, accounts for nearly all the impact, explaining 27 per cent of variance in 1983. Support for welfare principles cannot discriminate between parties, since virtually the whole electorate is united in favouring the welfare state. Nor can voters favouring traditional morality or opposing immigrants be much influenced, since the Conservative and Labour parties do not explicitly and consistently endorse these principles.

The electoral force of socialism benefits the Conservatives much more than Labour, because the majority of voters are *anti*-socialist. The mean voter is likely to reject three-fifths of the propositions that would be endorsed by adherents of socialist principles, and this has consistently been

228

MODELS OF PARTY CHOICE

the case. Electors who are consistently anti-socialist vote Conservative. The average Labour voter agrees with little more than half the statements defining the socialist principle.

IV Current performance of parties (19 per cent)

The voter's evaluation of parties during the life of a Parliament accounts for up to one-fifth of the variance in Conservative versus Labour voting. In 1983 the evaluation of party leaders collectively accounted for six per cent of the variance of the vote between Conservatives and Labour, a noteworthy amount but not large by comparison with the media publicity given the leaders. An index of voters' evaluation of the record of the Conservative government, based on judgements about its handling of unemployment, taxation, the cost of living and strikes, directly accounted for seven per cent of voting. Expectations of the ability of a party to improve the standard of living in the next four years accounted for another seven per cent of variance; these are linked to retrospective evaluation of the governing party's performance and that of party leaders in the past four years.

Transitory events and issues appear of little direct importance on election day. The Falklands War was an important event in 1982, when it had positive consequences for the Conservative Party's morale and mid-term standing in the Gallup Poll. But by the time of the June 1983 general election, it could directly add only an additional one per cent to the variance explained by what voters had earlier learned about parties. Similarly, views about the Common Market had no independent influence on voting in 1974. After taking into account a lifetime of previous learning, the campaign appears as a transitory event of limited influence upon voters.

V Party identification (11 per cent)

To a substantial extent, [using] party identification [as a predictor of votes] is tautological. Demonstrating a high correlation between party identification and party vote supports the hypothesis that these are but two names for one thing.

The test of party identification as an independent influence upon voting is to calculate its impact after accounting for the effect of all other factors. When this is done, party identification is largely redundant, adding little to [preceding influences].

Party identification is the only influence examined that is *not* consistently important. In 1983 it added only three per cent to the explanation of the variance in the Conservative versus Labour share of the vote. The apparently high level of influence of party identification in 1979 appears to reflect the fact that all other social structure and political influences were

LEARNING THROUGH A LIFETIME

less strong at this election, thus allowing more scope for the purely residual effect of party identification.

When tested across a decade of elections, the lifetime learning model gives a clear, coherent and parsimonious account of the division between Conservative and Labour voters. At each election since October 1974 it can account for four-fifths of the variance, an extraordinarily high proportion by comparison with conventional models of voting relying upon a single set of influences.

Political influences are more important than social structure in determining the vote. Five different types of influence affect voting behaviour. In order of their average importance they are: political principles (24 per cent); the current performance of parties (19 per cent); pre-adult socialization (15 per cent); socio-economic interests (12 per cent); and residual party identification (11 per cent). The greater importance of political principles and the current performance of parties is striking, inasmuch as the stepwise regression model measures their influence only *after* calculating the impact of pre-adult socialization and socio-economic interests.

Moreover, voters are increasingly open to political influence. In 1974, 40 per cent of the variance was explained by political principles and the current performance of parties, 10 per cent more than by social structure. By 1983, 50 per cent of the variance was explained by political principles and the current performance of parties, 23 per cent more than that explained by social structure.

5.6 The demise of party identification theory?

Anthony Heath and Sarah-K. McDonald

Since Butler and Stokes wrote *Political Change in Britain* there has been an intellectual revolution in political science with the apparent demise of the 'party identification' model of political behaviour which they advanced and the rise of rational choice theories, and in particular the theory of issue voting. Perhaps the most common view, shared by most writers [on issue voting], is that party identification theory held true for the earlier period with which Butler and Stokes were concerned but that it has declined in explanatory value since that time. This represents the new orthodoxy. The purpose of the present paper is to scrutinise its claims.

We shall begin by exploring the assumptions of party identification and issue theory. We shall then turn to the question whether their propositions hold true for certain categories of voter rather than others. And we shall move to the question of their changing explanatory force over time.

The assumptions of the theories

The assumption of party identification theory is that identifications have a real existence independent of vote; the assumption of issue voting theory is that voters have 'real' perceptions of where the parties stand as well as 'real' attitudes towards the issues.

One method by which the 'realness' of attitudes was assessed in Converse's pioneering work was by measuring their stability over time (Converse, 1964). Of course, even 'real' attitudes may change over time, but Converse noted that, in a three-wave panel study, many respondents' attitudes varied apparently randomly over time. Thus the correlation

From A. Heath and S.-K. McDonald, 'The demise of party identification theory?', *Electoral Studies* (1988), vol. 7, pp. 95–107.

THE DEMISE OF PARTY IDENTIFICATION THEORY? 231

between respondents' positions at times 1 and 2 was of the order of 0.3; between their positions at times 2 and 3 was 0.3; and between their positions at times 1 and 3 was also 0.3. It is this third correlation which is of crucial importance. If there had been systematic attitude change, this correlation would have been expected to fall to perhaps 0.09. The fact that it did not suggested to Converse that there were two types of respondent – some with constant 'real' attitudes and others with non-attitudes which varied randomly over time. He termed this the 'black–white' model.

Using the 1983–6–7 British General Election Panel Study we can follow Converse's method and compute the three correlations for party identification, vote (or vote intention in the 1986 wave of the panel), respondent's issue position, and respondent's perception of the party's issue position. The issue which we examine here is the one which proved to be one of the best predictors of party preference in 1983, namely nationalisation.

For simplicity, we present the results for the Conservative party only. Thus for vote and party identity we employ a binary variable, scored 1 if the respondent voted for or identified with the Conservative party, zero otherwise. Respondents who had no party identification or had not voted were scored 0.

The respondents' attitudes to nationalisation and their perceptions of the Conservative party's position on nationalisation were obtained using 20-point scales. Three per cent of respondents did not know where their own position was on the scale, and 5 per cent did not know the Conservative party's position. These respondents were excluded from the analysis, along with those who did not or refused to answer.

As can be seen from Table 5.6.1, for all four variables, the pattern found by Converse holds – the correlation for the 1983–7 period is much the same as that for the two shorter periods – suggesting that his 'black–white' model holds for identities, intentions, values and perceptions alike.

This is not in itself damaging to the theories, for the crucial question is not whether some voters change their attitudes at random but rather what proportion of the electorate have 'non-attitudes'. The detailed results of Table 5.6.1, however, offer much more encouragement for the party identification theory than for the issue voting theory. Thus party identification proves to be more stable than vote, and both party identification and vote are a great deal more stable than attitudes to nationalisation or perceptions of the Conservative party's position on nationalisation.

This suggests that the doubts which early writers like Converse and Butler and Stokes had about the stability of attitudes still have force in the 1980s. Despite the decline in the strength of party identification and the alleged rise in issue voting, the question mark which they raised against issue voting theory remains. Is it plausible to suppose that such unstable variables as, for example, attitudes to nationalisation can explain the much more stable one of voting behaviour?

232   MODELS OF PARTY CHOICE

Table 5.6.1 The stability of identification, vote, attitudes towards, and perceptions of party position on, the nationalisation issue

	Correlation coefficients			
	Party ID	Vote	Respondent's position	Party's perceived position
1983–86	0.70 (868)	0.64 (867)	0.29 (832)	0.29 (821)
1986–87	0.80 (873)	0.73 (859)	0.36 (849)	0.35 (852)
1983–87	0.72 (865)	0.62 (864)	0.32 (838)	0.33 (825)

Note: Figures in brackets give the number of respondents included in the computation of the correlation coefficient.

The next issue we must tackle is that of the measurement of attitudes. The 20-point scales [referred to] above were developed in order to deal with [criticisms of Converse's work]. However, we also included in the panel study a large number of further items which related to various aspects of the left–right dimension of British politics, for example income redistribution, private education, big business power and the like. While none of these individual items showed any greater stability over time than the nationalisation question already described, somewhat more impressive results were achieved when these items were combined to form an index of what might be termed 'left–right' principles. The index has reasonably good internal reliability and also much more impressive stability over time, the correlation between responses in the 1983 and 1986 waves being 0.73.

The methodological device of calculating an index of left–right values has, therefore, rescued issue voting theory from the accusation that a large proportion of the electorate exhibit non-attitudes. To be sure, the index which we have constructed should be thought of as measuring a *general normative principle* rather than an attitude to a specific issue like nationalisation. In this respect our findings confirm the approach adopted by Rose and McAllister (1986) who also give primacy to political principles rather than specific issues in their formulation of issue voting.

Versions of issue voting theory, on the other hand, which assume that voters weigh up the issues of the day are still in need of revision, or at least of methodological improvement. It may be that voters do have real attitudes towards the issues of the day, but the onus is on exponents of such versions to demonstrate that their measures have acceptable levels of reliability and validity. The present discussion indicates that political principles can be measured with an acceptable degree of reliability, and the next section will give some indication of validity as well. To the best of our knowledge, however, the comparable task for attitudes towards the specific issues of the day remains to be carried out.

Do the theories apply to different types of voter?

Both party identification theory and one version of issue voting theory (a version which we might term 'principled voting') have passed the first hurdle satisfactorily. Do they, however, apply to different groups of voters, party identification theory having more force for those in solidary social groups, issue voting theory for the more interested or educated voter?

We shall begin with one of the central claims of party identification theory, namely that party identity is inherited through the family. We first test the hypothesis that Conservative identification depends on whether the respondent's mother and/or father voted for the Conservatives when he (the respondent) was growing up. Following Rose and McAllister we shall define solidary social groups as unionised council tenants and non-union owner-occupiers respectively. 'Open' groups constitute the remainder of the population.

Since we are concerned to test whether parental partisanship affects the probability of the respondent identifying with the Conservative party, it is appropriate to use logit analysis. We shall report the coefficients for 'closed' and 'open' groups respectively. The data come from the 1983 British General Election Study. As expected [see Table 5.6.2(a)], the results of this test confirm the main claim of party identification theory, namely that party identification is inherited from one's parents. But it gives no support at all to the idea that the theory is more appropriate for members of closed than for members of open groups. The differences between the coefficients for the two groups are well within sampling error.

An alternative definition of 'closed' and 'open' groups would be in terms of class mobility. Thus we could define people who are intergenerationally stable as belonging to 'closed' or solidary groups, while the intergenerationally mobile could be defined as belonging to 'open' groups. This time we get a somewhat different picture [see Table 5.6.2(b)]. Among the intergenerationally stable respondents, the inheritance of partisanship is noticeably higher than among the mobile. This is of course entirely in line with party identification theory, but it also suggests that the definition of solidary social groups in terms of patterns of mobility is more fruitful than Rose and McAllister's definition in terms of housing tenure and union membership.

Turning next to issue voting theory, the most persuasive test is to see whether, controlling for party identity, attitudes in 1983 predict vote in 1987. In this way, we can be sure that our measure of attitudes is temporally prior to that of vote. As with the inheritance of party identity, we shall compare the coefficients for different groups of elector, first of all comparing those who said, in 1983, that they 'cared a good deal' which party won the election with those who said that they 'didn't care very

234 MODELS OF PARTY CHOICE

much'. Since interested respondents will be more likely to have 'real' attitudes, these attitudes might be expected to play a larger role in determining voting behaviour.

Table 5.6.3(a) provides a rather stringent test of issue voting theory, but it is one that it passes. It is striking, however, how modest the impact of 1983 attitudes is on 1987 vote in comparison with the impact of 1983 party identity.

It is also striking that the effects of both party identity and principles are much weaker among respondents who did not care very much about the election outcome. There is no sign here that issue voting (or principled voting) applies to the politically interested while party identification applies to the uninterested. The most plausible interpretation of Table 5.6.3(a) is that the uninterested are simply more random in their voting behaviour (a conclusion which would also conform with Converse's black–white model). While interested respondents may have rather more stable principles, they also have more stable identities too.

An alternative comparison is between more and less educated respondents. It is generally expected that the more educated will display greater political sophistication, and might therefore vote more according to principles than to identities. We accordingly distinguish 'qualified' respondents (those with degrees, A level or its equivalent) and 'unqualified' respondents (those with no formal school qualification) [Table 5.6.3(b)]. Here we see no statistically significant difference between the two categories of respondent. Qualifications, unlike political interest, do not appear to affect the nature of political decision-making.

It follows from this that the great expansion of educational qualifications which we have witnessed over the last quarter-century cannot be expected to have made any great contribution to the alleged rise of issue voting.

Has inheritance decreased or issue voting increased?

To answer the question whether issue voting has increased over the last twenty five years is not a straightforward matter. The problems are both technical and theoretical. First, on the technical side, the ways in which attitudes to the issues have been measured, and the types and numbers of issues covered, have all changed markedly over the years. As a result of this, it is not possible to determine whether issue voting has increased over the period. If, for example, we found that the variance in vote explained by issues had increased, it would be open to the critic to suggest that this merely reflected the improvements in measuring attitudes or the improved coverage of issues in the later surveys.

An alternative strategy is for the researcher to restrict himself to shorter periods during which the measurement techniques and the coverage of

Table 5.6.2 The inheritance of partisanship in open and closed groups and among intergenerationally stable and mobile respondents

	Logit coefficients				Logit coefficients	
	Closed groups	Open groups			Stable respondents	Mobile respondents
(a) Father's party	0.19 (0.04)	0.16 (0.04)	(b) Father's party		0.22 (0.05)	0.16 (0.03)
Mother's party	0.24 (0.04)	0.28 (0.04)	Mother's party		0.32 (0.05)	0.22 (0.03)
Unweighted N	1,926	1,845	Unweighted N		1,400	2,371

Note: Figures in brackets give the standard errors.

Table 5.6.3 The effect of attitudes on 1987 vote among interested and uninterested respondents and among qualified and unqualified respondents

	Logit coefficients				Logit coefficients	
	Interested respondents	Uninterested respondents			Unqualified respondents	Qualified respondents
(a) 1983 party identity	0.74 (0.05)	0.44 (0.10)	(b) 1983 party identity		0.76 (0.08)	0.68 (0.13)
1983 political principles	−0.06 (0.01)	−0.04 (0.02)	1983 political principles		−0.04 (0.02)	−0.02 (0.02)
Unweighted N	669	186	Unweighted N		316	127

Note: Figures in brackets give the standard errors.

issues stayed more or less constant. This is essentially the strategy followed by Franklin (1985a) and by Rose and McAllister (1986).

Even with this strategy, however, there are problems. In particular, the issues of the day will almost certainly change. It is not obvious, for example, that the salient issues of 1970 were the same as those of 1966. The fact that the same range of issues was covered at both time points does not therefore mean that the issues of the day were equally well tapped at both time points. It follows that all we can ever reasonably conclude is that a specific issue or set of issues explained more of the variance at one time than another. We could, for example, say whether attitudes to trade unions explained more of the variance in vote in 1970 than they did in 1966, since the same question was asked in standard form in both surveys. But we cannot say whether issue voting in *general* increased.

In the case of party identification theory, however, the problems are rather simpler. Since the crucial variables – vote, party identification and parental party – do not change their meaning from one election to another, it is possible to examine in a relatively unambiguous way the changes in their importance over time. Thus, while there is no sure way of determining whether issue voting in general has become more important over the last quarter century, it is possible to say whether the claims of party identification theory receive less support than they did formerly.

First, we shall examine the relative stability of party identification and vote at different periods. In Table 5.6.1 we showed that, as predicted by the theory, identification was somewhat more stable at the individual level than was vote over the four years of the 1983–87 panel. But it is quite possible that the difference in stability had been even greater in an earlier period such as the 1960s. Indeed, if party identification has lost some of its force, we would surely expect the gap between identity and vote to have narrowed.

In order to compare like with like, we shall use the 1966–70 panel study, which covers a similar length of time to the 1983–87 panel. We shall measure variables in the same way as in Table 5.6.1.

Table 5.6.4 reports both the correlation coefficients and the log odds ratios, but as we can see they tell the same story: the relative stability of party identification and vote was almost exactly the same in the late 1960s as it was in the mid-1980s. If anything the difference between the two concepts has tended to widen. In this respect at least, there has been no tendency for party identification theory to lose its force.

A second way to look at the changing force of party identification theory over time is to look at the extent to which party identity is inherited. Again, if the theory is weakening in its force, we should expect inheritance to weaken over time. The 1974 surveys did not obtain information on mother's party preference and we shall therefore, in order to provide a full time series, use father's party only. As before we shall construct binary

THE DEMISE OF PARTY IDENTIFICATION THEORY? 237

Table 5.6.4 The stability of party identification and vote, 1966–70 and 1983–87

	Party ID		Vote	
	Correlation	Log odds ratio	Correlation	Log odds ratio
1966–70	0.71	3.67 (1,088)	0.65	3.27 (1,097)
1983–87	0.72	3.85 (865)	0.62	2.98 (864)

Note: Figures in brackets give the unweighted *N*s.

variables measuring whether or not the respondent identified with the Conservative party and whether or not his or her father supported the Conservatives.

The overall picture from Table 5.6.5 is fairly clear. In the three Butler and Stokes studies of 1964, 1966 and 1970 the 'inheritance of party identity' was somewhat stronger than in the subsequent studies. The decline in inheritance is relatively small and in most cases is within the 95 per cent confidence interval. The 1983 coefficient, for example, is not significantly lower than that for 1964. Still, the pattern is clear and it would be fair to conclude that, post-1964, the inheritance of party identity has been slightly weaker.

It is rather unfortunate, however, that the decline in inheritance occurs at exactly the same time as a change in question wording. [Before 1974 the question asked was: 'Did [your father] have any particular preference for one of the parties when you were young?'; from 1974 onwards the question used was 'Do you remember what party your father usually voted for when you were growing up?'] The possibility therefore that the decline is a methodological artefact cannot be ignored. We would not, however, wish to press this point too hard, since the timing of the decline in inheritance matches rather neatly the decline which writers such as Sarlvik and Crewe have documented in the *strength* of party identification.

Table 5.6.5 The relationship between respondent's and father's party, 1964–83

	Logit coefficient	95% confidence interval	Unweighted *N*
1964	0.42 (0.03)	0.36–0.48	1,716
1966	0.48 (0.03)	0.42–0.54	1,806
1970	0.45 (0.03)	0.38–0.51	1,814
Feb. 1974	0.38 (0.02)	0.33–0.42	2,462
1979	0.36 (0.03)	0.31–0.42	1,847
1983	0.37 (0.02)	0.33–0.41	3,779

Note: Figures in brackets give standard errors.

238   MODELS OF PARTY CHOICE

The occurrence of a modest, once for all decline in inheritance in 1974 thus seems the safest conclusion. And while this conforms with the evidence on the decline of the strength of party identification, it provides a marked contrast with some other conclusions that have been drawn. For example, 1970 has often been pin-pointed as the election in which class voting declined and issue voting increased, but the evidence of Table 5.6.5 shows that inheritance of partisanship remained as strong in 1970 as it had been in the 1960s.

Again there is no parallel in Table 5.6.5 to the continuing erosion of class voting and rise of issue voting which writers such as Rose and McAllister claim to have found. We do not dispute Rose and McAllister's finding that the specific political principles which have been measured in standard form in the 1974, 1979 and 1983 surveys explain, in a statistical sense, an increasing proportion of the variance. But the interpretation of their finding is open to question.

Thus, if the variance explained in vote by a specific set of issues increases over time, we might plausibly attribute this increase either to a change in the electorate – their increased political sophistication perhaps – or to a change in the political situation facing the electorate – a shift in the positions taken by the parties on the issues for example.

As the Labour and Conservative parties became more sharply polarised on a number of issues in the late 1970s and 1980s, so the variance explained in vote by the specific set of issues covered in the relevant election studies might be expected to increase too. The increase in variance explained may well tell us more about the changing character of the parties or the changing nature of the issue choices facing the public than about changes in the public's disposition towards politics. Indeed, party identification theory itself would predict that, if the parties became more sharply differentiated on the issues, their respective identifiers would follow suit. Such movements would result in these issues 'explaining' a greater proportion of the variance in vote, but we would not be entitled to conclude that, in a causal sense, issues had become more important in determining vote. The changing variance explained is entirely consistent with the claim that party identification has continued to be of unchanged importance in determining vote.

We do not wish to claim that party identification theory will suffice on its own to explain political behaviour, much less political change. Rather, the evidence we have reported suggests that political principles must be taken seriously as influences on the vote. What the paper does suggest is that the changes over time in the relative importance of political principles and party identifications in determining vote may be much less than is commonly supposed. There may have been an intellectual revolution in political science, but we should beware of supposing that there has been an equivalent revolution in the behaviour of the electorate.

Part III

Economic performance and government popularity

6 | Economic performance and government popularity

Introduction

Politicians and political commentators have always believed that there was a close connection between economic prosperity and the popularity of the government of the day, and also that governments manipulate the economy in order to improve their chances of re-election. As long ago as the early nineteenth century the Whig politician Lord Brougham commented to a friend: 'A government is not supported a hundredth part so much by the constant, uniform, quiet prosperity of the country as by those damned spurts which Pitt used to have just in the nick of time' (quoted by Butler and Stokes, 1969, p. 368). The availability of regular and reliable opinion poll reports on party preference and accurate government statistics on basic economic indicators, such as the rate of growth of real incomes and the level of unemployment, together with advances in computing and in statistical techniques, have made it possible to carry out detailed explorations of the relationship between government popularity and the performance of the economy. In this section we reproduce a number of examples of work of this kind.

In our first extract, from *Political Change in Britain*, Butler and Stokes use a very simple technique – basically the visual inspection of graphs – to demonstrate that, during the period they consider, there was a marked similarity between trends in the popularity of the government and in economic performance, as indicated by the level of unemployment and the state of the balance of payments.

Simple inspection of graphs does not take us very far, however, and more complex statistical methods are required to enable us to be more specific about the form and nature of the relationships found. A glance at the remaining extracts in this section may perhaps prove rather daunting to those who are not too confident when it comes to interpreting statistical analyses – some of the material is very advanced. With a little effort, however, we think that it should be possible even for the reader with only a

241

242 ECONOMIC PERFORMANCE

moderate grasp of statistics to follow the general line of argument being put forward. It may have to be taken on trust that the statistical techniques being used are appropriate and that they are being correctly applied. Nonetheless, we think that the material is sufficiently interesting and important to be well worth including here.

The first statistically advanced analysis of opinion poll trends in party support in Britain was by Goodhart and Bhansali (1970). They used multiple regression techniques on data for the period 1947–1968 and experimented with a number of different independent variables. They found that a model giving a good statistical prediction of levels of government popularity could be produced by using just two economic variables (the level of unemployment lagged six months, and the rate of price inflation) and also assuming a regular inter-election cycle in which the popularity of the government declined in the mid-term but revived as the following election approached.

Miller and Mackie, in the second of our extracts, challenge Goodhart and Bhansali's interpretation. They argue that the apparent relationship between government popularity and economic indicators is in fact spurious. They show that variations in government popularity can be satisfactorily explained as the product of cycles in government popularity alone – their final model involves a short-term cycle between elections superimposed upon a long-term gradual downward trend in government popularity. They argue that although governments do engineer economic upturns as elections approach, their support would increase in any case because of the cyclical effect.

In the third extract, Alt draws attention to the difficulties of developing a model which will accurately account for the relationship between government popularity and economic performance over a long period of time. He points out the importance of taking account of voters' *expectations* about the likely movement of economic indicators – for example, a 1 per cent change in the inflation rate in the middle 1970s meant something very different to electors than did a 1 per cent change in the 1960s. Alt shows how the basic Miller/Mackie model can be modified to take account of voters' expectations and then goes on to present some evidence to support the view that governments' manipulation of the economy, in particular by raising real disposable personal income just before elections, does in fact affect their popularity. He suggests that the combination of such short-term manipulation together with the long-term decline in the strength of party identification can account for the cyclical pattern in government popularity revealed by Miller and Mackie's analysis.

Our fourth extract has undoubtedly produced the most surprising results of any piece applying the techniques illustrated in this section. Most political commentators have argued or assumed that the Tories' sweeping victory in the 1983 general election was at least partly due to a 'Falklands

ECONOMIC PERFORMANCE 243

factor' – the surge of support for the government associated with the Falklands war of 1982. Sanders, Ward and Marsh argue, however, that a perfectly adequate statistical explanation of the trend in government support in this period can be produced by equations using only economic variables – in particular the surge in government support in 1982 can, they claim, be explained as the product of increasing personal economic optimism, and a lagged effect of changes in the exchange rate and the Public Sector Borrowing Requirement.

Not unexpectedly, Sanders *et al.*'s startling conclusions have not gone unchallenged. In our final extract, Clarke, Mishler and Whiteley offer a powerful critique, arguing that a more careful analysis of the data using more appropriate techniques suggests that there was indeed a 'Falklands effect' of considerable proportions. Readers must make their own judgement about this debate – it is perhaps worth adding that Sanders *et al.* have replied to their critics, defending their analysis (see Sanders *et al.*, 1990). But, whoever is right, what this exchange demonstrates is the need for very great care in employing and in interpreting the results of the extremely complex statistical procedures that are increasingly used in electoral analysis.

Further reading

Detailed quantitative studies of inter-election trends in party support using opinion poll data and a variety of indicators of the health of the economy are a relatively recent addition to electoral analysis. The literature is now extensive, however, and Whiteley (1984) describes it as 'one of the few growth industries around'. Such studies have frequently been undertaken by econometricians (statistically oriented economists) and, as a consequence, undergraduates (and lecturers!) without specialised statistical expertise may find the details difficult to follow. Brief, non-technical discussions of this approach can be found, however, in Scarbrough (1987) and in Harrop and Miller (1987, ch. 8).

It is worth mentioning here some of the studies that have been made using British data, in addition to those from which we have reproduced extracts. As we pointed out above, Goodhart and Bhansali (1970) were the first to examine the effect of economic indicators on monthly opinion poll results in Britain. Further articles followed by Frey and Garbers (1971), Frey and Schneider (1978), Mosley (1978) and Hibbs (1982). Clarke *et al.* (1986) make a plea for including political as well as economic variables in statistical models explaining trends in party support, as is done by Norpoth (1987a, 1987b). Fuller lists of references are given in Whiteley (1984) and Clarke *et al.* (1986).

6.1 | The parties and the economy

David Butler and Donald Stokes

It would be surprising if the state of the economy did not colour the view of the Government taken by many people. The economic health of the country as a whole is given the widest coverage in Westminster and in the mass media. It would be astonishing [therefore] if this great national issue, or cluster of issues, altered the standing of the parties only in the segment of the electorate on which the penalties or blessings of economic change fell most directly. A Government's successes or failures in handling the country's economic affairs can alter the attitudes of many other people as well.

What the economy means as a national issue [however] depends on the economic debate between the parties and is capable of changing over time. During the 1960s attention was given to a series of economic problems – unemployment, sluggish economic growth, the balance of payments, rising prices. Among these, unemployment probably provided the leading test of a Government's handling of the economy from the end of the Second World War until the middle 1960s.

The rise of the opinion polls with their frequent readings of party strength greatly extended the opportunities for analyzing the political impact of changing employment levels and other changes in the economy. The importance of the parties' perceived ability to deal with economic affairs is plainly evident in the polling results for the early years of our own research. This is seen by superimposing, as is done in Figure 6.1.1, two statistical series that may be calculated from the Gallup Poll during these years. The first of these is the positive or negative lead which Labour enjoyed over the Conservatives in voting intentions as recorded by Gallup's monthly index. The second is the positive or negative 'lead' of

From D.E. Butler and D. Stokes, *Political Change in Britain* (2nd edn, 1974), London: Macmillan, chapter 18.

THE PARTIES AND THE ECONOMY

Labour over the Conservatives in terms of the proportions in successive Gallup samples that said they approved or disapproved of each party's handling of economic affairs. There is in fact a remarkable agreement of these two series over a period of nearly five years.

The difficulties in the way of placing too clear a causal interpretation upon such an agreement are familiar enough. Party preference may colour the voter's perception of the parties' ability to handle the economy. Some of the agreement shown by Figure 6.1.1 must therefore be due to the tendency of voters, having attached themselves to a given party, to see its performance on economic matters in a more favourable light. Indeed, the match of the two series is partly the result of nothing more than the accidents of sampling which have drawn into different samples different proportions of these who incline towards the same party both in voting intention and in perceptions of the parties' ability to cope with economic affairs.

These qualifications are genuine ones. Yet their force is somewhat lessened by two additional observations. First, if party bias and sampling error were mainly responsible for the agreement of the two series shown in Figure 6.1.1 they ought to produce equal agreement between the party lead in terms of votes and in terms of the handling of international affairs and health and housing and other areas about which Gallup questioned their samples. But if the agreement shown by Figure 6.1.1 is partly the result of the genuine impact of changing economic perceptions and if the impact of perceptions in other areas, for example pensions and housing, varied much less in the short run (as is almost certainly the case) then there ought to be a closer agreement between short-term variations of party strength and variations of the parties' perceived success in handling the economy. And this, indeed, is what we found.

Secondly, a causal interpretation of the agreement over the 1959–64 period of the two series in Figure 6.1.1 is strengthened when we disaggregate the electorate's comparative judgement of the two parties and examine separately its evaluation of government and opposition. This separation is accomplished by Figure 6.1.2. It is at once apparent from the contrast of Figures 6.1.1 and 6.1.2 that perceptions of the Government's economic performance were much more variable and matched more closely the movements of party strength. If party bias and the accidents of sampling accounted for the agreement of the series in the earlier figure, the party lead in votes ought to provide an equally good match with each of the two series showing the changing approval of the economic performance of government and opposition. The fact that the agreement with approval of the Government was much the closer of the two is evidence that we were tapping changes which had genuine influence on party strength in these years and is at the same time evidence that it was the Government's performance that was of greater salience for the electorate.

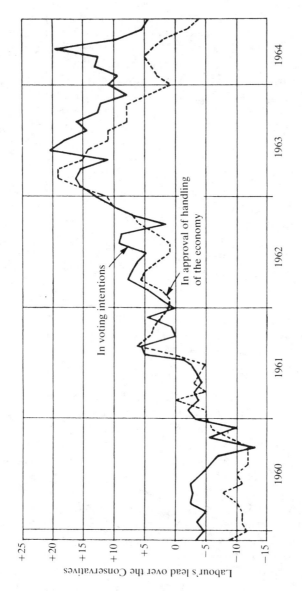

Note: These series are derived from the Gallup Poll's published figures for December 1959 to August 1964. Labour's lead in voting intentions is the arithmetic difference of the proportions giving their voting intentions as Labour and Conservative. Labour's lead in approval of parties' handling of the economy is the arithmetic difference of the proportions approving the Labour Opposition's and the Conservative Government's handling of economic affairs.

Figure 6.1.1 Labour's lead over the Conservatives in Gallup's monthly series on voting intentions and approval of parties' handling of the economy, December 1959 to August 1964

THE PARTIES AND THE ECONOMY

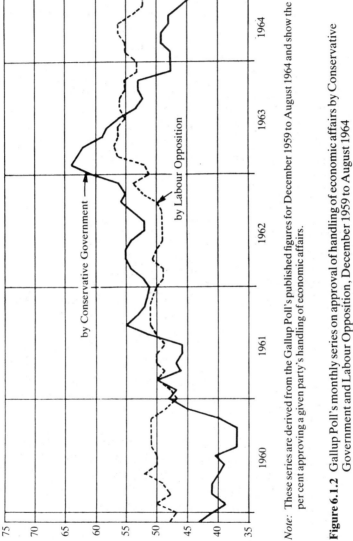

Note: These series are derived from the Gallup Poll's published figures for December 1959 to August 1964 and show the per cent approving a given party's handling of economic affairs.

Figure 6.1.2 Gallup Poll's monthly series on approval of handling of economic affairs by Conservative Government and Labour Opposition, December 1959 to August 1964

The most important analytical opportunity that these polling series provides is the possibility of measuring the relationship between fluctuations of party strength and fluctuations of the economy itself. A number of factors, including the time a party has been in office, will intervene between changes of party support and changes of the economic realities that are experienced by millions of electors. But it would be very surprising if approval of the Government's economic record were not systematically tied to the performance of the economy itself.

A strong presumption of unemployment's impact on party support in the early period of our research is raised if we plot together the time series for unemployment and the Gallup series for the party lead during the years from 1959 to 1964. A marked relationship between the two is evident in Figure 6.1.3. Closer inspection makes it plausible that changes in the level of unemployment precede changes of party support; Goodhart and Bhansali [1970] estimated that an average lag of four to six months separated a change of unemployment from its maximum political effect in this period. In particular, the decline of Conservative support between 1959 and 1963 and the partial Conservative recovery between 1963 and 1966 seem to have owed a good deal to changes of unemployment levels in 1961–2 and 1963–4.

But changes in unemployment were much less able to explain the variations in party support over the later years of the 1960s. If the unemployment and party support series for the years from 1966 to 1970 were superimposed, the fit between the two would be much less close than in Figure 6.1.3. Such a divergence is plainly damaging to the unemployment thesis. Labour won its 1966 victory at a time of low levels of unemployment. The rapid rise in unemployment after the severely restrictionist measures adopted by the Labour Government in July 1966 to defend the pound and the continued high unemployment throughout the 1966 Parliament must have been major factors in eroding Labour's support to very low levels. But the later variations in party support were not matched by large fluctuations in employment. In particular, Labour's remarkable recovery in the first six months of 1970 was not accompanied by a marked reduction in unemployment from the levels that had prevailed for three and a half years.

These facts led some observers to wonder whether there might not be a natural cycle of party support, not mainly dependent on economic conditions, under which a Government loses support in the middle of a Parliament and regains support as a new election approaches. The view was put forward that the earlier parallelism of changes of unemployment and party support was merely coincidental, since unemployment had happened to rise towards the middle of Parliaments and fall as the next election approached. It was further said that governments, believing their strength depended on reducing unemployment, tended to expand the

THE PARTIES AND THE ECONOMY

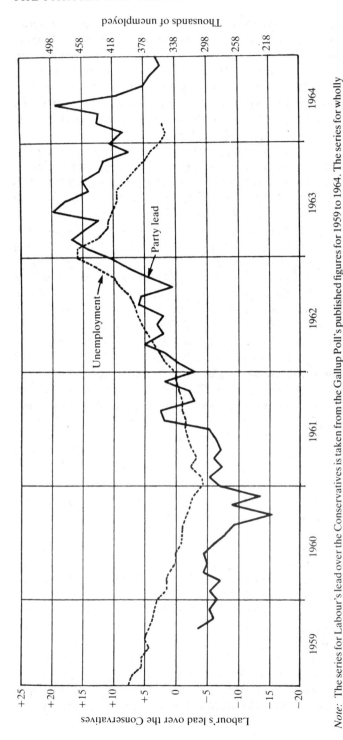

Note: The series for Labour's lead over the Conservatives is taken from the Gallup Poll's published figures for 1959 to 1964. The series for wholly unemployed, seasonally adjusted, is taken from the *Ministry of Labour Gazette*. That source gives a seasonally adjusted series only from June 1963. For the earlier period the figures given for actual number of wholly unemployed, excluding school leavers, were adjusted for seasonal variation by applying a constant seasonal adjustment factor computed as the mean of the adjustment factors used by the Ministry of Labour for the years 1964–7.

Figure 6.1.3 Gallup Poll's monthly series on Labour's lead over Conservatives and monthly series on thousands of unemployed, seasonally adjusted, 1959–64

250 · ECONOMIC PERFORMANCE

economy and bring unemployment down before going to the country, thereby strengthening a correlation which did not describe a true causal link since they would have regained support in the absence of such measures.

Nonetheless, there is a good deal about the size and timing of the shifts of party support that would remain unexplained if we were to see a rhythmic cycle of electoral support for the Government as the explanation. The shifts have, after all, varied greatly in magnitude and in detailed timing during the several post-war Parliaments.

An alternative view is that the electorate's judgement of the Government's economic performance has continued to shape the movements of party support, but that the test of economic success can change – and indeed, that it did change in the later 1960s and again in the early 1970s. The circumstances surrounding Labour's accession to power in 1964 and the substance of the economic debate between the parties in the 1966 Parliament promoted Britain's balance of payments to a more central place in the electorate's judgement of the economic performance of the Government. When Labour did eventually produce a payments surplus its standing in the country rose rapidly.

There is at the very least a suggestive fit between Britain's payments deficit (or surplus) and party strength over the latter years of the 1966 Parliament. This relationship is charted by Figure 6.1.4. The one interval in which the two series diverge widely is in the aftermath of the July measures of 1966. These policies brought a transient payments surplus but cost Labour dearly in public support, dispelling the goodwill left over from the party's victory in March. Thereafter the deterioration in Britain's trading position, which even the devaluation of November 1967 did not seem to check, was accompanied by further drops in Labour strength, until the appearance of a payments surplus in September 1969 set the stage for Labour's revival in the first six months of 1970.

The hypothesis that the country came in these years to judge Labour's economic performance mainly in terms of the balance of payments is consistent with evidence that in 1970 more of the electorate approved than disapproved of Labour's handling of the economy. It would be hard to reconcile this judgement with the state of other indicators of the country's economic health. The hypothesis is also consistent with Labour's success over its whole period in office from 1964 to 1970 in keeping alive the idea that it had inherited its main economic difficulties from the Conservatives.

We do not regard this alternative account of the role of the economy in the 1966 Parliament as more than a hypothesis. But it can explain much of the gross variation of party strength in these years without jettisoning the view that the electorate will judge a Government partly in economic terms.

There is no reason to believe that the balance of payments has permanently displaced other aspects of the economy as the major test of a

THE PARTIES AND THE ECONOMY

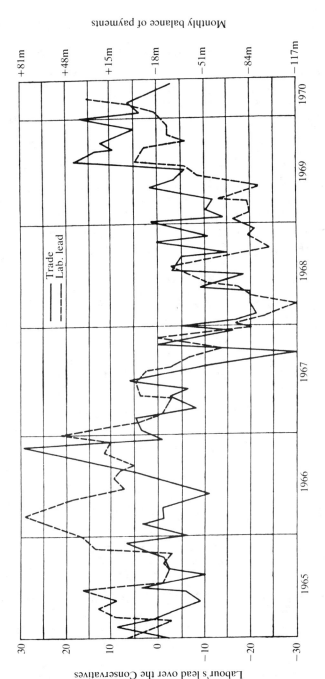

Figure 6.1.4 Gallup Poll's monthly series on Labour's lead over the Conservatives and previous month's announcement on the balance of payments, February 1965–May 1970

Government's economic performance. On the contrary, the way changes in the economy are translated into shifts of party strength is itself subject to change and will depend on the way economic issues are defined by the parties and the media as well as on the economic experiences of ordinary electors. Rising prices may, for example, at times dominate the economic responses of the electorate, and in the early 1970s they seemed to have usurped the position that the balance of payments had recently held.

Such changes in the terms of the electoral argument, in so far as it centres on political economy, will add to the difficulties both of interview studies and of studies which relate economic to electoral series. These changes will oblige the survey analyst to probe more deeply into the expectations and beliefs which give to the economy its political translation. And they will shorten the periods in which it is safe to fit a single aggregative model of economic and political change. They will also raise the importance of anchoring both types of studies in a better description of what the parties and the media say about the economy in a given period. But if we take account of these things we will hear more clearly one of the drums to which the electorate marches.

6.2 The electoral cycle and the asymmetry of government and opposition popularity

W.L. Miller and M. Mackie

Throughout the 1960s it was a common journalistic assumption that the level of government popularity was a response to the success of the country's economic performance. This assumption gained credence because the variables commonly used to explain the results of General Elections – ideology, party identification, social structure – were not suited to the explanation of large and rapid changes in government support. The evidence of both polls and by-elections was that the change in the level of government support between elections was on a scale never seen at post-war general elections. There is obviously no point in trying to explain such a change as the result of demographic or social structural change.

Goodhart and Bhansali used the monthly series [of government statistics] for unemployment and retail price inflation as predictors of [government] popularity and concluded that 'the apparent sensitivity of political popularity to economic conditions, as shown by the equations, seems almost too much to credit' [1970, p. 86].

We present here an alternative explanation of the data patterns. When two series are correlated either may indeed cause the other, but a third explanation is that they are both dependent on some third variable. Cyclical patterns in both popularity and unemployment can account for the correlation between them.

But not every writer saw the fluctuations in government popularity as primarily a response to economic success. Anthony King in *New Society*

From W.L. Miller and M. Mackie, 'The electoral cycle and the asymmetry of government and opposition popularity', *Political Studies* (1973), vol. XXI, pp. 263–79.

254 ECONOMIC PERFORMANCE

[1968] and Nigel Lawson in the *Spectator* [1968] proposed variants of a model of electoral cycles. Both put forward explanations of 'why all governments lose by-elections' irrespective of the success or failure of their policies.

In this paper the theory of economic influences on British government popularity is re-examined. Lawson's model of electoral cycles is developed and its fit to the data compared with the fit given by the economic influence model. Finally the electoral cycle model is used to show why Goodhart and Bhansali found such an apparently strong relationship between economic performance and popularity.

The economic performance models tested

Four measures of popularity are useful: the percentage of respondents who support the government, the percentage who support the main opposition party, and the sum and difference of these percentages. The measures represent (i) the absolute support for the government, (ii) for the opposition, (iii) the support for the two-party system and (iv) the government lead over the main opposition party, which is a second measure of government popularity and the one used by Goodhart and Bhansali. [Following Goodhart and Bhansali] we have used price inflation, the unemployment rate and the balance of trade as independent variables. We added the wage inflation rate, the net wage inflation rate (corrected for price inflation), the rate of house building and the bank rate. As an alternative measure of unemployment we have used the vacancies rate and also constructed a net unemployment rate (corrected for vacancies). This gives nine economic predictor variables.

Since neither the government nor the opposition share of the Gallup poll show much evidence of seasonal variation, the economic predictors are seasonally adjusted using a simple multiplicative adjustment technique.

The main method of evaluation is by stepwise multiple regression. Predictor variables are added into the equation one at a time, the variable with the greatest predictive power being added first, then the one that most improves the initial prediction of popularity and so on.

Each of the models tested can be defined by the transformations applied to the set of nine economic predictor variables described above. This set is denoted by *ECON*.

MODEL E1: *Immediate response.* In this model, the electorate pays attention only to the party in power and only to conditions during its current tenure of office.

$$\text{Predictor set} = ECON_t$$

(Nine variables)

THE ELECTORAL CYCLE

The subscript t is used to indicate that the popularity in month t depends upon the economic performance in month t.

MODEL E2: *Lagged response.* Goodhart and Bhansali found that unemployment six months previously affected popularity more than current unemployment. We allow the response to be immediate or lagged by three or by six months.

$$\text{Predictor set} = ECON_t, ECON_{t-3}, ECON_{t-6}$$

(27 variables, being the original set plus that set 3 months and 6 months ago)

MODEL E3: *Response to change.* We allow popularity to be a response to current levels of economic performance, and to the changes over the last three or six months.

$$\text{Predictor set} = ECON_t, ECON_t - ECON_{t-3}, ECON_t - ECON_{t-6}$$

(27 variables, being the current values and the changes in those variables over the previous three and six months)

Popularity may be a response to the difference between 'expected' and 'acceptable' economic performance. Harold Wincott in the *Financial Times* (23–iv–63) suggested that 'it is not necessarily the absolute state of affairs prevailing at any time which seems to count, but either people's ability to adapt themselves to those conditions or their belief that they will be temporary.' This relatively complex model can be operationalized in several ways depending upon how we measure the 'expected' and the 'acceptable' levels of performance. Some possibilities follow.

MODEL E4: *The detrended model.* This identifies the 'expected' performance with the current performance, and the 'acceptable' performance with the linear trend.

$$\text{Predictor set} = \text{Detrended } ECON_t$$

(Nine variables, being the deviations from linear trends in the economic variables)

MODEL E5: *The continuous adjustment model.* Using the linear trend to estimate the currently acceptable level is perhaps unnecessarily simple. As an alternative we have formed the weighted average $AECON$ based on the preceding 12 months, weighted by $0.95, (0.95)^2 \ldots (0.95)^{12}$. This weights the most recent months most highly on the assumption that memories fade.

$$\text{Predictor set} = ECON_t - AECON_t$$

(Nine variables)

256 ECONOMIC PERFORMANCE

MODEL E6: *The simple projection model.* Models E4 and E5 took the expected economic levels to be the current levels. One alternative is to project forward the trends over the last three months to estimate expected future levels of performance.

$$\text{Predictor set} = (ECON_t + (ECON_t - ECON_{t-3})) - AECON_t$$
$$= 2ECON_t - ECON_{t-3} - AECON_t$$

(Nine variables)

MODEL E7: *The prescient model.* A second alternative for the 'expected' economic performance is the actual future performance.

$$\text{Predictor set} = ECON_{t+3} - AECON_t$$

(Nine variables)

MODEL E8: *The cumulative effect model.* Models E4 to E7 are all based upon the assumption that the electorate adjust to changing economic conditions, that for example a run of high unemployment will gradually make higher levels of unemployment acceptable. Models E5 to E7 assume that this adjustment process is very rapid and occurs within a year. An opposite view is that in the very short term a run of poor economic performance figures might make the government cumulatively less popular rather than poor performance more acceptable. Thus

$$\text{Predictor set} = AECON_t$$

(Nine variables)

Table 6.2.1 shows the percentage of the variation in each popularity series that is explained by each of these eight models.

Table 6.2.2 shows which predictor variable was selected first by the automatic stepwise procedure, and the figure in brackets is the proportion of popularity variation which is explained by that variable alone.

The results shown in these two tables are in general accordance with those of Goodhart and Bhansali in that they show unemployment to be the best predictor of the government lead, but these tables examine more models and the results for the other models cast some doubt upon the simplicity of the finding for government lead. To summarize the evidence of these tables:

1. The expectations and acceptability models E5 to E7 are extremely poor predictors.
2. Model E8 shows why this is so: the cumulation of poor economic performance correlates with popularity in much the same way as current economic performance.
3. With models E1 to E4 and E8, which do display some predictive power, the correlation with economic performance is always higher for the government share of the Gallup poll than for the government lead over the opposition.

THE ELECTORAL CYCLE

Table 6.2.1 Percentages of variation in popularity series explained by various models

Model	Govt	Opp.	Govt lead	Two-party system
E1 immediate response	28	14	19	33
E2 lagged response	33	28	26	39
E3 response to change	32	28	26	39
E4 detrended	19	15	19	16
E5 continuous adjustment	3	1	2	4
E6 simple projection	3	1	2	3
E7 prescient	6	2	3	8
E8 cumulative effect	31	34	25	43

Table 6.2.2 The single best predictor and the percentage of popularity variation explained by it alone

Model	Govt	Opp.	Govt lead	Two-party system
E1 immediate response	UN(22)	BANK(5)	UN(16)	BANK(20)
E2 lagged response	UN(22)	$BAL_{t-6}(6)$	UN(16)	$BANK_{t-6}(23)$
E3 response to change	UN(22)	BANK(5)	UN(16)	BANK(20)
E4 detrended	UN(12)	UN(6)	UN(13)	UN(4)
E5 continuous adjustment	NETUN(2)	WI(0)	UN(1)	HOU(2)
E6 simple projection	UN(2)	WI(0)	UN(1)	NETUN(2)
E7 prescient	BANK(3)	BANK(1)	UN(1)	BANK(4)
E8 cumulative effects	UN(21)	WI(13)	UN(14)	BANK(24)

Note: UN = unemployment rate; NETUN = net unemployment rate; WI = wage inflation rate; PI = price inflation rate; BANK = bank rate; BAL = balance of trade; HOU = house building rate. Figures in brackets are the additional percent of popularity variation explained by the addition of the single variable specified.

4. In these models it is unemployment or its transformations which correlates most highly with the government share of the poll.
5. The opposition share of the poll does not correlate highly with unemployment or its transformations. Prediction of the opposition share is achieved by a combination of variables, none of them bearing a majority of the predictive load. The best of these predictors is the bank rate.
6. The proportion of Gallup respondents supporting one or other of the two main parties can be predicted more easily than any of the other three popularity measures, and the best predictor is the bank rate, except in the detrended variables model.

These results indicate a basic asymmetry between government and opposition shares of the poll. It is not true, for example, that the government's loss is the opposition's gain or vice versa. They also show that the relatively strong but still fairly weak predictive power of unemployment applies only to the government share of the poll, not to the opposition.

The electoral cycle models tested

The predictor variables used in the electoral cycle models are very simple series, even if their interpretation is not.

The cycle variables we have used are:

$NEAR$ = the number of months to the nearest election, past or future,
$SQNR$ = the square of the number of months to the nearest election,
$LAST$ = the number of months since the last election.

The first two, $NEAR$ and $SQNR$, were chosen because a table of the average government lead against the number of months away from a general election showed a strongly curvilinear pattern, the relationship being steeper in the immediate vicinity of elections. Including both $NEAR$ and $SQNR$ is equivalent to fitting a parabola to the pattern of popularity.

Anthony King's explanation of 'why all governments lose by-elections' is that elections are won by the temporary adherence of uncommitted voters with weak party identification. Between elections, when the political stimulus is low, these voters tend to revert to their 'normal' identification, splitting more evenly between Labour and Conservative, and they are also less likely to vote at all. This explains why there is a drop in turnout and in government support at by-elections. While the idea of a changing political context is valuable, the other details of this explanation do not fit the data. Between elections the government lead in the Gallup poll over the main opposition party does not just revert to zero as implied by the re-establishment of long run identification but consistently assumes negative values. Table 6.2.3 shows the average value of the government and opposition support at all distances from elections. As can be seen, the opposition share of the poll is almost constant, but the government share is particularly low in the mid-term and overall the government runs 3 per cent behind.

Nigel Lawson's 'new theory of by-elections' is that between elections government supporters feel mildly disenchanted and abstain whereas opposition supporters still turn out in full. This explanation also accounts for a rise in abstention and a drop in government support at by-elections. Lawson suggests that the mild disenchantment of government supporters between elections is so mild that it does not prevent them from returning to the fold as the election approaches. This provides the simplest cyclical model:

MODEL C1: *Pure cycles.* Expressed popularity drops after an election but rises again as the next election approaches.

Predictor set = $NEAR$, $SQNR$

(Two variables)

THE ELECTORAL CYCLE

Table 6.2.3 Average value of government and opposition support at all distances from elections

Months from nearest election	Average govt share %	Average opp. share %	Months from nearest election	Average govt share %	Average opp. share %
0	42	38	16	34	40
1	41	38	17	34	39
2	40	38	18	34	39
3	38	39	19	34	39
4	38	39	20	35	39
5	37	39	21	33	39
6	38	39	22	32	38
7	36	39	23	30	40
8	36	40	24	31	39
9	36	40	25	30	40
10	36	38	26*	33	39
11	36	39	27*	33	38
12	35	38	28*	32	34
13	34	40	29*	31	35
14	35	39	30*	29	35
15	34	40			
			All months	36	39

*Less than eight observations for 26 months or more.

MODEL C2: *Cycles plus trend*. Some at least of the disenchantment might not be so mild. As time progresses even the most pusillanimous government must offend a succession of minorities, if not majorities, and bring into being a 'coalition of minorities' opposed to it. Hence the model: in addition to mid-term effects there is a steady growth of disenchantment which is not reversed as the next election approaches.

$$\text{Predictor set} = NEAR, SQNR, LAST$$
(Three variables)

MODEL C3: *Time dependent cycles*. While there was a little evidence that governments became generally more unpopular over time, they were both more popular and more unpopular in the sixties than in the fifties. A possible explanation of this is that the respondents to the Gallup poll became as a group more volatile, that more of them came to see the polls as something different from general election voting. To test the fit of this growth of volatility model the regression equation of C2 can be modified by letting the regression coefficient of *NEAR* and *SQNR*, but not of *LAST*, be a linear function of the month of the century. Where *T* stands for the month of the century:

$$\text{Predictor set} = NEAR, SQNR, LAST, T \times NEAR, T \times SQNR$$
(Five variables)

260   ECONOMIC PERFORMANCE

MODEL C4: *Majority dependent cycles.* Alternatively, the increases in popularity and unpopularity can be attributed to the size of the government's parliamentary majority, on the assumption that governments with large majorities become less responsive to public demands over a wide range of issues, and less concerned about their public relations image, while the converse is true for governments with small majorities. Using J to stand for the government's overall majority in parliament,

Predictor set $= NEAR, SQNR, LAST, J \times NEAR, J \times SQNR, J \times LAST$
(Six variables)

Table 6.2.4 shows the percentages of variation in several popularity series explained by each of these models.
The results can be summarized:

1. The predictive power (R^2) of the cyclical models compared to the economic models of the last section is a little better for government lead and for the two-party system.
2. The cyclical models predict the government share of the poll much better than did the economic models.
3. The cyclical models hardly predict any of the variation in the opposition's share of the poll, whereas the economic models predicted about 30 per cent.

These results confirm the basic asymmetry of government and opposition shares of the poll, and in a dramatic way: governments suffer from mid-term unpopularity, but the opposition does not receive a corresponding rise in support. Our statistical tests show, [then], a surprising amount of truth in Lawson's hypothesis of cycles.

Economic performance and the electoral cycle

We have shown that the government share of the poll follows a cyclical pattern. Using only the number of months to the nearest election, and the

Table 6.2.4 Percentages of variation in the popularity series explained by various cyclical models

Model	Govt	Opp.	Govt lead	Two-party system
C1 pure cycles	31	1	19	29
C2 cycles plus trend	42	3	27	38
C3 time dependent cycles	63	3	37	62
C4 majority dependent cycles	44	19	30	48

THE ELECTORAL CYCLE

square of that value, we can explain 31 per cent of the variation in the government share of the poll and the slightly more complex models explain up to 63 per cent. Consequently any economic series which follows an electoral cycle will correlate with government popularity. Unemployment peaked in the middle of the 1955–9 parliament, and again in the middle of the 1959–64 parliament. In the 1966–70 parliament it rose in the mid-term but did not fall as the 1970 election approached. The coincidence of relatively high unemployment and relatively high unpopularity in the mid-term is certainly some evidence of a causal link, but very little. The number of separate data points is not the number of months in our analysis (about 300) but the number of full parliaments, i.e. four. Of these four, the 1955–9 and 1959–64 parliaments suggest that there is a causal link, and the 1951–5 parliament gives ambiguous evidence, while the 1966–70 parliament suggests that there is not. In the winter of 1969 through to the summer of 1970 the electoral cycle of government popularity continued in spite of the government's failure to reduce unemployment.

If the cyclical components of unemployment and popularity are retained in the regression analysis the conclusions may be based on little more than this counting of coincident cycles. It would be easy to claim that these coincidences produce a correlation between unemployment and popularity, that the variations in both series arise not from a direct link but from a common dependence upon electoral forces, the variations in the popularity series being the result of Gallup respondents switching to and fro between comparative and non-comparative evaluations of the government, and the variations in the unemployment series resulting from the government's mistaken belief that the unemployment level was the main determinant of their chances of re-election.

It is an elementary notion in causal modelling that if a correlation between two variables x and y is purely the result of their joint dependence on a third variable z, then the partial correlation between x and y controlling for z has an expected value of zero. Equivalently this can be restated in terms of percentages of variation explained: the prediction of y from z will not be improved by the addition of x to the predictor set.

Table 6.2.5 shows the increases in the percentage of variation explained when each of the economic predictor sets is added to the [best] cyclical prediction set C3. Table 6.2.6 shows which economic variable was selected first by stepwise regression, and by how much it improved the prediction by itself.

Comparing these tables with those for the predictive power of the economic models before decycling, the economic variables do as well as before in predicting the opposition share of the poll, and bank rate is again prominent, but they add relatively little to the cyclical prediction of government share of the poll.

262   ECONOMIC PERFORMANCE

Table 6.2.5 Percentages of variation in the popularity series explained by a cyclical model alone, and the increases when the cyclical model is augmented by various economic models

Model	Govt	Opp.	Govt lead	Two-party system
C3 time dependent cycles	63	3	37	62
C3 plus E1 immediate response	7	14	11	6
C3 plus E2 lagged response	11	29	18	11
C3 plus E3 response to change	11	29	18	11
C3 plus E4 detrended	10	13	12	9
C3 plus E5 continuous adjustment	1	1	1	2
C3 plus E6 simple projection	1	2	1	1
C3 plus E7 prescient	0	3	0	2
C3 plus E8 cumulative effects	9	36	20	10

Table 6.2.6 The variables from the economic models which are selected as the first to be added to the cyclical prediction model

Model	Govt	Opp.	Govt lead	Two-party system
C3	63	3	37	62
C3 plus E1 immediate response	HOU(3)	BANK(10)	HOU(3)	BANK(1)
C3 plus E2 lagged response	$HOU_{t-3}(3)$	$BANK_{t-6}(10)$	$BAL_{t-6}(6)$	$VAC_{t-3}(2)$
C3 plus E3 response to change	HOU(3)	BANK(7)	HOU(3)	BANK(1)
C3 plus E4 detrended	HOU(3)	UN(4)	UN(4)	HOU(4)
C3 plus E5 continuous adjustment	BANK(0)	BANK(0)	BANK(1)	UN(0)
C3 plus E6 simple projection	WI(0)	WI(0)	WI(1)	VAC(0)
C3 plus E7 prescient	BAL(0)	BANK(1)	BANK(0)	HOU(1)
C3 plus E8 cumulative effects	PI(4)	WI(18)	PI(12)	VAC(1)

Note: See note to Table 6.2.2. VAC = vacancy rate.

The implications

Our analysis has shown that the apparently strong link between two economic performance variables, unemployment and inflation, and government popularity in the 1959–70 period was not in reality so strong as has been thought. Either by coincidence, or through the government's misperceptions of the electoral importance of these variables, they followed an electoral cyclical pattern in those years. At other times they did not, yet the cyclical pattern of government popularity continued.

When the electoral cyclical component is removed from the government popularity series, none of our performance measures added much to the prediction of popularity, though collectively they explained about a third

THE ELECTORAL CYCLE

of the remaining variation. The evidence is against a simple view of politics in which the electorate choose between competing teams of economic managers, base their choice on only two economic variables, and take no account of the politician's verbal interpretations of these economic statistics.

6.3 | The economy and government support

Jim Alt

Estimating a popularity function for Britain

It has been a regular observation about British politics for some years that the popularity of the government (measured by voting intention in opinion polls) always falls steeply in mid-term, giving rise to some remarkable by-election defeats, only to recover to a large extent in time for the next General Election. This inter-election cycle is usually put forward as a 'great constant' of British political life, and its origins remain unclear. Figure 6.3.1 shows the expected shape of the cycle between elections, whether it is modelled as a parabolic curve (Miller and Mackie, 1973), or as short-term surges before and after elections with a depreciation of popularity in between (Goodhart and Bhansali, 1970), or most efficiently as a sum of time to the nearest election plus depreciation (Frey and Schneider, 1978). Superficial differences in estimation of this cycle, which is one variety of a first-order autoregressive process (that is, popularity in any month is well predicted by popularity the previous month) should not mask the fact that all these estimates propose a broadly similar inter-election cycle.

Economic effects on government popularity are modelled as the determinants of fluctuations in popularity around this cycle. The effect of high unemployment is expected to be seen in levels of government popularity lower than the cycle alone would predict. Similarly, relative to cyclical levels of popularity, high rates of inflation depress, and high rates of real economic growth increase, government popularity. Attempts to link popularity to trends in the balance of payments have failed to isolate significant independent effects (despite the claim of Butler and Stokes (1969)). Relative to the predictive power of the overall cycles, however,

From J. Alt, *The Politics of Economic Decline* (1979), Cambridge: Cambridge University Press, chapter 6.

(a) Goodhart and Bhansali (1970) model contains fall after election ('euphoria'), rise before election ('backswing') and downward trend in mid-term.

(b) Miller and Mackie (1973) model contains time-dependent inter-election parabolic curves whose troughs are deeper in successive periods.

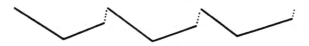

(c) Frey and Schneider (1978) model contains time to nearest election affected by downward inter-election time trend.

Figure 6.3.1 Models of inter-election cycles in government popularity (peaks in popularity coincide with elections)

economic effects, though statistically significant, are small, and lack explanatory power.

The existence of a recurrent cycle forms the basis for generalisation across governments and time periods, allowing for evaluation of the popularity of individual governments against some long-term standard. A five-point popularity deficit in mid-term is, according to the cycle hypothesis, less of a problem than a five-point deficit one year before or after an election. Moreover Miller and Mackie point out that the cycles are time-dependent, and that the decreased popularity of governments of the late 1960s relative to twenty years earlier is reflected in inter-election cycles whose troughs are deeper and longer-lasting.

Miller and Mackie's cyclical model covers all governments from 1948–72. However, when recent governments are considered, some difficulties arise. The Heath government [of 1970–74] was able to sustain a level of popularity in mid-term much higher than that of its predecessor, and the next Labour government did so as well throughout much of 1975–77. In fact, the best Miller–Mackie cycle equation explains only 30 per cent of the variance in government popularity from June 1970–January 1978, less than half its explanatory power from 1948–72.

The declining fit of popularity to the cyclical model is only one problem that merits investigation. A more serious problem is that the unprecedentedly high levels of inflation and unemployment during and after 1974 suggest that whatever magnitudes of effect might have been attributed to these economic variables in earlier years will no longer hold. It is inconceivable that the impact of one per cent of inflation in 1975 should be the same as the impact of one per cent of inflation in 1965. None of the published studies referred to above includes estimates from the last few years, but what is expected is exactly what happens: equation 1 in Table 6.3.1 shows that if the period 1959–77 is considered, the only terms which are well-determined are the downward trend and cycle elements within governments. Of the economic terms, only the growth rate of real income is (marginally) significant.

What is sought is a model which can be estimated correctly, sustain the impact of economic (and particularly inflation) expectations, and be estimated over a period including the years after 1974, as well as helping give an account of the apparently non-cyclical behaviour of government popularity during the years of the Heath government. This is an appropriate point to introduce the idea that people have by and large the greatest motivation to pay attention to economic conditions when these conditions are deteriorating. The government may well not benefit from economic conditions when these conditions are seen to be all right, since something like slow but steady real income growth may be taken for granted rather than seen as a credit to the government. It may be penalised when things are not all right, particularly if the electorate are more strongly motivated to notice economic conditions when these are deteriorating. In order to develop a model [which takes account of this], assume that members of the electorate are aware of the present rate of inflation [and] further that there is some average of recent experience which people see as critical. Since people's memories are not infinite, assume arbitrarily that this critical level of inflation can be represented by the average level of inflation over the last three years. When inflation has become worse than this critical standard, people are aware of it; if it is below recent experience, people pay no attention to the rate of inflation.

A straightforward extension of this argument is to hypothesise that economic conditions only affect government popularity when 'in crisis'. In other words, government popularity is diminished by inflation only when inflation is high relative to recent experience. A fall in the rate of inflation aids the government only when inflation is above satisfactory levels anyway; trends in inflation when it is below the critical standard are unnoticed, and therefore do not affect the popularity of the government. Table 6.3.1, equations 2 [for crisis periods] and 3 [for other periods] give empirical estimates relating to these hypotheses [for Jan. '61–Apr. '73].

These equations show that government popularity is determined by two entirely different processes, depending on whether inflation (expected) is

THE ECONOMY AND GOVERNMENT SUPPORT 267

Table 6.3.1 Popularity, cycles, and economic conditions

Equation	Period	Constant	Trend	Cycle	Annual rate of inflation: Observed	Expected	Unemployment rate	Growth rate of personal disposable income	R^2	F	obs.	DW	Estimation procedure
1	1959.1–1977.3	41.8 (29.5)	−0.50 (5.9)	−0.74 (3.8)	−0.11 (1.0)		−0.23 (0.4)	0.25 (1.6)	0.51	14.4	75	0.92	OLS
2	1961.1–1973.4	43.8 (15.5)	−0.32 (3.0)	−1.04 (3.4)		−0.74 (2.0)	−0.69 (0.5)	0.62 (2.2)	(0.79)	20.6	35	(2.07)	GLS ($\rho = 0.50$)
3	1961.1–1973.4	46.9 (11.5)	−0.77 (3.6)	−0.74 (8.6)		−0.19 (0.3)	−0.05 (0.3)	0.01 (0.3)	(0.78)	6.3	17	(1.95)	GLS ($\rho = 0.31$)

Note: Dependent variable is per cent intending to vote for government party, from *Gallup Political Index*, various, averaged over quarters. Trend and cycle as in Frey and Schneider (1978). Economic data from *Economic Trends*, various. Expected inflation from Carlson and Parkin (1975). Bracketed numbers beneath coefficients are t-statistics. Bracketed values of R^2 and DW indicate that dependent variable is differenced.

in crisis. When it is in crisis, the effects of inflation expectations and real income growth are marked and significant: independent of cycles each per cent of expected inflation knocks 0.74 of a percentage point off government popularity but each extra per cent growth of real income puts back 0.62 of that point. The coefficient of unemployment is not significantly estimated in inflation crises, but retains the right sign. In non-crisis periods, government popularity is all cycles and trends: the economic variables have insignificant effects. The fit in both cases is excellent. This represents a good foundation for a 'satisficing' model of economic effects on government popularity. Crisis levels of inflation, relevant to recent trends, represent a perceptual threshold. Only when inflation is in crisis are economic conditions perceived and brought to bear on government popularity.

[However, similar models, not shown here, taking account of the notion of 'crisis' in a different way and covering the longer period 1959–77, produce rather unclear results.]

While this discussion must end on a somewhat tentative note, it seems clear that the sort of models outlined offer the only hope for successfully estimating the impact of economic variables on popularity over long periods. These models must take account of expectations, and of the adaptive nature of expectations, considering the impact of the economy on government popularity in the light of constantly shifting perceptions and evaluations.

A reinterpretation of the electoral cycle

Some years ago, King (1968) put forward a hypothesis accounting for governments' mid-term by-election losses in terms of short-term factors involving party identification. At the heart of his model is the suggestion that general elections are 'high stimulus' events which move people to increase their support for parties. By-elections are commonly 'low stimulus' events, affecting people less, such that their voting is more in accord with levels and directions expected in 'normal' times. Briefly, it is the weaker identifiers who are more likely, having turned out and produced the pro-government swing at the last general election, to stay home and produce the government's mid-term losses. By extension, government popularity in the opinion polls should be seen as artificially raised by general elections, in between which it gradually returns to 'normal' levels, only to be disturbed again by the next election. Thus, it is less important to explain the decline in mid-term popularity than to explain the repeated surges at election time.

It [is] possible to decompose the question of economic effects on government popularity into two separate problems: a long-term problem

THE ECONOMY AND GOVERNMENT SUPPORT   269

and a short-term problem. There is an upswing in popularity before every election, compensated by a downswing afterwards, which is a *short-term* phenomenon. Between every pair of elections there is also a downward time trend: this is part of a *long-term* trend. In other words, since the Second World War there has been a consistent slippage of support for governments: the time trend observed in each government's popularity is a reflection of this long-term trend.

Clearly, elections and other events may move popularity around this long-term downward trend, though the trend, independent of these other effects, is always there, pulling popularity down. What can be said about this long-term trend? It is certainly something which affects both the major parties, which alternated in government over the period. This long-term trend is the same as the general decline in partisanship over this period in Britain. The proportion [of the electorate] having a 'very strong' identification with Labour or the Conservatives dropped from 40 per cent to 24 per cent between 1964 and 1974. This is the same long-term trend which produces the time-dependent cycles of the Miller–Mackie model.

Trends in government popularity are a function of trends in strength of attachment to the two major parties. Because of this, during each successive government, support at mid-term has fallen lower, as the government's support is reduced to its strongest adherents, though support continues to be available at election time (though decreasingly). To substantiate this claim, it ought to be the case that strength of party identification displays the same 'cyclical trends' that show up in series of government popularity. There are virtually no data with which to substantiate this point, but [such data as there are suggest] that *strength* as opposed to direction of party identification has a short-term 'cyclical' component, rising sharply at election times and falling away again after. This establishes something of an identity – or at least a functional relationship – between the general level of strength of identification for the two major parties and the drift of the popularity of the government, regardless of which party is in power. The fact that strength of identification varies with popularity in the short run suggests that it might do in the long run.

Whatever the exact causes, the decline in partisanship across the quarter of a century since 1950 lies at the heart of the persistent decline in government popularity reflected in increasingly exaggerated cycles between elections. As normal partisanship – and therefore mid-term popularity – has declined, however, the major parties have continued to be able to rally support at election time: this produces the apparent volatility of the electorate.

270 ECONOMIC PERFORMANCE

An interpretation of short-term surges in popularity

In the short term, how does the government manage to recruit the extra support observed in popularity before elections, and the increase in strength of party identification measured just after elections? It is probably the case that appeals to traditional loyalties, threats of the doom attendant upon the election of the opposing party, and so on, have something to do with it. These things tend to occur during the campaign only, however, and sometimes, as in 1970, there is evidence of a considerable backswing in popularity before the election campaign actually begins. More relevant therefore is the question of whether there is anything 'economic' going on in the months before elections which might account for the short-term backswing cycle – the government's ability to rally support again before the next election.

Miller and Mackie find an election component in fluctuations in the unemployment rate, and indeed unemployment does decline in the latter half of a number of governments in the period under consideration. There is no real evidence of any government attempting to hold down the rate of inflation in the short term to promote its own popularity at election time, except perhaps March–September 1974. When one considers the third variable usually included as a determinant of political popularity, personal disposable income, a slightly different picture emerges. Only election-time trends in *real personal disposable* income [RPDI] will be considered [here]: that is, personal income net of taxes and social security contributions, in terms of constant rather than current prices. RPDI increases throughout the whole of the period 1959–75, in line with general economic growth. The present interest is in short-term movements, and particularly in whether these tie up with the short-term movements in popularity around election times.

Consider the equation reported by Goodhart and Bhansali (1970), and summarised in Figure 6.3.1. The equation fits government lead to some economic variables, plus a downward time trend, plus two variables called euphoria and backswing. (Recall that euphoria describes the decline in popularity after an election and backswing its resurgence before the next election.) The argument of a decline in partisanship producing greater apparent 'volatility' in the long run implies that the coefficients of each of these variables should grow through this period. More ground has had to be made up to restore 'normal' partisanship levels at successive elections over the last two decades. [This means] that the coefficients measuring this election-time surge and decline should grow larger across the years. This can be tested directly by fitting the Goodhart–Bhansali model, not across the whole period, but within each individual government, and looking at the behaviour of the euphoria and backswing coefficients, with the

THE ECONOMY AND GOVERNMENT SUPPORT 271

expectation that they should grow in the equations relating to more recent governments.

With limited exceptions, as Table 6.3.2 shows, this is borne out. The coefficients attaching to 'euphoria', the post-election downswing, grow steadily, though there is (relative to trend, inflation and unemployment) no downswing after the 1959 election. Similarly, there is no evidence of a pro-government swing over the six months before the elections of 1955 and February 1974, independent of other factors. Thus, if what is sought is an economic account of euphoria and backswing, it lies in a variable which is getting 'better' in the six months before each election and 'worse' in the year following, save that there should be no deterioration after 1959 and no improvement before 1955 or February 1974.

Reasonably reliable data on RPDI are available on a quarterly basis only since 1959; they have been converted into a per capita figure to allow for the effects of a slowly growing population, and detrended to remove the effects of long-term growth. The series has then been recast as a difference between the current observation and the average of the previous two. Figure 6.3.2 plots trends in this variable around elections: enough observations are given to compare its behaviour with the 'cyclical' backswing and euphoria variables.

In terms of pre-election behaviour, [February] 1974 certainly stands out from other [elections] as the only case where immediately before an election real income was allowed to drop sharply over the previous half year; it goes without saying that the February 1974 election was also called

Table 6.3.2 Pre- and post-election trends in popularity

	Variable	
Government	'Euphoria' (post-election)	'Backswing' (pre-election)
1951–5	0.40	0.05*
1955–9	0.56	1.4
1959–64	0.10*	2.1
1966–70	0.89	2.7
1970–4	1.0	0.10*

Note: * indicates the coefficient is *not* statistically significant at (minimally) the 0.05 level. The coefficients are derived from OLS regressions of popularity on, jointly, a time trend, 'euphoria' (which takes the value 12 in the month after an election, decreasing by one each month over the first year of a government and zero thereafter) and 'backswing' (which takes the value one six months before a general election and increases by one each month until the election). The 1964–6 government is omitted as it was too short to incorporate these variables in a regression. Popularity data from Gallup.

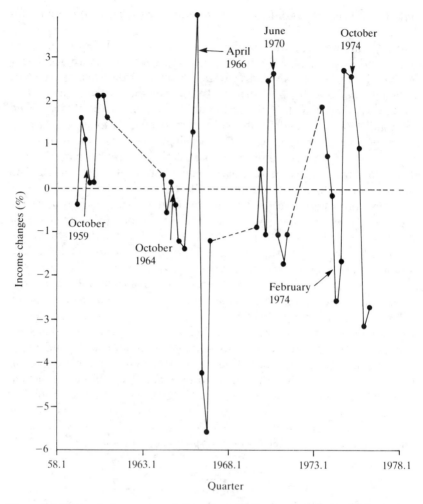

Figure 6.3.2 Quarterly movements in real per capita personal disposable income (detrended) around elections, 1958–75: each point reflects the difference between (annualised) growth rate of income in that quarter and the average over the two previous quarters

suddenly at a time when most expected the government to continue in office without an election for another year. The general upward movement of per capita RPDI is particularly marked in the months before the elections of 1966, 1970, and October 1974, and is evident also in the earlier years. Similarly, the decline in RPDI after each of the elections (except 1959, when the boom continued for another year) is also clear.

Before each of [the elections of 1964, 1966 and 1970], for a short period RPDI was rising at more than double its normal rate of growth; after each

THE ECONOMY AND GOVERNMENT SUPPORT

of these elections, it was actually falling. These trends coincide exactly with the short-term cyclical movements observed in government popularity, and suggest that RPDI movements may be a source of the repeated ability of governments (before 1974) to rally their supporters. Equally important, in [February] 1974 when for the first time in 20 years there was an election without the observable backswing to the government, there was also no cyclical movement in short-term changes of per capita RPDI. One must resist the temptation to make too much of Figure 6.3.2, however. Growth of RPDI was shown above not to be a significant predictor of government popularity. This is an illustration of how that prediction could come about, for it is short-term movements of RPDI which match trends in popularity around election times, when the higher stimulus of the campaign may bring considerations of personal well-being to bear on government popularity.

The principal analyses of government opinion poll popularity converge to a single account, which contains a long-term and a short-term component. The long-term component is the downward trend in strength of party identification. It produces the apparent volatility of the electorate reflected in deeper inter-election troughs in popularity. The short-term component consists of a rallying of support before elections and an accentuated fall in support after elections; short-term movements in personal disposable income are a factor in these sudden short-term recoveries. More generally, when modelling the economic determinants of government popularity, more attention needs to be paid to questions of timing. There is evidence that inflation expectations and changes in real disposable income may have different effects according to both the economic climate and timing with respect to elections. All this means that sophisticated models will be required to capture economic effects on popularity, but they appear to be worth seeking and testing.

6.4 Government popularity and the Falklands war: a reassessment

David Sanders, Hugh Ward and David Marsh (with Tony Fletcher)

For students of British political history, one of the more intriguing episodes of recent years was the revival in political fortunes experienced by the Thatcher Government during the course of 1982. In popular discourse, the favoured explanation for this transformation has centred on the domestic political effects of the Falklands war.

In this article we review the existing evidence that has been presented in support of the 'Falklands factor' interpretation of Mrs Thatcher's political resurgence. We then offer some alternative evidence, which casts a rather different light on the events of 1982.

The existing evidence for the Falklands effect

Quantitative studies of government popularity in Britain take as their dependent variable the month-by-month variations in the percentage of Gallup poll respondents who say that they would vote for the incumbent government 'if there were to be a general election tomorrow'. They then attempt to model these variations in terms of movements in various aggregate-level political and economic variables. Three recent studies have concentrated exclusively on the Thatcher years.

Dunleavy and Husbands [1985] estimate that the Falklands war led to a long-term increase in government popularity of over 16 percentage points. Clarke, Stewart and Zuk [1986] conclude that the Falklands affair produced a sustained and significant increase in Conservative popularity of about 7.3 percentage points.

From D. Sanders, H. Ward and D. Marsh (with T. Fletcher), 'Government popularity and the Falklands war: a reassessment' (1987), *British Journal of Political Science*, vol. 17, pp. 281–313.

GOVERNMENT POPULARITY AND THE FALKLANDS WAR   *275*

These analyses assume that the Falklands war had an 'abrupt–permanent' effect: government popularity jumped abruptly between April and May 1982 and this effect appears to have persisted right through to the 1983 election. Norpoth [1986] concludes that the Falklands war produced a gradual-temporary increase in popularity of eleven percentage points during May and June of 1982 but that this effect decayed at a rate of just under 0.7 of a percentage point per month thereafter. According to this model, the Falklands factor was still worth five percentage points by May 1983 and may have been crucial to the Conservatives' landslide victory.

The problem of mis-specification

All three of the studies of the Falklands effect referred to above are cogently argued and methodologically sound. But they are all open to the criticism that the models which they develop are mis-specified because some potentially relevant independent variable(s) has (have) been omitted from them. In particular there is one group of variables whose effects (as far as we are aware) have not been systematically investigated in previous analyses of the first Thatcher Government: measures relating to aggregate economic expectations about the future.

We would argue that in democratic societies expectations about the future – both for the economy as a whole and for the individual elector and her/his family – constitute a crucially important influence upon government popularity. Other things being equal, the more optimistic people are about the future – and, in particular, the more optimistic they are about the economic future of their immediate family – the more likely they are to support the incumbent government in order to sustain the very status quo that produced their optimism in the first place. If it could be shown that movements in *aggregate* levels of economic optimism are related (1) to aggregate movements in party support and (2) to objective macroeconomic changes, then the claim that those macroeconomic phenomena exert an indirect influence upon government popularity would be considerably enhanced.

But how can aggregate 'economic expectations' be measured? Our preferred measurement strategy is based on the regular Gallup poll questions concerned with whether or not respondents think that (a) the 'general economic situation' and (b) their 'own household's financial situation' will improve over the next twelve months. Our month-by-month measure of 'general economic expectations' is obtained by subtracting the percentage of respondents who think the 'general economic situation' will get worse from the percentage who think it will get better; our measure of 'personal expectations' is obtained from a similar arithmetic operation using responses about their 'own household's financial situation'.

276   ECONOMIC PERFORMANCE

In subsequent sections of this article, we show that personal expectations constitute a vitally important control variable, the effects of which must be taken fully into account before the impact of the Falklands factor upon government popularity can be properly assessed.

The data

The data analysed in our study are aggregate monthly time series covering July 1979 to June 1983. The variables examined fall into five broad categories: (1) assessments of government performance and popularity [6 variables]; (2) objective measures of various aspects of the state of the overall economy [20 variables]; (3) aggregate *retrospective perceptions* of the performance of the economy and how it has affected the individual [2 variables]; (4) aggregate *prospective expectations* about how the economy will perform in the future [2 variables]; and (5) 'political event' factors such as the 'Falklands dummy' and a dummy variable for the impact of the Alliance [2 variables].

In relation to category 1 the results reported here are confined solely to one measure: government popularity. All of the measures in category 1 are highly intercorrelated. We would argue that at the aggregate level at least (where measurements are necessarily crude) this results from the fact that *all* of the category 1 measures broadly record the extent to which public opinion is favourably disposed towards the government. The government popularity variable simply represents the most convenient way of operationalizing these general predispositions.

Informal data analysis: some obvious patterns

Figure 6.4.1 plots the movements in overall government popularity between July 1979 and June 1983. Two features of Figure 6.4.1 are immediately noticeable and both are extremely important. The first is the overall *trend*: popularity suffers a general decline until the beginning of 1982 and then experiences a recovery through to the 1983 election. Secondly, there is a marked – and critically important – acceleration or *discontinuity* in government popularity between April and May 1982; an increase in popularity of fully 11 percentage points.

Initially, we attempt to provide a few insights into the genesis of the decline–recovery sequence embodied in Figure 6.4.1. It seems relevant in the first instance to establish how far other, potentially explanatory, variables follow either (1) a similar decline–recovery or (2) an (obverse) increase–decline pattern. To put it another way given that a simple curvilinear trend function of the form $y_t = a + bt + ct^2$ fits the government

GOVERNMENT POPULARITY AND THE FALKLANDS WAR 277

Figure 6.4.1 Variations in government popularity over time, July 1979–June 1983

popularity trend remarkably well (see Table 6.4.1), are there any other variables (from those identified above) to which such an equation can also be fitted? Table 6.4.1 identifies nine such variables which exhibit either a decline–recovery or an increase–decline pattern. All can be plausibly linked in theoretical terms to the decline–recovery trend observed in government popularity.

In our view, the findings presented in Table 6.4.1 can be most plausibly interpreted in terms of the following model: 'objective economic conditions → subjective perceptions about the economy → preparedness to vote for the government'. Three pieces of evidence lead us to draw this inference. Firstly, as Table 6.4.1 indicates, three different measures of subjective economic perceptions follow the same broad decline–recovery sequence as several measures of the objective state of the economy; a finding which certainly supports the notion that general economic perceptions in some sense reflect 'real' economic conditions. Secondly, both government popularity and the subjective economic perceptions variables (a) follow the same general trend throughout 1979–83 and (b) shift from 'decline' to 'recovery' during the same four-month period (October 1981–January 1982). Thirdly, the 'personal expectations' variable shifts from decline to recovery at exactly the same point in time (January 1982) as

Table 6.4.1 Variables exhibiting either a decline–recovery or increase–decline trend, July 1979–June 1983

Variable	Trend equation estimated*	Graphical representation of trend equation estimated	R^2 of trend equation estimated ($N = 48$)
Tax and price index (% change on year earlier)	$\hat{Y}_t = 13.7 + 0.39(t) - 0.001(t^2)$		0.92
Taxation index	$\hat{Y}_t = -3.7 + 0.43(t) - 0.008(t^2)$		0.57
Exchange rate (£ against $)	$\hat{Y}_t = 2,250.0 + 5.06(t) - 0.46(t^2)$		0.84
Short-time working (manufacturing industry)	$\hat{Y}_t = 1.5 + 2.5(t) - 0.05(t^2)$		0.42
Consumer expenditure (durable goods; seasonally adjusted)	$\hat{Y}_t = 34.5 - 38.64(t) + 1.2(t^2)$		0.92
Retail sales (seasonally adjusted)	$\hat{Y}_t = 105.2 - 0.15(t) + 0.006(t^2)$		0.82
General retrospective economic perceptions (% thinking situation got better − % thinking got worse)	$\hat{Y}_t = 4.184 - 0.27(t) + 0.007(t^2)$		0.71
Personal retrospective economic perceptions (% thinking situation got better − % thinking got worse)	$\hat{Y}_t = 0.50 - 0.22(t) + 0.004(t^2)$		0.71
Personal economic expectations (% thinking own household situation will get better − % thinking will get worse)	$\hat{Y}_t = 0.29 - 0.12(t) + 0.002(t^2)$		0.56
Government popularity	$\hat{Y}_t = 39.7 - 1.05(t) + 0.02(t^2)$		0.50

* All coefficients more than twice their own standard error.

government popularity. We believe that such a pervasive and consistent decline–recovery pattern lends clear informal support to the sort of simple model in which government popularity is determined by subjective perceptions about the state of the economy while those perceptions are in turn determined by objective economic conditions.

Formal data analysis

Modelling the economic influences upon government popularity
The basic theoretical model underlying our more formal data analysis hypothesizes that government popularity is influenced by two basic sets of

GOVERNMENT POPULARITY AND THE FALKLANDS WAR   *279*

economic factors: (1) the objective performance of the overall economy and (2) people's expectations about their own living standards in the future. In essence, if a government is to achieve high poll ratings, it must not only ensure that the economy as a whole is performing relatively well, but it must also convince enough people that their own economic position is going to improve in the foreseeable future.

Employing a stepwise [regression] procedure and using as predictors all of the variables identified in categories (2) and (4) [above], we estimated a large number of equations which provided alternative operationalizations of this basic 'expectations/objective economic performance' model. The effects of all potential predictor variables were considered both unlagged at time t and lagged at time $t-1, t-2, \ldots t-12$. Our aim was to obtain a parsimonious model of government popularity which (a) was intuitively plausible; (b) maximized R^2; (c) ensured the significance and robustness of all parameters; and (d) avoided high collinearity between predictor variables. [Equation 1 in Table 6.4.2] summarizes the outcome of our investigations. With only four predictor variables – one that directly measures personal expectations and three (exchange rate, PSBR and unemployment) that indirectly measure the general state of the economy – we were able to explain some 87 per cent of the variance in government popularity.

Several observations need to be made about [this] 'best equation' model. Firstly, none of the other variables in categories 2–5 [above], either lagged or unlagged, made any additional contribution to the statistical explanation of government popularity over and above the effects of the four predictor variables specified in the model. Given the high level of R^2, this constitutes strong overall support for our hypothesized expectations/performance model. Secondly – and of considerable substantive importance – the absence of any Falklands factor variable indicates that the variance in Mrs Thatcher's first term popularity can be statistically explained quite satisfactorily without any direct reference to the Falklands factor whatsoever. Indeed, as [equation 2 in Table 6.4.2] shows, the addition of a Falklands dummy to the model yields a non-significant parameter, together with an increase in R^2 of only 0.006. This finding – on the face of it at least – casts considerable suspicion upon the claims of previous analyses that the Falklands war was a significant factor in Mrs Thatcher's electoral victory in 1983.

A third feature of [equation 1] is that one of the most important influences upon government popularity is personal expectations, a conclusion which is certainly consistent with our 'informal' analysis of trend patterns presented in the previous section. There is a potential problem of tautology here, however, and it needs to be confronted. It could be argued that the personal expectations index which we have employed is not truly independent of our measure of government popularity: both, after all, are

Table 6.4.2 Predictive models of government popularity, January 1980–June 1983

1. $GP_t = \underset{(14.15)}{74.32} + \underset{(4.51)}{0.371} \ PE_t - \underset{(5.59)}{0.01} \ ER_{t-12} - \underset{(3.81)}{0.61} \ UN_t - \underset{(2.53)}{0.0008} \ PSBR_{t-6}$

    $R^2 = 0.874 \quad N = 42 \quad$ Durbin–Watson statistic $= 1.70$

2. $GP_t = \underset{(8.73)}{66.45} + \underset{(4.53)}{0.37} \ PE_t - \underset{(2.54)}{0.004} \ ER_{t-12} - \underset{(3.42)}{0.92} \ UN_t - \underset{(1.82)}{0.0005} \ PSBR_{t-6} + \underset{(1.41)}{3.37} \ \text{Falkland dummy}$

    $R^2 = 0.880 \quad N = 42 \quad$ Durbin–Watson statistic $= 1.86$

Note: Figures in parentheses are t statistics. GP = government popularity; PE = personal expectations; ER = exchange rate; UN = unemployment; $PSBR$ = public sector borrowing requirement.

GOVERNMENT POPULARITY AND THE FALKLANDS WAR

based on Gallup poll survey questions and it is possible that the answers which respondents give to all 'political' questions in such circumstances reflect their general affective feelings towards the government of the day.

We reject this line of argument on both theoretical and empirical grounds. We are not convinced that simply because two or more survey responses are empirically related, it necessarily follows that they are merely artefacts of some deeper structure. That way lies a retreat into universal tautology which is just as absurd as the claim that all empirical correlations reveal causal relationships. In our view the Gallup question which elicits the respondent's voting intention is so clearly differentiated from the question which ascertains her/his degree of optimism about the future that it requires an unwarranted effort of imagination to regard the responses to them as mere expressions of the same underlying phenomenon.

The problem, of course, is that if we only possessed survey evidence, we would have no way of substantiating our interpretation empirically. [However] we can devise an empirical test of the validity of our survey-based measure of expectations. In subsequent models (see especially Figure 6.4.5) we show that a personal expectations variable constructed entirely from objective, aggregate-level macroeconomic indices correlates just as strongly with government popularity as the survey-based personal expectations measure which we have examined thus far. This leads us to the conclusion that the original Gallup question concerned with personal expectations does elicit something other than general affective predispositions towards government; that it does indeed measure people's expectations [and] is *not* tautologically related to voting intentions.

It could be argued that the idea that the electorate pays the slightest attention to distant macroeconomic intangibles like PSBR or the external value of sterling assumes a level of intellectual sophistication on the part of the British public that has never been demonstrated in micro-level research. We would argue, however, that the electorate does not need to be sophisticated in order to be affected by the 'more good news' or 'more bad news' interpretations which are offered by the mass media when they report on fluctuations in these macroeconomic indices. A second line of potential criticism concerns the question of why, according to our model, government popularity appears to be affected by PSBR after a period of six months and by the exchange rate after a period of twelve months. With aggregate-level data we are unable to specify why these particular lags seem to have been important during the first Thatcher term. None the less, in view of the fact that people's perceptions are rarely transformed instantaneously, it does seem reasonable to us that some sort of time-lag between macroeconomic changes and public predispositions towards government should be in evidence; the manner in which and the rate at

282   ECONOMIC PERFORMANCE

which they are transformed must primarily be matters for individual-level research.

In these circumstances, what we have demonstrated is that macroeconomic changes do appear to be empirically linked to variations in government popularity and that – without reference to political factors such as the Falklands effect – a very high proportion of the variance in government popularity can be explained by reference to straightforward personal expectations and objective macroeconomic variables.

The discontinuity in government popularity revisited

Figure 6.4.2 plots the predicted values from our expectations/ performance model against time for the period January 1980–June 1983. What is immediately noticeable about Figure 6.4.2 is that these predictions of government popularity exhibit the same sort of discontinuity as the actual government popularity scores shown in Figure 6.4.1. In other words, our expectations/performance model predicts a dramatic increase in government popularity in May 1982 purely on the basis of a linear combination of the independent variables identified in [equation 1 in Table 6.4.2].

[But] what characteristics – if any – of the independent variables in the expectations/performance model might be responsible for producing this discontinuity in predicted values? Figure 6.4.3 reveals [that] the source of the discontinuity is a similar discontinuity in the single most important variable in the expectations/performance model: the personal expectations variable.

But now we have another question to answer: why should aggregate personal expectations jump suddenly in May 1982? Could this not be an indirect consequence of the Falklands factor? In other words, is it not possible that the Falklands factor was responsible both for the spurt in popularity that Mrs Thatcher's Government enjoyed in May 1982 and for the rapid increase in personal expectations which coincided with it, the latter producing the discontinuity in predicted values observed in Figure 6.4.2? If these speculations were shown to be correct, the explanatory value of the expectations/performance model that we presented in [equation 1 in Table 6.4.2] would be enormously diminished. It is therefore essential that we attempt to establish how the discontinuity in aggregate personal expectations arose. In the next section we show that it can in fact be traced almost entirely to movements in objective macroeconomic variables.

Modelling the discontinuity in personal expectations

Using all of the variables in categories (2) and (5) [above, stepwise regression was again] employed in order to develop a predictive model of personal expectations. This 'best model' is presented in [equation 1 in Table 6.4.3]. It should be noted that the model maximizes explained

GOVERNMENT POPULARITY AND THE FALKLANDS WAR 283

Figure 6.4.2 Variations in predicted values from best model of government popularity over time, January 1980–June 1983

variance (R^2 is a respectable 0.76), ensures that all parameters are significant and avoids multicollinearity. As [equation 2 in Table 6.4.3] indicates, the inclusion of a Falklands dummy adds a mere 0.001 to R^2 and yields a clearly non-significant parameter.

In substantive terms, Table 6.4.3 has two major implications. Firstly, in order to provide a statistical explanation of the personal expectations variable, the inclusion of a Falklands factor is, quite simply, unnecessary. Secondly, what does seem to matter in the determination of personal expectations are movements in precisely those macroeconomic variables which common sense suggests have an obvious and direct impact upon the elector-as-consumer.

The crucial question arising from the results reported in [equation 1 in Table 6.4.3], however, is whether the model produces the same sort of discontinuity in (the predicted values of) personal expectations that was observed in Figure 6.4.3. Figure 6.4.4, which plots the predicted values from the model in [equation 1 in Table 6.4.3] against time, reveals that this is indeed the case: the model predicts an upward discontinuity in personal expectations at exactly the appropriate point, between April and May 1982. Critically, this discontinuity is produced entirely by movements in

Figure 6.4.3 Variations in 'personal expectations' over time, July 1979–June 1983

objective macroeconomic indices: it does not require any reference whatsoever to a specific Falklands factor.

Of course, having demonstrated that we can reproduce the discontinuity in personal expectations purely from four macroeconomic variables, another question poses itself: what characteristics (if any) of those macroeconomic variables could be responsible for producing such a discontinuity? Having reached a trough in December 1981, consumer spending had been rising for five months prior to the Falklands conflict; interest rates had been falling for six months; and short-time working had been falling since its peak in October 1981. It is unlikely that the joint effects of these three upswings could alone have provided the upward discontinuity in personal expectations in May 1982. However, when the effects of these three variables are combined with the reduction in the personal taxation index which occurred in April 1982 in the wake of Geoffrey Howe's March budget, it is relatively easy to appreciate why personal expectations experienced an upward surge one month later. Howe's 1982 Budget was cautiously expansionary. In the spring of 1982 the electorate, having experienced a prolonged dampening in personal expectations as a result of three aggressive budgets, appears to have been favourably surprised by the new 'wet look' package and reacted

Table 6.4.3 Predictive models of personal expectations, January 1980–June 1983

1. $PE_t = -44.38 + 0.01\ CDE_{t-12} - 1.45\ TI_{t-1} - 0.12\ STW_{t-1} - 0.82\ IR_{t-1}$
       (3.16)   (4.18)   (4.28)   (2.73)   (2.75)
   $R^2 = 0.764$ $N = 42$ Durbin–Watson statistic = 1.609

2. $PE_t = -44.27 + 0.015\ CDE_{t-12} - 1.50\ TI_{t-1} - 0.14\ STW_{t-1} - 0.91\ IR_{t-1} - 0.85\ \text{Falklands dummy}$
       (3.12)   (3.86)   (3.85)   (2.32)   (2.15)   (0.29)
   $R^2 = 0.765$ $N = 42$ Durbin–Watson statistic = 1.62

Note: Figures in parentheses are *t* statistics. *PE* = personal expectations; *CDE* = consumer durables expenditure; *TI* = taxation index; *STW* = short-time working; *IR* = interest rates.

Figure 6.4.4 Predicted values from best model of personal expectations over time, January 1980–June 1983

accordingly. In essence, the tax changes in the 1982 Budget constituted a discontinuous shock to expectations: a modest reduction in taxation bought a decisive increase in personal expectations.

Predicting the discontinuity in government popularity entirely from objective macroeconomic factors

In this section we combine the results and models of the two previous sections to demonstrate that the leap in government popularity which occurred between April and May 1982 can be plausibly explained entirely in terms of objective macroeconomic variables.

Figure 6.4.5 combines our best equation for government popularity [equation 1 in Table 6.4.2] with our best equation for personal expectations [equation 1 in Table 6.4.3]. It offers a summary of the main factors which according to our analysis were most responsible for variations in government popularity during Mrs Thatcher's first term of office. The model employs a modified version of Two-Stage Least Squares by which the equation for government popularity is estimated using the predicted rather than the observed values of the personal expectations variable.

The use of these predicted values ensures that all of the independent

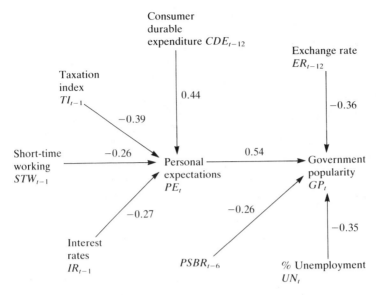

Note: The path coefficients reported are standardized regression coefficients derived from the following equations (t statistics in parentheses):

[i] $\hat{PE}_t = -44.38 + 0.01CDE_{t-12} - 1.45TI_{t-1} - 0.12STW_{t-1} - 0.82IR_{t-1}$
$\phantom{[i] \hat{PE}_t = -44.38 + }(4.18) \phantom{CDE_{t-12}} (4.28) \phantom{TI_{t-1}} (2.73) \phantom{STW_{t-1}} (2.75)$

$(R^2 = 0.764;$ Durbin–Watson statistic $= 1.6;$ N $= 42)$

[ii] $\hat{GP}_t = 70.98 + 0.53\hat{PE}_t - 0.01ER_{t-12} - 0.86UN_{t-1} - 0.0009PSBR_{t-1}$
$\phantom{[ii] \hat{GP}_t = 70.98 + }(4.41) \phantom{\hat{PE}_t} (3.36) \phantom{ER_{t-12}} (4.36) \phantom{UN_{t-1}} 3.62$

$(R^2 = 0.872;$ Durbin–Watson statistic $= 1.81;$ N $= 42)$

Figure 6.4.5 Full recursive model of government popularity, January 1980–June 1983

variables are composed entirely of objective macroeconomic effects. Crucially, even with this restriction, over 87 per cent of the variance in government popularity is explained by the model. What is even more significant is that the predicted values from this constrained government popularity equation, when plotted against time (see Figure 6.4.6), exhibit exactly the same upward discontinuity between April and May 1982 that was observed in Figure 6.4.1. To be sure, the discontinuity in Figure 6.4.6 is not as marked as that evident in Figure 6.4.1, but it still constitutes the largest monthly change in predicted values during Mrs Thatcher's first term of office. The crucial point is that the broad macroeconomic forces already operating in the six months or so before the outbreak of the Falklands conflict would in all probability have led to a dramatic resurgence in government popularity anyway. The interposition of the Falklands crisis merely served to mask the effects of these macroeconomic changes and to give the false impression that the revival of Mrs Thatcher's electoral

Figure 6.4.6 Predicted values from full 2SLS model of government popularity over time, January 1979–June 1983

fortunes was the consequence principally of an uncontrived but well-managed foreign policy entanglement rather than the result of clever macroeconomic management.

Over and above the effects of the various macroeconomic variables we have identified, the Falklands factor does not help us explain the overall variations in the popularity of Mrs Thatcher's first administration. In the first months of the Falklands crisis, government popularity did surge forward slightly ahead of what we would have anticipated solely on the basis of the movements on macroeconomic variables. Specifically, government popularity in May was some 2.6 per cent ahead of our prediction; in June 2.8 per cent ahead; and in July again 2.8 per cent ahead. By August, however, the effect had disappeared altogether. In short, there was a genuine Falklands effect upon the popularity of Mrs Thatcher's Government but it was extremely small (in the region of 3 per cent) and highly ephemeral (lasting three months at the most). The real achievement of the first Thatcher Government was its ability to raise personal expectations through skilful (or fortunate) macroeconomic management. It was this latter factor which was by far the most influential in the revival of Mrs Thatcher's electoral fortunes after January 1982.

6.5 | Recapturing the Falklands: models of Conservative popularity, 1979–83

H.D. Clarke, W. Mishler and P. Whiteley

In a thought-provoking article, David Sanders, Hugh Ward and David Marsh (henceforward SWM) appear to refute what has become a conventional wisdom in British politics, namely that victory in the Falklands war played an important, perhaps decisive, role in rebuilding support for the Conservatives in 1982 and paving the way for Mrs Thatcher's landslide re-election in 1983. Criticizing previous studies for failing to employ properly specified controls, SWM contend that the 'Falklands effect' observed in those studies is largely spurious.

SWM are correct in asserting the importance of a properly specified model. They also make a compelling case for the inclusion of subjective economic variables (i.e. public perceptions and expectations of the economy's performance) in models of government popularity. However, their analysis suffers from a variety of theoretical and methodological problems. This article outlines these problems and demonstrates that when theoretically attractive models are estimated with suitable techniques the 'Falklands effect' appears highly significant.

The theoretical and methodological problems of the SWM models

Our central theoretical criticism of the SWM models is the same as their criticism of the previous literature on the Falklands. Their models are not properly specified.

From H.D. Clarke, W. Mishler and P. Whiteley, 'Recapturing the Falklands: models of Conservative popularity 1979–83' (1990), *British Journal of Political Science*, vol. 20, pp. 63–81.

290   ECONOMIC PERFORMANCE

SWM acknowledge the importance of theory to model specification when they advocate the inclusion of economic expectations and perceptions, in addition to standard aggregate economic indicators, in their models. However, in identifying the specific variables to be incorporated, and in specifying the lag structure, they ignore theory and rely instead on statistical technique. Having collected twenty aggregate economic indicators which are assumed to be predictors of government popularity, they enter these into a stepwise regression analysis along with four measures of public perceptions/expectations of economic performance and two dummy variables reflecting the Falklands war and the formation of the Liberal–SDP alliance. They also included lagged measures of each of the twenty economic variables from times $t - 1$ up to $t - 12$. This means, in effect, that the stepwise regression included a total of 266 variables, many of which were very highly correlated with each other.

Following standard stepwise procedures, these variables were entered into the model of government popularity one at a time depending on their contribution to the variance explained (R^2), controlling for the other variables in the model. This procedure yielded the model [SWM's Table 6.4.2, equation 1; see p. 280 above] in which government popularity is predicted by the unemployment rate at time t, personal expectations also at t, the exchange rate at time $t - 12$, and the Public Sector Borrowing Requirement at $t - 6$. The Falklands variable was not statistically significant, and thus does not appear in this model.

Although the use of stepwise regression is a great temptation when theory is scarce, it is not a sufficient substitute. It is particularly inappropriate when the number of cases is relatively small ($N = 42$) and the number of independent variables is large and [they are] highly correlated. Not surprisingly, the model resulting from the stepwise regression procedure contradicts existing findings in several important respects. It is mis-specified in several critical respects.

Firstly, the aggregate economic variables included in the SWM model are difficult to justify by any reasonable ideas about how macroeconomic trends might influence individual political behaviour. To influence individual political attitudes or behaviour, aggregate indicators of economic performance should be both visible and salient to the everyday lives of the electorate. It is now well established that inflation and unemployment are both visible, in the sense of being highlighted by the media, and salient to the voters. In contrast, there is no evidence of which we are aware that these conditions are met in the case of the Public Sector Borrowing Requirement, the exchange rate or even tax rates which SWM include in their final model. Indeed, SWM had to resort to a relatively complicated statistical transformation to calculate their tax-rate measure, because there is no publicly accessible series which measures tax burdens over time. SWM do not explain how individual voters make or attempt to make this calculation on their own. Furthermore, individual-level survey evidence suggests that a majority of the electorate oppose the devaluation of the pound and reductions in the PSBR by means of cuts in public expenditure. This is, of course, inconsistent with SWM's findings that voters reward the government for devaluing the pound and reducing the PSBR.

Secondly, even if a theoretical justification can be provided for including the PSBR and exchange rates as predictors of government popularity, the particular lags SWM specify for these variables pose additional problems. It is not obvious why the current level of popularity should be influenced by changes in the PSBR that occurred six months previously or the exchange rate twelve months previously (and not one, two, three or some other number of months). The exchange rate lag is especially curious since the pound was falling in 1982 in relation to the dollar, whereas by 1983 it had stabilized and, for a time, rose slightly. The SWM formulation suggests that voters rewarded the government in 1983 for a devaluation of the currency a year earlier, ignoring the fact that the pound was already increasing in value – bizarre behaviour by any standards.

Thirdly, although SWM experiment with numerous lags for the economic variables, they do not appear to consider the possibility that the Falklands effect was similarly delayed. Yet there are good reasons to believe that it was. Norpoth [1987a], whose analysis is the central focus of the SWM critique, argues explicitly that the Falklands effect was lagged. Moreover, a brief review of the key events in the Falklands war supports Norpoth's findings.

Given that the most dramatic events of the war did not occur until late April or early May and given also that Gallup's monthly polls report the aggregated responses to interviews conducted at several different times across a month, it is reasonable to suppose that the full effect of the Falklands crisis would not register in public opinion surveys until May – the month after the crisis began. The SWM model does not allow for this possibility.

Nor does the SWM model consider the possibility that the Falklands effect was non-linear as Norpoth also suggests. Instead, by treating the war as an unlagged variable in a linear model, the implicit assumption is that the full effect of the crisis on government popularity occurred instantaneously in April 1982 and persisted undiminished until June 1983 – assumptions clearly contrary to both historical record and to previous research. An alternative possibility is that the Falklands effect was permanent during the estimation period, but was realized gradually rather than abruptly. Another alternative is that the effect was temporary, rather than permanent, but took some time to diminish. Indeed, such dynamic non-linear models are highly plausible given the timing of significant events in the Falklands conflict.

Fourthly, SWM assume that expressed satisfaction with the leadership

292 ECONOMIC PERFORMANCE

of Margaret Thatcher is synonymous with satisfaction with the performance of the Conservative government. However, recent research suggests that although related, leadership satisfaction and party popularity are conceptually distinct and empirically separable. Given also the evidence that leadership satisfaction bears significantly on government popularity, failure to consider the impact of the Falklands war on public evaluations of prime ministerial performance leaves open the possibility that the war may also have had indirect effects on government support.

Fifthly, SWM argue persuasively for focusing attention on the economic expectations of the electorate, but they do so in a way which is inconsistent with a good deal of micro-level literature on the relationship between perceptions of economic performance and party popularity. A number of studies have argued that national rather than personal economic judgements are important in influencing political support. In contrast, SWM focus exclusively on personal economic expectations, because they allow the stepwise regression procedure to determine which variables are included in the equation. Thus additional work on the influence of general as well as personal economic expectations is required.

Finally, difficulties with SWM's analyses are not confined to questions of model specification. We show below that their estimates are suspect because of severe multicollinearity. In addition, their OLS [ordinary least squares] and pseudo-GLS [generalized least squares] regressions and accompanying diagnostics are inherently unable to detect and control for time-series dependencies in the model residuals other than simple first-order autocorrelation. If such dependencies are unattended, they can produce biased and misleading inferences and cause a model to appear to have a much more impressive fit than is actually the case.

The SWM model: a reanalysis

Taken together, these several theoretical and methodological problems raise serious questions about the validity and reliability of SWM's estimates, and undermine confidence in their conclusions about the importance of the Falklands war. To demonstrate that these problems are not simply hypothetical, we replicated SWM's analysis. We begin by replicating their basic model, which includes unemployment, personal economic expectations, the PSBR $(t-6)$, the exchange rate $(t-12)$, and of course the Falklands variable. As reported by SWM, the Falklands effect was not statistically significant when forced to enter a stepwise regression model that includes the other predictors.

Significantly, however, an examination of the correlations among the five independent variables clearly hints that multicollinearity may be a problem (see Table 6.5.1). Indeed the average inter-item correlation

RECAPTURING THE FALKLANDS

Table 6.5.1 Matrix of zero-order correlations (r) among independent variables in SWM model

Variable (lag)	2	3	4	5	R^2
1 Personal expectations (t)	−0.74	−0.61	0.46	0.74	0.91
2 Exchange rate ($t - 12$)		0.56	−0.28	−0.81	0.96
3 PSBR ($t - 6$)			−0.27	−0.63	0.84
4 Unemployment (t)				0.70	0.94
5 Falklands (t)					0.97

$N = 42$.
R = Multiple correlation of independent variable with other independent variables.

among all variables (excluding unemployment) is nearly 0.70. The right-most column in Table 6.5.1 reports the R^2-coefficient for each independent variable when the other five independent variables are regressed against it. It demonstrates that several of the variables, particularly the Falklands variable and the exchange rate, are almost perfectly collinear with the rest. In practical terms this means that there is virtually no independent variation in several of the predictors in the model which can be used to estimate their separate effects on government popularity. In the presence of such severe multicollinearity, even small sampling or measurement errors can produce large changes in the coefficients.

This problem is underscored by an examination of the step-by-step results of the regression analysis of the SWM model. Because it has the highest zero-order correlation with government popularity, the first variable entered into the stepwise model is the exchange rate. The relationship between personal expectations and popularity, controlling for the exchange rate, is the strongest among the variables not entered on the first step, and this enters the equation on the second step. Unemployment enters third by the same criterion. At this point the partial correlation between popularity and the Falklands variable (0.375) controlling for the exchange rate, personal expectations and unemployment is only very slightly smaller than the partial correlation between popularity and the PSBR (−0.384) with the same controls. Since the latter coefficient has a p value (0.0157) which is slightly smaller than the former (0.0184), the stepwise algorithm selects the PSBR for entry at step four, rather than the Falklands variable. Once entered, the PSBR together with the other variables in the equation reduce both the Falklands and the Alliance effects to insignificance and the stepwise procedure stops. If the Falklands variable had had a slightly stronger partial correlation with popularity, and thus a smaller p value (0.004 or less) it would have entered the equation before the PSBR, and been statistically significant in the SWM model. This

ECONOMIC PERFORMANCE

means that the key result of the SWM article depends upon a completely trivial difference between the strength of relationships in a model where the relationships are suspect anyway because of multicollinearity. Far from proving the Falklands and Alliance effects to be spurious, all this analysis shows is that they are collinear with a handful of economic variables whose theoretical relevance to government popularity is suspect in the first place.

In an effort to assess the robustness of the SWM model we repeated their analysis with the Falklands variable lagged one month (i.e. $t - 1$). This specification is more consonant with our hypothesis that the war's impact became significant in May 1982, although it does not address the possibility that the effect was non-linear, a point we consider later. The OLS estimates of this model are as follows:

$$GP_t = 46.59 + 0.36PE_t - 1.84UN_t + 10.91FK_{t-1}$$
$$\quad (25.84) \ (4.74) \qquad (8.33) \qquad (7.73)$$

Adj. $R^2 = 0.88$ $\qquad F = 106.67$ (df 3/38) $\quad DWS = 1.36$ $\quad N = 42$

(where GP = government popularity; PE = personal expectations; UN = unemployment; FK = the Falklands variable; DWS = Durbin–Watson Statistic; and t statistics are in parentheses).

As expected, when the Falklands variable is lagged one month, it proves highly significant. In this revised model the exchange rate, the PSBR and the Alliance variable are not significant and thus do not enter the equation. This three-predictor model (hereafter, the CMW model) has a slightly better fit than the original SWM model (R^2 of 0.88 rather than 0.87), and because it requires one less degree of freedom it achieves a higher significance level. The CMW model is also preferable because the only macro-economic variable included (unemployment) clearly meets the criteria of visibility and salience discussed previously. Finally, the lag structures are also more reasonable than in the SWM model.

The Falklands coefficient in the revised model indicates that the war increased government popularity by an average of nearly 11 per cent from the period beginning in May 1982, and this continued through to the June 1983 election. This conforms more closely with existing literature than the estimates provided by SWM.

Although preferable to the SWM model, the alternative CMW model shares several important shortcomings with it. Principal among these are the problem of multicollinearity, the possible non-linearity of the Falklands variable, the omission of some theoretically interesting variables, and the problem of autocorrelation in the residuals.

At this point we have carried the analysis as far as ordinary least squares procedures can take us. Further exploration of the Falklands effect requires that we respecify the model in the light of our earlier discussion and re-estimate it using more sophisticated time-series methods.

Alternative models and estimates

The use of time-series data, although vital for understanding the effects of the Falklands war on government popularity, introduces special problems of analysis which ordinary least squares procedures are poorly suited to handle. In particular, time-series analyses are confounded by the tendency of time-related observations to be correlated such that the value of a series at one time is dependent, at least partly, upon one or more earlier values of the same series. When this occurs, the series is said to be serially or autocorrelated. Ordinary least squares procedures assume, however, that the error terms associated with different observations in a series are independent.

A variety of procedures have been developed to address these problems. We rely on Box–Jenkins transfer function modelling procedures to re-estimate our revised model of government popularity. Instead of making assumptions about the form of the error terms in the popularity function models, Box–Jenkins procedures allow us to identify and estimate empirically the nature and extent of autocorrelation in a series prior to the analysis.

The set of potential predictor variables in the models [we test below] includes not only macroeconomic conditions, but also subjective evaluations and perceptions, public feelings about party leaders and various salient political events. Although construction of a fully specified model would entail investigating all these possibilities, doing so is beyond the scope of the present enquiry. Here we shall focus on variables that are particularly relevant for extending our analysis of the SWM and CMW models. These include, unemployment, personal economic expectations and three alternative specifications of the Falklands effect. The [likely] importance of the economic variables suggests that the impact of the Falklands war should be assessed by using controls for various combinations of them.

The three Falklands specifications include the one-month lag abrupt–permanent effect model, and gradual–permanent and gradual–temporary models with initial and secondary effects occurring in May and June 1982 – these effects continuing in subsequent months [see Figure 6.5.1]. The latter two dynamic specifications are plausible in the light of both the unfolding of events associated with the war and the empirical support provided in Norpoth's analyses.

There is little theoretical guidance for specifying the precise lags at which these variables affect Conservative support. As noted, lags of several months or longer such as those in the SWM model seem unlikely, according to any plausible account of the transmission process. A variety of short-lag effects are possible, however, and the bivariate cross-correlations indicate that unemployment and personal expectations operate con-

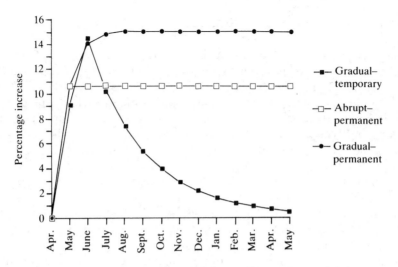

Figure 6.5.1 Alternative models of the Falklands effect on Conservative popularity, April 1982–May 1983

temporaneously, whereas inflation does so with a one-month delay. Accordingly the models were specified with those lags.

[Details of the results of this analysis are not shown here but, for example,] the estimates for models [which] treat the Falklands effect as an abrupt–permanent impact starting in May, this being estimated in conjunction with different combinations of inflation, unemployment and personal economic expectations, [give] results [which] are unequivocal and massive – the Falklands coefficient is always strongly significant ($p < 0.01$). Expressed in absolute terms, since Conservative popularity averaged 29.3 per cent before the Falklands war, the increases would produce postwar popularity levels averaging between 39.3 and 41.6 per cent. [Estimates for models which treat the Falklands war as having a gradual–permanent or a gradual–temporary effect also produce good results.]

All three models of the Falklands effect employed in the Box–Jenkins analyses indicate that the war had a significant impact on Conservative popularity, net of any influences associated with inflation, unemployment and personal economic expectations. However, the permanent and temporary effects models tell very different stories about the war's influence in the post-Falklands period. As in the CMW model, the abrupt–permanent and gradual–permanent effects imply that the Conservatives enjoyed a large and lasting increment in support as a result of public reactions to the war. The former estimates this to be 10.6 points; the latter 14.1 points. Given that Conservative popularity averaged slightly over 29 per cent before the Falklands war and 38 per cent after, these models suggest that the war alone accounted for virtually all of the government's comfortable lead in the polls in the year preceding the 1983 election. The gradual–temporary effect model indicates that the war quickly produced large increases in Conservative support, these reaching 14.5 percentage points by June 1982 (Figure 6.5.1). However, the impact subsequently eroded, such that it was worth less than 1 percentage point by May 1983.

The long-term significance of the war thus seems very different if one accepts the gradual–temporary instead of the abrupt–permanent model as the correct specification of the Falklands effect. However, it is important to note that all of the models consider only the direct effects of the war. In this regard, Norpoth's [1987a] analyses of prime ministerial approval reveal that Mrs Thatcher's performance ratings increased by nearly 20 percentage points during May and June 1982, and that a year later the war was still worth between 7 and 8 percentage points to her.

This is important because individual and aggregate-level analyses show that party leader images have strong and significant effects on party support; thus the war may well have had important indirect effects that persisted well after its direct impact had dissipated. Relatedly, and contrary to SWM, Box–Jenkins analyses of subjective economic variables, including personal expectations, reveal that the war had a positive impact, net of macroeconomic trends and other factors. The significance of personal expectations in the Conservative popularity function again suggests that the Falklands war may have had important indirect influences on Conservative support. Mrs Thatcher's handling of the war seems to have dramatically altered public judgements about her competence as prime minister, and thereby prompted the development of more sanguine expectations about the future course of the nation's economy under her stewardship.

Conclusions

We can see that the argument that the Falklands war was inconsequential, although intriguing, is quite simply incorrect. Whether the impact of the war is measured using permanent or temporary specifications, it had a major influence on Conservative popularity. Other plausible influences on Conservative support such as rates of inflation and unemployment, and economic expectations, fail to eliminate the Falklands effect when they are included in an estimating equation. The persistence of the Falklands effect in the face of controls for personal expectations is especially notable given SWM's claim that changes in expectations produced virtually all of the dramatic increase in Conservative popularity which occurred in the spring of 1982. Certainly, expectations did become more optimistic at this time and they did have a positive influence on government support, but the Falklands war mattered as well.

We shall never know whether the Conservatives would have lost the 1983 general election in the absence of the South Atlantic war. But considering the low ebb to which their political fortunes fell in late 1981, there is a plausible case for the proposition that the Thatcher hegemony of contemporary British politics owes a lot to General Galtieri.

Part IV

Recent themes in voting behaviour research

7 | Regional differences in voting behaviour

Introduction

The emergence of a North–South electoral divide was one of the most remarked-upon aspects of British general election results during the 1980s. The idea that there is a simple North–South division is, of course, too crude but it does highlight a major feature of the pattern of party support in Britain in this period, as Table 7.1 shows.

The obvious weakness of the Conservatives in Scotland, Wales and the North of England and of Labour in the South led to a number of more detailed analyses of regional voting patterns (see Johnston, Pattie and Allsopp, 1988), and stimulated a flood of publications by geographers, economists and others exploring regional disparities in employment and

Table 7.1 Regional patterns of party support, 1983 and 1987

1983	England			Wales	Scotland
	South %	Midlands %	North %	%	%
Conservative	50.6	46.8	38.4	31.0	28.4
Labour	19.8	28.1	36.7	37.5	35.1
Alliance	28.6	24.5	24.4	23.2	24.5
Nationalist	–	–	–	7.8	11.8
Other	1.0	0.5	0.5	0.4	0.3
1987	England			Wales	Scotland
	South %	Midlands %	North %	%	%
Conservative	51.8	47.8	36.6	29.5	24.0
Labour	20.9	30.0	42.1	45.1	42.4
Alliance	26.8	21.8	21.0	17.9	19.2
Nationalist	–	–	–	7.3	14.0
Other	0.5	0.4	0.3	0.2	0.3

Source: Butler and Kavanagh, 1984, 1988.

301

302 RECENT THEMES

unemployment, investment, housing, health and so on (see, for example, Smith, 1989).

In the first extract in this section, however, Curtice and Steed, analysing data for the period 1955–1979, show that the electoral divergence of Scotland, Wales and the North from the rest of the country is nothing new, but dates back at least to the 1950s. Moreover, this regional divergence has been overlaid by a second spatial divergence – between more rural and more urban areas – with the former becoming relatively more and the latter relatively less Conservative. Curtice and Steed suggest three explanations for these trends. Firstly, there have been slow changes in the socio-economic make-up of the electorate in different parts of the country. Partly as a consequence of migration and partly due to the changing industrial structure, the South and rural areas have become more middle class. Secondly, there is evidence that voters have increasingly responded differentially to the social context in which they live. Thirdly, there is a more directly political explanation. When third parties do well, as the Nationalists in Scotland and Wales have done since the 1960s and the Alliance did in the 1980s, it tends to be the locally weaker major party which suffers more – the Conservatives in the North, and Labour in the South – thus further accentuating regional disparities in their support.

The fact that at least part of the explanation for variations in the voting behaviour of different parts of the country seems clearly to be their differing socio-economic make-up has led some commentators to argue that there is in fact no truly regional variation. However our second and third extracts contradict this view. William Miller examines the electoral history of Scotland and Wales in some detail, arguing persuasively that there are genuine regional variations in voting behaviour. In the remainder of the article, not reproduced here, he goes on to analyse the roots of Scottish and Welsh nationalism arguing that there are important differences between them. Welsh nationalism has a long tradition, largely focused on preserving the Welsh language, and has in many ways been successful. As a result it has not demonstrated itself particularly strongly in elections. By contrast, Scottish nationalism has had as its goal political independence for Scotland and the SNP has been able to mobilise widespread but not particularly intense electoral support for this goal. Miller suggests that recent Labour success in Scotland can be explained as a result of the party successfully aligning itself with some key Nationalist policies, in particular its support for some limited form of devolution. Thus Labour has come to be seen, in Scotland, as a 'Scottish' party.

In the third piece in this section Johnston and Pattie, who have produced many publications on the question of regional variations in voting behaviour, argue strongly that there is a clear regional effect. They show that the trends observed by Curtice and Steed between 1955 and 1979 have continued since 1979, and they suggest that they are a product of Britain's

REGIONAL DIFFERENCES IN VOTING BEHAVIOUR 303

changing economic geography, particularly in terms of unemployment and house prices. They go on to reanalyse Gallup data to show that *perceptions* of economic well-being also exhibit regional variations, and they conclude that voters increasingly take the local and regional environment into account when deciding how to vote.

Further reading

The 'raw material' for describing regional patterns in voting behaviour is the election results themselves. Figures for the distribution of party support within standard regions and sub-regions are regularly presented in the appendices of the Nuffield studies of British general elections (see, for example, Butler and Kavanagh, 1988, p. 284) and detailed voting figures for English and Welsh counties and Scottish regions are to be found in The Times *Guide to the House of Commons* published after each general election.

In their commentaries on election results, also to be found in the Nuffield studies, Curtice and Steed regularly analyse and comment upon regional patterns (see, for example, Curtice and Steed, 1984, 1988). The same two authors have also provided an influential account of the implications of regional divergence for the operation of the electoral system (Curtice and Steed, 1986; see also pp. 325–33 below). McAllister and Rose (1984) use the 1983 election results together with census data to analyse voting patterns in Scotland, Wales and England separately. The most recent detailed survey studies of Scottish and Welsh voting behaviour are reported in Miller (1981) and Balsom *et al.* (1983). For a discussion of electoral volatility in Scotland see Denver (1985).

By far the most prolific authors on regional voting patterns in the 1980s have been R.J. Johnston and his colleagues. Their book *A Nation Dividing?* contains a wealth of data and analysis and they have also produced a large number of articles and book chapters (see, for example, Johnston and Pattie, 1989b, and other references in Johnston, Pattie and Allsopp, 1988). McAllister (1987a, 1987b, 1987c), particularly criticising Johnston (1987), argues that once other variables are taken into account there is no genuinely *regional* variation in British voting behaviour.

7.1 | Electoral developments, 1955–79

John Curtice and
Michael Steed

Since [1955] the long-term change in the relative strength of the Conservative and Labour parties within constituencies has been marked by two major cleavages – between the North and the South, and between urban areas and rural ones. A North–South cleavage began to emerge in the 1955–59 swing (with Labour doing particularly well in Scotland and North-West England) while the urban–rural cleavage became clearly evident in the 1959–64 swing. Prior to that, the 1950–51 and 1951–55 swings had been notable for the absence of systematic geographical variations. This feature of the 1950–55 period was termed 'uniform swing', i.e. the whole country moved from one major party to the other to a similar extent, and the limited variation that did occur around the national swing was randomly distributed amongst constituencies. It has since become a widely accepted nostrum about British electoral behaviour that this has been a regular feature of post-war elections. But, in fact, since 1955 the variation in swing has been cumulatively systematic and, viewed in the long term, far from uniform.

[Between 1955 and 1979] the only change in [constituency] boundaries was implemented at the February 1974 election (hereafter 1974(F)). The gap in the series of comparable constituency results that this causes between 1970 and 1974(F) can be bridged by the use of the notional results, computed by Michael Steed, for the 1970 election as if it were fought on the boundaries used from 1974(F); these are referred to as 1970(NT). This means that figures indicating the change in the various parties' fortunes in each constituency can be calculated for two long-term periods – 1955–70 and 1970(NT)–1979. The break at 1970 has no theoretical justification, but

From J. Curtice and M. Steed, 'Electoral choice and the production of government: the changing operation of the UK electoral system since 1955', *British Journal of Political Science*, vol. 12 (1982), pp. 249–98.

304

ELECTORAL DEVELOPMENTS, 1955–79

it will in fact be seen that for some purposes a division of the total period into those two segments is heuristically useful.

The pattern of change that started shortly after 1955 has proved remarkably consistent, with the North and urban areas moving cumulatively towards Labour and the South and rural areas cumulatively towards the Conservatives. Although, as in 1955–59 and 1959–64, the urban–rural or the North–South cleavage was usually more important at any one election, almost all the variation in swing at each election contributed in some part to the cumulative trend. The only long-term reversal of the secular trend was in Wales. The majority of the principality's constituencies – the more urban ones – moved towards Labour before 1970, but thereafter most of Wales drifted, in some cases rapidly, towards the Conservatives.

Table 7.1.1 sets out the pattern of swing for the two periods. We have combined the eight standard regions of England into two broader regions.

Table 7.1.1 Mean swing, 1955–79, broken down by region and rurality

	South and Midlands	North of England	Wales	Scotland	Mean
(a) 1955–70: overall (United Kingdom) swing +0.09					
City	−1.93	−7.51	–	−9.53	−3.92 (113)
Very urban	+0.08	−5.60	−4.55	−9.02	−2.78 (110)
Mainly urban	+1.19	−2.09	−4.47	−6.81	−1.08 (123)
Mixed	+3.01	−0.22	−4.16	−5.74	+0.40 (147)
Mainly rural	+3.59	−1.35	+5.16*	−2.06	+2.17* (77)
Very rural	+4.97	+1.29	+0.42	−1.40[†]	+1.68[†] (36)
Mean	+1.21	−2.98	+2.89*	−5.82[†]	−0.98
	(335)	(171)	(31)	(69)	(606)
(b) 1970 (NT)–79: overall (United Kingdom) swing +2.44					
City	+0.24	−4.74	–	−8.12	−1.98 (99)
Very urban	+1.48	−1.81	+1.45	−7.15	−0.28 (100)
Mainly urban	+4.26	−0.60	+2.42	−4.22	+1.67 (144)
Mixed	+6.24	+2.77	+6.17	−2.17	+4.48 (158)
Mainly rural	+7.87	+3.75	+10.49	+0.31	+6.27 (76)
Very rural	+8.82	+7.99	+15.16	+4.03	+8.45 (40)
Mean	+4.24	+0.10	+7.60	−2.84	+2.49
	(344)	(170)	(34)	(69)	(617)

Note: Two-party swing is used in this table. Seats where there was a split Conservative or Labour candidature, or an absence of a Labour or Conservative candidate in one of the elections concerned, are omitted in the calculation of mean swing.

* These figures are heavily influenced by a very strong, untypical swing in Anglesey (viz. +20.52); if Anglesey is excluded, the following figures apply: −2.52 (Wales, mainly rural); +1.90 (mean, mainly rural); −3.67 (Wales, mean).
[†] These figures are similarly influenced by a strong swing in Caithness & Sutherland (−28.26); if Caithness & Sutherland is excluded, the following figures apply: +0.84 (Scotland, very rural); +2.53 (mean, very rural); −5.49 (Scotland, mean).

306 RECENT THEMES

We have kept Scotland distinct because it departed more strongly from the national norm than the three northernmost regions of England, and Wales because of its inconsistent behaviour. Constituencies are arranged into six urban–rural categories. The rural categories are defined by the proportion of the employed population engaged in agriculture [and] we use a categorization of the urban character of constituencies based on the electorate density, i.e. the number of electors per hectare.

Little systematic effort has been put into discovering the reasons for the geographical variations in swing. [Our] purpose [here] is to see whether the most plausible explanations of the changes reinforce or negate our impression that we have witnessed a long-term, fundamental change in electoral geography that is more likely to be continued further than to be reversed.

In a society in which voting behaviour is principally determined by class, perhaps the simplest explanation of a long-term change in a constituency's political affiliation is a change in its class composition. In Britain there has been considerable evidence to suggest that the relationship between class and voting has changed and that other factors have become significant determinants of voting behaviour. However, Miller (1977) has shown that the percentage of employers and managers in a constituency remains not only the best but also an accurate predictor of the Conservative share of the two-party vote in a constituency, and that, despite whatever changes may be occurring in the relationship between class and voting at the individual level, the predictive ability of that percentage remained largely unimpaired throughout the period we are examining. It would thus seem probable that if it could be shown that the proportion of employers and managers who live in rural areas and in the South of Britain had increased, a strong *prima facie* case will have been made for the argument that changes in the distribution of the nation's classes underlie some of the changes in the distribution of the relative strength of its two principal parties.

Migration statistics derived from recent censuses confirm the expectation that the flight from the inner city has been disproportionately a middle-class one. In all of the conurbations, the rate of net loss in the professional and managerial socio-economic groups [has been] greater than the rate of loss in the manual occupation groups. It is true that, as a consequence of a general upgrading in the skill level of the workforce, the percentage of economically active males in professional and managerial occupations rose in conurbations between the 1961 and 1971 censuses; but the rise in the conurbations was noticeably less than in the rest of the country. Thus the tendency for urban Britain to move towards Labour and rural Britain towards the Conservatives has been matched by congruent changes in the spatial distribution of the classes.

It also seems possible that the North–South difference might be partly accounted for by changes in the distribution of the classes. The increase in the average percentage of economically active and retired males who were employers and managers between 1966 (old boundaries) and 1971 (new boundaries) was 2.3 per cent in parliamentary constituencies in the South and Midlands, 2.0 per cent in Wales and 1.6 per cent in both the North of England and Scotland. But be this as it may, it is clear that changes in the distribution of classes have not been solely responsible for the long-term variation in the swing since 1955. Thus there was variation in the swing between February and October 1974 as between more urban and more rural areas, and between Scotland and the rest of the country. As the two 1974 elections occurred on the same electoral register this variation could not have been affected by migration. It must have reflected differences in the behaviour of otherwise similarly socially situated voters according to some characteristic of the area in which they live.

We offer two suggestions to help account for such behaviour. Labour's support has haemorrhaged badly in rural areas to the benefit of both the Conservatives and third parties. This may be accounted for by differences in the social environment of rural and urban working-class supporters. Rural workers are less strongly unionized and are, perhaps, more likely to be in an atomized social situation where their patterns of social intercourse are not characterized by regular contact with other workers who might help to reinforce their partisanship. If, as Miller has argued, the predominant class in a voter's environment has become a more important influence on voting behaviour in Britain, the different environmental position of the urban and rural worker may help to explain some of the difference in the behaviour of urban and rural constituencies. The rural worker, whose environment provides less reinforcement of his Labour partisanship, would seem more likely to leave the Labour fold than his urban counterpart. However, the evidence of rural mining constituencies, pre-eminently a case of Labour and working-class predominance, but also showing a swing to the Right, indicates that this explanation may have its limitations.

To a considerable extent, the North–South and urban–rural differences correspond with the variation in the post-war distribution of economic well-being in Britain. The North of England and Scotland have generally had higher levels of unemployment in the post-war era than most of the South and Midlands. Similarly, inner-city areas tend to have higher levels of unemployment than the surrounding hinterland. Finding that time and time again an upward turn in the trade cycle does not solve the economic problems of their area, voters of all classes in the relatively disadvantaged parts of Britain may gradually have been led to transfer their support to Labour. Since the Labour party evidently has a greater commitment to governmental intervention in the economy, in particular to regional policy and policies which help the inner cities, such behaviour has a political logic.

But besides this speculation, there is one remaining definite reason for the pattern of Table 7.1.1. The period between 1955 and 1979 has seen a marked improvement in the voting strength of minor parties. There have been three major sources of this increased strength. Firstly, there were two waves of revival in the fortunes of the Liberal party from the nadir of 1951. The first peaked, so far as general elections were concerned, in 1964 when they won 11.4 per cent of the poll in Great Britain. In the two years prior to the February 1974 general election there was a sudden and dramatic increase in their level of popular support which enabled them to win 19.9 per cent of the poll in Great Britain at that election. Secondly, the Scottish National Party has emerged as a major force in Scottish politics, gaining ground at each successive election up to October 1974 when they were the second largest party in terms of electoral support in Scotland with 30.4 per cent of the Scottish vote. Although both the Liberals' and the SNP's fortunes declined after their respective peaks in 1974, both performed better in 1979 than in 1955 or 1970.

It has been the pattern of the Liberals' and SNP's success which has to some extent influenced the figures in Table 7.1.1. Two-party swing is unaffected by movements to and from the major parties and third parties so long as they are in proportion to the major parties' relative strength. However, both Steed [1965] and Berrington [1965,1966; Berrington and Bedeman, 1974] have shown that in any constituency the Liberals tend to take their vote disproportionately from the weaker of the two major parties. The same appears to be true of the Scottish Nationalists. Steed has further shown that, on occasions, the Liberals and the Nationalists have benefited from 'tactical voting' whereby supporters of the weaker of the two major parties in a constituency appear to switch to a third-party candidate where that candidate is seen as having a chance of defeating the other major-party candidate. These features, especially the latter, will generate a two-party swing to the stronger of the two major parties in a constituency when a third party is gaining ground. This phenomenon has been most important in rural seats in the South and Midlands where the Liberals have won votes at the particular expense of Labour, and so the swing to the Conservatives in those categories of seats in Table 7.1.1, especially in the 1970s, at least partly reflects the manner of the success of the Liberals there, rather than an increased preference for the Conservatives over Labour. Furthermore, it would appear that in its impact on the relative strength of the two major parties, a strong third-party challenge has an effect which can outlast a later decline in that party's fortunes.

Thus there is good reason to conclude that the change in the spatial distribution of the two-party vote during the last quarter of a century reflects three sorts of changes, each reinforcing the other – change in the distribution of social and economic characteristics of the electorate, the differential behaviour of voters of the same social group according to where they live, and the local political impact of third parties. The first

ELECTORAL DEVELOPMENTS, 1955–79

trend, very probably, will continue; the impact of the current recession, which has badly affected the North of Britain, could well produce a continuation of the second change, while on current electoral evidence, there does not seem to be any reason to anticipate a significant fall in the Liberal and SNP vote – if anything, the opposite. We conclude, therefore, from this tentative exploration of its causes that the direction of the change in the distribution of the two-party vote is more likely to continue than to be reversed.

7.2 Voting behaviour in Scotland and Wales

W.L. Miller

The classic model of nationalised politics in Britain focused on electoral behaviour and political partisanship. Spatial variation was explained in terms of class variation and temporal variation in terms of transient issues with nation-wide (i.e. UK-wide) impact.

Since the end of the 1950s, however, the limitations of this uniform response model have become increasingly apparent. Partisan dealignment has permitted and encouraged partisan denationalisation (and vice versa). When large numbers of electors deserted Labour and Conservative in 1974, their choice of alternatives differed sharply according to whether they lived in Scotland, England, Ireland or Wales. And over a longer period the balance of Labour versus Conservative support has trended in different directions in different regions.

Electoral uniformity: in decline or not?

Declining support for Scots and Welsh nationalist parties at the 1979 election reopened the question of whether there was significant regional variation in voting patterns and whether such variation as did exist was decreasing. Two authoritative analyses of the 1979 results concluded that 'national (i.e. Scots v. Welsh v. English) differences never enter as significant determinants of party choice when the British electorate is analysed as a whole' [Rose, 1982] and even more dramatically 'one part of Britain broke with its long-term trend . . . This time Wales behaved like the rest of South Britain . . . the switch was unmistakable and in consequence the Conservatives won their highest Welsh parliamentary

From W.L. Miller, 'The denationalisation of British politics: the re-emergence of the periphery', *West European Politics*, vol. 6 (1983), pp. 103–29.

310

VOTING BEHAVIOUR IN SCOTLAND AND WALES

representation since 1874' [Curtice and Steed, 1980]. But the reason why Scots/Welsh/English differences never constitute a statistically significant explanation of party choice 'when the British electorate is analysed as a whole' lies not in the lack of substantial political variation but in the huge population imbalance between Scotland, Wales and Northern Ireland – which now comprise respectively only nine per cent, five per cent and two per cent of the UK electorate – and England which accounts for 84 per cent. Indeed the political significance of the Scots, Welsh and Irish derives almost exclusively from their geographic concentration, not their numbers. Geographic concentration fosters their sense of identity; reinforces their political tendencies; facilitates their organisation for party, pressure group and violent purposes; and under the UK electoral system it guarantees them over a fifth of the seats in Parliament.

The extent to which Scotland [and] Wales have deviated from the voting pattern in England at various times over the last century is shown in Table 7.2.1. Generally, the pattern of Welsh electoral deviance over the last century shows more continuity than change, more evidence of traditional bias than of a dynamic system of regional politics. Even the modest

Table 7.2.1 National voting deviations

	Difference from English voting pattern in terms of:							
	% Con. lead over Lab. (% Unionist lead over Liberal in 1885 and 1910)		% Lib.		% Nat.		% (Lib. + Nat.)	
	Wales	Scotland	Wales	Scotland	Wales	Scotland	Wales	Scotland
1885	−16	−15	–	NR	0	0	–	NR
Jan. 1910	−27	−21	–	NR	0	0	–	NR
1929	−24	−8	10	−6	0	0	10	−5
1945–55 average	−29	1	5	−2	1	0	6	−1
1959–66 average	−29	−7	−3	−3	5	3	2	0
1970	−29	−11	−1	−2	12	11	10	9
Feb. 1974	−24	−6	−5	−13	11	22	5	9
Oct. 1974	−24	−10	−5	−12	11	30	6	19
1979	−27	−21	−4	−6	8	17	4	11
1983	−27	−26	−5	−2	8	12	3	10

Note: 1983 figures are provisional.

NR = not relevant because the Liberal party was the main Left party at this time, part of the two-party system, not an alternative to it.

312

electoral support for Welsh nationalists in recent years has been offset by a Welsh bias against the Liberals when compared to England. Wales' strong and traditional bias towards the Left did not in fact decline in 1979. Curtice and Steed's conclusion was based on averaging swings in Welsh constituencies and the average misrepresented the nation as a whole because the largest swings to the Conservatives were in constituencies with the smallest electorates. Though the Conservative recovery in rural Wales is interesting in itself, Wales as a whole did *not* move sharply into line with Southern England in 1979.

Changes in the Scottish figures, however, reflect real changes in the Scots electorate. Though Scotland behaved much like Wales before the First World War its leftist bias was generally small thereafter, disappearing completely for a decade after 1945 but reappearing later, doubling in 1979, and increasing still further in 1983.

South of the border, the three most northerly regions of England also deviated towards the Left between the 1950s and the 1970s and again during the 1970s. They shared with Scotland feelings that Labour represented their interest in inter-regional conflict. They took special interest in moves towards devolution for Scotland. But they lacked Scotland's integrated set of public and political institutions; they lacked Scotland's capacity to sustain an intra-regional political debate; they did not produce regional parties in any way comparable to the SNP in Scotland or even [Plaid Cymru] in Wales; and they drifted towards the Left according to a different time schedule and generally by only half as much as Scotland (both before 1970 and after).

Overall, the 1979 general election showed a decline in nationalist party support in Scotland and Wales. But in terms of the balance between Labour and the Conservatives, regional differentiation increased both within England and between England and the rest of Britain. At the 1983 election both England and Scotland swung towards the Conservatives but the swing was almost three times as high in England; so that national differences were greater in 1983 than in 1979. Electorally, therefore, centre/periphery differences in terms of Labour versus Conservative voting have been maintained or have increased.

Uniform response as an explanation of electoral non-uniformity

Since we know that the periphery differs from England on a number of social and economic dimensions it might seem possible that partisan variation is no more than a reflection of social variation. Scotland and Wales have traditionally suffered more unemployment than England, their

VOTING BEHAVIOUR IN SCOTLAND AND WALES

occupational structure is a little more working-class and the Anglican church is weaker than in England. GDP per capita is specially low in Wales and socialised housing specially widespread in Scotland. Moreover some of this social variation may be amplified when objective characteristics are transformed into social attitudes. There is evidence that the sense of working-class identification varies even more sharply than class itself and higher levels of unemployment may produce still higher levels of concern about jobs.

Within Britain if not within the whole of the UK this uniform response model is at least plausible. We can test it most directly by comparing the partisan responses of similar people in different parts of Britain (see Table 7.2.2).

Regional differences remain strong even when we control for objective social characteristics. *Within* social classes, the Scots and Welsh in 1979 were much more pro-Labour and also pro-third party than the English. Variations in house tenure seem at first more promising but the explanation of regional political differences in these terms does not survive closer inspection. Welsh tenure patterns are very similar to those in England yet the Welsh deviate most strongly to Labour. In Scotland house tenure patterns are very different: twice as many Scots as English live in socialised housing. But in consequence, Scots council tenants are significantly more middle class than English council tenants; and Scots house owners are also very much more middle class than English house owners (paradoxical though that sounds). So Scots living under the same house tenure arrangements as Englishmen should be considerably *more* Conservative than the English, purely on class grounds. Controlling for class and tenure in combination explains a part of Scots pro-Labour deviance in 1979 but only a part. Moreover Scots political deviance is variable and contingent rather than traditional and persistent. The same procedures of control for class and tenure which explain half of the Scots pro-Labour deviance in 1979 suggest that after taking social background into account, Scotland was deviating towards the Conservatives as recently as February 1974. In Scotland, what we need to explain is not its deviant partisanship in 1979 but the sharp changes in its deviance during the 1970s, and slowly changing tenure patterns cannot do that.

Political attitudes can change more rapidly but they also fail to explain partisan variation on the periphery. Plausible though it sounds, the evidence is against the view that the Scots and Welsh were biased towards Labour because they were more concerned about unemployment. English/ non-English partisan differences remain little altered by controls for the salience of prices, unemployment or industrial relations. Perceptions of whether the British economy was getting better or worse had almost no influence on peripheral deviance. Ideological positions on government

RECENT THEMES

Table 7.2.2 Scots and Welsh partisan bias within subgroups, 1979

Source	Subgroup	% Lab. lead in Scotland minus Lab. lead in England[1]	% Lab. lead in Wales minus Lab. lead in England
	Amongst all voters	21	27
G	Amongst middle class (by occupation)	15	35
G	Amongst working class (by occupation)	23	20
G	Amongst owner-occupiers	3	40
G	Amongst council tenants	9	14
G	Amongst middle-class owner-occupiers	7	40
G	Amongst middle-class council tenants	8	22
G	Amongst working-class owner-occupiers	9	39
G	Amongst working-class council tenants	11	13
G	Amongst those for whom prices are most imp. issue	24	28
G	Amongst those for whom unemployment is most imp.	17	18
G	Amongst those for whom strikes are most imp.	19	40
G	Amongst self-described middle class	18	36
G	Amongst self-described working class	18	16
G	Amongst Anglicans	NR[2]	26
G	Amongst Nonconformists	NR	37
E	Amongst Anglicans	NR	30
E	Amongst Nonconformists	NR	43
E	Amongst those who feel 'welfare gone too far'	14	26
E	Amongst those who feel 'welfare not far enough'	5	22
E	Amongst those who feel 'govt should redistrib.'	12	27
E	Amongst those who feel 'govt should not redistrib.'	12	5

Notes:
1. % Lab. lead = % Labour minus % Conservative (adjusted for discrepancies between survey results and actual election outcomes).
2. NR = not relevant, too few Anglicans or Nonconformists.

Sources: G = 1979 Gallup merged pre-election samples of 2,056 Scottish respondents, 389 Welsh, 7,693 English. Similar patterns show up in Gallup surveys for 1970 and 1974. E = 1979 Scots, Welsh and British election studies with 623 Scottish, 734 Welsh and 1,336 English respondents.

provision of welfare or the redistribution of income explain a part of regional deviance but not the major part. Freely assumed self-identification with class clearly explained very little about Welsh deviance, though Gallup and BES surveys disagree on whether it explains some or none of Scots deviance.

VOTING BEHAVIOUR IN SCOTLAND AND WALES

Even religious nonconformity fails to explain Welsh electoral deviance. Welsh nonconformists and Welsh Anglicans were both very much more pro-Labour than their English co-religionists. Sectarian differences totally fail to explain Welsh deviance in 1979 despite their importance in the last century of Welsh political history. However, Welsh respondents to the 1979 election survey report a very high tendency to follow the partisanship of their fathers and mothers. They differ from the English in this only because the children of Labour parents in England display an unusually low level of loyalty to family traditions in 1979. Even allowing for that difference, persistent family traditions explain a great deal of Welsh/ English differences. Another variable which helps explain Welsh deviance is place of birth. Fully 21 per cent of the Welsh sample were born outside Wales, mainly in England, and they voted Conservative even more strongly than the English who lived in England. They voted for third parties to exactly the same degree as their Welsh-born neighbours but their third-party vote went heavily towards the Liberals rather than the Nationalists.

These findings reinforce the view suggested by the steady relationship between Welsh and English voting: namely, that Welsh electoral deviance owes more to political tradition than current issues or current social and religious structures. By contrast the variability of Scots deviations from the English voting norm suggests more active current influence.

7.3 The changing electoral geography of Great Britain

R.J. Johnston and C.J. Pattie

Increased spatial polarisation, 1979–87

The changing electoral geography of Great Britain is a major unsolved puzzle for electoral analysts. Analyses of the 1983–7 trends suggest that the regional polarisation [identified in earlier work] continued during the latest inter-election period – if anything, the pace accelerated. Here we extend those analyses, using two classifications of the 633 constituencies. (For the detailed statistical material, see Johnston, Pattie and Allsopp, 1988.) Our *geographical regionalisation* comprises twenty-two regions defined to separate out the urban and rural portions of the major regional divisions of the country and is thus finer-grained than the Standard Regions conventionally used. Our *functional regionalisation*, based on a cluster analysis of 1981 census data (Crewe and Fox, 1984), identifies thirty-one separate groups of constituencies with common socio-economic and demographic characteristics.

Table 7.3.1 shows the change in the percentage of the electorate who voted Conservative, Labour and Alliance in each geographical region for the periods 1979–83, 1983–7 and 1979–87. By geographical region, the general north–south divide is clearly evident in the changing pattern of support for both Conservative and Labour Parties. Over the full eight-year period 1979–87, for example, the Conservative share of the electorate fell on average by 0.6 percentage points. In most of the regions north and west of a Severn–Wash line the fall was substantially greater (Rural North, Rural Wales and West Yorkshire were exceptions); south and east of that line the Conservative vote increased in all regions on average, except in

From R.J. Johnston and C.J. Pattie, 'The changing electoral geography of Great Britain', in J. Mohan (ed.), *The Political Geography of Contemporary Britain*, London: Macmillan, 1989.

316

Table 7.3.1 Inter-election changes in the percentage of the electorate voting for each party, 1979–87, by geographical region

	Conservative			Labour			Alliance		
	79–83	83–87	79–87	79–83	83–87	79–87	79–83	83–87	79–87
Strathclyde	−3.3	−2.4	−5.7	−3.9	10.5	6.6	11.2	−4.0	7.2
East Scotland	−0.9	−0.9	−1.8	−4.6	7.9	3.3	11.0	−3.3	8.6
Rural Scotland	−0.3	−0.3	−0.6	−4.0	5.2	1.3	8.1	1.0	9.1
Rural North	−0.2	0.4	0.1	−7.1	3.7	−3.4	6.2	−0.9	5.2
Industrial North East	−2.3	−1.2	−3.6	−8.6	7.3	−1.3	9.6	−2.4	7.2
Merseyside	−5.0	−3.5	−8.5	−4.5	7.7	3.1	6.8	0.7	7.5
Greater Manchester	−4.0	0.8	−3.1	−6.3	4.6	−1.7	6.9	−1.8	5.1
Rest of North West	−2.5	0.4	−2.1	−5.7	4.9	−0.8	7.4	−2.1	5.3
West Yorks	−1.4	1.8	0.4	−8.2	5.6	−2.6	7.8	−2.8	5.0
South Yorks	−2.7	−1.4	−4.1	−7.9	7.8	−0.1	7.9	−2.5	5.4
Rural Wales	−0.1	0.7	0.6	−6.8	6.1	−0.7	6.1	−0.2	5.9
Industrial South Wales	−2.6	0.7	−1.9	−8.4	10.2	1.8	10.1	−4.2	5.9
West Midlands Conurbation	−3.4	1.4	−2.0	−6.2	2.9	−3.3	8.7	−1.9	6.7
Rest of West Midlands	0.3	1.2	1.5	−7.4	2.3	−5.1	8.3	−0.8	7.5
East Midlands	−0.3	2.8	2.5	−8.0	2.7	−5.3	7.6	−1.6	6.0
East Anglia	0.4	2.1	2.5	−8.8	1.5	−7.3	9.3	−1.2	8.0
Devon and Cornwall	−0.9	−1.1	−2.0	−6.8	4.3	−2.5	8.4	−2.0	6.4
Wessex	−0.1	1.8	1.7	−7.8	1.2	−6.6	7.9	0.9	8.8
Inner London	−3.8	2.6	−1.2	−7.4	3.2	−4.1	7.8	−0.1	7.7
Outer London	−3.2	3.7	0.5	−9.0	1.6	−7.3	8.3	−2.3	6.0
Outer Metropolitan	−0.5	2.9	2.4	−8.4	1.1	−7.3	8.5	−1.2	7.2
Outer South East	−0.4	1.8	1.4	−7.7	1.3	−6.4	8.1	0.4	8.5
National	−1.7	1.1	−0.6	−7.2	4.1	−3.1	8.3	−1.4	6.9

Source: Computed by the authors (see also Johnston, Pattie and Allsopp, 1988).

318   RECENT THEMES

Devon and Cornwall and in Inner London. Similarly, the Labour vote fell
overall by 3.1 percentage points on average, but it increased in four of the
northern regions and fell by less than the national average in five others
there; it fell by more than the national average in nine of the ten southern
regions. The Alliance vote increased more in southern than northern
England, on average, though it increased by well above the average in
Scotland.

The thirty-one functional regions also show substantial variations about
the national averages (Table 7.3.2). In general terms, the more deprived
regions are at the top of the table, and the economically more buoyant and
prosperous are lower down. In most of the former (the major exception
being the Black Country grouping) the Conservative loss was greater than
average, whereas in many of the latter the Conservative vote grew between
1979 and 1987; increasingly its support came from those constituencies that
were benefiting most from the industrial restructuring over which the
Conservative governments of 1979 and 1983 presided. Complementing
this, Labour lost fewer votes in the less prosperous regions, and its share of
the poll increased substantially in three regions most of whose member
constituencies are in Scotland. This suggests a growing spatial polarisation
of the electorate that sees Conservative and Labour increasingly drawing
their support from particular geographical regions of Britain and also from
particular types of constituency.

Accounting for the new geography

The main reason for this growing spatial polarisation of the electorate since
1979 appears to be the changing economic geography of the country during
that period. Several indices illustrate those changes: among the most
directly apparent to the electorate are levels of unemployment and the
prices of residential properties. During the period of Conservative rule,
the official unemployment rate increased from 4.3 per cent in 1979 to a
peak of 12.3 per cent in January 1986, and was at 10.4 per cent in June 1987.
The increases were not uniform across the country, however, but were
much higher in the northern and western regions (including Devon and
Cornwall). The geography of property value changes was more or less a
mirror image of that of unemployment. The 1980s have seen a great boom
in the prices for residential units in the southern regions but property prices
have increased much less elsewhere.

These two indicators may directly influence people's voting. Those made
unemployed, those never able to get work, and those in a household where
somebody either is or becomes out of work, will be quite likely to blame the
Government and, if they previously voted Conservative, to switch to
another party in protest. In contrast, those benefiting from the increased

Table 7.3.2 Inter-election changes in the percentage of the electorate voting for each party, 1979–87, by functional region

	Conservative			Labour			Alliance		
	79–83	83–87	79–87	79–83	83–87	79–87	79–83	83–87	79–87
Inner city/immigrant	-3.2	3.0	-0.2	-6.9	2.6	-4.3	7.5	-1.4	6.2
Industrial/immigrant	-2.6	1.3	-1.3	-6.7	4.4	-2.3	7.3	-2.2	5.1
Poorest immigrant	-3.5	1.5	-2.0	-4.6	4.7	0.1	6.9	-4.8	2.1
Intermediate industrial	-1.8	0.9	-0.9	-8.1	4.5	-3.6	8.5	-1.8	6.7
Old industrial/mining	-2.4	1.3	-1.1	-8.1	7.1	-1.0	7.5	-3.2	4.4
Textile	-1.8	1.3	-0.5	-6.6	4.7	-1.9	6.6	-2.6	4.0
Poorest domestic	-2.6	0.4	-2.2	-8.4	10.6	2.2	8.2	-0.7	7.5
Conurban local authority	-3.3	-0.4	-3.7	-7.8	6.2	-1.6	8.2	-2.5	5.8
Black Co.	-2.2	2.6	0.5	-6.3	2.2	-4.1	9.1	-2.2	6.9
Maritime industrial	-3.4	-1.0	-4.4	-8.6	7.4	-1.2	10.0	-2.7	7.4
Poor inner city	-2.3	0.9	-1.4	-6.6	4.4	-2.2	7.8	-0.5	7.3
Clydeside	-4.1	-0.9	-5.0	-5.1	11.5	6.4	9.2	-3.7	5.6
Scottish industrial	-1.2	-2.1	-3.4	-3.4	9.7	6.3	12.8	-4.0	8.8
Scottish rural	-0.3	0.1	-0.2	-4.0	3.4	-0.6	8.4	0.7	9.1
High status inner metropolitan	-5.4	2.3	-3.1	-5.6	3.4	-2.2	6.5	-1.7	4.7
Inner metropolitan	-4.4	2.0	-2.4	-6.6	4.1	-2.6	7.4	-0.7	6.7
Outer London	-3.3	3.4	0.2	-8.2	2.0	-6.2	8.3	-1.8	6.5
Very high status	-2.0	1.9	-0.1	-7.3	1.7	-5.6	7.3	-0.7	6.6
Conurban white collar	-4.0	1.0	-3.0	-7.3	3.4	-3.9	8.3	-0.6	7.7
City service	-3.3	0.1	-3.3	-7.7	4.5	-3.2	8.5	0.4	8.9
Resort/retirement	-1.0	1.2	0.2	-6.3	2.1	-4.3	6.1	0.6	6.7
Recent growth	0.9	1.2	2.1	-6.7	3.7	-3.1	11.1	-1.4	9.6
Stable industrial	-1.0	1.7	0.7	-8.0	3.6	-4.4	9.8	-2.5	7.4
Small towns	-0.4	1.2	0.8	-8.0	2.6	-5.4	7.7	-0.2	7.5
Southern urban	0.4	2.3	2.6	-8.4	0.9	-7.5	9.4	-0.2	9.2
Modest affluence	-1.5	0.9	-0.6	-8.5	3.2	-5.3	9.2	-1.1	8.1
Metropolitan industrial	-1.1	3.4	2.4	-9.8	2.9	-6.9	9.7	-3.2	6.5
Modest affluent Scotland	-1.8	-0.4	-2.2	-4.3	8.4	4.2	10.7	-3.7	7.0
Rapid growth	1.7	2.7	4.4	-7.7	1.9	-5.9	8.0	-1.6	6.4
Prosperous/non-industrial	-0.3	0.6	0.3	-7.1	2.5	-4.6	6.6	0.6	7.2
Agricultural	0.6	0.9	1.5	-6.5	2.2	-4.2	6.4	-0.3	6.1
National	-1.7	1.1	-0.6	-7.2	4.1	-3.1	8.3	-1.4	6.9

Source: Computed by the authors (see also Johnston, Pattie and Allsopp, 1988).

320 RECENT THEMES

property prices could decide to vote Conservative to protect their enhanced equity holdings. More importantly, however, these indicators point to major geographical differences in social and economic circumstances across the country, differences that provide the contexts within which people evaluate the future and the promises of the contenders for political power.

Sanders, Ward and Marsh (1987) suggest that people's perceptions of their likely immediate futures have been major influences on their voting choice during the 1980s. [They] suggest that the major cause of the revival in Conservative fortunes [before the 1983 election] was a belief that economic recovery was beginning; an increasing proportion of the electorate responded optimistically to questions about their perceptions of their own and the country's economic future.

Such optimism was probably more common in the relatively prosperous regions of the country – those with low unemployment rates and rapidly increasing property prices. If so, the swing to the Conservative Party in the south and east (or to the Alliance as a second choice), but towards Labour in the north and west, is readily appreciated. Similarly, the poor performance of Labour in Greater London in 1987 (relative to its vote-winning in Merseyside and Strathclyde in particular) can be appreciated as a function of the relative strength of the London economy rather than the claimed impact of the Conservative and Alliance campaigns against the so-called 'loony left' councils in some London boroughs and the targeting of London Labour Party candidates as left wing.

Table 7.3.3 presents data drawn from the 1979, 1983 and 1987 Gallup polls conducted on election day for the BBC, each of which included a question relating to respondents' perceived household financial situations over the previous twelve months. Those data show, for five aggregated regions: 1) the B:W ratio, between the number who thought things had got better and the number who thought things had got worse; and 2) the percentage voting Conservative, Labour and Alliance (Liberal in 1979) among those who thought things had got better, stayed the same, and got worse. There were clear regional variations in people's levels of economic satisfaction, especially in 1983 and 1987 when southerners (including Londoners) were generally more satisfied than their northern counterparts. These variations were matched by voting in 1983 and 1987. (In 1979, the incumbent government was Labour, and people who thought things had got better recently were more likely to vote Labour, especially in the northern regions.) In each region in 1983 and 1987, the less satisfied people were with their situations, the less likely they were to vote Conservative and the more likely they were to vote either Labour or Alliance. Given the spatial variations in economic satisfaction, therefore, the voting pattern is clearly related to perceived economic well-being. But there were further inter-regional variations: dissatisfied southerners were twice as likely to

CHANGING ELECTORAL GEOGRAPHY

Table 7.3.3 Vote by perceptions of personal economic situation over the last twelve months and aggregated region

	Got better			The same			Got worse			B:W ratio
	C	L	A	C	L	A	C	L	A	
1979										
London	33	39	12	28	42	10	40	13	15	0.55
South	37	32	17	41	28	12	58	15	13	0.73
Midlands	31	48	9	41	26	8	60	13	7	0.85
North urban	20	50	8	29	39	6	40	21	13	0.99
Scotland/Wales	14	51	7	24	38	10	30	28	8	0.75
1983										
London	74	4	17	53	26	14	19	51	22	0.77
South	71	5	18	56	11	25	21	28	43	1.15
Midlands	54	16	15	41	26	17	21	39	26	0.61
North urban	60	15	20	47	23	18	16	49	26	0.61
Scotland/Wales	53	15	18	34	28	25	13	46	21	0.49
1987										
London	45	33	13	34	40	17	12	60	15	0.98
South	67	8	18	48	14	26	18	35	34	1.55
Midlands	59	17	17	44	27	19	17	42	22	1.29
North urban	43	22	25	33	34	20	10	58	17	0.75
Scotland/Wales	43	17	20	22	43	16	10	57	11	0.88

Source: Computed by the authors from BBC/Gallup survey tapes (see also Johnston, Pattie and Allsopp, 1988).

vote Alliance as dissatisfied Scots and Welsh, for example, and people who thought things had stayed 'about the same' were more likely to vote for the incumbent government in the South and Midlands than were people with similar beliefs in London, the urban North and Scotland and Wales.

These results suggest a growing local and regional consciousness regarding economic and social welfare in Britain during the 1980s. This is probably an extension of trends that began in the 1950s, which clearly contradict the notion of a uniform British political culture promoted by many psephologists and by the political parties whose campaigning activity increasingly focuses on the national mass media and the projection of their leaders' images via television. The implication is that although most effort at mobilising voters – at influencing their processes of political evaluation – is national in its content, an increasing number of people are responding to this through their interpretations of the local rather than the national context.

8 | Elections and the electorate in the 1980s

Introduction

In this last section we bring together a number of commentaries on developments in British electoral politics in the 1980s. That decade was dominated by the Conservative party, which won overwhelming victories – at least in terms of seats in the House of Commons – in 1979, 1983 and 1987, and by the extraordinary influence of Margaret Thatcher. The fact that the Conservatives were able to win large majorities in the House of Commons while receiving a relatively small minority of the votes cast (together with the enormous disparity between the share of votes and number of seats won by the Liberal–SDP Alliance) pushed the question of reform of the electoral system on to the political agenda. In the first extract in this section Curtice and Steed, in one of a number of analyses they have undertaken, demonstrate that a consequence of cumulative swings in party support over the past thirty years has been that the single-member simple plurality system, as it operates in contemporary Britain, no longer has the exaggerative effect which results in decisive election results, which its defenders claim as one of its central virtues. Though Curtice and Steed are not concerned in this piece to get involved in the debate about electoral reform, their work provides the detailed statistical evidence upon which many sophisticated contributions to the debate rest.

The two main questions addressed in the remaining extracts are first, why the Conservatives so clearly outstripped their rivals, and second, whether Mrs Thatcher has had an enduring influence on the values and political attitudes of British voters. The second and third extracts are analyses of the elections of 1983 and 1987. The first, by Miller, is in the form of a commentary on an immediately post-election analysis by Ivor Crewe. Miller's arguments are unusual and even tendentious at times. His central argument, however, is that Labour's problem was not that the party was unpopular because of its positions on the important issues, but that its divided and fractious leadership undermined the electorate's confidence in the party's ability to govern.

322

ELECTIONS AND THE ELECTORATE IN THE 1980s

In his report on the 1987 BBC/Gallup election day survey Crewe brings out two central points. The first is Labour's continuing problems in realising its potential working class support. Among skilled manual workers Labour's vote continued to decline – in 1987 only 34 per cent of skilled manual workers voted Labour. Second, Crewe offers an overall assessment of why Labour lost, in spite of what had been widely thought to be a very professional campaign. He argues that the main reason for the Conservatives' success was economic prosperity. Although Labour was the preferred party on many of the issues, Crewe suggests that when it came to making up their minds about how to vote the electors were swayed by their sense of economic well-being and prosperity.

The remaining two extracts consider whether a new ideology of *Thatcherism* has been absorbed by the British electorate. Anthony Heath explores two central elements of the Thatcherite programme – privatisation and council house sales – to see whether there is any evidence that the beneficiaries have been converted to support for the Conservative party. Broadly their answer is 'no'. He argues that the more normal pattern is that those who took advantage of the opportunities to buy shares in privatised industries or to purchase their council houses were already Conservative supporters before they did so.

Finally, in a wide-ranging article, Crewe considers evidence, mainly from Gallup polls, about the electorate's attitudes on a wide variety of issues. He concludes that there is again little evidence to support the claim (or hope) of Mrs Thatcher's more ardent supporters that she has managed to transform British voters' attitudes on central social, economic and political matters. He sums up his conclusions as follows: 'Voters oppose the government on the vast array of its specific policy initiatives. They say they prefer Labour on the issues that matter. Their economic values are solidly social democratic, their moral values only half-Thatcherite, and on both fronts they have edged to the Left since 1979. There has been no ideological sea-change.' (p. 369 below) Why then did the Conservatives win the general elections of the 1980s so handsomely? Crewe suggests that it is because the electorate recognised and admired Mrs Thatcher's qualities as a political leader – her 'statecraft'. It is interesting to note that both this analysis and Miller's explanation of the 1983 election result place a good deal of emphasis on the electors' assessment of the political abilities and image of party leaders, as opposed to their assessment of the parties' stands on the issues of the day.

Further reading

Electorally speaking 'the 1980s' could be said to have begun with the Conservative victory in the 1979 general election. For that reason, the Nuffield study of the 1979 election (Butler and Kavanagh, 1980) should be

324 RECENT THEMES

included with the 1983 and 1987 studies (Butler and Kavanagh, 1984, 1988) as major sources on British electoral politics over the period. These volumes provide detailed analysis of the election results, descriptions and assessments of the campaign at local and national level and analysis of the characteristics of candidates and of the role of the media in campaigns.

There are also two volumes in the excellent 'Britain at the Polls' series (Penniman, 1981; Ranney, 1985), though unfortunately there is no corresponding study of the 1987 election.

The major BES study of the 1987 election is, of course, Heath, Jowell and Curtice (1985) and their report on the 1987 contest is forthcoming (Heath *et al.*, 1991). There are also many other books and articles based on the BES data – see, for example, Rose and McAllister (1986 and 1990).

Ivor Crewe's influential analyses of voting behaviour in 1979 and 1983, using Gallup data (Crewe, 1981a, 1985) are found in the 'Britain at the Polls' series referred to above, while his report on the 1987 election is reproduced below. A brief account of the 1987 campaign can be found in Norris (1987).

Alderman (1978) provides an easily accessible overview of the controversy about the British electoral system. A clear statement of the attack on the single-member simple plurality system can be found in Bogdanor (1981), while a thoughtful defence can be found in Chandler (1982).

Harrop and Shaw (1989) consider Labour's electoral predicament in the late 1980s and come to generally gloomy conclusions, but a more optimistic note is sounded by Heath and McDonald (1987).

The literature on Mrs Thatcher and Thatcherism is voluminous. Kavanagh (1990) is a useful introduction while more advanced treatments are found in Skidelsky (1988) and, from a broadly Marxist perspective, Hall and Jacques (1983).

8.1 Proportionality and exaggeration in the British electoral system

John Curtice and Michael Steed

Introduction

The advent of the Liberal/SDP Alliance and its past and possible future electoral performance has put the issue of electoral reform firmly in the centre of British political debate. Despite only winning 2 per cent less of the vote than the Labour party at the 1983 general election it won 29 per cent less seats; the result was unusually disproportional even by the normal standards of the single member plurality system. The electoral system, it is claimed, has reached a threshold of unfairness which it is no longer possible to tolerate.

This argument has one main drawback; it evaluates the single member plurality electoral system by different criteria than those used by its defenders. The system has been defended not on the grounds that it produces a 'fair' result, but rather that it enables the electorate to choose between alternative governments and that it encourages governments to be responsive to the wishes of the electorate. These qualities are ascribed to the system because it supposedly exaggerates leads in votes into larger leads in terms of seats, that is, systematic 'unfairness' can be a virtue.

Four years ago (Curtice and Steed, 1982) we argued that significant changes in the country's electoral geography had seriously undermined the exaggerative quality of the electoral system. In this article we will demonstrate that apart from one important point – the exceptional size of the Conservative lead over Labour – the result of the 1983 general election proved to be a dramatic confirmation of our thesis. The exaggerative quality of the single member plurality electoral system is contingent upon

From J. Curtice and M. Steed, 'Proportionality and exaggeration in the British electoral system', *Electoral Studies* (1986), vol. 5, pp. 209–28.

326 RECENT THEMES

the existence of certain circumstances which no longer pertain at Westminster elections. In consequence, even if the Alliance remains the third party in terms of votes the electoral system can no longer be defended on the grounds commonly used by its defenders.

In the next two sections we summarise why the single member plurality system was believed to be suitable for the ends of its proponents and how the changing political geography of Great Britain has undermined its exaggerative quality. Although we discover that the exaggerative quality of the electoral system in its relative treatment of Conservative and Labour is close to disappearing entirely, the following section shows that important exaggerative features still exist.

The exaggerative quality

Central to the defence of the single member plurality electoral system has been its exaggerative quality. There are two elements to this. The first is relatively straightforward. It is argued that the system makes it difficult for small parties to win seats and thus representation in parliament tends to be dominated by two parties who compete with each other for office. It is now widely appreciated that this claim is only partly true. The single member plurality electoral system discriminates against small (and not so small) parties with a geographically evenly spread vote (such as the Liberal party) but not against those parties whose vote is geographically concentrated, such as the Northern Ireland Unionists. But it is clear that the system does make it difficult for a small party with a nationwide basis of support (and thus perhaps a party with the potential to become a national party) to achieve effective representation.

The second element in the claimed exaggerative quality of the single member plurality electoral system is a little more complex. The system not only helps larger parties at the expense of smaller ones, but also benefits the largest party at the expense of the second largest. The lead of the winning party over the second party in terms of seats is an exaggerated reflection of its lead in terms of votes. This exaggerative quality has been modelled in the form of a cube law. If the two largest parties share their joint vote between them in the ratio $A:B$, they will divide their seats in the ratio $A^3:B^3$. This means that [with] a result close to a 50:50 division of the vote, a 1 per cent transfer of votes [would] produce a 3 per cent switch of seats. Research suggested that the law applied not only in Britain, but also in the other Anglo-Saxon democracies using the same or a similar electoral system. The law has thus become widely regarded as an integral feature of the single member plurality electoral system.

With these two elements of exaggeration, the single member plurality electoral system was able to achieve the objectives of its advocates. The

PROPORTIONALITY AND EXAGGERATION

squeeze on (some) small parties together with the operation of the cube law meant that the largest party usually won a safe overall majority despite having less than 50 per cent of the vote. In consequence, the government was chosen directly by the people rather than determined by coalition bargaining. Further, the security of office given to governments helped to produce stable and effective government.

While the exaggerative quality of the electoral system gives one party unfettered power for a period of years, it also encourages its responsible use. Because the winning party's overall majority is vulnerable to a small loss of votes it has to be responsive to a wide range of public opinion. Under a Downsian logic (Downs, 1957), it is encouraged to stay in the ideological centre and thus much public policy will be operated under a Butskellite-type consensus. Equally, the vulnerability of a significant proportion of its seats to a small switch of votes means that the government will take cognizance of a wide range of geographical interests.

In their seminal work which demonstrated the statistical underpinning of the cube law, however, Kendall and Stuart (1950) demonstrated quite clearly that the cube law would only operate if certain conditions were met. As in the case of its treatment of small parties, the single member plurality electoral system only exaggerated the distance between the two largest parties in conformity with the cube law if a certain geographical distribution of the vote existed. The distribution of the votes of the two main parties across the constituencies had (approximately) to represent a normal distribution with a standard deviation of 13.7. Although a number of writers have suggested reasons why these conditions should be fulfilled, the operation of the cube law never has been inevitable. This is now evident in the case of Britain. The last thirty years have seen a persistent and dramatic change in its electoral geography which has all but removed this second element in the exaggerative quality of its electoral system.

The decline of the cube law

In order to understand the decline of the cube law in Great Britain we need to examine the constituency by constituency variation in the net movement between the Conservative and Labour parties ('swing') over the last 30 years. At each of the last eight general elections, starting in 1959, the variation in swing since the previous election has reflected a socio-geographic pattern of two overlapping cleavages, North/South and urban/rural. At most elections one of the two has been the stronger, but at almost every election both have been present.

Table 8.1.1 measures these movements in terms of the deviation from the national (mean) swing over three periods. The periods were determined by the incidence of boundary changes. We have had to construct a

Table 8.1.1 Socio-geographical deviations in swing, 1955–83

	South of England	Midlands	North of England	Scotland	All
(a) 1955–70					
City	−1.0		−6.5	−8.5	−3.9
Very urban	+1.1		−4.6	−8.0	−2.8
Mainly urban	+2.2		−1.1	−5.8	−0.1
Mixed	+4.0		+0.8	−4.8	+1.4
Mainly rural	+4.6		−0.4	−1.1	+3.2
Very rural	+6.0		+2.3	−0.4	+2.7
All	+2.2		−2.0	−4.8	0
(b) 1970 (NT)–79					
City	−2.2		−7.2	−10.6	−4.5
Very urban	−1.0		−4.3	−9.6	−2.8
Mainly urban	+1.8		−3.1	−6.7	−0.8
Mixed	+3.8		+0.3	−2.7	+2.0
Mainly rural	+5.4		+1.3	−2.2	+3.8
Very rural	+6.3		+5.3	+1.5	+6.0
All	+1.8		−2.4	−5.3	0
(c) 1979 (NT)–83					
City or very urban	−0.6	−4.1	−5.6	−8.4	−2.9
Mainly urban	+3.8	+1.0	−3.1	−6.7	−0.4
Mixed	+4.7	+1.9	−0.8	−3.9	+1.1
Mainly or very rural	+3.3	+5.1	+0.0	+0.9	+2.9
All	+2.4	+1.0	−2.8	−3.7	0

Note: Each entry is the difference between the mean swing in the category and the mean swing in all constituencies. A plus sign (+) indicates a deviation in the Conservatives' favour, and a minus sign (−) a deviation in Labour's favour. (NT = notional results based on new boundaries).

'bridge' across the boundary changes by using both the actual election results in 1970 and 1979 and a recalculation of those results on the constituency boundaries used at the following election. But the most striking feature of Table 8.1.1 is the consistency of movement during the three periods.

The consequence of this consistency of variation is that cumulatively the variation has been massive. At one extreme, Scottish cities have experienced a total deviation of some 27.5 percentage points towards Labour, while rural constituencies in Southern and Midland England have moved altogether some 15 percentage points towards the Conservatives. This cumulative systematic variation in swing has fundamentally altered the exaggerative quality of Britain's electoral system.

The key to understanding how variation in swing can affect the exaggerative quality of an electoral system lies in its impact upon the

PROPORTIONALITY AND EXAGGERATION

distribution of the two-party vote. Any uniform swing will leave the distribution of the two-party vote unaffected. Equally, so will any non-uniform swing whose variation is randomly distributed among constituencies so that there is no correlation between swing and past performance. But any swing which is correlated with past performance will affect the distribution of the two-party vote. If both parties do well in their weaker areas the standard deviation of the distribution of the two-party vote will fall and the exaggerative quality of the electoral system will increase; if both do well in their stronger areas the opposite will happen.

These a priori considerations lead us to anticipate therefore that the long-term variation in swing seen in Great Britain since 1955 would eventually increase the spread of the two-party vote. The variation may not initially have had much impact – it might even have resulted in an increase in the exaggerative quality of the electoral system – but we would expect that ultimately it would start to decline.

The actual impact of the long-term variation in swing upon the exaggerative quality of the electoral system is shown in Table 8.1.2. This shows the standard deviation of the two-party vote in Great Britain at each election since 1955. It also shows the number of marginal seats both in terms of absolute numbers and as a proportion of all seats. A marginal seat is defined as a seat which, at a 50:50 division of the overall two-party vote, would be held by the winning party by a majority of 10 per cent of the two-party vote or less. For the cube law to operate, 30 per cent of seats should lie within this crucial area.

Table 8.1.2 shows that there has been a dramatic change in the distribution of the two-party vote. In 1955 Britain did largely conform to the cube law, though a somewhat flatter than anticipated distribution meant that there were slightly less marginal seats than would have been

Table 8.1.2 Changing distribution of two-party vote, 1955–83

	Standard deviation	Marginal seats	
		No.	%
1955	13.47	166	27.2
1959	13.79	157	25.7
1964	14.12	166	27.3
1966	13.77	155	25.6
1970	14.34	149	24.5
1970 (NT)	14.32	149	24.3
1974 (Feb.)	16.10	119	19.9
1974 (Oct.)	16.82	98	16.4
1979	16.86	108	17.8
1979 (NT)	16.56	100	16.1
1983	20.02	80	13.2

expected. By 1983 the standard deviation of the two-party vote had increased considerably, and the number of marginal seats [had] been more than halved. Until 1970 the fall was slight, but thereafter there has been a sharp fall in the number of marginal seats. More and more Labour seats became more Labour, and more and more Conservative seats more Conservative.

The limited ability of the British electoral system operating with the 1983 distribution of the vote to exaggerate the lead of the largest party over the second party is illustrated in Table 8.1.3. It shows what the distribution of seats between Conservative and Labour would be if the allocation of seats were strictly proportional, and if it were according to a square or cube law. This is contrasted with the actual distribution of seats that would occur as a consequence of a uniform shift from the 1983 result, assuming that no seats were won by third parties. It is clear that for any result likely to occur so long as Conservative and Labour remain the principal competitors for power the exaggerative power of the British electoral system is now very mild, being less not only than that of the cube law but also less than that of a square law.

This decline in the exaggerative power of the electoral system acquires additional significance because of the increase in the number of third party MPs in the House of Commons. This has been brought about not only by the increase in the number of Liberal/Alliance and Nationalist MPs from Great Britain but also by the divorce of Northern Ireland politics from that on the mainland and an increase (in 1983) in the province's total representation from 12 to 17. The decline of the ability of the electoral system to exaggerate the lead of the largest party over the second has occurred at a time when it was increasingly needed if elections were to continue to produce safe overall margins for one party.

An indication of the prospects for a hung parliament in the continued absence of a parliamentary breakthrough by the Alliance is given in Table 8.1.4. The table assumes that the Alliance wins the same share of the vote in Britain (26 per cent) and in each constituency as it did in 1983 and then explores the impact of successive transfer of 1 per cent of the total British vote from Conservative to Labour. We find that the Conservatives need to retain at least a 4.2 per cent lead over Labour if they are to have an overall majority, while Labour need to acquire a lead of at least 6.4 per cent.

Such a lead (in Great Britain) has not been common in post-war elections. Only on three occasions, since 1950 – in 1966, 1979 and 1983 – has it been achieved. The 1983 lead of 15 per cent in particular was wholly exceptional, being more than twice that achieved by either party in any other election since 1950. But should British elections return to the post-war norm of close competition between Conservative and Labour, the electoral system will demonstrate a profound inability to produce single-party government with safe overall majorities.

PROPORTIONALITY AND EXAGGERATION

Table 8.1.3 Exaggerative quality of electoral system

	Distribution of the 633 seats			Actual 1983	
Voting ratio	Proportional	Squared	Cubed	Con.:Lab.	Lab.:Con.
50:50	316:316	316:316	316:316	326:307	307:326
52.5:47.5	332:301	348:285	364:269	345:288	326:307
55:45	348:285	379:254	409:224	365:268	353:280
57.5:42.5	364:269	409:224	451:182	387:246	371:262
60:40	380:253	438:195	488:145	414:219	400:233
60.6:39.4	384:249	445:188	497:136	417:216	– –

Table 8.1.4 The current seats/votes relationship

% vote (GB)		Seats (UK)					
Con.	Lab.	Con.	Lab.	All.	Other	Maj.	
43.5	28.3	397	209	23	21	Con.	144
42.5	29.3	387	217	25	21	Con.	124
41.5	30.3	370	233	26	21	Con.	90
40.5	31.3	355	246	27	22	Con.	60
39.5	32.3	340	259	28	23	Con.	30
38.5	33.3	332	266	28	24	Con.	14
38.0	33.8	326	271	29	24	Con.	2
37.5	34.3	318	277	31	24	None	
36.5	35.3	305	290	31	24	None	
35.5	36.3	297	300	29	24	None	
34.5	37.3	286	310	29	25	None	
33.5	38.3	273	318	34	25	None	
32.7	39.1	265	326	34	25	Lab.	2
32.5	39.3	259	331	36	24	Lab.	12
31.5	40.3	244	345	37	24	Lab.	40

The exaggeration that remains

We have demonstrated so far that the single member plurality electoral system has now almost lost its ability to exaggerate the relative electoral strength of the Conservative and Labour parties in terms of the seats that they win. But while the relative sizes of the Conservative and Labour parliamentary parties are little different from what would be produced under a system of proportional representation their composition is very different. For while the electoral system fails to exaggerate the lead of one party over the other at national level, it still produces substantial exaggeration of the lead of one party over another in any particular region.

This point is demonstrated in Table 8.1.5. The regions in the table have been defined in such a way as to distinguish those parts of the country which

Table 8.1.5 Parliamentary geography

	1951 Seats		1974 (Feb.) Seats		1983 adjusted to 50:50 voting ratio Seats		Votes %	
	Con.	Lab.	Con.	Lab.	Con.	Lab.	Con.	Lab.
South and East shire counties	118	24	135	21	151	17	66.2	33.8
Outer London	36	18	35	19	36	14	55.9	44.1
Midland shire counties	26	35	35	27	41	27	53.4	46.6
Conservative Britain	180	77	205	67	228	58	61.4	38.6
Inner London	14	33	7	31	3	27	35.9	64.1
West Midland met. county	7	22	7	25	8	23	42.2	57.8
Wales	6	27	8	24	8	25	34.7	65.4
North of England	70	101	49	114	41	115	40.5	59.5
Scotland	35	35	21	40	11	49	34.1	65.9
Labour Britain	132	218	92	234	71	239	38.6	61.4
House of Commons	312	295	297	301	299	297	50.0	50.0

are predominantly Conservative and those which are predominantly Labour. Table 8.1.5 shows the distribution of seats between Conservative and Labour within each region in 1951 and February 1974 (when the two parties almost tied with each other in terms of votes) and what the distribution would have looked like in 1983 assuming the existing electoral geography but overall national equality of votes. The final two columns show what the distribution of the two-party vote would have been in 1983 on the same assumptions.

The exaggerative quality of the electoral system at sub-national level is immediately apparent. In the South and East shire counties, for example, the Conservatives would, in an evenly contested election, win two-thirds of the two-party votes, but 90 per cent of the seats. Across the whole of Conservative Britain the Conservatives would win just over three-fifths of the vote, but nearly four-fifths of the seats, while the result in Labour Britain would be almost a perfect mirror image. The distribution of seats in the two halves of the country separately is indeed close to the predictions of the cube law!

The use of the single member plurality electoral system therefore results in a substantial amplification of the geographical variation in the electoral strength of the Conservative and Labour parties. Both parliamentary parties are dominated by representatives from areas of their electoral strength and, as can be seen, to a far greater extent than was true in 1951, or even in February 1974. Whereas in 1951 less than three-fifths of the

Conservative parliamentary party came from 'Conservative Britain', the same result in 1983 would have seen over three-quarters do so.

The sometime exaggerative quality of the electoral system at the national level supposedly encouraged political parties to aggregate a wide range of interests and thus to operate not far from the consensus of the political centre. In so far as it has any consequences for the policy stances adopted by the political parties now it appears to encourage dissensus. The electoral system ensures that both parliamentary parties are dominated to a far greater extent than they would be under most forms of proportional representation by representatives from one half of Britain.

Conclusion

The claim that the exaggerative quality of the single member plurality electoral system ensured that the electorate could directly choose between alternative governments has been fundamental to the argument in its favour. That exaggerative quality is, however, contingent upon circumstances. In Britain the last thirty years has demonstrated that fact quite clearly. Some parties have been able to secure parliamentary representation on relatively small shares of the overall vote because of the geographical concentration of their support. More importantly, [the system's] tendency to exaggerate the lead of the Conservatives over Labour or vice versa at Westminster elections has all but disappeared. The continued use of the single member plurality system now seems likely to produce hung parliaments even in the absence of an Alliance break-through. The traditional defence of that electoral system has been rendered unconvincing.

8.2 | There was no alternative: the British general election of 1983

W.L. Miller

There may be widespread agreement that the 1983 election was lost by Labour rather than won by the Conservatives, but there will be less agreement on the nature, extent and causes of Labour's defeat. Focusing on an intensive analysis of the BBC/Gallup election-day poll Crewe [1983b] reaches the following conclusions.

1. The result was 43% Conservative, 28% Labour and 26% Alliance.
2. Class depolarization continued in 1983.
[3.] The Falklands Affair had little effect on the outcome.
[4.] The outcome was the result of the electorate's judgement on issues, not personalities.
[5.] The issues were overwhelmingly against Labour.

Such conclusions flow naturally enough from analysis of the BBC/Gallup survey. None the less, I want to suggest that every one of these conclusions is arithmetically correct but politically misleading.

1. Was the result 43% Conservative, 28% Labour and 26% Alliance?

[According to Crewe] 'this was Labour's poorest showing since 1900. Thus, what needs to be explained about 1983 is not why the Conservatives did so well, but why Labour did so badly, and the Alliance not quite well enough.'

But shares of the vote have little political significance and no constitutional significance at all. Two other facets of the result – party identification

From W.L. Miller, 'There was no alternative: the British general election of 1983', *Parliamentary Affairs* (1984), vol. 37, pp. 364–84.

334

THERE WAS NO ALTERNATIVE: THE ELECTION OF 1983   *335*

and seats in Parliament – have much greater significance now and for the future.

When surveys tried to measure party identification, the Labour party came out far ahead of the Alliance. In the BBC/Gallup survey 44% said they 'generally thought of themselves as Conservatives', 38% Labour and only 16% Alliance. In the past, voting behaviour in Britain has closely followed party identification, but not in 1983 [see Table 8.2.1]. Labour won the votes of only just over two-thirds of those who identified with the party: 16% of Labour identifiers voted for the Alliance, 5% for the Conservatives and 10% did not vote at all. Overall, 69% of Labour identifiers loyally voted Labour [but] amongst those whose Labour identification was 'not very strong', only 41% actually voted Labour. That defection by Labour identifiers explains why Labour's vote was so much less than its level of identification. But the basic fact that many non-Labour voters retained a Labour party identification is of more significance than a detailed analysis of the defectors.

Party identifications, like votes, have no constitutional significance. Only seats in Parliament matter for government. And in terms of seats in Parliament the result was 397 Conservative, 209 Labour and a mere 23 for the Alliance. So both in terms of parliamentary seats and in terms of party identification we do not have to explain 'why Labour did so badly, and the Alliance not quite well enough.' By either of these measures the result was not a near miss for the Alliance – it was a total rout.

But surely this is a trivial point? I think not: the fact that neither seats nor identifications reflected votes has several important implications.

First, we cannot explain the re-election of a Conservative government with a landslide majority simply by explaining the party shares of the vote: the spatial distribution of the vote has come to be as important as the party distribution.

Second, while the numbers of seats won by the different parties do not reflect shares of the vote at all well, the numbers of seats won fit much better with party shares of party identification. The Alliance came a poor third in Parliament just as it came a poor third in terms of party identification. [In addition] commitment to the Alliance by its voters was outstandingly weaker than commitment by Labour and Conservative voters to their parties. Just over one third of Labour and Conservative identifiers said they 'very strongly' identified with their party, but only one sixth of Alliance identifiers [see Table 8.2.2]. Contrary to the trends found by Sarlvik and Crewe during the seventies, both Labour and Conservative party identification strengthened in 1983. Since many Alliance voters did not identify with the Alliance at all, the differences between parties on strength of identification are even more striking if we look at voters for the different parties: 32% of Conservative voters strongly identified with the Conservative party, and fully 37% of Labour voters strongly identified

336 RECENT THEMES

Table 8.2.1 Voting by party identifiers

	Percent voting for			
	Con.	Lab.	Alliance	No vote
Amongst:				
Con. identifiers	84	1	7	8
Lab. identifiers	5	69	16	10
Lib. identifiers	13	5	76	6
SDP identifiers	10	1	77	12
Those with no party identity	27	10	23	38

Source: Author's reanalysis of BBC/Gallup election-day poll.

Table 8.2.2 Strength of identification

	Percentage 'very strongly' identifying with		
	Con.	Lab.	Alliance
Amongst the party's own identifiers in			
1964	48	51	32
1966	49	50	35
1970	51	47	26
1974 (Feb.)	32	41	12
1974 (Oct.)	27	36	14
1979	24	29	14
1983	36	33	17
Amongst the party's actual voters in			
1983	32	37	10

Sources: 1983 author's reanalysis of BBC/Gallup election-day poll; 1964–79 B. Sarlvik and I. Crewe, *Decade of Dealignment* (Cambridge University Press, 1983), p. 337.

with the Labour party, but only 10 % of Alliance voters strongly identified with the Alliance (6% with the Liberal party and 4% with the SDP).

Third, it will be difficult for [the Alliance] to consolidate their vote and they will not be the natural beneficiaries of the 'swing of the pendulum' if and when the public turns against the Conservative government. There is an enormous political gap between 26% of the vote with 23 MPs and 28% of the vote with 209 MPs, and that gap has almost nothing to do with shares of the vote.

2. Did class depolarization continue in 1983?

For two decades now, opinion polls have shown a steady decline in class polarization – in the sense that the voting choices of middle-class individuals and working-class individuals have become ever more similar

THERE WAS NO ALTERNATIVE: THE ELECTION OF 1983   *337*

to each other. In 1983 the BBC/Gallup survey shows that [this trend continued]. But if class had not polarized the vote much more strongly than these polls imply, then Labour's 2% voting margin over the Alliance would not have given it ten times as many seats.

If we look at constituency election results over the last two decades, two features of class polarization are immediately apparent: *first*, class polarization between constituencies is vastly greater than that implied by a simplistic interpretation of nationwide opinion poll results; *second*, class polarization between constituencies has not declined over the past two decades. In short, the votes of individuals may no longer be very easily predictable from their social class, but the votes of parliamentary constituencies do remain easily predictable from their social class characteristics.

[Calculations not reproduced here show that] class polarization between constituencies did not decline in 1983, and [that] it ran at four times the level implied by nationwide opinion polls.

Class polarization has increasingly become an attribute of communities rather than individuals; and the depolarization of individuals may even be a cause of the polarization of constituencies. But whatever the reasons for it, the consequences are highly significant for parliamentary election outcomes. The high level of class polarization between constituencies explains (1) why the Labour party won so many more seats than the Alliance with so few more votes, and (2) why the Labour party came third in so many constituencies. As long as [this] degree of class polarization persists, the Alliance can have little real prospect of a substantial number of MPs.

[3.] Did the Falklands Affair have little effect on the outcome?

According to respondents in the BBC/Gallup poll, only 1.4% of them were influenced in their voting choice by the Falklands Affair. That tells us something about the superficial nature of opinions elicited in the poll, but it does not prove the Falklands had little effect on the outcome.

Just before the Falklands crisis, indeed throughout the winter of 1981–82, the Conservatives were running between one and two per cent behind Labour, though both were gaining at the expense of the Alliance. Three months later, in June 1982, the Conservatives were 29% ahead of Labour. For three months of the crisis, large percentages of Gallup respondents quoted foreign affairs as the most important issue facing the country. As soon as Port Stanley was retaken, however, foreign affairs dropped right out of the list of salient issues. The Conservative party lead dropped much more slowly however. Mrs Thatcher's personal rating as Prime Minister also shot up during the crisis and only partially dropped

338 RECENT THEMES

back again afterwards. Roughly, MORI figures suggest that half the Falklands boost in both party support and leadership approval was retained after the crisis had passed.

By the summer of 1983 the Falklands crisis was no longer in the forefront of people's minds but it was evoked by all kinds of codes and symbols. Thatcher was photographed against the world's biggest Union Jack. She seized on the defence issue in order to portray Labour as divided and unpatriotic. And in somewhat more subtle vein she chose 'The Resolute Approach' as her campaign theme.

Winning the Falklands War added a touch of verisimilitude to the tattered image of a nationalistic authoritarian like Thatcher. Image and event matched perfectly. By 1983 the event had been pushed back into the public subconscious, leaving only the refurbished image to directly influence voting behaviour. Even those who judge that the Falklands Affair had a major impact on the 1983 outcome would not expect very many of the BBC/Gallup respondents to quote it as a major determinant of their vote. The link between event and vote was not that direct.

[4.] Was the outcome a result of the electorate's judgement on issues rather than personalities?

If we cross-tabulate BBC/Gallup respondents' voting choices by which party they thought had the 'best policies' and the 'best leader', it seems that policies rather than leaders determine votes: when people prefer the policies of one party but the leader of another, they split (their votes) 83% to 17% in favour of the first. However, that does not mean that the personality of the leadership is irrelevant; the function of the party leadership is to sell their party, not themselves. British party leaders are not American presidential candidates. When *Panorama* or *TV Eye* give them prime time television, it is to make the case for their party. In 1983 only 13% chose Foot as the 'best for Prime Minister', only 17% said Labour had 'the best team of leaders' and only 25% said Labour had 'the best policies', although 28% voted for Labour and 38% said they 'generally identified with Labour'. Judged against that 38% standard, Labour policies were unpopular, Labour leaders were very unpopular and Michael Foot extremely unconvincing as a potential Prime Minister.

The unpopularity of Foot and the 1983 Labour leadership rubbed off on the party. Table 8.2.3 shows the trends in party support during the election campaign. Compared to the last few months before the announcement of an election on 8th May, the first fortnight of the campaign showed a very steady picture with Conservative and Labour doing a little better than earlier in the year, and the Alliance clearly under pressure – its support down to an average of 18%. From the 25th May, however, there was a

THERE WAS NO ALTERNATIVE: THE ELECTION OF 1983   *339*

Table 8.2.3 Short-term trends, 1983

Opinion polls	Percent voting intention of		
	Con.	Lab.	Alliance
Last 17 polls before election announcement on 8th May	45	32	22
First 20 polls of campaign (9th–25th May: no trend apparent within this period)	47	33	18
7 polls to 1st June	45	30	23
7 polls to 3rd June	46	28	24
4 polls to 7th June	46	25½	26½
5 polls on 8th June	46	26	26
Result 9th June	43	28	26

Sources: Calculated by author from reports published in daily and weekly press.

progressive collapse of Labour support and a surge in Alliance support. Labour had been 15% ahead of the Alliance in the first two weeks of the campaign but sank to parity with the Alliance by the fourth week, recovering slightly in the election itself.

The main headlines on 25th May were reserved for quarrels within the Labour leadership. Earlier in the campaign Healey had attempted to define Labour's defence policy in such a way as to turn unilateralism into multilateralism. Foot had tried to clarify Labour's policy by defining it in more unilateralist terms. The *Times'* main headline on 25th May was about an alleged ultimatum by Healey threatening that he would withdraw from the campaign if Foot insisted that Labour's defence policy involved unilateral abandonment of all British nuclear weapons. The press focused on each Labour leader's personal defence policy. Foot clearly had a different policy from his Deputy, Healey, and from his predecessor, Callaghan.

In such circumstances we could hardly expect many voters to rate Foot as the best for Prime Minister, nor could we expect many to describe Labour as having the 'best *team* of leaders'. Nor, indeed, could we expect them to rate Labour has having the 'best policies'. What team? What policies? But equally, it is hardly likely that policy evaluation was entirely self-contained. Poor and divided leadership was bound to produce negative evaluations of policy. Voting choices correlate with policy better than with explicit leadership evaluations mainly because those leadership evaluations were so very negative.

The reason why the 'best team of leaders' question fails to discriminate between [Labour] loyalists and [Labour] defectors is simply that even [the] loyalists were unimpressed by the party's team of leaders. Technically that prevents the 'leadership' question from predicting whether Labour partisans would or would not defect, but it does not support the argument

340   RECENT THEMES

that the Labour leadership had little effect upon defection. A universally recognized failing in a party can never be a good statistical discriminator between those who defect and those who stay loyal. Yet it may well be a powerful cause of defection amongst those whose other ties to the party are weak.

[5.] Were the issues overwhelmingly against Labour?

Even the BBC/Gallup survey itself hardly sustains the argument that the issues were overwhelmingly anti-Labour. Only a few issues were quoted by more than ten per cent of respondents as 'one of the two most important' in influencing their vote. They were the NHS (quoted by 11%), prices (20%), defence (38%) and unemployment (72%). On these issues Labour had a lead of 4% on unemployment and 15% on the NHS but lagged behind the Conservatives by 47% on defence and 21% on prices. If we restrict attention only to those who declared the issue important, these four party preferences on issues rise to 16%, 46%, 54% and 40% respectively.

So Labour was ahead on two of the top four issues, including the most important issue of all: unemployment. But Labour had only a small lead on unemployment and relatively few people put the NHS as a major issue. By contrast, the Conservatives were well ahead on two issues that were quoted by moderately large numbers of respondents.

Some issues that were not quoted by respondents as important may nonetheless have been so, even if respondents were less immediately conscious of them – but once again they were not overwhelmingly anti-Labour: 72% supported stricter laws against trade unions, but only 57% supported the idea of selling off parts of British Steel and British Leyland to private enterprise, while a massive 80% opted for maintaining public services in health, education and welfare rather than cutting taxes.

How could the Labour party do so badly in an election when the main issue was unemployment and the Conservative government had pushed unemployment up to well over three million? When the public were antagonistic towards trade unions but unenthusiastic about privatization and massively in favour of public services rather than tax cuts? That was *not* a bad background for a Labour election campaign. Labour's problems were of its own making.

The issues were not inherently against Labour. Instead, disunity and incompetence in the Labour leadership destroyed Labour's credibility on its own natural issues and allowed its opponents to put their issues on the agenda.

Even though popular attitudes [on defence] at the start of 1983 matched Labour's Manifesto policy, the subject was never likely to be a great

THERE WAS NO ALTERNATIVE: THE ELECTION OF 1983   *341*

vote-winner for Labour, especially at an election held on the anniversary of the Falklands Affair. But the Labour leadership turned it into a vote loser by allowing the Conservatives to redefine the issue as unilateral disarmament instead of a new round in the arms race, and by disagreeing with each other on what Britain's defence policy should be, while agreeing on its vital importance. Labour leaders were guilty of making defence a major issue at all.

The unemployment issue provides the clearest evidence that Labour was defeated by disunity and incompetence as much as by unattractive policies. Labour's desire to bring down unemployment was widely accepted but people doubted its ability to fulfil that desire. Polls consistently showed that (except during the short Falklands crisis) unemployment was quoted as the major issue. But could Labour do anything about it? Early in May 1983 Gallup reported a 34% majority for the proposition that a Conservative victory would increase unemployment. Late in May they reported a 4% majority saying Labour had the best policies on unemployment. These Labour majorities on such a natural Labour issue were low enough, but at the end of May Harris reported a Conservative majority of 7% on the question of which party respondents 'trusted most to take the right decisions on unemployment'. Earlier in the parliament Labour had failed to get as much advantage out of the unemployment issue as it might have hoped, because people were not entirely convinced that it could do better; but by the time of the election Labour had lost its advantage even on the unemployment issue.

In the end, specific issues may not have been very important to the outcome. Overall, about a third of Labour identifiers either stayed at home or went out to vote against Labour. However, the rate of defection was very little affected by which issues were uppermost in their minds. Labour's chaotic mishandling of one issue [defence] probably damaged its credibility even amongst those who were primarily interested in other issues.

General images seemed more influential than specific issues. The BBC/Gallup election-day poll asked quite explicitly whether Labour's alleged extremism and disunity had influenced respondents' votes. Almost half the Labour identifiers who voted Conservative or Alliance quoted one or other of these factors as influencing their vote: 14% mentioned disunity, 20% extremism and 10% mentioned both.

Labour's disunity was consciously recognized and quoted as a reason for switching away from Labour. But it also operated on the unconscious: much of Labour's reputation for extremism in 1983 derived from its disunity, from its consequent inability to put its case on policy, and from the charges of extremism that various Labour (and ex-Labour) factions hurled at each other. Labour was so divided at the top, its most prominent

342 RECENT THEMES

leaders so clearly disagreed with each other on matters that they judged critically important, that they were unable to convince the electorate about anything, even the government's responsibility for unemployment.

Prospect

Everything considered, 1983 was kind to Labour. Identification with the party held up well – slipping a little behind the Conservatives but remaining far ahead of the Alliance. And the electoral system coupled with continued class polarization (of areas) protected Labour from the consequences of its own folly.

I have suggested that dissension at the top rather than spontaneous desertion at the bottom was the cause of Labour's very poor performance in 1983. That does not mean that policies are irrelevant. If Labour leaders cannot agree policies amongst themselves on what they define as the central issues in politics then they will not succeed in convincing the electorate either that Labour has the policies or that it has the men to form a government. The personal bitterness and unrestrained hostility between Labour leaders that has been so evident in recent internal disputes has been more damaging than any policy proposals. Labour was not ready for government in 1983 and the electorate knew it.

8.3 | The 1987 general election

Ivor Crewe

The voting patterns

In renewing Mrs Thatcher's landslide majority [in 1987] the British electorate gave the impression of massive continuity. The small net changes in the parties' parliamentary strength reflected modest shifts in their share of the Great Britain vote. The Conservatives went 17 seats down but held on to all but 0.3 per cent of their 1983 vote; Labour added a mere 20 seats and 3.2 per cent of the vote to its post-war nadir of 1983; and the Alliance [vote] slipped by 2.9 per cent [and its seats] from 23 to 22. Thus there are three obvious questions. Why did the Conservative vote hold rock steady? Why did Labour fail to recover more than a third of its 1983 losses? Why did the Alliance decline but not quite collapse?

The answers probably do not lie in the campaign itself. The polls of polls recorded next to no movement in party support after the manifestos were launched. In the BBC TV/Gallup election survey fully 81 per cent of respondents claimed to have decided their vote before the campaign began, a higher proportion than for any election since 1966.

Beneath the surface stillness of the parties' national vote, however, flowed complex currents and counter-eddies (see Table 8.3.1). The 1983 Conservative vote was marginally more solid than the Labour or Alliance vote but was far from a granite block. Almost a quarter defected, half to the Alliance and the rest in almost equal numbers to Labour and abstention. But the Conservatives recouped most of these losses by enticing almost (but not quite) as many defectors from Labour and the Alliance.

From I. Crewe, 'A new class of politics' and 'Tories prosper from a paradox', *The Guardian*, 15/16 June 1987.

344   RECENT THEMES

Table 8.3.1 The flow of the vote from 1983 to 1987

	Vote in 1983				
	Con. %	Lab. %	L/SDP %	Did not vote %	Too young %
Vote in 1987					
Con.	77	4	10	21	28
Lab.	5	75	12	19	24
L/SDP	12	11	70	14	14
Other	–	1	1	1	1
Did not vote	6	8	8	45	32
Total	100%	99%	101%	100%	99%

Note: Columns do not always add up to 100% exactly because of rounding.

Similarly, the Alliance's retreat in the face of Labour's advance was not the simple product of a direct transfer from Alliance to Labour. On the contrary, the traffic between the parties went both ways.

Labour's mini-recovery flowed from a number of streams in combination. First, it grabbed an extra 1 per cent of the vote by losing fewer deserters to the Conservatives than the Conservatives lost to them. Secondly, it gained a further 1 per cent from differential voting by previous abstainers. The proportion of previous non-voters voting Labour jumped from 12 per cent in 1983 to 19 per cent in 1987, a reflection perhaps of its success in mobilising its traditional, but unreliable, working class support. Thirdly, among those who had died since the previous election the Conservatives' majority over Labour in 1983 was at least 15 per cent whereas among first-time voters in 1987 it was only 4 per cent. The sheer physical replacement of the electorate gave Labour its third extra percentage point.

Let us place some sociological flesh on these bones of electoral change by asking: who switched? Differences between men and women were minuscule (see Table 8.3.2). For the third election running the traditionally higher Conservative vote among women than men failed to materialise: the old gender gap has evidently disappeared.

Young voters once again defied stereotypes and post-war psephological conventions. Labour's self-consciously 'pop' youth campaign did produce a 5 per cent increase in its vote but still yielded a mere 0.5 per cent swing because the Conservative vote rose by almost as much. The real loser among 18–22 year olds was the Alliance, whose vote fell from 30 per cent to 21 per cent (see Table 8.3.2).

However, class rather than age or sex remains the primary shaper of the vote and the stark North–South variation in the swing immediately

THE 1987 GENERAL ELECTION

Table 8.3.2 Vote by sex, age and class

	Vote in 1987			Change 1983–87			Change 1979–87		
	Con. %	Lab. %	All. %	Con.	Lab.	All.	Con.	Lab.	All.
Men	44	33	22	−2	+4	−2	−3	−6	+9
Women	44	31	25	+1	+2	−3	−3	−8	+10
First-time voters	45	34	21	+4	+5	−9	+2	−7	+4
Professional/managerial	59	14	27	−3	+2	–	−8	−4	+12
Office/clerical	52	22	26	−3	+1	+2	−6	+1	+6
Skilled manual	43	34	24	+4	−1	−3	−2	−11	+14
Semi-/unskilled manual	31	50	19	+2	+6	−8	−1	−5	+5
Unemployed	32	51	17	+2	+6	−9	−8	+2	+6

Note: All. = Alliance. In this and later tables, the Conservative, Labour and Alliance vote is their share of the three-party vote.

suggests a sharpening of the class polarisation in the vote. But Table 8.3.2 refutes any such simple notion, at least on a conventional definition of social class. In both the 'core' middle class of the professions, administration and management and the 'lower' middle class of office and clerical workers the Conservative vote fell by three per cent. Its share of the total non-manual vote shrank for the third consecutive election, falling to little more than half (55 per cent) – its lowest level since the two 1974 elections. The unique appeal of Thatcherism is clearly not to the middle classes.

The erosion of the Conservative middle class, however, is confined to particular segments, in particular the intelligentsia and the public sector salariat (see Table 8.3.3). The Conservative vote fell by nine per cent among the university-educated, to the special benefit of the Alliance, which has become the leading party in the 'thinking electorate'.

A similar socio-political division within the middle classes is portrayed by the contrast between the private and public sector. In the private sector the Conservative vote remained high and stayed solid; among the public sector salariat it was much lower. Mrs Thatcher's personal preference for businessmen over bureaucrats and profit-makers over professors is, it appears, fully reciprocated.

Nonetheless, the Conservative party's vote only held steady because they made further inroads into the working class. At 36 per cent its share of the manual workers' vote was the largest for any post-war election. Its success among the newly affluent working class of the South was crucial. Among working-class home-owners it led Labour by 44 per cent to 31 per cent. In the South manual workers alone gave the Conservatives a larger lead (by 46 per cent to 28 per cent) than the electorate as a whole.

It is in the contrasting shifts of a divided working class that Conservative

346 RECENT THEMES

Table 8.3.3 The new divisions in the middle classes

	University educated		Public sector		Private sector	
	1987 %	1983–87	1987 %	1983–87	1987 %	1983–87
Con.	34	−9	44	−4	65	+1
Lab.	29	+3	24	–	13	–
Lib./SDP	36	+4	32	+4	22	−1

success and Labour failure is most apparent. Labour's 1987 campaign was geared to recovering those working class supporters whose large-scale desertion had produced the debacle of 1983. It concentrated unswervingly on what has always appealed most to its traditional class base: full employment, the welfare state and the authentic working class roots of its leaders.

The strategy only half worked. Labour partly remobilised the 'rank and file' working class of semi- and unskilled manual workers, among whom its vote rose by a full six percentage points, twice the national average. But it failed spectacularly in the other half of the working class, the 'NCOs' of foremen, supervisors, craft and high-tech workers who make up the market researchers' 'C2' category of 'skilled manual workers'. Here there was a further swing to the Conservatives of 2.5 per cent since 1983 (see Table 8.3.2).

Comparisons with the 1970s starkly underline Labour's diminishing appeal to skilled workers. In October 1974, the last election it won (just), Labour took half the skilled worker vote (49 per cent), and the Conservatives less than a third (31 per cent). In 1979 – an election it lost – it took 45 per cent of their vote, level pegging with the Conservatives. In June 1987, it secured barely over a third (34 per cent) of their vote, trailing the Conservatives by 9 per cent. There could be no starker electoral testament to Thatcherism.

The Alliance's decline was not a direct mirror image of Labour's advance. True, its vote fell most (by 8 per cent) where Labour did best, among semi- and unskilled workers. This was paralleled by the regional pattern to the swing from Alliance to Labour which was largest in Wales (6.7 per cent) and Scotland (5.8 per cent) and lowest in the South West (1 per cent) and South East (1.4 per cent). Many of these lost working class voters had probably been gained only in the course of the 1983 election, once Labour's campaign had fallen into disarray. But the Alliance held its 1983 vote among non-manual workers (slightly increasing it among office and clerical workers) and there was next to no swing from the Alliance to Labour among skilled workers. Thus almost all of Labour's inroad into the Alliance occurred within Labour's social – and political – heartland.

THE 1987 GENERAL ELECTION

My post-mortem survey of the 1983 election concluded that Labour's claim to be the party of the working class was sociologically threadbare. The Labour vote remained largely working class; but the working class was no longer largely Labour. The party had come to represent a declining segment of the working class – the traditional working class of the council estates, the public sector, industrial Scotland and the North, and the old industrial unions – while failing to attract the affluent and expanding working class of the new estates and the new service economy of the South. It was a party neither of one class nor one nation; it was a regional class party.

The 1987 survey reinforces each of these conclusions. Labour remains the largest party among manual workers (42 per cent), but a minority party, only 6 per cent ahead of the Conservatives. The political gulf between the traditional and new working class remains (see Table 8.3.4). The Conservatives are the first party of manual workers in the South, among owner-occupiers and non-unionists and only 1 per cent behind in the private sector; Labour retains massive leads among the working class of Scotland (+43 per cent), the North (+16 per cent), council tenants, trade unionists and the public sector. Although the housing gap has slightly narrowed, regional differences have widened further.

In one important sense the picture is even gloomier for Labour this time. Government policies are producing a steady expansion of the new working class, and diminution of the old. Council house sales, privatisation, the decline of manufacturing industry (on which the old unions are based) and the steady population drift to the South have restructured the working class. The new working class is not only the dominant segment, but increasingly dominant. Demography and time are not on Labour's side. Its need to break out of its old class fortresses is more urgent than ever but on present evidence no nearer in sight.

The paradox of Labour's failure

Every party has a 'natural' level of support. Election campaigns can add or subtract a few percentage points, depending on the particular issues, personalities and events of the time. Labour's natural base appears to lie between 35 and 38 per cent; its proportion of 'identifiers' in the electorate (36 per cent in 1983, 35 per cent in 1987), its 1984 Euro-election vote, its local election vote from 1983 to 1986 and its opinion poll average since Neil Kinnock became leader have all fallen within this narrow range.

In 1983 Labour badly under-polled its natural support, but an amateurish campaign, public disarray at the top over defence, the shadow of Militant and, above all, an implausible pretender to Downing Street provided numerous alibis. At the 1987 election Labour again under-polled

Table 8.3.4 The division in the working class

	The new working class				The traditional working class			
	Lives in South	Owner-occupier	Non-union	Works in private sector	Lives in Scotland/ North	Council tenant	Union member	Works in public sector
Con.	46	44	40	38	29	25	30	32
Lab.	28	32	38	39	57	57	48	49
Lib./SDP	26	24	22	23	15	18	22	19
Con./Lab. maj. 1987	Con. +18	Con. +12	Con. +2	Lab. +1	Lab. +28	Lab. +32	Lab. +18	Lab. +17
Con./Lab. maj. 1983	Con. +16	Con. +22	Con. +6	Lab. +1	Lab. +10	Lab. +38	Lab. +21	Lab. +17
Category as % of all manual workers (change from 1983 in brackets)	40 (+4)	57 (+3)	66 (+7)	68 (+2)	37 (−1)	31 (−4)	34 (−7)	32 (−2)

THE 1987 GENERAL ELECTION

by a wide margin. It retrieved only a third of the vote it lost between 1979 and 1983, ending up with its lowest share of the vote, 1983 excepted, since its calamity of 1931.

This time, however, its campaign offers few excuses. By common consent it fought a professional, disciplined election under a personable and effective leader, pushing the Government on to the defensive and forcing its own best issues to the top of the agenda. What went wrong?

Perhaps the received wisdom about the excellence of Labour's campaign should be re-examined. It did indeed lead the others in the BBC TV/Gallup survey as 'coming over most effectively on television'. [But] setting aside the crushing counter-evidence of the actual result, a closer look at the data raises doubts. For example, those who switched to Labour or only plumped for Labour during the campaign mentioned a Labour party election broadcast (PEB) less often than their Alliance counterparts mentioned an Alliance broadcast (see Table 8.3.5).

Reinforcing evidence comes from the chronology of the campaign polls which show that Labour reached its 33 per cent plateau before the broadcast of its first and perhaps over-celebrated PEB devoted to Mr Kinnock.

Kinnock's electoral advantage to Labour has also been over-estimated. It largely consisted of not being Michael Foot. Thirty-one per cent chose him as a potential prime minister, well above Foot's tiny 13 per cent in 1983 but still behind the 41 per cent for Thatcher (see Table 8.3.6). Among Labour voters he was far more acceptable (79 per cent) than Foot had been (44 per cent), but less popular than Thatcher was among Conservatives (86 per cent). His standing did improve in the first week of the campaign – the real benefit of the opening PEB – but only from the extraordinarily low base of 25 per cent to which it had ebbed after his trip to Washington, and it failed to rise any further.

Table 8.3.5 The impact of parties' election broadcasts (PEBS)

% saying vote influenced by	Switches to			Decided during campaign to vote for		
	Con. %	Lab. %	All. %	Con. %	Lab. %	All. %
Conservative PEB	16	2	5	21	4	6
Labour PEB	8	23	6	9	26	9
Alliance PEB	4	1	26	8	4	30

350 RECENT THEMES

Table 8.3.6 The best (and worst) person for Prime Minister

		Thatcher	(Foot) Kinnock	Steel	(Jenkins) Owen	
Who would make the best PM	1983	46	13	35		100%
	1987	42	31	10	17	100%
And the worst PM	1983	25	63	2	10	100%
	1987	34	44	12	10	100%
Best minus worst	1983	+21	−50	+33	−4	
	1987	+8	−13	−2	+7	

Moreover, he led the field as the *worst* choice for prime minister. His combined 'best and worst' score of minus 13, while puny in comparison with Foot's minus 50 in 1983, suggests that on balance he was more of an electoral liability than an asset, especially when compared with Thatcher and Owen.

It would be a mistake, too, to assume that Labour's campaign successfully expunged its 'extremist' image. References to Labour 'extremism' rose sharply from 19 per cent to 27 per cent among the general public and from 25 per cent to 42 per cent among Labour defectors. The party's campaign organisers managed to keep its so called 'hard' and 'loony' left out of sight but not, apparently, out of mind.

Labour's poor performance remains a puzzle, because its campaign did succeed in placing its favourable issues much further up the agenda than in 1983 (see Table 8.3.7). The single most important issue remained unemployment (mentioned by 49 per cent), although far less overwhelmingly than in 1983 (72 per cent), followed by defence, the National Health Service, education and pensions. No other issue reached double digits (respondents could choose two).

Had electors voted solely on the main issues Labour would have won. It was considered the more capable party on three of the four leading issues – jobs, health and education – *among those for whom the issue was important*. Its lead over the Conservatives as the party for jobs doubled from 16 per cent in 1983 to 34 per cent in 1987; only part of this electoral advantage was eroded by the declining saliency of the issue. Its precedence over the Conservatives on the NHS edged forward from 46 to 49 per cent among a group of concerned voters that had trebled in size since 1983. On all three social issues there was widespread agreement, even among Conservatives, that matters had deteriorated (see Table 8.3.8).

By wide margins the public believed [that] over the 'last few years' unemployment, NHS waiting lists and the quality of education [had 'got worse']. So Labour was manifestly vulnerable only on defence: it lagged

Table 8.3.7 The issues that mattered

	All %	Change 1983–87	Con. recruits %	Con. defectors %	Lab. recruits %	Lab. defectors %	Lib./SDP recruits %	Lib./SDP defectors %	Party preference on issue (among those citing it as important)	
Per cent mentioning an issue as one of the two most important influencing their vote*									1987	1983
Unemployment	49	−23	29	50	59	51	50	44	Lab. + 34	Lab. + 16
NHS/hospitals	33	+22	18	33	45	44	43	36	Lab. + 49	Lab. + 46
Education	19	+13	14	26	23	22	26	25	Lab. + 15	N/A
Defence	35	−3	59	32	25	38	33	41	Con. + 63	Con. + 54
Pensions	10	+2	5	12	10	10	12	7	N/A	N/A

*This was an open-ended question. The issues above were those most frequently mentioned. N/A = not available.

352 RECENT THEMES

Table 8.3.8 Perceptions of recent change

	Got better	Stayed the same	Got worse	% better − % worse
Unemployment	10	10	80	−70
NHS waiting lists	4	28	68	−64
Quality of education	10	22	68	−58
Opportunities to get ahead	46	27	27	+19
The general economic situation	45	25	30	+15
Your household's financial situation	30	41	28	+2

behind the Conservatives by a huge 64 per cent (even wider than the 54 per cent gap in 1983) among the 35 per cent of the public for whom the defence issue mattered.

This interplay of issue concern and party preference was broadly reflected by the pattern of vote switching (see Table 8.3.7). Defence swung voters away from Labour (twice as many Labour defectors as Labour loyalists cited it) and, to a lesser extent, from the Alliance to the Conservatives. Jobs produced a swing in the opposite direction. Health, education and pensions clearly cost the Conservatives votes, although the Alliance appears to have benefited as much as Labour did.

The final balance sheet favoured Labour. Admittedly, its disadvantage on defence outweighed its advantage on any one of the three social issues. But an election confined to these four issues, where voters faithfully supported the party they preferred on the issues they claimed mattered, would have put Labour 2 per cent ahead of the Conservatives.

The puzzle of the Opposition's failure is only dissolved if, looking again at Table 8.3.8, we give due prominence to three other verdicts on the recent past, all of them more favourable [to the Conservatives]. By clear if modest margins the public agrees that the economy has improved, its living standards have risen, and 'opportunities to get ahead' have expanded.

In this conjunction of public poverty and private prosperity lies the key to the policy *paradox* of the Opposition's failure. When answering a survey on the important issues respondents think of public problems; when entering the polling booth they think of family fortunes. 'Prosperity' is not an issue or a problem but a blessing, and by a decisive 55 per cent to 27 per cent majority the public regarded the Conservatives as more likely to bestow it. Here, quite simply and obviously, lies the key to Conservative victory.

There are two pieces of supporting evidence. First, since autumn 1986 more people believe that both the economy in general and family living standards in particular are improving. On the economy the balance of perceptions moved from a minus 32 per cent deficit in September 1986 to a

THE 1987 GENERAL ELECTION

Table 8.3.9 Prosperity and the vote

	Believe that the economy has		Believe that family finances have	
	Improved %	Worsened %	Improved %	Worsened %
Switched from Con. 1983–87	11	67	12	41
Switched from Lab. 1983–87	36	10	38	14
Switched from All. to Con. 1983–87	23	3	34	1
Switched from All. to Lab. 1983–87	3	29	5	23
Abstained 1983 but in '87 voted:				
Con.	64	5	56	13
Lab.	16	69	18	65

surplus of +15 per cent by election day. On family finances perceptions moved from a minus 12 per cent deficit in September 1986 to a 2 per cent surplus on June 11 1987. Both perceptions were decisively more favourable than at the previous election. More voters than before believed more voters than before had more money than before.

The second piece of evidence is the close coincidence between economic perceptions and the Conservative/Labour vote. Only 3 per cent of Conservatives believed the economy had deteriorated; only 15 per cent of Labour voters believed it had improved. Perceptions like these were directly linked to movements of the vote (see Table 8.3.9). For example, one in six of those who voted Conservative in 1983 said their living standards had declined; of those fully 41 per cent defected. Among the two in five whose family fortunes had improved only 12 per cent switched. Similarly, Labour lost almost three times as many supporters among the one in five whose living standards had improved as among the two in five whose living standards had got worse.

It is tempting to attribute the Alliance's dismal performance to a mishandled campaign. After all, it began the campaign with the 27 per cent support it secured at the local elections; it was granted equal media coverage for the first time; and it had not lost support during previous campaigns, at least since regular opinion polls began.

Table 8.3.10 suggests that the current scapegoat, the double leadership [of Steel and Owen], was not the main culprit. Among the 23 per cent of respondents who claimed to have voted or seriously considered voting Alliance but eventually decided against, the overwhelming reason given was some variation of the classic 'wasted vote' argument. Altogether 68 per cent said that the Alliance could not win or that voting Alliance would let in

354 RECENT THEMES

Table 8.3.10 Why the Alliance didn't do better

Reason for not voting Alliance	Lib./SDP defectors	Respondents who seriously considered voting Alliance but eventually did not (23% of voters)
Obvious that they could not win	43	37
Would have let Labour in	8	15
Would have let Conservatives in	23	16
Would have led to coalition	1	5
Lack of clear policies	17	17
Two leaders	16	22
No experience of government	19	16
Saw no reason to change from usual party	10	19

Note: Multiple responses per respondent.

one of the major parties – an even larger proportion than in 1983 (58 per cent). Much smaller proportions referred to the double leadership, unclear policies or inexperience. Among actual defectors from the Alliance fear of letting the Conservatives in was twice as potent a factor as fear of letting Labour in (the ratio was the reverse in 1983), as the collapse of the Alliance vote to Labour in many two-party marginals revealed. Once again, the Alliance was doubly penalised by the electoral system: unable to convert votes into seats, it is unable to convert support into votes.

None of the Opposition parties, therefore, should lay too much blame (or future hope) on the campaign. They were beaten by that old maxim for winning elections 'prosperity at home and peace abroad'. They were also beaten by a changing social structure and an unbending electoral system. Therein lies both immediate solace but long-term despond.

8.4 The extension of popular capitalism

Anthony Heath
with Geoff Garrett

The Thatcher government has not sought simply to change the direction of government policy but to mould the social structure and attitudes of the British population. It has wished to promote a more entrepreneurial spirit and to encourage people to secure their welfare by their own efforts rather than rely upon the state. And one of the most widely espoused policies that it has pursued with that intention in mind has been the disposal of state assets to private individuals. In particular it has vigorously pursued the sale of council houses to their tenants and sold off major nationalised industries to private shareholders.

The sale of council houses was promoted from the beginning of the first Thatcher term. Over one million council houses, approximately 5% of the total housing stock, were sold to their tenants in the period 1980–1987. The terms of the sales were highly advantageous to buyers.

Participation in the government's privatisation of publicly-owned corporations has been even more extensive. It has been estimated that the programme of sales almost doubled share ownership to around a quarter of the population. There were only a few small privatisations in the first Thatcher administration, but the programme expanded rapidly after the government's re-election in 1983 with the sales of British Aerospace, British Airways, British Gas, British Telecom, Britoil, Jaguar, Rolls-Royce and the TSB. As was the case for purchasers of council houses, the benefits of purchasing shares in privatised companies were very large. In both cases, then, there were important windfall profits to the purchasers,

From A. Heath, R. Jowell, J. Curtice, Geoff Evans, Julia Field and Sharon Witherspoon, *Understanding Political Change* (1991) Oxford: Pergamon, chapter 8; and A. Heath, R. Jowell, J. Curtice and G. Evans, 'The extension of popular capitalism', *Strathclyde Papers on Government and Politics*, no. 60 (1989).

356   RECENT THEMES

which might be expected to lead to short-term electoral benefits to the Conservative party. On the usual theories of retrospective voting, we might expect the voters affected to reward the Conservative government which had provided these windfalls and to punish the Labour party which had opposed them, and which might conceivably take away these benefits in future.

More substantial electoral claims have also been made for the Conservative government's policy. Home and share ownership have often been shown to be close correlates of voting behaviour. Because of this association, it has widely been argued that the sale of council houses and shares has been of long-term electoral benefit to the Conservatives. Both sorts of purchasers have a new-found stake in property and in the price of that property, and hence have a longer-term interest in political arrangements that protect and enhance these investments. The government, it is therefore claimed, has succeeded in expanding its social base and in undermining Labour's.

At the [1987] election home owners and shareholders were more likely to vote Conservative than were tenants and people without shares. [But] it does not necessarily follow from this that, when individuals become owner-occupiers or shareholders, they then also change their voting behaviour. We therefore need to see if their behaviour has changed since making the purchase.

In order to investigate these questions about change, we conducted a small panel study, separate from the main 1987 cross-section survey. That is to say, we reinterviewed respondents to the 1983 survey and we can thus relate changes in their voting behaviour to changes in their social and demographic characteristics.

Share purchase

Table 8.4.1 explores the relation between changes in share ownership and changes in voting between 1983 and 1987. Since the bulk of the privatisations took place between these two elections this is a reasonable period to focus on. We asked our respondents in the 1987 wave of the panel 'Do you (or your partner) own, or have you ever bought shares in any of these recently privatised companies?' and we gave them a checklist of the major share issues since 1983. We also asked them whether they owned any other shares quoted on the stock exchange, including unit trusts.

On the basis of this information we have divided our respondents into four categories; first [there] are respondents who reported that they neither purchased any of the privatised share issues nor owned any other shares. These respondents make up 61% of the panel respondents but, because of selective attrition, this is certainly an underestimate of their

THE EXTENSION OF POPULAR CAPITALISM

Table 8.4.1 Share purchase and vote

	Non-purchasers		'New' recruits		Enthusiasts		Other share owners	
	1983 %	1987 %	1983 %	1987 %	1983 %	1987 %	1983 %	1987 %
Conservative	45	42	55	53	64	70	56	62
Labour	26	31	14	16	14	10	16	14
Other	29	27	31	32	22	20	29	24
(*N*)	(438)	(471)	(127)	(135)	(95)	(102)	(69)	(70)

Source: 1983–87 panel study.

numbers in the electorate as a whole. (Our cross-sectional data give an estimate of 71% of households without shares.)

Second, we have respondents who purchased the privatised issues but owned no other shares. They make up 17% of the panel respondents. They can be thought of as the new recruits to Mrs Thatcher's popular capitalism. Third, we have respondents who both purchased the privatised issues and owned other shares. They make up 13% of the sample and can be thought of as the enthusiasts for popular capitalism. And fourthly we have respondents who owned other shares but failed to take advantage of the windfall gains of the privatisations.

As we had expected, there are quite marked differences between the four sets of respondents in their voting behaviour. The non-purchasers have the lowest propensity to vote Conservative while the enthusiasts have the highest propensity. The new recruits fall about midway between (at least as far as Conservative voting is concerned).

However, the striking feature of the table is how little change in the voting patterns of these four groups took place between 1983 and 1987. We might have expected that the new recruits would have moved away from the non-purchasers and would have become more similar to the other members of the property-owning democracy in their pattern of voting. As we can see however, there was little change in their relative propensities to vote Conservative, Labour or Alliance. The new recruits were already more inclined to the Conservatives in 1983, and they remained that way. The 10 point differential barely changed. And the new recruits, just like the non-purchasers (and of course the electorate overall), showed a modest net increase in Labour voting between 1983 and 1987.

There are however signs of change [among enthusiasts and other share owners]. In both these [cases] we see an increase in Conservative voting and a decline in Labour voting. Insofar as there is any pattern of change, then, it is that the new recruits are akin to the non-purchasers while the

358   RECENT THEMES

enthusiasts are akin to the other share owners. In other words, Table 8.4.1 divides up, as far as change is concerned, not into purchasers versus non-purchasers of the privatised shares but into owners versus non-owners of other shares.

So while the privatisations have certainly extended popular capitalism perhaps to a quarter of the electorate, it is not clear that this has had any direct effect on the purchasers' voting behaviour. The purchasers were already more inclined to vote Conservative before they bought the privatised share issues, and the new recruits show no sign of rewarding the Conservatives for their windfall gains.

Nor is there any sign that their increased stake in capitalism has made the new recruits any more supportive of the existing order. In both waves of the panel we asked our respondents 'whether you agree or disagree that income and wealth should be redistributed towards ordinary working people'. Table 8.4.2 shows how their attitudes changed between 1983 and 1987.

The pattern of change is not unlike that of Table 8.4.1, and clearly refutes the hypothesis that the new recruits would become more attached to the existing economic order. To the contrary they show a clear swing to the left (as do the non-purchasers). Once again, moreover, the enthusiasts and the other share owners show a common pattern, their attitudes towards redistribution remaining more or less unchanged.

Our analysis fails, then, to show that privatisation per se had any electoral impact on the purchasers. In particular, the new recruits have neither rewarded the Conservatives for their windfall gains nor become more attached to the economic order. Claims about the effects of popular capitalism simply failed to recognise that the share purchasers were not a random selection of the electorate in the first place.

The distinctive character of share purchasers becomes very clear from Table 8.4.3. Share purchasers and share owners were generally more advantaged than the non-purchasers. They were less likely to be working

Table 8.4.2 Share purchase and attitudes

	% opposing redistribution	
	1983	1987
Non-purchasers	39 (531)	34 (533)
New recruits	46 (147)	38 (146)
Enthusiasts	61 (109)	60 (111)
Other share owners	52 (77)	50 (76)

Note: Figures in brackets give the base frequency.

Source: 1983–87 panel study.

THE EXTENSION OF POPULAR CAPITALISM 359

Table 8.4.3 The characteristics of share purchasers

	Non-purchasers	New recruits	Enthusiasts	Other share owners
% working class	44	23	12	23
% in paid employment	53	62	59	66
% income over £8,000	50	61	78	78
% home owners	63	88	93	85
% living in South and Midlands	55	64	67	65

Source: 1987 cross-section survey.

class and more likely to be in paid employment and to have above-average incomes. These are of course characteristics which tend to go with Conservative voting anyhow.

It is not unreasonable to conclude, therefore, that the extension of popular capitalism largely extended share ownership to a group that was already relatively privileged and relatively inclined to the Conservatives. It was a case of the windfall gains going to people who were already well-off, or to put the matter somewhat differently, of the Conservative party rewarding their own supporters.

Council house purchase

Houses are rather larger assets than most of the share holdings we have been discussing. So they might well have more electoral impact on the purchasers. The buyers of council houses are also a rather different group from the new shareholders, being more likely to have social characteristics typical of Labour rather than of Conservative voters. Here then there is more potential for the Conservatives to reach beyond their own supporters and to inflict electoral damage on Labour.

The council house purchasers are also a much smaller group than the shareholders. Unfortunately this means that there are too few such respondents in our panel study to undertake a sensible analysis. We have instead to turn to our cross-section data, using respondents' recall of how they voted at previous elections.

Table 8.4.4 shows how home owners, council house purchasers, and council house tenants reported voting in 1979, 1983 and 1987. Only those respondents who were eligible to vote in all three elections are included in the table. We look at this longer time period because many of the council house purchases took place between 1979 and 1983, and thus some of the electoral consequences could already have occurred by 1983.

360 RECENT THEMES

Table 8.4.4 Council house purchase and vote

	Local Authority tenants			Council house purchasers			Other home owners		
	1979 %	1983 %	1987 %	1979 %	1983 %	1987 %	1979 %	1983 %	1987 %
Conservative	21	22	21	36	42	35	59	58	54
Labour	70	64	61	52	42	35	29	24	21
Other	10	15	18	11	16	30	13	18	25
(N)	(531)	(531)	(483)	(149)	(149)	(139)	(1,587)	(1,587)	(1,472)

Source: 1983 cross-section survey, respondents who were eligible to vote in all three elections.

The [left] panel of Table 8.4.4 covers the 21% of respondents who were council tenants in 1987. The middle panel covers the 6% of respondents who bought their council houses between 1979 and 1987. And the [right] panel covers owner-occupiers other than those who had bought council houses. They make up 64% of respondents. There is also a residual category, making up 8% of respondents, who were in tenures such as private renting, housing co-operatives, tied cottages and the like.

As we had expected, there are quite marked differences in the voting behaviour of the three categories. In particular, we see that the purchasers were about midway between the council tenants and the home owners in 1987 in their support for the Conservative and Labour parties. More importantly, however, we can see that the purchasers were already more prone to vote Conservative in 1979 than were the other council tenants and the gap does not widen between 1979 and 1987. Reported Conservative voting was 15 points higher among the future purchasers in 1979; it was 20 points higher in 1983, when some of this group had completed their purchases; but it was only 14 points higher in 1987 when the whole of the group had purchased their council houses. There is little indication, therefore, that the sale of council houses produced *new* recruits for the Conservatives.

However, inspection of Table 8.4.4 does suggest that perhaps council house sales did hurt Labour. Among the continuing tenants reported Labour voting fell by 9 points; among the other home owners it fell by 8 points; but among the purchasers it fell by 17 points. The Labour vote does therefore seem to have declined rather faster among the purchasers than it did among the other two groups. More rigorous [logit] analysis confirms the conclusion that the purchasers were more likely than the continuing tenants to defect from Labour.

There is also some evidence of change in the purchasers' attitudes towards the economic order. In Table 8.4.5 we look at the attitudes

THE EXTENSION OF POPULAR CAPITALISM

361

towards redistribution of those who said, in 1983, that they were likely to purchase their council houses and of those who said, in 1987, that they actually had done so.

As we can see, the continuing tenants and the other home owners both show the shift to the left that we saw earlier in Table 8.4.2. The purchasers, on the other hand, have moved if anything to the right. Compared with the other two groups, then, the purchasers do stand out. They seem to have resisted the more general move to the left, and the hypothesis that council house purchase has influenced political attitudes cannot be rejected.

Clearly, we must be cautious about these conclusions since we do not have adequate panel data to test them. However, the various pieces of evidence on the attitudes and voting behaviour of the purchasers are quite consistent and make good sociological sense. [Evidence from the 1987 BES survey shows that] direct switching from the Labour party to the Conservatives is relatively rare. If the general effect of council house purchase is to shift people's attitudes somewhat towards the right, then the natural consequence would be for their political preferences to move somewhat towards the right as well. In other words, a modest shift in attitudes, of the kind we saw in Table 8.4.5, is likely to lead to a modest shift across the political spectrum from Labour towards the centre parties rather than all the way to the Conservatives.

The impact of this on Labour's fortunes will not have been very great, however. 6% of these respondents were purchasers, and among the purchasers the Labour vote appears to have fallen by perhaps 8% more than it fell among the tenants. 8% of 6% comes out as 0.5% of the electorate as a whole. In contrast, the total Labour share of the vote in the electorate fell from 37% in 1979 to 31% in 1987.

The major social process, therefore, is not conversion from one party to another but selective mobility. As with share purchase, the council house purchasers were not a random selection of local authority tenants. They

Table 8.4.5 Council house purchase and attitudes

	% opposing redistribution	
	1983	1987
LA tenants	19 (888)	12 (799)
Likely/actual purchasers	21 (123)	23 (101)
Other home owners	44 (2,564)	33 (2,579)

Note: Figures in brackets give the base frequency.

Sources: Column 1 – 1983 cross-section survey. Column 2 – 1987 cross-section survey, respondents who were eligible to vote in 1983.

differed beforehand in ways that made them more inclined to the Conservatives than those who stayed behind. Council house purchase, for example, is not likely to have the same feasibility for older, retired tenants as it does for those with secure, well-paid employment. Nor are some council flats as desirable properties to buy as some of the semi-detached houses. It is hardly surprising, therefore, to find that purchasers were much more likely than the other local authority tenants to be in paid employment. They were also less likely to be working class, and accordingly their household income was substantially higher than that of people who stayed behind in council housing [see Table 8.4.6].

To be sure, the house purchasers were not as advantaged as the share purchasers, at least with respect to social class. The programme of council house sales thus did reach a rather different group from the privatisation programme. Nor was the government rewarding its own supporters through the council house sales to the same extent that it was with the share issues. Whereas in 1979 the Conservatives got over 50% of the votes of the future recruits to popular capitalism, they received less than 40% of the votes of the future home owners.

In both cases, however, there were marked prior differentials between purchasers and non-purchasers. It is this fact, and the pattern of selective mobility that followed from it, that largely explains the association between vote and property ownership with which we began this chapter.

Conclusion

We have shown that the electoral claims made for the extension of popular capitalism cannot be substantiated. We find that the new shareholders and the new owner-occupiers *were already* more likely to be Conservatives than were non-shareholders or council tenants. In choosing to become shareholders and owner-occupiers these voters were more evidently affirming their existing social and political values rather than changing them.

Table 8.4.6 The characteristics of council house purchasers

	LA tenants	Purchasers	Other home owners
% working class	68	50	26
% in paid employment	37	72	61
% income over £8,000	23	70	71
% living in South and Midlands	43	60	63

Source: 1987 cross-section survey.

THE EXTENSION OF POPULAR CAPITALISM

In politics giving your own supporters what they want can be as important as trying to win recruits from the other side. And undermining one's opponent's image amongst the electorate at large can be more fruitful than securing the support of some small target group of supporters. And on these grounds the extension of popular capitalism may have assisted the Conservatives' cause. But as an attempt to undermine Labour's long-term social base and expand its own, it must on the available evidence so far be adjudged a failure.

8.5 | Has the electorate become Thatcherite?

Ivor Crewe

How are we to assess Mrs Thatcher's election hat trick? Does it reflect an enduring realignment to the Right – the forging of a new popular Conservatism – or merely a remarkable, yet temporary, run of political luck? And how are we to assess the role of the electorate? Has it voted in Conservative governments because it is Thatcherite, or Thatcherite governments because it preferred the Conservatives?

Political commentators frequently claim that a social realignment underpins the Conservative ascendancy. Thatcherism is both creator and beneficiary of a new social order and, within it, of a new working class. In fact three quite separate claims are being made. The first is that gradual, inexorable mutations in the social structure have benefited, and will continue to benefit, the Conservatives. The second is that Thatcherism has accelerated the process by deliberately recreating the social structure in its favour. The third is that over and above these changes, Thatcherism has a special appeal to important sections of the working class. All three claims are true, but all three need qualification.

Certainly social trends are on the Conservatives' side. Almost all the expanding groups in the British electorate are predominantly Conservative, almost all the contracting groups predominantly Labour. The working class has become Britain's newest minority. By the next election [manual workers] will be outnumbered by the professional and managerial salariat, there will be fewer trade union members than shareholders, and owner occupiers will exceed council tenants by five to two in the electorate and by almost two to one amongst the working class. These trends alone have been worth a swing from Labour to Conservative of at least 5 per cent

From I. Crewe, 'Has the electorate become Thatcherite?', in R. Skidelsky (ed.), *Thatcherism*, Oxford: Blackwell, 1988.

HAS THE ELECTORATE BECOME THATCHERITE?

since 1964. But this is only part of the story. For reasons that are not entirely clear, region and community have been exerting a steadily stronger electoral influence. And here too the Conservatives are at an advantage. Migration from the Labour-voting north to the Conservative-voting south and from inner city to suburbia and commuter village will continue apace. Even electoral demography is Conservative: increasing longevity combined with the decline in the 1970s' birthrate means that job- and welfare-dependent new voters will be outnumbered, for the first time, by the fixed and investment income old voters. The greying rentier class will matter more than the employed – let alone unemployed – youth vote.

One must not be too mechanistic. There are counter-trends: women are entering the labour force in growing numbers and, partly as a result, trade union membership has started to reverse its post-1981 decline: there is scope here for the radicalisation of a hitherto Conservative group, white collar women. We should not automatically assume, either, that voting patterns must remain the same within each social group. Labour voters do not immediately abandon lifelong loyalties on moving south or buying a council house. And fluctuations of political fortune could counteract the social trends. Social trends do not preclude a Labour victory, let alone guarantee unending Conservative rule. It is not impossible to climb to the top of a downward moving escalator, just difficult.

Whether Thatcherites can be said to have *created* a new social base remains to be seen. Herbert Morrison promised to build the Conservatives out of London; have the Conservatives privatised and gentrified themselves back in again? Cause and effect are difficult to disentangle. Certainly council house owners voted Conservative in 1987 in larger numbers (40 per cent) than council house tenants (25 per cent), but then they were Conservative before they bought the house. Panel surveys refute the idea that voters switch from Labour to Conservative after buying their council house or, for that matter, their shares. House- and share-owners do not become Conservatives; rather Conservatives become house- and share-owners.

Other structural consequences of Thatcherism have hurt rather than helped the Conservatives. The squeeze on the public sector has alienated the administrating, educating and caring classes; the unemployed have swung sharply anti-Conservative.

What of the final claim, that Mrs Thatcher, like Disraeli a century ago, has created a new Conservative working class, but this time a self-advancing post-industrial one rather than a self-effacing pre-industrial one? Thatcherism, it is said, has a special appeal to the working class because it speaks to their actual experience in language (and, nowadays, accents) it understands about unwanted strikes, work dodging, welfare cheating and crime on the streets.

It is on this issue that there is some academic controversy. [But] what is beyond dispute is that the Conservative vote in the working class, however defined, grew at a faster rate than in the electorate as a whole, while the Labour vote declined at a faster rate in the working class than the electorate as a whole. Two comparisons make the point. Between the elections of 1959 and 1987, among manual workers, the Conservative vote was actually 5 per cent higher in 1987 than in 1959, whereas among non-manual workers it fell 12.5 per cent, i.e. twice the national average. Between 1979 and 1987, in the electorate as a whole, there was a 2.2 per cent swing to the Conservatives, but the classes diverged. In the middle classes the swing was zero; in the working class over 4 per cent. Quite simply, the Conservative advance over both the long and short term has been entirely within the working class. How has it been done? And how, in particular, was it done when segments of the working class were bearing the brunt of the recession?

At this point New Right and Neo-Marxist Left unite in a common answer: Thatcherism has fashioned an ideological realignment within the electorate in which free market doctrines and authoritarian populism [are] fused into a new 'reactionary common sense'.

Future historians will probably say that the Thatcher governments were both more authoritarian and more populist than their predecessors. But the survey evidence fails to reveal any parallel trend in the electorate. True, it portrays a public that was already taking a hard line on immigration control, the death penalty and crime before 1979, as the simmering discontents brought to boil by Powellism in the previous decade suggest. In these respects there was a Thatcherite consensus before Thatcher. But this mood did not spread or intensify; on the contrary, the picture is one of a slow, halting advance for tolerance and liberalism. In 1974 the British Election Study asked respondents about a series of social trends: had they gone too far or not far enough? The identical questions were repeated in 1979 and, by Gallup, in November 1987. Between 1974 and 1979 the electorate grew slightly more conservative about pornography, modern teaching methods, racial equality, sexual equality and the availability of welfare benefits. But between 1979 and 1987 public sentiment reversed direction. The proportion of social conservatives fell by 33 per cent on 'the availability of welfare benefits', 14 per cent on 'changes towards modern teaching methods', 11 per cent on 'attempts to ensure equality for women', 10 per cent on 'nudity and sex in films and magazines', 8 per cent on 'the availability of abortion on the NHS', and 4 per cent on 'challenges to authority'. Over a similar period support for the return of capital punishment – surely the core of authoritarian populism – fell by 12 per cent.

Of course, the electorate remains socially illiberal on many issues, but less so in 1987 than in 1979. This does not suggest that public sentiment in

HAS THE ELECTORATE BECOME THATCHERITE?

these areas underlay or responded to the Conservatives' election wins. The most that can be claimed for the thesis of authoritarian populism is that between 1974 and 1979 Mrs Thatcher worked with rather than against the popular grain, softening them up for the true ideological crusade on the economic front.

A distinctive feature of Thatcherism is its pedagogic impulse. It has been at pains to educate the electorate about economic realities. Not since Gladstone has Britain been led by such an opinionated and evangelical Prime Minister as Mrs Thatcher. But there is precious little evidence that she has succeeded. Her missionary preaching has fallen on deaf ears. Let me now pepper you with polling evidence that the public has not been converted to economic Thatcherism – not to its priorities, nor to its economic reasoning, nor to its social values.

First, priorities. The Thatcherite refrain is that the reduction of inflation to near-zero levels is both a necessary and sufficient condition for bringing unemployment down in the long term. In 1980 the public agreed, just: 52 per cent wanted the government to give priority to curbing inflation, 42 per cent to cutting unemployment. By mid-1986, however, these priorities were massively rejected, by over six to one, and 75 per cent agreed that the government 'should always keep unemployment as low as possible, *even if this means some inflation with rising prices*'.

Mrs Thatcher believes in holding down government spending in order to facilitate tax cuts. But the electorate disagree: they want expansion of public expenditure. The Gallup poll has asked at regular intervals whether, if forced to choose, they would prefer tax cuts – even at the expense of some reduction in government services such as health, education and welfare – or for these services to be extended even if this means some tax increases. In May 1979, when Mrs Thatcher entered Number Ten, there were equal numbers of tax-cutters and service-extenders. By 1983 there were twice as many service-extenders as tax-cutters; by 1987 six times as many.

Perhaps the public disliked the Government's economic medicine, but accepted that There Was No Alternative. Not a bit of it: in the public's eyes unemployment was neither justifiable nor inevitable. For example, in July 1984 a 56 to 44 per cent majority said that unemployment 'is always a bad thing' rather than 'sometimes necessary during a period of adjustment'; by June 1985 the majority had increased to 61 to 39 per cent. Similarly, a 56 to 44 per cent majority rejected the fatalistic proposition that 'high unemployment is something we shall just have to learn to live with as best we can' in July 1985; by December 1986 that majority had grown to 62 to 37 per cent. Indeed, the public turn out to be unreconstructed Keynesians.

Asked 'How likely do you think it that a cut in taxes would help reduce unemployment?' only 26 per cent replied 'very' or 'fairly' likely; 63 per cent

368 RECENT THEMES

said 'not very' or 'not at all' (October 1987). On the other hand, 85 per cent thought that 'spending more on building roads, houses, hospitals, etc. would help to reduce unemployment' and only 10 per cent demurred. Tough Thatcherite talk about the futility of throwing taxpayers' money at unemployment and about the creation of 'real' rather than 'paper' jobs on a base of zero inflation and a thriving private sector has so far made few converts.

As for Victorian values, Samuel Smiles fares no better than Milton Friedman. In 1977, before Mrs Thatcher came to power, Gallup reported that 35 per cent of voters thought that, if people were poor, their own lack of effort was probably to blame; by 1985 that figure had fallen to 22 per cent and 50 per cent blamed 'circumstances'. Asked in November 1987 whether the unemployed have usually themselves to blame, only 13 per cent agreed; 87 per cent disagreed.

Thus Mrs Thatcher's message of self-reliance has fallen mainly on deaf ears. In 1984 Gallup asked voters whether they thought the Government's most important job was to provide good opportunities for everyone to get ahead, or whether its job was to guarantee everybody steady employment and a decent standard of living. Only 30 per cent said they were content with good opportunities; 65 per cent wanted a Government guarantee. The proportion believing in self-reliance was actually higher when the identical question was put under Mr Attlee's Government in 1945.

Finally, Thatcherism claims to have instilled a new sense of national pride, to have put the Great back in Britain; but surveys suggest otherwise. In 1985 Gallup asked voters whether they had more or less pride in Britain than five years earlier: only 18 per cent said they had more pride now; 42 per cent said they had less. More recently, only 18 per cent said they believed Britain as a nation was on the way up; 50 per cent thought it was standing still, while 32 per cent thought it was on the way down. The strong sense abroad that Britain is no longer the sick man of Europe does not appear to have penetrated opinion at home.

The electorate, in other words, is hardly suffused with Thatcherite values on either the economic or moral plane. Not surprisingly, therefore, it has consistently opposed a raft of specifically Thatcherite policies and decisions. These are [some] examples:

	Approve	Disapprove
Abolition of GLC	21%	79%
Banning of trade unions at GCHQ	31%	69%
Privatisation of British Gas	43%	57%
Privatisation of British Telecom	44%	56%
Community charge	29%	71%
Privatisation of electricity and water supply	28%	72%
Attempt to prevent the publication of *Spycatcher*	35%	65%

So Conservative success remains a puzzle. Voters oppose the Government on the vast array of its specific policy initiatives. They say they prefer Labour on the issues that matter. Their economic values are solidly social democratic, their moral values only half-Thatcherite, and on both fronts they have edged to the Left since 1979. There has been no ideological sea change. The economic record might account for 1987, but not 1983. The changing class structure explains only a fraction.

What jigsaw pieces are left? Mrs Thatcher herself? The long-running 'satisfaction' ratings in the polls suggest that Mrs Thatcher has been the second most *un*popular Prime Minister since the war, surpassed only by Edward Heath. Admittedly, this is a crude measure because it ignores intensities and combines assessments of performance with those of personality. The truth is more complicated. In effect, she is *both* intensely admired and deeply loathed. Not much liked as a human being, she is widely if grudgingly respected as a leader. Therein lies her electoral appeal, and it offers a clue to solving the electoral puzzle.

For policy-based party preferences to be translated into votes, a prior condition is probably crucial: the party in question must be regarded as 'fit to govern'. In 1983 and 1987 both Labour and the Alliance fell at this first hurdle, allowing the Conservatives to win because the voters judged that indeed There Was No Alternative – no governing alternative. This primary judgement by the voters has been neglected in the surveys, which ask respondents which party is better on this or that policy, but not 'which is better at governing?' *tout court*. The ingredients of 'fitness to govern' include strong leadership within party as well as over country; party unity; clarity of policy goals; and personal probity.

Thatcherism's 'statecraft', to use Bulpitt's happy term (Bulpitt, 1986), is at least as distinctive as its economic and cultural prejudices and is the neglected element of its electoral success. Mrs Thatcher's warrior style – setting objectives, leading from the front, confronting problems, holding her position – *did* make a major electoral impact in both 1983 and 1987. So did her austerely centralist conception of the role of government: that it should rule untrammelled by organised interests, or by other governments, whether local or European; and that within the Government she should be unimpeded by doubting ministers or officials.

The results of a set of questions on Thatcherism as statecraft asked in the BBC's 1983 and 1987 election surveys are revealing (see Table 8.5.1). Voters were asked, for example, whether it was better for government to stick firmly to their beliefs or meet opponents half-way; whether it was better for governments to be tough or caring in economically hard times; whether governments by themselves could do much to create prosperity; whether governments should involve major interests in making decisions or keep them at arm's length. Voters turned out to be fairly evenly split overall, with anti-Thatcherites in a slight majority in 1983 and an increased

370 RECENT THEMES

Table 8.5.1 Thatcherism as a style of governing

Question: 'When dealing with political opponents, what is better – sticking firmly to one's political beliefs, or trying to meet them halfway?'

Month/ year	Sticking to beliefs	Meet half way	Neither, both, don't know	Balance of approval for 'Thatcherism'
6/83	50	39	11	+11
5/87	45	48	7	−3

Question: 'In difficult economic times, what is better – for the government to be caring or for the government to be tough?'

	Tough	Caring	Neither, etc.	
6/83	46	34	20	+12
5/87	36	50	14	−14

Question: 'When governments make decisions about the economy, what is better – to involve major interests like trade unions and business, or to keep them at arm's length?'

	Keep at arm's length	Involve interests	Neither, etc.	
6/83	28	60	12	−32
5/87	22	69	9	−47

Question: 'It is sometimes said that no government of any party can in fact do much to create economic prosperity, that it is up to people themselves. Do you agree or disagree?'

	Agree	Disagree	Neither, etc.	
6.83	48	37	15	+11
5/87	39	48	13	−9

Question: 'In its relations with the rest of the world, what is better – for Britain to stick resolutely to its own position, or for Britain to meet other countries half way?'

	Stick to own position	Meet half way	Neither, etc.	
6/83	30	58	12	−28
5/87	28	63	9	−35

	1983	1987
Average percentage supporting Thatcherite position	40.4%	34.0%
Average percentage opposing Thatcherite position	45.6%	55.6%

majority in 1987; there was certainly no consensus for Thatcherism. Of course it correlated with the vote, but more closely with the 1983 vote than with that of 1979. In other words, it was an important component of vote-switching between the two elections.

HAS THE ELECTORATE BECOME THATCHERITE? 371

Table 8.5.2 Thatcherism as statecraft and the flow of the vote, 1979–83

Vote in 1979	Vote in 1983		
	Con.	L/SDP	Lab.
Con.	+37	−21	−39
L/SDP	+12	−23	−88
Lab.	+25	−53	−48
Did not vote	+27	−43	−61
Too young	+13	−43	−38

Note: Cell entries are the percentage majority of 'Thatcherites' over 'anti-Thatcherites', as defined in Table 8.5.1. For example, among those voting Conservative in both 1979 and 1983 the proportion of Thatcherites exceeded the proportion of anti-Thatcherites by 37%.

There is an important technical point to make here. Responses to attitude questions can be expected to correlate with party preference if the questions deal with policies that have been associated with one party or another for many years, or if they call for an evaluation of the government's record. The Thatcherism scale does not fall into this category. It neither contains specific policy references, nor [calls] for a judgement of the government's performance; rather it is concerned with the more abstract issues of statecraft. Yet it is strongly associated with the constancy and switching of votes between 1979 and 1983 (see Table 8.5.2). Take 1979 Conservative voters as an example. Among the majority who remained Conservatives in 1983 there was a clear majority of Thatcherites (+37 per cent). But among the minority who switched to Labour (−39 per cent) or the Alliance (−21 per cent) they were outnumbered by anti-Thatcherites. The differences are very sharp. There is a similar, but reverse, pattern among 1979 Labour voters. Attitudes to Thatcherism as statecraft had a powerful discriminating impact in the 1983 election.

Whether a distinctive statecraft can form the basis of an enduring party realignment, however, seems doubtful. Style of government is bound up with the personality of the Prime Minister, and this Prime Minister, who so much prefers to bypass than reform political institutions, will bequeath few structural legacies for continuing the style after her departure.

Almost every government defeated at an election in this century lost authority before it lost office. Governments defeated at the polls forfeit votes for lack of authority, not authority for lack of votes. This is evidently true of four of the five defeats of governments since the war – 1951, 1964, February 1974 and 1979. Among electors policy and ideology have been mere cloaks for applying a *coup de grace* to a government already crippled by failure, division, scandal or sheer exhaustion. Cohesion, purpose and success take precedence over policy and ideology in voters' eyes; that is the lesson of Mrs Thatcher's and Thatcherism's astonishing success.

Glossary of Statistical Terms

The entries given below are intended to provide some basic guidance on statistical terms which will have been encountered in this volume. But the guidance is necessarily *basic*. For further details the reader should consult a reliable textbook on statistical methods in the social sciences, such as A. Bryman and D. Cramer, *Quantitative Data Analysis for Social Scientists* (London: Routledge, 1990) or B.H. Erickson and T.A. Nosanchuk, *Understanding Data* (Milton Keynes: Open University Press, 1979). (Below, terms in bold type have separate entries.)

AID analysis
Automatic Interaction Detector is a multivariate statistical technique (i.e. one involving many **variables**) which is analogous to stepwise multiple **regression** and is used to assess the relative contribution of a set of dichotomous nominal variables (e.g. sex, class) to explaining variation in a dependent variable (e.g. party choice). Cases are successively divided into dichotomous groups on the basis of the predictor variable which maximises the amount of remaining variation in the dependent variable which is explained. This technique is also known as tree analysis.

Autocorrelation, autoregression
When data are in a time series (e.g. monthly opinion poll results) then the score for one point in time is likely to **correlate** with the score for immediately preceding and succeeding time points. The data are said to be autocorrelated. In estimating a **regression** equation to fit the data we may include a term or terms which assume that the dependent variable at one point in time is a function of the same variable at some other point in time. Such an equation is autoregressive.

Beta weights
A (linear) multiple **regression** equation takes the form:

$$y' = a + b_1 x_1 + b_2 x_2 + b_3 x_3, \text{ etc.}$$

where y' is the estimate of the dependent **variable** and x_1, x_2, x_3, etc. are the independent or predictor variables. The coefficients of the independent variables are not directly comparable because the different variables may be measured in

GLOSSARY OF STATISTICAL TERMS

373

different units. To make the coefficients comparable they may be standardised (by dividing by the standard deviation of the variable). They are then known as Beta weights, and within one equation comparison of Beta weights gives an indication of the relative importance of the variables.

Box–Jenkins methods
A set of procedures for dealing with **autocorrelation** in a time series. Very simply, the procedures involve making an estimate of the level of autocorrelation and then transforming the scores in the series to take account of it. For further details see R. McCleary and R.A. Hay, *Applied Time Series Analysis* (Beverly Hills, CA: Sage, 1980).

Chi-squared test *See* **significance tests**

Contingency tables *See* **cross-tabulation.**

Correlation
Simple correlation (or zero-order correlation) refers to association between two **variables**. The strength of the association is measured by a correlation coefficient.

In the case of two interval-scale variables the usual measure is the product moment correlation coefficient, or Pearson's 'r'. Strictly speaking this is a measure of the closeness of fit of data points around a straight least squares **regression** line drawn through a scatter diagram in which cases are plotted in two dimensions. The values of r may range from $+1$ (perfect positive correlation) through 0 (no linear correlation at all) to -1 (perfect negative correlation). The closer to $+1$ or -1 r is, the stronger is the association between the variables, though in practice extreme values are never found. The square of r (r^2) is a measure of the proportion of variation in the values of one variable which is statistically explained by variations in the values of the other. It is usually multiplied by 100 to give a measure of the percentage of variation explained.

The association between one dependent variable and two or more independent variables taken together is measured by the multiple correlation coefficient (also r), and here r^2 measures the proportion of variation in the value of the dependent variable which is statistically explained by variations in the values of the independent or predictor variables.

Rank order correlation coefficients are used to measure association between pairs of ordinal variables. A common measure is Kendall's tau-b. This can be interpreted in the same way as a simple r (but does not have the same statistical properties).

Cross-tabulation
This is the standard method of presenting and investigating the relationship between two or more nominal **variables**. Tables (sometimes called contingency tables) are created by defining a series of row and column categories and assigning cases to the appropriate cells in the table. The total numbers of cases in each column and row are known as 'marginals'. More sophisticated analysis of contingency tables may use **odds ratios** or **log-linear analysis.**

Dummy variables
Dichotomous nominal or ordinal **variables** can be treated as if they were interval variables by assigning the values one and zero to the categories. Vote, for example,

374 GLOSSARY OF STATISTICAL TERMS

could be scored 1 = voted Conservative, 0 = did not vote Conservative. Variables transformed in this way are known as dummy variables. This technique is useful because it allows more powerful statistical analysis than is otherwise normally possible for nominal or ordinal data.

Durbin-Watson statistic
Regression analysis assumes that errors in estimating values for the dependent variable are random. If this is not the case then the estimate of the regression equation will be unreliable in various ways. The Durbin–Watson test is a procedure for testing whether the error terms are random.

Factor analysis
This is a technique which can be used when a dataset contains a large number of related **variables** to detect which variables tend to hang together. It identifies a number of 'factors' and estimates factor loadings for each variable which give an indication of the **correlation** between the variable and the factor in question, and which therefore show which variables 'go together' in a particular factor. The factors are sometimes interpreted as latent variables. More precisely delineated clusters of variables can be produced by 'rotating' the factors and one technique by which this is done is known as 'varimax' rotation. Each factor produced by a factor analysis has an associated 'eigenvalue' which indicates the amount of variation in the data which is statistically explained by that factor.

Generalised least squares (GLS)
The ordinary least squares method assumes that the error terms in the **regression** equation are independent of each other and have the same **variance** for all values of the independent **variables**. Generalised least squares methods allow the estimation of regression equations when, in some respects, these assumptions do not hold.

Kendall's tau-b *See* **correlation**

Logit analysis
A form of **regression** analysis often used when the dependent variable is dichotomous (e.g. when it is a **dummy variable**) since the relationship between a dichotomous variable and an interval variable will be linear only in most exceptional circumstances. The assumption is made that the expected values of the dependent variable will form not a straight line but on a logistic curve.

Log-linear analysis
This is a relatively recently developed technique for analysing the relationships between nominal variables in large **contingency tables**. The numbers actually in the cells of a table are compared with the numbers that would be there under various models, i.e. hypotheses about the relationship between the variables involved. When the best fitting model is identified an estimate can be made of the **significance** of each of the variables and the interactions between them.

Marginal(s) *See* **cross-tabulation**

Multicollinearity
It is a condition for the reliable estimation of multiple **regression** equations that there should not be a strong correlation between the independent **variables**. A situation in which some or all of the independent variables in a regression equation are strongly inter-correlated is known as multicollinearity.

GLOSSARY OF STATISTICAL TERMS

Odds ratios
A method for analysing or summarising the relationships in a **contingency table**. Odds ratios are calculated as the odds of a case in a column category being in one row category rather than another divided by the odds of a case in another column category being so.

Ordinary least squares (OLS) *See* **regression**

Panel survey
A survey design in which the same respondents are interviewed on more than one occasion.

Partial correlation
A partial **correlation** coefficient indicates the correlation between two **variables** when controlling for one or more other variables. **Beta weights** derived from **regression** equations are sometimes interpreted as indicating the strength of the partial correlation between a predictor variable and a dependent variable controlling for the other predictor variables. (Beta weights and partial correlation coefficients both measure associations after controlling for other variables, but they are not identical.)

Pearson's r *See* **correlation**

Regression
A technique for estimating the relationship between one or more independent **variables** and a dependent variable. Simple regression analysis involves estimating the line (the regression line) that best fits a distribution of points on a scatter diagram which plots the dependent variable against one independent (or predictor) variable. In linear regression the line is assumed to be straight and is a 'least squares line' (i.e. that line which minimises the sum of the squares of the vertical distances from each point to the line). It can be described by an equation of the form $y' = a + bx$, where a is a constant and b measures the slope of the line. The goodness of fit of the line to the data is measured by the **correlation** coefficient r. Non-linear regression, such as **logit** and probit analysis, assumes that the expected value of y is a non-linear function of x.

By extension, multiple regression is used to predict a dependent variable on the basis of more than one independent variable, and the equation is of the form:

$$y' = a + b_1x_1 + b_2x_2 + b_3x_3, \text{ etc.}$$

The goodness of fit of the multiple regression line to the data is measured by the multiple correlation coefficient (r), and r^2 again gives an estimate of the proportion of variation in the dependent variable statistically explained by the equation.

Residuals
Regression equations can be used to predict values for a dependent variable from the values of the independent variable(s). The differences between predicted and actual values are called 'residuals'. Analysis of residuals can give some indication of important variables which have been omitted from the regression analysis.

Significance tests
Significance tests measure the probability that a statistical relationship at least as large as that observed might have occurred by chance if there were no relationship

376 GLOSSARY OF STATISTICAL TERMS

in the whole population. There are a variety of such tests including the chi-square test, which is used for **contingency tables**, and the **t-test**. Normally researchers take a probability of 0.05 or less as providing *prima facie* evidence that a relationship does exist and that the observed result is unlikely to be due to sampling variation. This is sometimes referred to as the 95% level. It is important to remember that the *statistical* significance of a variable does not necessarily imply that it is *theoretically* or *substantively* significant.

Standard deviation
A measure of the spread or dispersion of a set of values on an interval-scale variable.

Standard error
If a large number of samples are randomly drawn from a population, then the standard error of the sample mean is the standard deviation of the means of those samples. A standard error may be estimated for any sample statistic and provides a measure of the precision with which the statistic estimates the corresponding population parameter. In **regression** and **logit** analysis a common practice is to assume that estimated coefficients indicate the presence of a systematic relationship when they exceed twice their standard errors. This is equivalent to a significance test conclusion at approximately the 95% level that the population coefficients are non-zero.

Statistical Package for the Social Sciences (SPSSX)
A commercial statistics package for use either on mainframe or personal computers, widely used in social science research. It includes programmes for carrying out all of the common statistical procedures.

Stepwise multiple regression
In estimating multiple regression equations the order in which **variables** are entered into the calculations may be critical. Statistics packages such as **SPSSX** usually offer a variety of techniques for deciding what the order should be, of which stepwise regression is one. Independent variables are entered into the equation one at a time, the programme either selecting whichever variable is most **significant** (according to some criterion) at each step, or eliminating a variable which has ceased to be significant.

t-test
In a variety of statistical techniques a t-statistic may be calculated as a test of statistical **significance**. In interpreting **regression** equations, for example, t-statistics may be calculated to test whether particular coefficients are statistically significant and their relative sizes can be interpreted as indicating the relative statistical importance of the **variables** in the equation.

Two-stage least squares (2SLS)
A development of ordinary least squares multiple **regression**. The method can be used, in particular, for estimating the parameters of two simultaneous regression equations when the dependent **variable** of one equation is an independent variable in the other.

GLOSSARY OF STATISTICAL TERMS

377

Variables
Variables are characteristics which vary from person to person, place to place, time to time, etc. They fall into three types:

1. Nominal (or categorical) variables are simply categories, attributes or classes into which cases can be put – people are either male or female, for example – with no implication that any category is higher or lower than another.
2. Ordinal variables can be classified in a rank order, but the magnitude of the difference between the ranks is imprecise and unknown – thus people could identify with a party very strongly, fairly strongly, not very strongly or not at all.
3. Interval variables, by contrast, can be measured precisely on a scale – all variables which can be expressed as percentages, for example, are interval variables.

In **regression** analysis, it is important to distinguish between a dependent variable – the characteristic whose variation is to be explained – and the independent variable(s) – the characteristic(s) which explain(s) variations in the dependent variable. Independent variables are sometimes called 'predictor' variables since they 'predict' to a greater or lesser extent the values of the dependent variable.

Variance
Variance is the square of the **standard deviation**. It gives a measure of the average amount of variation in a set of values.

References

Abramson, P.R. (1983), *Political Attitudes in America*, San Francisco: Freeman.
Alderman, G. (1978), *British Elections: Myth and reality*, London: Batsford.
Alford, R. (1963), *Party and Society*, New York: Rand McNally.
Allen, A.J. (1964), *The English Voter*, London: English Universities Press.
Alt, J. (1979), *The Politics of Economic Decline*, Cambridge: Cambridge University Press.
Alt, J. (1984), 'Dealignment and the dynamics of partisanship in Britain', in P. Beck, R. Dalton and S. Flanagan (eds), *Electoral Change in Advanced Industrial Societies*, Princeton: Princeton University Press.
Anwar, M. (1986), *Race and Politics*, London: Tavistock.
Asher, H.B. (1984), *Presidential Elections and American Politics*, 3rd edn, Homewood, IL: Dorsey Press.
Balsom, D., Madgwick, P.J. and Van Mechelen, D. (1983), 'The Red and the Green: patterns of partisan choice in Wales', *British Journal of Political Science*, **13**, 299–325.
Bealey, F., Blondel, J. and McCann, W.J. (1965), *Constituency Politics*, London: Faber.
Benney, M., Gray, A.P. and Pear, R.H. (1956), *How People Vote*, London: Routledge and Kegan Paul.
Berelson, B., Lazarsfeld, P. and McPhee, W. (1954), *Voting*, Chicago, IL: University of Chicago Press.
Berrington, H. (1965), 'The general election of 1964 (with discussion)', *Journal of the Royal Statistical Society*, Series A, **CXXVIII**: 17–66.
Berrington, H. (1966), 'The general election of 1966: an analysis of the results', *Swinton Journal*, **XII**: 3–10.
Berrington, H. (ed.) (1984), *Change in British Politics*, London: Frank Cass.
Berrington, H. and Bedeman, T. (1974), 'The February election', *Parliamentary Affairs*, **XXVII**: 326–32.
Birch, A.H. (1959), *Small Town Politics*, Oxford: Oxford University Press.
Bishop, G.F., Oldendick, R.W. and Tuchfarber, A.J. (1978), 'Effects of question wording and format on political attitude consistency', *Public Opinion Quarterly*, **42**: 81–92.

378

REFERENCES 379

Blewett, N. (1972), *The Peers, the Parties and the People: The general elections of 1910*, London: Macmillan.

Blumler, J.G. and McQuail, D. (1968), *Television in Politics*, London: Faber.

Bogdanor, V. (1981), *The People and the Party System*, Cambridge: Cambridge University Press.

Budge, I. and Urwin, D.W. (1966), *Scottish Political Behaviour*, London: Longman.

Budge, I., Crewe, I. and Farlie, D. (eds) (1976), *Party Identification and Beyond*, New York: Wiley.

Bulpitt, J. (1986), 'The discipline of the New Democracy: Mrs Thatcher's statecraft', *Political Studies*, **XXXIV**: 19–39.

Butler, D.E. and Kavanagh, D. (1974), *The British General Election of February 1974*, London: Macmillan.

Butler, D.E. and Kavanagh, D. (1975), *The British General Election of October 1974*, London: Macmillan.

Butler, D.E. and Kavanagh, D. (1980), *The British General Election of 1979*, London: Macmillan.

Butler, D.E. and Kavanagh, D. (1984), *The British General Election of 1983*, London: Macmillan.

Butler, D.E. and Kavanagh, D. (1988), *The British General Election of 1987*, London: Macmillan.

Butler, D.E. and King, A.S. (1965), *The British General Election of 1964*, London: Macmillan.

Butler, D.E. and Pinto-Duschinsky, M. (1971), *The British General Election of 1970*, London: Macmillan.

Butler, D.E. and Stokes, D. (1969), *Political Change in Britain*, 1st edn, London: Macmillan.

Butler, D.E. and Stokes, D. (1974), *Political Change in Britain*, 2nd edn, London: Macmillan.

Cain, B.E. (1978), 'Dynamic and static components of political support in Britain', *American Journal of Political Science*, **22**, pp. 849–66.

Cain, B. and Ferejohn, I. (1981), 'Party identification in the United States and Great Britain', *Comparative Political Studies*, **14**, pp. 31–48.

Campbell, A., Converse, P., Miller, W. and Stokes, D. (1960), *The American Voter*, New York: Wiley.

Campbell, A., Converse, P., Miller, W. and Stokes, D. (1966), *Elections and the Political Order*, New York: Wiley.

Campbell, A., Gurin, G. and Miller, W. E. (1954), *The Voter Decides*, Evanston, IL: Row, Peterson & Co.

Carlson, J. and Parkin, M. (1975), 'Inflation expectations', *Economica*, **42**: 123–38.

Chandler, J. (1982), 'The plurality vote: a reappraisal', *Political Studies*, **XXX**: 87–94.

Clarke, H.D. and Stewart, M.C. (1984), 'Dealignment of degree: partisan change in Britain, 1974–83', *Journal of Politics*, **46**: 689–718.

Clarke, H.D., Mishler, W. and Whiteley, P. (1990), 'Recapturing the Falklands: models of Conservative popularity, 1979–83', *British Journal of Political Science*, **20**: 63–81.

Clarke, H.D., Stewart, M.C. and Zuk, G. (1986), 'Politics, economics and party popularity in Britain, 1979–83', *Electoral Studies*, **5**: 123–41.

380 REFERENCES

Converse, P.E. (1964), 'The nature of belief systems in mass publics', in D. Apter (ed.), *Ideology and Discontent*, Glencoe: The Free Press.

Crewe, I. (1974), 'Do Butler and Stokes really explain political change in Britain?', *European Journal of Political Research*, **2**: 47–92.

Crewe, I. (1976), 'Party identification theory and political change in Britain', in Budge *et al.* (1976).

Crewe, I. (1981a), 'Why the Conservatives won', in Penniman (1981).

Crewe, I. (1981b), 'Electoral participation', in D. Butler *et al.* (eds), *Democracy at the Polls*, Washington, DC: American Enterprise Institute.

Crewe, I. (1983a), 'The electorate: partisan dealignment ten years on', *West European Politics*, **6**: 183–215; also in Berrington, (1984).

Crewe, I. (1983b), 'Why Labour lost the British election', *Public Opinion*, June/July: 7ff.

Crewe, I. (1985), 'How to win a landslide without really trying', in Ranney (1985).

Crewe, I. (1986), 'On the death and resurrection of class voting: some comments on *How Britain Votes*', *Political Studies*, **XXXIV**: 620–38.

Crewe, I. (1987), 'A new class of politics' and 'Tories prosper from a paradox', *The Guardian*, 15/16 June.

Crewe, I. (1988), 'Has the electorate become Thatcherite?', in Skidelsky (1988).

Crewe, I. and Denver, D. (eds) (1985), *Electoral Change in Western Democracies*, London: Croom Helm.

Crewe, I. and Fox, A. (1984), *British Parliamentary Constituencies: A statistical compendium*, London: Faber.

Crewe, I. and Payne, C. (1971), 'Analysing the census data', in Butler and Pinto-Duschinsky (1971).

Crewe, I., Fox, T. and Alt, J. (1977), 'Non-voting in British general elections, 1966–October 1974' in C. Crouch (ed.), *British Political Sociology Yearbook*, **3**: 38–109, London: Croom Helm.

Crewe, I., Sarlvik, B. and Alt, J. (1977), 'Partisan dealignment in Britain, 1964–1974', *British Journal of Political Science*, **7**: 129–90.

Curtice, J. and Steed, M. (1980), 'An analysis of the voting', in Butler and Kavanagh (1980).

Curtice, J. and Steed, M. (1982), 'Electoral choice and the production of government: the changing operation of the UK electoral system since 1955', *British Journal of Political Science*, **12**: 249–98.

Curtice, J. and Steed, M. (1984), 'Analysis of the results', in Butler and Kavanagh (1984).

Curtice, J. and Steed, M. (1986), 'Proportionality and exaggeration in the British electoral system', *Electoral Studies*, **5**: 209–28.

Curtice, J. and Steed, M. (1988), 'Analysis', in Butler and Kavanagh (1988).

Denver, D. (1985), 'Scotland', in Crewe and Denver (1985).

Denver, D. (1989), *Elections and Voting Behaviour in Britain*, Oxford: Philip Allan.

Denver, D. and Hands, G. (1974), 'Marginality and turnout in British general elections', *British Journal of Political Science*, **4**: 17–35.

Denver, D. and Hands, G. (1985), 'Marginality and turnout in general elections in the 1970s', *British Journal of Political Science*, **15**: 381–8.

REFERENCES   *381*

Denver, D. and Hands, G. (1990), 'Issues, principles or ideology? How young voters decide', *Electoral Studies*, **9**: 19–36.

Downs, A. (1957), *An Economic Theory of Democracy*, New York: Harper and Row.

Dunleavy, P. (1979), 'The urban basis of political alignment: social class, domestic property ownership and state intervention in consumption processes', *British Journal of Political Science*, **9**: 409–43.

Dunleavy, P. (1980a), *Urban Political Analysis*, London: Macmillan.

Dunleavy, P. (1980b), 'The political implications of sectoral cleavages and the growth of state employment', Part I: 'The analysis of production cleavages', *Political Studies*, **28**: 364–83: Part II: 'Cleavage structures and political alignment', *Political Studies*, **28**: 527–49.

Dunleavy, P. (1987), 'Class dealignment in Britain revisited', *West European Politics*, **10**: 400–19.

Dunleavy, P. and Husbands, C.T. (1985), *British Democracy at the Crossroads*, London: Allen and Unwin.

Eagles, M. and Erfle, S. (1989), 'Community cohesion and voter turnout', *British Journal of Political Science*, **19**: 115–25.

Franklin, M.N. (1982), 'Demographic and political components in the decline of British class voting', *Electoral Studies*, **1**: 195–220.

Franklin, M.N. (1983), 'The rise of issue voting in British elections', *Strathclyde Papers in Government and Politics*, no. 3, University of Strathclyde, Glasgow.

Franklin, M.N. (1985a), *The Decline of Class Voting in Britain*, Oxford: Clarendon Press.

Franklin, M.N. (1985b), 'Assessing the rise of issue voting in British elections since 1964', *Electoral Studies*, **4**: 36–55.

Franklin, M.N. and Mughan, A. (1978), 'The decline of class voting in Britain: problems of analysis and interpretation', *American Political Science Review*, **75**: 523–34.

Franklin, M.N. and Page, E. (1984), 'A critique of the consumption cleavage approach to British voting studies', *Political Studies*, **XXXII**: 521–36.

Frey, B. and Garbers, H. (1971), 'Politico-econometrics: on estimation in political economy', *Political Studies*, **XIX**: 316–20.

Frey, B. and Schneider, F. (1978), 'A politico-economic model of the United Kingdom', *Economic Journal*, **88**: 243–53.

Goldberg, A.S. (1966), 'Discerning a causal pattern among data on voting behaviour', *American Political Science Review*, **60**: 913–22.

Goldthorpe, J., Lockwood, D., Bechhofer, F. and Platt, J. (1968), *The Affluent Worker: Political attitudes and behaviour*, Cambridge: Cambridge University Press.

Goodhart, C.A.E. and Bhansali, R.J. (1970), 'Political economy', *Political Studies*, **XVIII**: 43–106.

Hall, S. and Jacques, M. (1983), *The Politics of Thatcherism*, London: Lawrence and Wishart.

Harrop, M. and Miller, W.L. (1987), *Elections and Voters: A comparative introduction*, London: Macmillan.

Harrop, M. and Shaw, A. (1989), *Can Labour Win?*, London: Unwin.

382   REFERENCES

Heath, A. and McDonald, S.-K. (1987), 'Social change and the future of the left', *Political Quarterly*, **58**: 364–77.

Heath, A. and McDonald, S.-K. (1988), 'The demise of party identification theory?', *Electoral Studies*, **7**: 95–107.

Heath, A., Jowell, R. and Curtice, J. (1985), *How Britain Votes*, Oxford: Pergamon.

Heath, A., Jowell, R. and Curtice, J. (1987), 'Trendless fluctuation: a reply to Crewe', *Political Studies*, **XXXV**: 256–77.

Heath, A., Jowell, R. and Curtice, J. (1988a), 'Class dealignment and the explanation of political change: a reply to Dunleavy', *West European Politics*, **11**: 146–8.

Heath, A., Jowell, R. and Curtice, J. (1988b), 'Partisan dealignment revisited', unpublished paper presented to the PSA annual conference.

Heath, A., Jowell, R., Curtice, J. and Evans, G. (1989), 'The extension of popular capitalism', *Strathclyde Papers on Government and Politics*, no. 60, University of Strathclyde, Glasgow.

Heath, A., Jowell, R., Curtice, J., Evans, G., Field, J. and Witherspoon, S. (1991), *Understanding Political Change*, Oxford: Pergamon.

Hibbs, D.A. (1982), 'Economic outcomes and political support for British governments among occupational classes', *American Political Science Review*, **LXXVI**: 259–79.

Himmelweit, H.T., Humphreys, P. and Jaeger, N. (1981), *How Voters Decide*, London: Academic Press.

Johnston, R.J. (1987), 'The geography of the working class and the geography of the Labour vote: England, 1983: a prefatory note to a research agenda', *Political Geography Quarterly*, **6**: 7–16.

Johnston, R.J. and Pattie, C.J. (1983), 'The neighbourhood effect won't go away: observations on the electoral geography of England in the light of Dunleavy's critique', *Geoforum*, **14**: 161–8.

Johnston, R.J. and Pattie, C.J. (1989a), 'The changing electoral geography of Great Britain', in J. Mohan (ed.), *The Political Geography of Contemporary Britain*, London: Macmillan.

Johnston, R.J. and Pattie, C.J. (1989b), 'Voting in Britain since 1979: a growing North–South divide', in J. Lewis and A. Townsend, *The North South Divide*, London: Paul Chapman Publishing.

Johnston, R.J., Pattie, C.J. and Allsopp, J.G. (1988), *A Nation Dividing?*, Harlow: Longman.

Kavanagh, D. (1990), *Thatcherism and British Politics*, Oxford: Oxford University Press.

Kendall, M.G. and Stuart, A. (1950), 'The law of cubic proportions in election results', *British Journal of Sociology*, **1**: 183–97.

King, A. (1968), 'Why all governments lose by-elections', *New Society*, 21 March: 413–15.

Lawson, N. (1968), 'A new theory of by-elections', *Spectator*, 8 November: 650–2.

Lazarsfeld, P., Berelson, B. and Gaudet, H. (1944), *The People's Choice*, New York: Columbia University Press (3rd edn, 1968).

Marshall, G., Newby, H. and Rose, D. (1988), *Social Class in Modern Britain*, London: Hutchinson.

REFERENCES

McAllister, I. (1987a), 'Social context, turnout and the vote: Australian and British comparisons', *Political Geography Quarterly*, **6**: 17–30.

McAllister, I. (1987b), 'Comment on Johnston', *Political Geography Quarterly*, **6**: 45–9.

McAllister, I. (1987c), 'Comment on Johnston and Pattie', *Political Geography Quarterly*, **6**: 351–4.

McAllister, I. and Mughan, A. (1986), 'Differential turnout and party advantage in British general elections, 1964–83', *Electoral Studies*, **5**(2): 143–52.

McAllister, I. and Rose, R. (1984), *The Nationwide Competition for Votes*, London: Frances Pinter.

McKenzie, R. and Silver, A. (1968), *Angels in Marble*, London: Heinemann.

McLean, I. (1982), *Dealing in Votes*, Oxford: Martin Robertson.

Miller, W.L. (1977), *Electoral Dynamics*, London: Macmillan.

Miller, W.L. (1978), 'Social class and party choice in England: a new analysis', *British Journal of Political Science*, **8**: 257–84.

Miller, W.L. (1979), 'Class, region and strata at the British general election of 1979', *Parliamentary Affairs*, **32**: 376–82.

Miller, W.L. (1981), *The End of British Politics?*, Oxford: Clarendon Press.

Miller, W.L. (1983), 'The denationalisation of British politics: the re-emergence of the periphery', *West European Politics*, **6**: 103–29.

Miller, W.L. (1984), 'There was no alternative: the British general election of 1983', *Parliamentary Affairs*, **37**: 364–84.

Miller, W.L. (1988), *Irrelevant Elections?* Oxford: Clarendon Press.

Miller, W.L. and Mackie, M. (1973), 'The electoral cycle and the asymmetry of government and opposition popularity', *Political Studies*, **XXI**: 263–79.

Miller, W.L., Tagg, S. and Britto, K. (1986), 'Partisanship and party preference in government and opposition: the mid-term perspective', *Electoral Studies*, **5**: 31–46.

Milne, R.S. and Mackenzie, H.C. (1954), *Straight Fight*, London: Hansard Society.

Milne, R.S. and Mackenzie, H.C. (1958), *Marginal Seat*, London: Hansard Society.

Mosley, P. (1978), 'Images of the "floating voter": or the political business cycle revisited', *Political Studies*, **XXVI**: 375–94.

Mosteller, F. (1968), 'Association and estimation in contingency tables', *Journal of the American Statistical Association*, **63**: 1–28.

Mughan, A. (1981), 'The cross-national validity of party identification: Great Britain and the United States compared', *Political Studies*, **XXIX**: 365–75.

Mughan, A. (1986), *Party and Participation in British Elections*, London: Frances Pinter.

Nie, N.H., Verba, S. and Petrocik, J. (1976), *The Changing American Voter*, Cambridge, MA: Harvard University Press.

Niemi, R.G. and Weisberg, H.F. (eds) (1976), *Controversies in American Voting Behavior*, San Francisco, CA: W.H. Freeman.

Norpoth, H. (1986), 'War and government popularity in Britain', paper given at the annual meeting of the American Political Science Association, Washington, DC.

REFERENCES

Norpoth, H. (1987a), 'Guns and butter and government popularity in Britain', *American Political Science Review*, **81**: 949–59.

Norpoth, H. (1987b), 'The Falklands War and government popularity in Britain: rally without consequences or surge without decline', *Electoral Studies*, **6**: 3–16.

Norris, P. (1987), 'Four weeks of sound and fury . . . the 1987 British election campaign', *Parliamentary Affairs*, **4**: 458–67.

Penniman, H. (ed.) (1981), *Britain at the Polls, 1979*, Washington, DC: American Enterprise Institute.

Pomper, G.M. (1972), 'From confusion to clarity: issues and American voters 1956–68', *American Political Science Review*, **62**: 415–28.

Powell, G.B. (1980), 'Voting turnout in thirty democracies: partisan, legal and socio-economic influences', in Rose (1980).

Pulzer, P.G. (1967), *Political Representation and Elections in Britain*, London: Allen and Unwin.

Ranney, A. (ed.) (1985), *Britain at the Polls, 1983*, Washington, DC: American Enterprise Institute.

Robertson, D. (1984), *Class and the British Electorate*, Oxford: Blackwell.

Rose, R. (1974), 'Britain: simple abstractions and complex realities', in R. Rose (ed.), *Electoral Behavior: A comparative handbook*, New York: The Free Press.

Rose, R. (1980a), 'Class does not equal party', Occasional Paper no. 74, Centre for the Study of Public Policy, University of Strathclyde, Glasgow.

Rose, R. (ed.) (1980b), *Electoral Participation*, London: Sage.

Rose, R. (1982), 'From simple determinism to interactive models of voting', *Comparative Political Studies*, **15**: 145–69.

Rose, R. and McAllister, I. (1986), *Voters Begin to Choose*, London: Sage.

Rose, R. and McAllister, I. (1990), *The Loyalties of Voters*, London: Sage.

Runciman, W. G. (1966), *Relative Deprivation and Social Justice*, London: Routledge and Kegan Paul.

Sanders, D., Ward, H. and Marsh, D. (1987), 'Government popularity and the Falklands war: a reassessment', *British Journal of Political Science*, **17**: 281–313.

Sanders, D., Ward, H. and Marsh, D. (1990), 'A reply to Clarke, Mishler and Whiteley', *British Journal of Political Science*, **20**: 83–90.

Sarlvik, B. and Crewe, I. (1983), *Decade of Dealignment – The Conservative Victory of 1979 and the Electoral Trends of the 1970s*, Cambridge: Cambridge University Press.

Scarbrough, E. (1984), *Political Ideology and Voting: an exploratory study*, Oxford: Oxford University Press.

Scarbrough, E. (1987), 'The British electorate twenty years on: electoral change and election surveys', *British Journal of Political Science*, **17**: 219–46.

Sharpe, L.J. (1962), *A Metropolis Votes*, Greater London Paper no. 8, LSE.

Skidelsky, R. (ed.) (1988), *Thatcherism*, Oxford: Blackwell.

Smith, D. (1989), *North and South*, Harmondsworth: Penguin.

Steed, M. (1965), 'An analysis of the results', in Butler and King (1965).

Studlar, D. and Welch, S. (1986), 'The policy opinions of British non-voters: a research note', *European Journal of Political Research*, **14**: 139–48.

Sullivan, J.L., Pierson, J.E. and Markus, G.B. (1978), 'Ideological constraint in

REFERENCES

the mass public: a methodological critique and some new findings', *American Journal of Political Science*, **22**: 233–49.

Swaddle, K. and Heath, A. (1989), 'Official and reported turnout in the British general election of 1987', *British Journal of Political Science*, **19**: 537–51.

Todd, J. and Butcher, B. (1982), *Electoral Registration in 1981*, London: Office for Population Censuses and Surveys.

Trenaman, J. and McQuail, D. (1961), *Television and the Political Image*, London: Methuen.

Wallas, G. (1910), *Human Nature in Politics*, London: Constable.

Weakliem, D. (1989), 'Class and party in Britain, 1964–83', *Sociology*, **23**: 289–97.

Whiteley, P. (1984), 'Inflation, unemployment and government popularity: dynamic models for the United States, Britain and West Germany', *Electoral Studies*, **3**: 3–24.

Whiteley, P. (1986), 'Predicting the Labour vote in 1983: social background versus subjective evaluations', *Political Studies*, **XXXIV**: 82–98.

Index

We have included references to individual political parties and to particular general elections only where there is a specific and/or extended discussion of them.

abortion, 366
absolute class voting, *see* class
age
 and party choice, 138–40, 144, 344
 and turnout, 22–4, 28–9, 37–9
 see also cohorts
aggregate data analysis, 2–4, 16, 52
Alford Index, 63, 66, 77, 86, 90, 91,
 101–3, 108, 109, 116
Alford, R., 5
Allen, A.J., 3
Alliance, 11, 67, 73, 89, 98, 276, 293–4,
 330, 353–4
Allsopp, J.G., 301, 316
Alt, J., 16, 36–7, 51, 119, 127, 128, 149,
 152, 156, 209, 242
American Voter, The, 7, 170
Anwar, M., 5
attitudes, 220, 313, 323
 and class, 70–2, 82–4
 see also issues

balance of payments/trade, 250–1, 254,
 264
bank rate, 254, 257, 261
Bealey, F., 4
Bedeman, T., 308

Benney, M., 4, 215
Berelson, B., 6–8
Berrington, H., 308
Bhansali, R.H., 242, 248, 253–6, 264–
 5, 270
Birch, A., 4
Blewett, N., 3
Blumler, J., 4
British Election Study (BES), 5, 9, 11,
 16, 20, 31–4, 52, 120, 128, 146,
 162, 171–2, 198–9, 220, 231, 233,
 314, 356, 366
Britto, K., 128, 169
Budge, I., 4, 10
Bulpitt, J., 369
Butcher, B., 34, 40
Butler, D.E., 5, 6, 8,–10, 12, 57, 61,
 118–20, 127, 157, 170, 230–1, 237,
 241, 264

Cain, B., 152
Callaghan, James, 151, 339
Campbell, A., 7, 170
censorship, 366
census data, 3, 55, 118, 125, 306–7
Clarke, H.D., 128, 243, 274

386

INDEX 387

class
  absolute class voting, 52, 76, 77,
    85–6, 89–91, 98–101, 103, 106,
    115–6
  changing sizes/structure, 63, 66, 79,
    82, 86, 92, 94–7, 364
  core classes, 125–6
  dealignment, 10, 11, 51–2, 61–7, 74,
    76–8, 85–7, 89, 92–8, 107–17
  definition of, 54–7, 65–6, 68–70,
    111–12, 118–19
  interests, 58–60, 65, 69, 70, 74, 86,
    223, 226, 229
  relative class voting, 52, 76–8, 85–6,
    89, 98–101, 103, 106, 113, 115–17
  and turnout, 21–2, 39
  subjective, 54–6, 104–5, 314
  voting, 8, 10, 51–126, 150, 198, 201–
    2, 205–7, 238, 306, 323, 344–7, 366
cohorts, age, 145, 149, 150
  see also generations
Conservative party, 63–5, 72–3, 156–7
Converse, P., 170, 230–2, 234
council housing
  purchase/sales of, 323, 355–6, 359–
    62
  see also housing tenure
Crewe, I., 4–6, 9–11, 16, 35–40, 51–2,
    97–106, 119, 127, 128, 149, 156–7,
    159, 160, 162, 167, 171–2, 209,
    237, 316, 322, 334–5
cube law, 3, 326–7, 329, 330, 332
Curtice, J., 2, 5, 11, 12, 52, 107, 108,
    111, 113, 115, 117, 171, 215, 302,
    311–12, 322–3, 325
cycles, electoral, 242, 248, 253–73

dealignment
  class, *see* class
  partisan, 10, 46, 141–54, 160–9, 310
  see also party identification
death penalty
  attitudes to, 366
Decade of Dealignment, 10, 171
defence
  attitudes to, 212, 216, 340–1, 350–2
Denver, D.T., 4, 17, 41–2, 172
Downs, A., 18, 327

Dunleavy, P., 5, 52, 66, 274

economic expectations, 242, 255–6,
    266–8, 275–88, 290, 292–7, 320–1
economic growth, 264
economic indicators, 241–2, 253, 281,
    290
economic perceptions of voters, 245–7,
    313, 352–3
economy and government popularity,
    241–98
education
  attitudes to, 70, 72, 216–17, 350–2,
    366–7
  and party choice, 234–5
  and turnout, 21, 22
election expenditure, 45–6
electoral system, 134, 322, 325–33, 342
environmental effect, 52–3, 120–3, 126
European Economic Community
  attitudes to, 152–3, 177–8, 186–9,
    192–4, 228
European elections, 11, 347
exchange rate, 279–81, 290–4

Falklands War, 228, 242–3, 274–98,
    334, 337–8, 341
Foot, Michael, 338–9, 349–50
Fox, A., 16, 36–7, 316
Franklin, M.N., 10, 65, 171–2, 206–7,
    236
Frey, B., 264–5

Gallup poll, 199, 228, 244–9, 251,
    254–9, 261, 274–5, 281, 291, 314,
    320, 323, 334–5, 337–8, 341, 343,
    349, 366–8
Gaudet, H., 6
general elections
  1959, 271
  1974 (Feb.), 128, 157–9, 161, 271–3
  1979, 185–97
  1983, 52, 208–18, 330–42
  1987, 31–40, 343–54
generations, 127–8, 209
  see also cohorts
Goldberg, A., 200
Goldthorpe, J.H., 4, 107

Goodhart, C.A.E., 242, 248, 253–6, 264–5, 270
Green party, 11

Hands, H.T.G., 4, 17, 41–2, 172
Harris poll, 341
Harrop, M., 167
Healey, Denis, 339
Heath, A., 5, 11, 12, 16, 17, 52, 85, 87, 89, 90, 92–6, 107–8, 111–17, 171–2, 215, 323
Heath, Edward, 265–6, 369
Himmelweit, H.T., 10, 171
homing tendency, 157–9, 167–8
housing tenure
    and attitudes, 360–2
    and party choice, 226, 356, 359–60, 365
    and turnout, 21–2, 24, 37–9, 42–4
How Britain Votes, 11, 12, 52, 85–99, 104, 107, 110, 117, 171
Howe, Geoffrey, 285
Husbands, C.T., 5, 274

ideology, 70–2, 183–4, 219–21, 223, 313–14, 323
    and party choice, 11, 172, 215–18
income
    growth, 266–7
    and turnout, 22, 24, 39
    see also RPDI
incomes policy, 186–9, 192–4
inflation, 252, 254, 262, 264, 266–8, 270–1, 296–7, 313
inflation policy
    attitudes to, 152–3, 209–11, 252, 340, 367
interactionist model, 11, 12, 214–15
issues
    importance/salience, 193–5, 213–14, 236
    and party choice, 189–93, 195–7, 200–5, 215–17, 232–4
    perceptions of, 152–4, 186–91, 340–2
issue voting model, 10–12, 170–238

job creation
    attitudes to, 70–2, 188–9, 192–4, 216

Johnston, R.J., 301, 316
Jowell, R., 5, 11, 12, 52, 107, 108, 111, 113, 115, 117, 171, 215

Kendall, M.G., 327
King, A., 253, 268
Kinnock, Neil, 110, 347, 349

Labour party, 63–5, 72–3, 94–6, 160–1, 182–3, 338–42, 347–53
    leadership, 338–42
Lawson, N., 254, 258
Lazarsfeld, P., 6
leadership, *see* party leaders
left/right, 171, 178–84, 189–90, 215–16, 252
Liberal party, 57–8, 65, 89, 98, 308–9
Liberal/SDP Alliance, *see* Alliance
Lockwood, D., 4
log-linear analysis, 52, 78–9, 99, 101–3, 106, 113–15
Logit analysis, 38–9, 168, 233, 360

McAllister, I., 4, 5, 11, 162, 167, 172, 232–3, 236, 238
McDonald, S.-K., 172
McKenzie, R.T., 4
Mackenzie, H.C., 4
Mackie, T., 242, 264–5, 269–70
McQuail, D., 4
marginality of constituencies, 17, 41–7, 329
marital status and turnout, 21–2, 24, 37–9
Market Research Society, 55–6, 68
Marsh, D., 243, 289–98, 320
Michigan model, 7, 8, 11, 51, 170–3
migration, 306–7, 365
Miller, W.L., 4, 5, 52, 128, 167, 169, 242, 264–5, 269–70, 302, 306–7, 322
Milne, R.S., 4
Mishler, W., 243
mobility, *see* migration, social mobility, residential mobility
MORI poll, 338
Mosteller, F., 166

INDEX

National Health Service
  attitudes to, 340, 350–2, 367
nationalisation
  attitudes to, 70, 72, 93–4, 104, 106,
    152–3, 174–5, 177–8, 189, 192–5,
    212, 216–17, 231–2
neighbourhood effect
  see environmental effect
Nie, N., 171
non-voting, 16, 18–40
Norpoth, H., 275, 291, 295, 297
North/South divide, 64, 301–2, 304–9,
  316–18, 320, 365
nuclear weapons, 339, 341
  attitudes to, 175–6, 212
Nuffield studies, 2–4

occupation, *see* class
  and turnout, 21–2, 42–3
odds ratios, 52, 76–79, 83, 85, 86,
  89–94, 100–3, 106–12, 117
opinion polls, 5, 6, 46, 128, 146, 147,
  241, 244, 273, 291, 336–7, 341
Owen, David, 350, 353
owner occupation, *see* housing tenure

parent's party, 9, 135–7, 201–5, 225,
  227, 233, 236–7, 315
partisan self-image,
  see party identification
party identification, 7–10, 51, 120, 127–
  69, 202, 204–5, 218, 228–9, 230–8,
  334–6
  and age, 138–9
  decline of, 29–30, 128, 141–5, 148–
    50, 160–1, 163, 237–8, 269–70, 273
  and turnout, 25–30
party leaders, 151, 152, 154, 227–8,
  292, 322–3, 338–42, 349–50, 354,
  369
Pattie, C.J., 301, 316
Payne, C., 4
pensions, 350–2
People's Choice, The, 6–7
Plaid Cymru, 302, 310, 312
polarisation, electoral, 118–26, 238,
  316–21, 336–7, 345

Political Change in Britain, 8, 9, 51,
  127, 170, 230, 241
Pomper, G.M., 171
popular capitalism, 355–63
principles, 172–3, 219–29, 232–4, 238
privatisation, 323, 355–9
  attitudes to, 72, 212, 340
PSBR (Public Sector Borrowing
  Requirement), 243, 279–81, 290–3
Pulzer, P., 51, 54

race
  attitudes to, 186–9, 192–4, 222, 224,
    227
rational choice theory, 18, 19, 230
redistribution of income/wealth,
  attitudes to, 70, 72, 216–17, 314, 358,
    361
region, 304–9, 312–14, 316–21, 328,
  331–2, 346, 365
registration, electoral, 15, 18, 32–4, 40
relative class voting, *see* class
religion, 313, 315
residential mobility
  and turnout, 21–4, 34, 37–9
response bias, 33–4
Rose, R., 4, 5, 10, 11, 15, 65, 125, 162,
  167, 172, 232–3, 236, 238, 310
RPDI (real personal disposable
  income) 270–3
Runciman, W.G., 4

Sanders, D., 243, 289–98, 320
Sarlvik, B., 5, 9–11, 51, 119, 127, 128,
  149, 156–8, 160, 171–2, 209, 237,
  335
Scarbrough, E., 11
Schneider, F., 264–5
Scotland, 11, 61, 64, 301–2, 306–8,
  310–14, 321, 328, 346–7
SDP, 11
sectoral cleavages, 64, 66, 365
sex
  and party choice, 344
  and turnout, 21–4
Sharpe, L.J., 4
Silver, A., 4
Smith, D., 302

SNP, 302, 308–10
social mobility, 66–7
social services spending
  attitudes to, 152–3, 189, 192–4, 212,
    340
socialisation, 8, 59, 131, 135–8, 201–5,
    208–9, 218, 225–7, 229
socialism, 221–5, 227–8
Steed, M., 2, 302, 304, 308, 311–12,
    322, 325
Steel, David, 353
Stewart, M.C., 128, 274
Stokes, D., 5, 6, 8–10, 12, 51, 61,
    118–20, 127, 157, 170–1, 230–1,
    237, 241, 264
strikes
  attitudes to, 152–3
Stuart, A., 327
subjective class, *see* class
survey analysis, 4–6, 16, 52, 101–2,
    118, 155–6
  question wording, 185, 200, 209,
    231–2, 234–7, 356, 369–71
Swaddle, K., 16–7
swing, 3, 63, 128, 146, 304–5, 307–8,
    312, 322, 327–9

tactical voting, 308
Tagg, S., 128, 169
tax cuts
  attitudes to, 186–9, 192–4, 212, 340,
    367
taxation, 278, 290
television, 4, 143
Thatcher, Margaret, 151, 274–5, 279,
    281–2, 286–9, 292, 297–8, 322–3,
    337–8, 343, 349–50, 355, 357, 364–
    71

Thatcherism, 12, 323, 345, 364–71
Todd, J., 34, 40
trade unions, 364–5
  attitudes to TU power, 186–9, 192–
    4, 216–7, 340
  membership and party choice, 63,
    226, 347
  membership and turnout, 22
Trenaman, J., 4
turnout, 15–47

unemployment, 244, 248–9, 250, 253–
    7, 261–2, 264–8, 270–1, 279, 290,
    292–7, 312–13, 318, 320, 340–1,
    350–2, 367
  attitudes to policy, 186–9, 192–4,
    209–11
United States, 4, 6–8, 127, 131–5,
    170–1
Urwin, D.W., 4

volatility, electoral, 10–11, 67, 128,
    145–7, 165–7, 269–70, 273
Voter Decides, The, 7

Wales, 11, 61, 301–2, 305, 309, 310–15,
    321, 346
Wallas, G., 130
Ward, H., 243, 289–98, 320
welfare, 221–2, 224–5, 227, 366–7
welfare benefits
  attitudes to, 314
Whiteley, P., 10, 243
Wilson, Harold, 128, 161
Wincott, H., 255

Zuk, G., 274